W9-BHD-986

DEFENSE CONVERSION

A Critical East-West Experiment

Studies in
Geophysical Optics and Remote Sensing
Series Editor: Adarsh Deepak
Selected Volumes

DEFENSE CONVERSION

A Critical East-West Experiment

Edited by

Alex E.S. Green

with Former Soviet Union perspectives by

Victor V. Chernyy

A. DEEPAK Publishing   **1995**

A Division of Science and Technology Corp.

Hampton, Virginia USA

A. DEEPAK Publishing
A Division of Science and Technology Corporation
101 Research Drive
Hampton, Virginia 23666-1340 USA

Library of Congress Cataloging-in-Publication Data

Green, Alex Edward Samuel, 1919–
    Defense conversion : a critical East-West experiment / edited by
Alex E.S. Green.
        p. cm
    Includes bibliographical references.
    ISBN 0-937194-36-0
        1. Economic conversion. 2. Defense industries. 3. Disarmament.
    4. Nuclear nonproliferation. 5. World politics—1989– I. Title.
    HC79.D4G73   1995
    338.9—dc20   95-22514

Foreword

World War II and the Cold War that followed created a siege mentality in America's psyche and precepts, which contributed to the way we planned and practiced both our national and our personal lives for five decades. For all those years the nation's great science and technological enterprise was influenced pervasively by the Cold War. In some measure "big science" such as the national space program became a surrogate form of warfare. Today that 50-year heritage is hard to relinquish and we might have lost the ability to see other perspectives from which we might structure our goals and efforts.

In the Former Soviet Union (F.S.U.) these trends were substantially magnified since their military-industrial complex produced a much larger share of their gross national product than did the defense enterprises of the United States. Thus, the countries arising out of the F.S.U. now have two difficult adjustments to make: (1) changing from an authoritarian centrally controlled military dominated economy to a democratic market economy, and (2) changing defense industries to civilian or dual purpose industries.

With the end of the Cold War, the U.S.A. and F.S.U. must clearly turn their attention to converting sectors of their defense enterprises to civilian or dual purposes. Such programs might regain some value out of our large investment in military production, defense facilities and hardware that were built up during the Cold War. The opportunity also exists to market civilian adaptations of recent defense technologies.

The initiation of such efforts should serve to substantially lower the potentially destructive level of global armaments. These threat reduction measures should naturally lead to economic savings in the form of reduced defense costs. If big science is placed on an international basis rather than on a competitive basis the cooperation engendered should lead to further development towards peace and understanding between nations.

Just as scientists and engineers in the U.S.A. and F.S.U. considered themselves duty bound to apply their knowledge and skills to their national interests during the Cold War, they need now and in the future to work for national and international betterment. In fact, I consider it a moral imperative to enlist science and technology in a campaign for more productive and humane societies in which all can enjoy the benefits of an improved quality of life.

The deterioration of our environment, the proliferating disparities between the rich and the poor, the absence of affordable health care and the growing popular discontent with political governance are just the beginning of a new agenda for the next 50 years, to which research and development must be directed as effectively as it has been to military enterprises over the past 50 years.

To begin moving in this direction, we must look at issues and problems in a new way. Although economic prosperity has been a consistent and commanding concern throughout American history, from now on economics and environmental concerns must be increasingly integrated. We should conceptualize a science and technology agenda that moves us in the direction of sustainable development—a life pattern that promotes economic and social survivability while preserving the planetary habitat that supports such activity.

The United States' concern for its national interests naturally includes our support and encouragement of defense conversion programs in Russia, Ukraine, and other countries arising from the former Soviet Union. Thus the United States' interests would best be served if the F.S.U. succeeds in these efforts and establishes stable democratic societies that could join the U.S.A. toward achieving Isaiah's goal *"Nation shall not lift up sword against nation and neither shall they experience war anymore."*

George E. Brown, Jr.
Ranking Democratic Member
Committee on Science
U.S. House of Representatives

CONTENTS

Preface

And they shall beat their swords into plowshares
And their spears into pruning hooks
Nation shall not lift up sword against nation
Neither shall they experience war anymore   Isaiah 2

This effort to examine and develop effective defense conversion (DC) methods essentially began at a conference on Climate Change at Los Alamos National Laboratory in October 1991. Scientists from the (then) Soviet Union participated, and it became clear that after over a half century of Hot and Cold Wars the Soviet Union was experiencing great economic difficulties. The U.S.A., over $4 trillion in debt, in significant part as a result of the Cold War, was also hurting, although not as badly. Its military-industrial complex was involved with a much smaller fraction of its GNP than the Soviets'. Glasnost, Perestroica and the beginnings of defense conversion efforts in the Soviet Union marked a thawing of the Cold War. This trend accelerated with the break-up of the Soviet Union in December 1991. A DC program in the U.S.A. was also getting under way, but without an overall national perspective.

It appeared that a bilateral defense conversion program based upon systems, economic, environmental, energy and externality analyses could preferentially help the U.S.A. and the former Soviet Union (F.S.U.). Despite abundant natural resources, these "winners" of WWII are suffering from a half-century of investment in military facilities, hardware and personnel resulting in severe capital depletion problems. In retrospect, these problems were greatly exacerbated by blunderings into the Vietnam and Afghanistan wars.

On the other hand the military production complexes of Japan and Germany were largely destroyed and these countries were prohibited from rebuilding their war machines. In amazingly successful defense conversions based upon investments in civilian industries, the main "losers" of WWII generated and accumulated capital and may now have the world's strongest economies. Cooperative bilateral U.S.A.-F.S.U. defense conversion endeavors might not only lead to military threat reduction but also help restore some of the civilian industrial vitality needed to compete for world markets.

It must be recognized at the outset that the conversion of long ingrained economic systems is exceedingly difficult and thus will take time and labor. By focusing on specific examples of successful defense conversions, our hope was that a pattern might evolve that could guide a general defense conversion program towards success. Hovering like swords of Damocles over the world are the vast supply of weapons-grade nuclear fuel produced during the Cold War and the proliferation of nuclear weapons capability that unfortunately is physically linked to peaceful uses of nuclear energy.

Working through the Committee for Academic-Industrial Research (CAIR) of the Fuels and Combustion Technology (FACT) Division of the American Society of Mechanical Engineers (ASME), I initiated a "Swords to Plowshares" shirt-sleeve session for a meeting of the International Joint Power Generation Conference (IJPCG) held in Atlanta in October 1992. In this effort I was joined by Mr. Victor Chernyy of Ukraine's Bureau of Defense Conversion who served as Keynote Speaker and introduced F.S.U. perspectives into this DC endeavor.

The Atlanta session was very stimulating and led to a "Spears to Pruning Hooks" shirt-sleeve session held at the IJPCG meeting in Kansas City, Missouri in October 1993. This was followed up by a specialized symposium on defense conversion with the theme "Nation Shall Not Lift Up Sword Against Nation" held in Orlando, Florida in February 1994. This book and the abstracts constituting the Executive Summary consist of contributions by speakers at these three conferences plus several contributions by distinguished persons recruited to broaden the overall perspective. The theme of the book is "Neither shall they experience war anymore."

I would like to thank Victor Chernyy, coeditor of this volume, and other fellow authors for valuable contributions that range from historical overviews and anecdotal experiences with defense conversion to social, economic and technical analyses intended to foster successful DC endeavors. Additionally, the editorial assistance of Dr. E. David Hinkley, Science and Technology Corporation, is acknowledged. I would also like to thank the Gatorade Foundation and the College of Engineering of the University of Florida and the Science and Technology Corporation for sponsoring our Defense Conversion Symposium and this book. The participation of the American Society of Mechanical Engineers in conferences leading to this work is also noted. Finally, manuscript preparation by Freda Green, editorial and organizational work by Diana McQuestion, advice by Erwin Cohen and encouragement by Adarsh Deepak are acknowledged with deep appreciation.

Alex E.S. Green
Editor

Executive Summary

Background and Dimensions of the Defense Buildup
Victor V. Chernyy, Bureau of Defense Conversion of Ukraine

Following the victory of the Great October Socialist Revolution of 1917 the Communist Party's national strategy basically was a continual adversarial struggle with the West. This required a total integration of political, military, and economic components of the Soviet national power that eventually led to the militarization of the Soviet economy and to the emergence of one of the largest military-industrial complexes in the world. After the U.S.A.-Soviet cooperation in defeating Hitler's Germany in World War II, the Cold War developed and the Soviets gave highest priority to strategic nuclear forces. The centralized management appropriated huge resources to meet military requirements, especially in high technology and heavy industry, often at the expense of living standards and investment in industries essential for civilian economic growth. The United States did not lag behind the former Soviet Union (F.S.U.) in its Cold War military build up, often taking the lead in the development of new weapons systems. Indeed, in the 1980s the U.S. annual military budget grew to more than $300 billion, amounting to approximately 5 percent of the U.S.A.'s gross national product (GNP). This chapter gives a correlation of basic types of F.S.U.-U.S.A. armaments in the late '80s. The end of the Cold War and the breakup of the Soviet Union led to unprecedented opportunities for developing a cooperative relationship between the former adversaries that could act in the interest of universal peace and stability.

Approaches to Defense Conversion
George L. Donohue, Federal Aviation Administration

Post-Cold War cuts in American military spending are forcing firms and employees in various defense-related industries to make the often difficult transition to the civilian economy. In adopting a policy toward this process of "defense conversion," the Government may choose to (1) let normal market forces determine the most successful conversion routes or (2) intervene to ease the conversion process by providing special assistance to those companies and workers that have been hurt by loss of defense contracts. The basic question is, Can the Government's current, small-scale policy of intervention be effective? The author addresses several common misconceptions about the ways in which defense spending cuts are affecting the nation's economy and concludes that government retraining efforts need to be targeted more effectively. He notes that retraining subsidies for laid-off defense workers would have more practical value if they were provided to employers who hire such workers. If the costs of training were offset it would give these employers greater incentive to take on former defense workers, and since the subsidized training would be directly job related, the effectiveness of the program would be almost guaranteed. Such an approach would certainly have a much better chance of reemployment success than current government or community college retraining programs that are often poorly directed and have not proven their worth to date. While well-aimed and timely government intervention could ease the conversion process somewhat, it seems very likely that the conversion process will be finished before many government programs can come into play. Thus, firms and individuals hurt by defense cutbacks will mostly understand that waiting for such assistance to arrive is probably not the wisest approach.

Defense Conversion: An Operations Analysis Approach
Alex E. S. Green, University of Florida

Operational analysis originated just prior to World War II when it was recognized that operational aspects of a national defense problem, as opposed to the purely technical aspects, were often paramount in the solution of the problem. Over the past half-century, operations analysis (or systems analysis) has developed a substantial body of theory and applications, and its current strength prompts it to attack difficult large-scale problems. In consideration of problems of the U.S.A. and F.S.U. the author takes an operations analysis approach to help define a general defense conversion program, reserving nuclear issues for broader and more detailed treatment. Using People, Economic, Environmental, Energy and Defense problems as drivers, he identifies a large number of programs that could utilize defense personnel, technologies and facilities for civilian, dual or multiple purposes. For example, the conversions of Defense Technologies to "Green Technologies" and defense products to "Green Products" (products whose manufacture, use and disposal place a reduced burden on the environment) could have a receptive market at this juncture in world affairs. Thus, operations analyses can lead to the development of civilian, dual or multiple purpose industries. Defense conversion applied to the restoration of environmental quality and industrial competitiveness would provide a challenging domain for cooperation between the U.S.A. and the F.S.U. that would enable both to benefit from peace dividends associated with the end of the Cold War.

Defense Conversion Techniques in the Mid-1990s
Erick G. Highum, Florida State University

Converting United States military industry workers and U.S. military personnel to commercial industries is one of the most important opportunities for the U.S. Government in this post Cold War era. Displaced military sector employees have skills and educational training that can aid in the economic recovery. This chapter assumes that "national security" involves many arenas—military, economic and ecological. Defense conversion is an ongoing process of moving managers, executives, engineers, other military industry workers and U.S. military personnel into commercial free-market enterprises in Russia, the United States and other countries. The federal reinvestment appropriations of 1994 are presented and the system of cooperative research and development arrangements (CRDAs) are described. Illustrations are given of commercially promising examples of CRDAs arising from Navy, Army and Air Force programs. For example, satellite-imaging systems developed by the intelligence community for espionage activities lend themselves to commercial applications and scientific research on the environment as well as mapping for geological survey purposes, and oil and mining exploration. The author concludes that conversion efforts have the potential for ameliorating large-scale social, economic, and environmental threats to U.S. national security.

Military-Industrial Complex of Russia and the Conversion-Related Problems
Victor V. Chernyy, Former Senior Staff of the U.S.S.R./Russian Embassy in Washington and Valeri V. Semin, Russian Academy of Sciences

The Russian Federation (R.F.) has inherited about 60 percent of the F.S.U. gross national product and population and the biggest share of the military-industrial complex. This sector of Russia's economy comprises more than 1700 enterprises, employing about 6 million workers, the elite of the Russian workers and researchers, operating in the best equipped R&D and industrial facilities. Among the former Soviet Republics, Russia has emerged as the only one capable of producing all types of weapon systems developed in the F.S.U. Despite considerable efforts, the conversion of these plants to civilian production has led to great transitional hardships. Thus, the Russian military-industrial complex finds it necessary to continue developing and producing high-class modern weapons, such as jet fighters, tanks, rocket systems, submarines, etc. However, the end of the Cold War paved the way for American-Russian partnerships or joint ventures, and very recently concrete examples have cleared obstacles in both countries. A 1992 resolution confirmed the R.F.-U.S.A. intention to settle disputes between them by peaceful means and to refrain from the threat or use of force against each other, to unite their efforts toward strengthening international peace and security, to prevent and to settle regional conflicts and solve global problems. This enables them to share common ideals and principles on the basis of mutual trust and respect for democracy, the primacy of the rule of law, and human rights and fundamental freedoms. As the two nations struggle with many very difficult transitional defense conversion problems, largely associated with insufficient capital, it is imperative that these goals be maintained.

Conversion of the Military-Industrial Complex of Ukraine: Problems and Solutions

Victor V. Chernyy, Bureau of Defense Conversion of Ukraine

On August 24, 1991 Ukraine, the second largest Soviet Republic, declared itself a sovereign state, a move widely supported by the Ukrainian people. Ukrainians saw in their declaration of independence a great opportunity for themselves and their country to take control of their destiny and their abundant natural resources to become a modern and prosperous state and a recognized member of the civilized world. Despite its formal independence Ukraine, like other F.S.U. Republics, was an integral part of a highly centralized state entity where Moscow monopolized the political decision-making process as well as economic planning and management. Ukraine had to develop a new mechanism of state Government, to assume a much greater responsibility for the development of internal and external policy, and to create a new brand of presidential, executive and professional legislative branches of power. Despite many difficult transitional problems, Ukraine (in 1994) not only celebrated the third anniversary of its independence but witnessed dramatic changes in its political, social and economic life by electing a new Parliament and a new President. Among the new leaders in the executive branch are President Leonid Kuchma, Valeri Shmarov, Vice-Premier and Defense Minister and Victor Petrov, Minister of Machine Building who came to the political arena from the military-industrial complex. Hence, they know its problems and will be looking for solutions and towards economic stabilization and reforms. The agreement Ukraine President Kuchma reached with the International Monetary Fund indicates that he is prepared to live up to his promises. These developments give reason to believe in economic recovery of the country as a whole and that its defense industries would contribute to the development of the independent Ukraine.

The Ukrainian Experiments
Neal B. Mitchell, Jr., Neal Mitchell Associates

The author has extensive experience in Ukraine-U.S.A. joint venture development in housing construction, air freight, computer software development and other potentially commercial defense conversions. Lack of entrepreneurial capital and the great chasm between Ukrainian and American business experience have been major obstacles. In the housing and air freight endeavors, working with retired military officers he has developed promising bartering arrangements that might overcome this problem. In computer software development, their joint venture partnership with the Institute of Cybernetics, the leading Mathematical Institute of the F.S.U., shows considerable promise of developing sophisticated products that are marketable abroad, although lack of knowledge in investments and commercialization presents difficulties. The author concludes that to be successful in defense conversion will require courage, creativity, and commitment (CCC). The crisis is severe enough in the F.S.U. to demand action so that CCC seems to be in abundance in the F.S.U. However, it is hard to find the required ingredients here in the United States. While conversion of weapons is a state-to-state program that requires both trust and mutual guarantees, defense conversion cannot succeed as a totally government initiative, since the major skill of any government is in spending money and not making it. It might succeed as a private exercise. The real essence of Defense conversion is that it can create large scale opportunities for regional development so that the conversions themselves are considered within a changing social and economic fabric and not as individual vignettes. How well we do will directly impact the lives of our children and grandchildren. We can't afford to fail.

The Middle Ultraviolet (MUV)
Alex E. S. Green, University of Florida

This chapter illustrates how a feasibility analysis of a military satellite system for detecting hostile rocket launches became a program of research and development on environmental applications of the middle ultraviolet (MUV). The defense study, supported in 1962 by Convair San Diego, then a division of General Dynamics, examined special features of the middle ultraviolet defined as the 340–170-nanometer spectral region. The study led to a Convair report that addressed the MUV emissions of fires, particularly rocket plumes; absorption by the ozone layer; background sources such as aurora and airglow; active atomic and molecular species, and quantitative optical techniques. Some far-sighted Department of Defense (DoD) program managers of the 1960 period encouraged the author to sanitize the report and convert it into a scientific monograph. The report was thus converted into the first monograph "The Middle Ultraviolet, Its Science and Technology" that focused primarily on scientific topics arising in the spectral region where stratospheric ozone and atmospheric oxygen are the dominant absorbing species. Government funding for peacetime applications of the MUV developed several years later when the author returned to academic work leading to a MUV-ozone aeronomical-environmental research program productive in scientific works and graduates. Most recently the program is concentrating on tests of proposed replacements for halon fire suppressants whose purpose is to protect the stratospheric ozone layer. Here MUV spectral analysis of fires is proving very informative. Thus, while making a defense conversion, the program has come full circle.

Laser Remote Sensing and Defense Conversion
Vladimir E. Zuev, Institute of Atmospheric Optics, Tomsk, Russia

The unique characteristics of laser radiation are of considerable current use both in military science and in different nonmilitary areas. A typical example of double application of lasers is their use for atmospheric sounding, whose data can be applied, e.g., in gun fire as well as in meteorology or for assessment of ecological condition of the atmosphere. In this connection it is clear that for the case of the use of lasers for remote sensing of the atmosphere the processes of defense conversion should present no problems. In the F.S.U., the problems of remote sensing of the atmosphere have been developing mainly at the Institute of Atmospheric Optics Siberian Branch of the U.S.S.R. Academy of Sciences (now SB of the Russian Academy of Sciences). These programs encompass all the basic aspects of the problem, namely: (1) Development of sounding techniques, (2) Creation of surface-based, ship-, air- and space-borne lidars, (3) coverage of maximum number of the parameters being sounded, (4) solution of corresponding inverse problems, (5) The interaction of laser radiation with the atmosphere, and (6) the use of different lasers for remote sensing in the IR, visible and UV. This chapter describes the most important original results obtained at the Institute of Atmospheric Optics in the last 25 years of its existence and is directly related to the problems of laser remote sensing of the atmosphere. The publications are in the form of monographs, papers and conference reports; the scientists were awarded various degrees and the honors and awards of institute members are summarized. In spite of the difficult years the Institute has preserved its main intellectual potential and unique experimental base that has made it possible to promote the scientific-engineering cooperation between the Institute and leading firms of the F.S.U. as well as International Associations.

Global Positioning System: A Successful Example of Dual-Use Technology
Helmut Hellwig, USAF Office of Scientific Research and
E. David Hinkley, Science and Technology Corporation

The U.S. Global Positioning System (GPS) is a U.S. Department of Defense satellite-based navigation system that provides precise navigation, time recovery and frequency control capabilities to users located anywhere in the world. It was made possible by technologies developed under basic research grants from the U.S. military. Conversion to civilian applications has led to a commercial industry that promises to be a major factor in the U.S. aerospace economy for many years to come. This chapter describes the key technological aspects of GPS and how and why they were supported through the research and development phases. Also covered is the crucial role of industry in recognizing the inherent value of GPS, and how the private sector "leapfrogged" the military in providing small, portable, and low-cost instrumentation available to the "average" person. GPS is an excellent and timely example of Defense Conversion and Dual Use.

Fire Suppression
Charles J. Kibert, USAF Wright Laboratory, and the University of Florida

The phaseout of certain Halon fire suppressants has led to the development of numerous innovative approaches to the fire suppression as well as to a degree of degradation in performance for the current industry offerings of gaseous Halon replacements. Industry offerings for occupied facilities have been generally limited in the United States to chemicals that are supported by the National Fire Protection Association (blends of HCFCs and blends of inert gases and CO_2). These have undergone extensive industry and military testing for a wide variety of applications, and although adequate for many applications, each has performance characteristics that will force the using community to carefully assess the criteria for each application. A recent development has been the emergence of the fluorocarbon family of chemicals as potential across-the-board drop-in replacements for Halons 1211 and 1301. Extensive testing on CF_3I has indicated that it is virtually identical to Halon 1301 in fire suppression performance and toxicity. C_3F_7I is being tested as a replacement for Halon 1211 and has most of the same performance characteristics. Non-gaseous solutions are also being identified, such as aerosols, to include solid particulate aerosols, water mists, and halocarbon mists. This chapter describes U.S. Air Force efforts to find replacements for Halons 1211 and 1301 with test information to date. The development of aerosol fire suppression systems holds great promise in offering an excellent option for consideration for several fire protection roles. An ongoing Air Force research program is examining the basic physics and chemistry of fire suppression aerosols and assessing the employment of aerosol delivery systems for a variety of applications.

Scientific and Technological Aspects of the Problem of Utilization of Military Stores
S. G. Andreev, V. S. Solov'ev, and N. N. Sysoyev, Moscow State University

In the problem of utilization of military stores (MS), great importance is now assigned to the extraction of explosive material (EM) from the casings of artillery projectiles, ammunition, mines, aerial bombs, engineering supplies, and their parts. In this chapter adequate methods are presented for engineering solutions and technology constructed on their bases. The authors consider not only each form of MS, but also different calibers. There will be choices of proper techniques, which both in technological, and also organizational features, are substantially different. The authors attempt to find and consider the possibility of describing the overall action and response mechanisms, with the aim of developing the scientific basis for a theory of safety in the utilization of MS. An investigation of the problem of utilization of MS confirms that one of the main problems is extraction of the explosive charge from the shell of the MS, as this process is especially difficult and dangerous. A cycle of investigations, including a broad spectrum, both of fundamental development and development of models of different principles of extraction of EM from the shell, permits demonstrating not only the effectiveness of these methods, but also the limits of their safe application with sufficiently high efficiency.

Retrofit Engineering: A Methodology for Conversion
Ali Seireg, University of Florida and University of Wisconsin

This chapter presents a dichotomy for the conversion process and outlines the framework of a systematic methodology for the economic conversion of military technology, products and production systems to commercial use. Since the objectives, the economics, management philosophy, and markets are different, successful conversion requires new approaches and new considerations. The proposed methodology provides the guidelines for determining the best match between existing military resources and the needs of the civilian economy. Economic conversion, when applicable, can be achieved by retrofitting, segmenting, and restructuring of existing products, components or processes for optimum utilization. An important and potentially dangerous situation facing the world today is the vast stockpiles of nuclear, chemical, biological and conventional arms which have to be disposed of. This is creating a "flea market" of military hardware and production facilities. Careful attention should be given to their conversion or disposal for maximizing the extraction of any value they can add to the civilian economy and minimizing the impact of disposal on world security and the environment.

Nuclear Technological Perspectives
Alex E. S. Green, University of Florida

This chapter lays the groundwork for discussions of options for reducing weapons-grade uranium and plutonium. It presents (1) the fundamental nuclear physics principles underlying the use of nuclear energy, (2) elementary descriptions of the early nuclear reactors and bombs, (3) a 1994 overview of world nuclear energy facilities, (4) a summary of the development of inherently safe nuclear reactors, and (5) some technical aspects of potential options for the disposition of weapons-grade uranium (WGU) and weapons-grade plutonium (WGP). The denaturing of WGU is readily accomplished by blending with natural uranium (99.3%U-238 and 0.7% U-235) to produce reactor-grade low enriched uranium (LEU) (about 3% U-235). An agreement between the U.S.A. and Russia has been adopted in which Russia will convert 500 tons of HEU to diluted U-235 and sell it to the U.S.A. for further conversion to LEU. The disposition of weapons-grade plutonium is much more difficult and is discussed in the chapters that follow. Economically, with the low cost of oil, natural gas and coal and the relative capital costs of gas-fired combined cycle systems (about $500/kW), coal plants (about $1500/kW) and nuclear plants (on the order of $2500/kW), the direct economic incentive for the construction of new inherently safe reactors at this time is not favorable. The longer range picture, however, must reflect our long-range national interests in maintaining advanced nuclear energy options and must consider long-range environmental and defense externalities.

Plutonium Options
John W. Landis, Chairman, Public Safety Standards Group

Plutonium is an extremely poisonous element that must be handled very carefully and not taken into the body in more than trace quantities. However, the main cause of our concern about plutonium is the hundreds of metric tons of this element that now reside in nuclear warheads, in weapons plants, in weapons scrap piles, in nuclear generating stations, in military and civilian nuclear waste, and in reprocessing plants. There is the possibility that these sources of plutonium will not be tightly controlled and that substantial quantities will be acquired by renegade nations or terrorist groups and used to make bombs or non-explosive critical masses for criminal purposes. Nuclear nations can be categorized into those with: (1) extensive programs in both nuclear power and nuclear weapons, (2) extensive programs only in nuclear power, (3) minor programs in nuclear power and nuclear weapons, (4) minor programs only in nuclear power, (5) minor programs only in nuclear weapons, or (6) no programs in nuclear power or nuclear weapons, but which have possession of weapons-grade plutonium made by the nuclear nations. The options for plutonium disposal include (1) recycling in commercial generating stations, (2) destruction in specially designed power producing reactors, (3) storage in retrievable form at centers supervised by the IAEA, and (4) storage in adulterated form in permanent depositories. Unfortunately, the most attractive options for the disposition of WGP and spent reactor fuel plutonium by different countries varies. There is, of course, much more to say about the options available for the use or disposal of weapons-grade plutonium.

Plutonium: Military and Civilian
W. K. H. Panofsky, Stanford Linear Accelerator Center

The management of plutonium, the only man-made element produced in large quantities, poses unprecedented challenges to man's wisdom. Physically, all isotopes of plutonium can be used to make nuclear explosives, and separation (reprocessing) of plutonium in the civilian fuel cycle increases the risk that that material can be diverted to military use. Yet it is such reprocessing which can extend the energy value of the finite uranium resources of the world by perhaps two orders of magnitude. In this discussion the author addresses first the problem engendered by the release of unprecedented amounts of military plutonium resulting from the reduction of the nuclear weapons stockpiles of the U.S. and Russia, then briefly the future and controversies of civilian plutonium. Before an optimum policy can be developed, the following questions must be answered: (1) What are the current forecasts for the availability of uranium for different parts of the world and the demand forecasts for nuclear electricity? (2) What are the proliferation risks inherent in civilian use of plutonium and how can they be reduced? (3) What is the lead time with which the question on the future role of civilian plutonium must be addressed? (in particular in respect to the needs of the less developed world), (4) When will the scarcity cost of uranium make the civilian plutonium use economically attractive and how large a lead time is required for developing a reliable breeder technology? (5) To what extent should one seek international agreement and standardization of a worldwide approach to the future role of civilian plutonium, or to what extent is it acceptable that countries with varying resources should pursue diverse policies? The author suggests that studying these questions in a manner not distorted by ideological viewpoints or special interests is a matter of urgency.

Nuclear Options: Russian Perspectives
MINATOM, Moscow

The success of the reforms of Russia's economy depends very much on the effectiveness of defense conversion. Russian defense enterprises, at the start of economic restructuring, produced up to 60 percent of the total volume of civil products and consumer goods. A significant portion belonged to MINATOM industry. During the last three years this portion has grown. Russia derives approximately 12 percent of its electricity from 24 operating nuclear power plants all supplied by MINATOM. MINATOM's concept for using plutonium is based on the evolutionary development of technologies mastered in Russia: (1) solution to the problem of reliable and safe pre-reactor storage of recovered weapons-grade plutonium (WGP); (2) the initial use of plutonium in FBRs; (3) orientation for the use of WGP and reactor-grade plutonium (RGP) within the scope of nuclear power centers; (4) the development of a safe fast breeder reactor as an efficient "utilizer" of plutonium and producer of uranium-233; (5) an analysis of the potential for development of a light water reactor (LWR) for the use of WGP; (6) the development of enhanced safety LWR that operates on uranium-233 fuel; and (7) the development of a technology for a safe closed fuel cycle based on plutonium and uranium-233. Taking into consideration all the above, MINATOM proposes WGP utilization, based on the evolutionary development of reactor technologies traditional to Russia. Any short-term plutonium management program must be based on the safe and reliable storage of WPG until it can be used in reactors. RGP should be utilized first, and WGP should be utilized later and its reprocessing technology should be initially tested on the BN-600. The future orientation on nuclear power centers should include a reliable solution to the non-proliferation problem.

Afterword
Alex E. S. Green, University of Florida

   This chapter summarizes important recent developments in defense conversion with emphasis on nuclear weapons control, the central problem of the Cold War. The recent "Nuclear Posture Review" (NPR) by the U.S. Department of Defense that directly addresses the issue of nuclear weapons is described. This was the first review of U.S. nuclear policy in 15 years, and the first study ever to include policy, doctrine, force structure, command and control, operations, supporting infrastructure, safety and security, and arms control in a single study. The Nunn-Lugar Cooperative Threat Reduction Program that provides U.S. Government funds to help dismantle the former Soviet nuclear arsenal and convert the Soviet weapons industry to civilian production is next summarized. Other United States funding organizations fostering defense conversions in the F.S.U. are then listed. Recently much larger sources of funding for joint ventures have developed for economic conversion. These programs are relevant because the same centralized authority formerly controlled both the civilian and defense sectors of the F.S.U. economy. Next, Russian-American collaborations in space, the scene of the most intense U.S.A.-F.S.U. Cold War competition, are described. Finally, the feasibility of defense conversion is assessed, and it is concluded that cooperative nuclear threat reduction from MAD (mutually assured destruction) levels, while pursuing defense conversion to recover as much as possible of Cold War costs, should help lower the indebtedness of former antagonists and help restore them to their rightful places among the nations of the world and set the stage for international cooperation towards further disarmament.

CHAPTER 1

Background and Dimensions of the Defense Buildup

Victor V. Chernyy
Bureau of Defense Conversion, Technological
Industrial Development of Ukraine
Arlington, Virginia.

Introduction

The twentieth century witnessed an arms race and stockpiling of weapons which had no precedent in human history. The major reason for that was not so much imperial ambitions of the major capitalist powers, but a deep ideological division of the world which emerged as one of the most important factors influencing historic developments of our time. In this context, events that took place in Russia in 1917 had a major significance.

Background of the Soviet Military Buildup

The victory of the Great October Socialist Revolution of 1917 and the establishment of the dictatorship of the proletariat brought about radical changes in the political system of Russia. Those developments had serious implications for the whole world.

The October Revolution fundamentally changed the position of the Communist Party, which became the governing party in the world's first Socialist State of workers and peasants. The new rulers of Russia were confronted with a number of historic tasks: the building up and strengthening of the Soviet State, the reorganization of society along Socialist lines, the organization of the country's defense against hostile international encirclement, and the strengthening of contacts with the proletarians of other countries in order to spread the Socialist Revolution worldwide.

The Soviets took great pride in what they believed to be superiority of their political and economic system. Buttressed by military power it elevated the Soviet Union to a superpower status. A fundamental goal of Soviet national strategy was to achieve the status that would guarantee "equal participation in world affairs" and "freedom from any criticism or interference in Soviet internal affairs."

Based on the Marxist-Leninist ideology, which taught that the Soviet Russia was engaged in a long-term struggle between two basically irreconcilable political, economic and social systems, the Soviet national strategy envisaged a basically adversarial relationship and engagement of the Soviet Union in a continual struggle with the West.

That conflict required a total integration of political, military, and economic components of the Soviet national power that eventually led to the militarization of the Soviet economy, to the emergence of one of the largest military-industrial complexes in the world. The economic cost of creation of the Soviet defense industry was immense. The Soviet system of centralized planning and management facilitated appropriation of huge resources, often at the expense of living standards and investment in industries essential for civilian economic growth, to meet military requirements especially in high technology and heavy industry. Practically at all levels of the party and government decision making there existed institutional mechanisms to enforce defense production priorities.

Several factors complimented the economic planning and management system in the maintenance of military priorities. The military five-year and long-term defense plans were prepared before national economic plans were formulated, ensuring that the military was given priority over other sectors and that military resources requirements were incorporated into national plans. The long administrative tenure of many managers throughout the military-industrial complex promoted stability and continuity in weapons development and production. Weapons systems were approved at the highest levels of the party and government. Funding was typically authorized for a system's entire production cycle. That process enabled the Soviet Union to select weapons for priority development while avoiding the uncertainties of annual budgetary reviews and funding adjustments that occurred in western democracies.

The Military-Industrial Complex of the Soviet Union

The military-industrial complex of the Soviet Union, according to various estimates, comprised more than two thousand enterprises employing up to 10 million people in the labor force including best qualified workers and managers operating in the most modern facilities (Nunn and Lugar, 1992).

By the 1980s the defense industry of the Soviet Union had expanded dramatically and was better equipped to produce large quantities of advanced weapons than ever before. In accordance with the estimates, the U.S.S.R. accounted for one-half of the world's output of military material, turning out three-quarters of the world's ballistic and surface-to-air missiles, more than one-half of its tanks and bombers, and better than a third of its artillery submarines, fighters, cruise missiles, light armor and military helicopters (DoD, 1988a).

In terms of conventional forces, the output of ground force systems has remained generally stable, although production of some weapons systems such as tanks and self-propelled artillery has increased. Tank industries of the Soviet Union have produced more than 40,000 modern tanks including the T-64, T-72 and T-80 which were equipped with new technology such as laser rangefinders, reactive armor and improved tank guns (DoD,1988a). To support ground forces the Soviet Union was investing heavily in modernizing its air tactical assets, including production of more technologically advanced and combat capable helicopters.

New programs were launched to modernize the Soviet Navy. Their primary goal was to build fewer but much more capable surface warships, submarines and auxiliary ships. The first unit of a new class of aircraft carrier displacing 65,000 metric tons, approaching the size of U.S. carriers, was under construction.

Strategic nuclear forces were accorded a high priority in the Soviet military program. The strategic ballistic missile industry was engaged in continuous expansion and modernization. In the 1980s the U.S.S.R. completed series production of its fourth generation ICBM force and has produced significant numbers of fifth generation systems. To enhance the capabilities of its strategic forces the Soviet Union developed nuclear-armed, long-range cruise missiles to be stationed on strategic bombers and submarines. New classes of nuclear powered ballistic missile submarines like the Typhoon and the Delta IV, as well as other types of nuclear attack submarines, were put into production. Considerable attention was paid to the upgrading and the modernization of the Soviet long-range bomber force, involving development of such systems as Bear H cruise missile carriers and Blackjack. As of January 1, 1988, the Soviet Union had approximately 10,000 charges on strategic delivery vehicles (Yazov, 1988).

Soviet strategic forces were the core of the Soviet military machine. In accordance with various estimates during the 1980s, the Soviet Union allocated resources equivalent to approximately $400 billion for strategic offensive and defensive programs. Strategic forces have been upgraded when deployment of a forth generation of ICBMs was completed. The SS-17, SS-18, SS-19 and road mobile SS-25 were put into operation. A new ballistic missile submarine (Typhoon) carrying 20 SS-N-20 MIRVed missiles was introduced followed by the new Delta IV with even more capable SS-N-23. Soviet long-range bomber capabilities were enhanced by the introduction of the Bear H armed with the AS-15 nuclear-armed cruise missile.

The Soviets have invested enormous effort and resources in increasing the survivability of their strategic weapons against nuclear attack. For example, they placed missiles in rebuilt hard silos and introduced the road-mobile system SS-25. Modernization of ICBMs was accompanied by the introduction of the intermediate-range and medium-range ballistic missiles—the number of them exceeded 400.

Within the framework of a military buildup increasing attention was paid to the development of space-related strategic offensive and defensive systems. Their primary goal was to support military operations on Earth. The Soviet Union conducted approximately 100 space launches annually. The high launch rate allowed the U.S.S.R. to maintain an increasing number of active satellites in orbit, up to 150 in 1987, including a space-based global navigation satellite system and radar-carrying satellite systems.

A significant role in the space efforts of the U.S.S.R. was played by the manned space program. In the mid '80s the Soviet Union launched a new generation space station MIR to replace SALYUT-7. With the launch of MIR, which represented a space station module and regular crew rotation with the SOYUZ-TM capsule, the U.S.S.R. began its permanent manned presence in space. In 1987, in the Soviet Union made the first flight test of the "Energiya," a space vehicle designed to launch the Soviet space shuttle orbiter.

To be able to implement all these programs the Soviet government had to spend enormous financial and material resources. It is estimated that Moscow's military expenditure amounted to 15–17 percent of the gross national product of the U.S.S.R. (DoD, 1988b).

The United States Military Buildup

One has to be fair and say that the United States was not lagging behind the Soviet Union in military buildup, often taking the lead in the development of new arms. Initiative in the production of new weapons systems was often taken by the American side and not by the Soviets. Table 1 illustrates major weapons systems indicating the initiation dates by the U.S.A. and the U.S.S.R. (Anon., 1984).

In the 1980s the U.S. annual military budget grew to more than $300 billion, amounting to approximately 5 percent of the GNP (Carlucci, 1990). In the 1980s, the United States proceeded with a number of new weapons programs designed to upgrade and modernize existing systems.

Nuclear Strategic Forces: Three new weapons systems were deployed in large numbers. Five hundred fifty Minuteman III ICBMs with three warheads each were put into service. Among them 300 were ready for reequipment with the highly accurate new MK12A reentry vehicles, with three 350 kt warheads; 496 Poseidon C-3 SLBMs, each with 10 to 14 warheads, were

Table 1. Major Weapon Systems Indicating the Init
by the U.S.A. and the U.S.S.R. (Anon., 198

Weapon System	U.S.A.	U.S.S.R.
Nuclear Weapons	Mid-1940s (used Aug. 1945)	Late 1940s
Intercontinental Strategic Bombers	Mid-1950s	Late 1950s
Nuclear-powered Submarines	Mid-1950s	Late 1950s
Nuclear-powered Aircraft Carriers	Early 1960s	None
Multiple Independently Targetable Re-entry Vehicles	Late 1960s	Mid-1970s
Neutron Weapons	Late 1970s to early 1980s	None
Long-range Cruise Missiles	Mid-1970s	Mid-1980s

installed on 31 nuclear-powered missile submarines. The strategic bomber force acquired the SRAM system; 268 B-52G and B-52H heavy bombers were fitted to take 20 SRAM attack missiles and 65 FB-111A medium-range bombers to take six. Plans were developed that visualized deployment of M-X intercontinental ballistic missiles, Pershing-II medium-range ballistic missiles, and the B-1 strategic bomber.

A second generation of air-launched cruise missiles with increased range and STEALTH technology went into production. Work was expanded on the development of a fundamentally new strategic STEALTH advanced technology bomber.

The U.S. Navy put into service Trident (Ohio-class) nuclear-powered submarines armed with Trident I missiles. The U.S. was also proceeding with a program for the development and deployment of a new SLBM Trident (D-5).

General Purpose Forces: As part of its buildup the U.S. military leadership attached great importance to expanding the theater nuclear forces. As a result of repeated modernizations obsolete tactical and carrier-based nuclear-capable aircraft were discarded and replaced with new, more accurate and longer range weapons: Pershing IA and lance missiles and F-4, F-III, A-6 and A-7 aircraft that can deliver nuclear weapons within a range of 30 to 2000 km.

The U.S. Army received a new tank, the more powerful M60A3 battle tank, and a new M-1 ABRAMS. The outdated antitank guided missiles were replaced by improved TOW and DRAGON versions. In reequipping the Army, great importance was attached to saturating it with antitank weapons systems, including helicopter borne. The new AH-64-A helicopter gun ship equipped with Hellfire ATGMs was delivered to the Army. Large-scale deliveries to the Army of M-2 infantry fighting vehicles were aimed at considerable improvement of the fighting capabilities of the Army's motorized infantry units.

To increase the capability for airlifting troops, plans were made to modernize the C-5A aircraft, to purchase new KC-10 cargo/tanker aircraft, C-5B aircraft and C-17 heavy transport aircraft designed primarily for use by the Rapid Deployment Force.

In structuring the tactical air force, much attention was given to increasing its striking capabilities. The force was equipped with F-15 all-weather fighters and its modification, an A-10 attack aircraft for close ground support, and F-16 fighter-bombers. The striking power of the force was also increased by equipment of the air units with guided missiles and guided bombs of various types and by mounting weapons control laser devices on the aircraft. Dozens of E-3A AWACS aircraft were supplied to make the tactical air force more effective.

The U.S. persistent policy of building up its military strength was leading to an unprecedented expansion of arms production and its military-industrial complex. For example, in 1983 the Pentagon placed contracts with various sectors of the economy for 140 billion dollars. Nearly half of this amount went to the 25 biggest arms and equipment manufacturers, including McDonnell Douglas, United Technologies, General Dynamics, Boeing and General Electric. The U.S. military production in the 1980s accounted for three fourths output of aircraft and missiles, approximately one half of artillery and small arms, and more than two thirds of naval ships produced by all NATO member-states.

By the mid '80s the arms race reached unprecedented and dangerous scales and enormous military potentials emerged, both in the East and West. Table 2 (Yazov, 1988) and Table 3 (WTO, 1989) show quantities of strategic offensive arms of the U.S.S.R. and the U.S.A. (as of January 1, 1988).

Improvement in East-West Relations

Since 1985 substantial improvements in East-West relations eventually led to an end of the "Cold War" and significantly transformed the world security environment. An important impulse to the process was given in 1985

**Table 2. Quantities of Strategic Offensive Arms of the U.S.S.R. and the U.S.A.
as of January 1, 1988 (Yazov, 1988)**

	U.S.S.R.	U.S.A.
ICBM launchers	1,390	1,000
including MIRVed ICBM launchers	812	550
SLBM launchers	942	672
including MIRVed SLBM launchers	388	640
Total no. of ICBM and SLBM launchers,	2,332	1,672
including MIRVed ICBM and SLBM launchers	1,200	1,190
Heavy bombers,	162	588
including heavy bombers equipped to carry cruise missiles	72	161
Total no. of ICBM and SLBM launchers and heavy bombers,	2,494	2,260
including ICBM and SLBM launchers and heavy bombers, MIRVed and equipped to carry cruise missiles	1,272	1,351
Total no. of charges on strategic delivery vehicles (approx.)	10,000	14,000-16,000

at the Geneva meeting between President R. Reagan and the General Secretary
of the CPSU Central Committee M. Gorbachev. The leaders of the United
States and the U.S.S.R. recognized the special responsibility of the two
countries for safeguarding peace and declared jointly that nuclear war should
never be unleashed. They also declared that neither side would seek military
superiority. These statements were followed by further East-West political
declarations.

The Paris Charter for a New Europe, signed in the French capital by the
Conference on Security and Cooperation in Europe (CSCE) countries on
November 21, 1990, declared that the era of confrontation and division of
Europe had ended. The states signatories also pledged their commitment to a
pluralist democracy, the rule of law and human rights, which were essential to
lasting security on the continent (TASS, 1990a).

Table 3. Correlation of Basic Types of Armaments (WTO, 1989)

	WTO	Ratio	NATO
Tactical combat aircraft of the air forces, air defense forces and navies	7,786	1.1:1	7,130
Tactical combat aircraft of the air force and air defense forces	5,355	1:1	5,450
AD interceptors that cannot be employed against ground targets	1,829	36:1	50
Naval combat aircraft	692	1:2.4	1,630
Total number of attack aircraft in the air force and naval tactical aviation	2,783	1:1.5	4,075
Combat helicopters, including those in the navies	2,785	1:1.9	5,270
Tactical missile launch systems	1,608	11.8:1	136
Tanks	59,470	1.9:1	30,690
Anti-tank missile launchers	11,465	1:1.6	18,070
Infantry fighting vehicles and armored personnel carriers	70,330	1.5:1	46,900
Multiple launch rocket system, artillery pieces (75mm calibre and larger) and mortars (50mm calibre and larger)	71,560	1.3:1	57,060
Submarines, conventional (except strategic ballistic missile submarines)	228	1.1:1	200
Submarines, nuclear-powered	80	1:1	76
Large surface ships and amphibious ships with 1,200+ ton displacement	102	1:5	499
Ships capable of carrying aircraft, aircraft carriers	2	1:7.5	15
Cruise missile ships	23	1:11.9	274
Amphibious ships (1,200 ton displacement+)	24	1:3.5	84

The joint declaration of 22 states, members of NATO and the Warsaw Treaty Organization signified another important step towards improvement of the international climate. It stated that the signatories were no longer adversaries and that they would build new partnerships and extend to each other the hand of friendship (TASS, 1990b).

Political pronouncements of the confronting parties were supported by very important political steps. In 1986, in Stockholm, the 35 participants at the Conference on Security and Cooperation in Europe reached an agreement on Confidence and Security Building Measures (CSBM) which substantially reduced military confrontation and advanced confidence in the building process in Europe.

The second agreement on Confidence and Security Building Measures was adopted by CSCE participating states in March 1992, in Vienna. This agreement was an important step forward as it superseded all previous CSBM agreements. The 1992 Vienna Document, which expands upon the 1990 Vienna Document and extends the zone of application to cover the territories of new CSCE members, entered into force on May 1, 1992. It contains a number of improved provisions and some new CSBMs including: annual exchange of data on stationed troops and equipment, lowered military exercise notification thresholds (from 13,000 troops and 300 tanks to 9,000 troops and 250 tanks); lowered observation thresholds for large-scale military exercises (from 17,000 troops to 13,000 troops and 300 tanks for ground force activities and from 5,000 troops to 3,500 troops for amphibious landing and airborne assaults); provisions for demonstration of new weapons and equipment types; constraints on size, frequency and scheduling of notifiable military exercises (State, 1992).

Provisions of the CSBM agreements were supplemented by other steps aimed at confidence and security building in Europe. The first Annual Implementation Assessment Meeting was held in Vienna on November 11–15, 1991. A seminar on military doctrine (October 8–18, 1991) and seminars on defense conversion (February 19–21, 1992) and Western concepts of civil-military relations (March 4–6, 1992), were held in Vienna by the CSCE Conflict Prevention Center. Political measures, aimed at further improvements in East-West relations, establishment in Europe and in the world of a new, more secure environment, were supplemented by a number of important practical steps in terms of reduction of conventional and nuclear forces.

It took less than 21 months to complete the Treaty on Conventional Armed Forces in Europe (CFE). Signed on November 19, 1990, the Treaty signified an historic event which reflected a mutual desire of former adversaries to establish a stable and more secure balance of NATO and Warsaw Pact conventional forces. It aimed to eliminate force disparities prejudicial to stability and security and, according to the negotiation mandate, to eliminate "the capability for launching a surprise attack and for initiating large-scale offensive action."

At the same time, the agreement to a certain extent represented a compromise between the major military superpowers, the U.S.S.R. and the U.S.A. The Soviet Union agreed among other things to the application of the openness principal to arms reduction in terms of acceptance of intrusive verification measures. It revealed good faith in implementing unilateral and negotiated withdrawal and reduction commitments, abandonment of the so-called "Brezhnev doctrine" and military disengagement from Eastern and Central Europe.

In its part, the U.S. Administration put on its high priority list the early completion of the CFE accord and accepted the inclusion into the Treaty of aircraft, helicopters and U.S. and Soviet foreign stationed manpower. This American proposal was endorsed by U.S. Allies at the May 29 NATO summit and formally presented on July 13, 1989.

The CFE Treaty covers very wide territory in a 2.5 million square mile area extending from the Atlantic Ocean to the Ural Mountains and stipulates the reduction of the equipment essential for a large-scale attack. The CFE Treaty includes limits on five items: battle tanks, armored combat vehicles, artillery pieces, combat aircraft and attack helicopters. It also sets limits on the quantity of bridging equipment that can be kept at any one time in active forces (CRS, 1990). The Treaty is complemented by a separate politically binding declaration committing each side not to increase its land-based naval aircraft beyond an agreed ceiling.

The guiding principle adopted for CFE reductions was that the holdings of the two groups of states, in each of the Treaty limited equipment categories, had to be brought down to an equal level set at some 10–15 percent below the lowest levels held by either side. A total limit on the number of arrangements acceptable in the ATTU area was agreed upon and divided by two, according to the principle of parity.

As a result, each group of states is able to keep a maximum of: 20,000 tanks; 30,000 armored combat vehicles; 20,000 artillery pieces; 6,800 combat aircraft and 2,000 attack helicopters. Armored vehicle launched bridges, although not subject to reductions, will be limited to 740 pieces in active forces on each side. In addition, each group of states has committed itself in a separate declaration not to raise its holdings of land-based naval aircraft to more than 430 planes, no more than 400 of which can belong to a single country.

The development by NATO of new mechanisms of cooperation with the Newly Independent States, such as the North Atlantic Cooperation Council and the Partnership for Peace Program, added an unprecedented dimension to the relationship of the Alliance with its former adversaries. Russia joined the Partnership for Peace on June 22, 1994. Thus, NATO and the major inheritor of the Soviet Union took a significant step in furthering their partnership and in formulating innovative approaches to promoting pan-European stability and security. NATO and Russia recognized that their constructive relations of mutual respect, benefit and friendship are a key element of security and stability in Europe and in the interest of all other states in the CSCE area. The parties emphasized the importance of Russia's joining the Partnership for Peace for further development of their cooperation through practical steps in the fields covered by this program. NATO and Russia agreed to pursue a broad, enhanced dialogue and cooperation in areas where Russia has unique and important contributions to make, commensurate with its weight and responsibility as a major European, international and nuclear power through: sharing of information on issues regarding politico-military related matters having a European dimension; political consultations, as appropriate, on issues of common concern; and cooperation in a range of security-related matters including, as appropriate, peacekeeping (NATO, 1994).

Nuclear Disarmament

A new era in a nuclear disarmament was opened by the U.S.-Soviet Treaty on Intermediate Nuclear Forces (INF) which was signed in Washington on December 8, 1987, by General Secretary of the CASU Central Committee M. S. Gorbachev and President Ronald Reagan. It was the first but very significant step towards nuclear disarmament. The goal of the INF Treaty was to eliminate the most destabilizing component of both superpowers' armed forces, all existing intermediate-range and shorter-range missiles, as well as the launchers and certain support facilities for those missiles, and to prohibit such missiles and equipment thereafter (State, 1987).

For the Soviet Union, U.S. land-based missiles such as the Pershing II and the BGM-109G as well as the Pershing IA have been perceived as having a first-strike potential. Their flight time to targets on the European part of the Soviet Union was only 8–10 minutes. In these circumstances it was very difficult, if possible at all, to build an antimissile defense. As a result, many military and sensitive facilities were exposed to the U.S. military threat.

On the other hand, for the United States, Soviet intermediate-range and short-range missiles SS-20, SS-4, SS-5, SS-12 and SS-23 have been regarded as designed to intimidate Western Europe and to drive a wedge between the United States and its European allies in their collective defense commitments.

The INF Treaty reflected a positive change in the dynamics of the East-West confrontation. In agreeing to the elimination of intermediate-range and short-range missiles, the Soviet side accepted a couple of very critical principles: on-site inspection and asymmetrical reductions, which showed greater Soviet willingness to accommodate Western concerns in other negotiations including those on strategic nuclear arms. Achievement of agreements on the INF and CFE facilitated completion of the START negotiations held since 1982.

Most of the outstanding issues were resolved in early July 1991. President Gorbachev and President Bush resolved the final issues during the Economic Summit in London in mid-July and signed START at the end of July 1991. START was the third strategic offensive arms control agreement negotiated by the United States and the Soviet Union. It followed the 1972 SALT Agreement, which capped the number of strategic offensive launchers on both sides, and the 1979 SALT II Treaty, which was never ratified but set new launcher limits that would have required some Soviet but no U.S. reductions and also constrained force modernization.

The Treaty represents the most complicated and comprehensive arms control agreement ever negotiated: reducing the strategic offensive arsenals (ICBMs, SLBMs, and manned strategic bombers and their weapons) of both nations by roughly 25–30 percent and setting certain limits on future force modernization within the new limits. In addition to the treaty itself, the agreed, joint, and other statements totaled 280 pages, reflecting the trend in arms control agreements with more specificity and detail to avoid ambiguities or misinterpretations of treaty obligations. To this must be added the May 23, 1992 protocol signed between the U.S. and the four Soviet successor states that have weapons covered by START, Russia, Belarus, Kazakhstan, and Ukraine.

The central limits that the Soviet Union and the United States agreed to include in START are shown in Table 4 (USACDA, 1992). Besides that, the treaty allows "downloading" of warheads on some MIRVed missiles and promotes extensive notifications and inspections to facilitate compliance with the monitoring provisions. The START monitoring regime is based on the precedents of the INF (Intermediate Nuclear Forces, 1987) and CFE

(Conventional Armed Forces in Europe, 1990) Treaties. It combines the use of national technical means (NTM) and extensive notifications and on-site inspections (OSI), including continuous monitoring of some facilities in both nations. In addition, the treaty addresses concerns of the United States in the area of test flight data, called telemetry, which is crucial to monitoring various quantitative and qualitative limits. Telemetry now must be broadcast and the tapes of telemetry exchanged after flight tests. Table 4 shows the central limits agreed upon by the Soviet Union and the United States to be included in START (State, 1987).

Another step by the United States and Russia to sharply reduce their strategic nuclear weapons was made on January 9, 1992, during the Moscow Summit (TASS, 1992a). Presidents Yeltsin and Bush signed a Treaty on Further Reduction and Limitation of Strategic Offensive Armaments (START-2). The purpose of this document is to eliminate many of the 9,500 U.S. weapons and 6,500 Russian weapons which might have been deployed under START. The new agreement bans all land-based, multiple warhead ballistic missiles (MIRVed ICBMs) and cuts in half the number of warheads carried on U.S. submarine launched ballistic missiles (SLBMs). In addition, all weapons deployed on bombers will count under the new limits on total weapons. (Most bomber weapons would not have counted under the limits in START.) Finally, the new agreement will not impose equal limits on each side's forces. Instead, it sets a range within which each nation can choose a force level that satisfies its own national security, political and economic needs. START weapons elimination rules will pertain.

Reductions and limitations on strategic offensive armaments will be achieved in two stages. At the first stage, seven years after the START Treaty comes into force, each of the sides will reduce its strategic offensive armaments to the following levels:

Overall number of warheads—3,800–4,250 units;
Warheads on MIRVed ICBMs—1200 units;
Warheads on heavy intercontinental ballistic missiles—650 units;
Warheads on submarine based ballistic missiles—2160 units.

At the second stage before January 1, 2003, all other measures to achieve strategic offensive armaments limits established for the sides will be executed.

Table 4. Central Limits Agreed Upon by the Soviet Union and the United States to be Included in START (State, 1987)

	U.S.A.	F.S.U.
Strategic Nuclear Delivery Vehicles (SNDVs): Deployed ICBMs and their launchers, Deployed SLBMs and their launchers and Deployed Heavy Bombers	1600	1600
Accountable Warheads	6000	6000
Total Warheads deployed on ICBMs and SLBMs	4900	4900
Warheads on Mobile ICBMs	1100	1100
Warheads on 154 Heavy ICBMs	1540	1540
Heavy Bombers equipped for long-range nuclear ALCMS (LRNA)	10 warheads-1st 150 bombers. Each additional bomber its LRNA capacity. No LRNA heavy bombers > 20 ALCMs.	8 warheads-1st 180 bombers Each additional bomber its LRNA capacity. No LRNA heavy bombers > 16 LRNA.
Heavy Bomber Aircraft equipped for nuclear weapons other than LRNA (warhead per bomber)	1	1
Throw-weight ceiling: Aggregate payload of ICBMs and SLBMs (metric tons)	3600	3600

The total number of nuclear warheads on strategic offensive armaments of Russia and the United States will decrease to 3,000–3,500 units. All MIRVed ICBMs, the most destabilizing elements of the strategic forces of both countries, will be removed from their positions. Each side shall reduce the number of nuclear warheads on their submarine-based ballistic missiles to 1,700–1,750 units (White House, 1992).

The visit of President Yeltsin to Washington on September 26–27, 1994 gave a fresh impulse to the nuclear disarmament of the U.S. and Russia. The parties committed themselves to accelerate the disarmament process and lay the groundwork for a third-stage Strategic Arms Reduction treaty

(START-3). This is supposed to be accomplished by the immediate start of removal of nuclear missile warheads as START-2 is retired, instead of phasing the removal in years that the 1992 treaty allows. The parties also reached an agreement regarding exchange of information on stocks of nuclear armaments and fissile materials, and moved forward towards a formal understanding sought by the White House that would draw a distinct boundary between theater missile defenses and the long-range ballistic missile defenses that are restricted by the ABM Treaty of 1972 (Aviation Week & Space Technology, 1994).

Nuclear disarmament was accompanied by substantial improvements in East-West relations. A significant step in East-West reconciliation was created under the auspices of NATO of the North Atlantic Cooperation Council to engage former Warsaw Pact nations in the Western military security system. This event reflected a growing transatlantic recognition that the overriding goal of European security policies at the end of the Cold War should be the development of a cooperative system of security in the Euro-Atlantic area, which would operate in a more cooperative political environment and be embodied in the diplomacy of conflict resolution, operated principally through the Conference on Security and Cooperation in Europe.

A positive evolution in international affairs, i.e., their transformation from confrontation to cooperation and partnership, resulted in dramatic changes in national goals and security priorities of the former Soviet Union's republics. As it has been declared by the Supreme Soviet of the Russian Federation, new Russian military concepts are to be based on the perception of strengthened international security, diminishing the threat of new military regional and global conflicts (TASS, 1992b).

Ukraine, the second biggest Republic of the former Soviet Union, proclaimed its national goal to be a neutral and nuclear free state.

In absence of the Soviet threat, dramatic changes in the international environment had serious implications for U.S. national military strategy. The new U.S. military concept is based on the perception that today's world is evolving from a bipolar to multi-polar environment. That resulted in the change in the strategy from a focus on global war footing to a focus on regional contingencies, and on the ability to deal with individual crises without their escalating to a global conflict. This put on the agenda the restructuring of the armed forces, first of all, in terms of making them more capable and threat oriented.

U.S. military planners refer to these type of forces as "the Base Force." Smaller in size, but more mobile and capable, they are located in the United

States and focus on the Atlantic region, the Pacific rim, contingencies in other regions and on continued nuclear deterrence.

President Clinton in his statement before the World Affairs Council on August 13, 1992, revealed his plans to (1) reduce U.S. forces, (2) to review the list of defense industries and laboratories that will be needed, and (3) promised to make security and savings compatible. These developments mean that the huge military complexes of the former adversaries are facing a difficult period of adaptation to new internal conditions and a new international security environment.

The success of the former Soviet Union and the United States in this field depends a lot on whether they will be able to combine their efforts to overcome the difficulties, to be partners in preserving and defending the stability and security of the world.

References

Anon, 1984: *Whence the Threat to Peace,* Third edition, Military Publishing House, Moscow.

Aviation Week & Space Technology, 1994: October 3.

Carlucci, F. C., 1990: Secretary of Defense Annual Report to the Congress, p. 219-221.

CRS Report, 1990: for the Congress, "Treaty on Conventional Armed Forces in Europe: A Primer," December 17.

DoD, 1988a: *Soviet Military Power: An Assessment of the Threat,* U.S. Department of Defense, 37- 38.

DoD, 1988b: ibid DoDa, 32.

Dipl., 1992: Diplomatic Vesnik, Moscow, #13-14, July 15-31.

NATO, 1994: #4, August Review.

Nunn, S. and R. Lugar, 1992: Senators Trip Report: A Visit to the Commonwealth of Independent States, March 6-10.

State, 1987: "Treaty on the Elimination of the Intermediate-Range and Shorter Range Missiles," Publication 9555, December.

State, 1992: Vienna Document, Dispatch Supplement Vol. 3, Supl. #3, July.

TASS Report, 1990a: Paris Charter, Nov. 20.

TASS Report, 1990b: The Joint Declaration of the 22 States, Nov. 20.

TASS Report, 1992a: START-2 Treaty, Jan. 9

TASS Report, 1992b: April 14.

USACDA, 1992: Fact Sheet, June 22.

White House, 1992: Fact Sheet START II, Dec. 30.

WTO and NATO, 1989: *Correlation of Forces in Europe,* Novosti Press Agency Publishing House, Moscow.

Yazov, D., 1988: *On the Military Balance of Forces and Nuclear Missile Parity*, Novosti Press Agency Publishing House, Moscow

CHAPTER 2

Approaches to Defense Conversion

George L. Donohue*
Project AIR FORCE
RAND

Background

Post-Cold War cuts in American military spending are forcing firms and employees in various defense-related industries to make the often difficult transition to the civilian economy. In adopting a policy toward this process of "defense conversion," the Government may choose one of two options. The first option is simply to let normal market forces determine the most successful conversion routes. The other option is to intervene: to ease the conversion process by providing special assistance to those companies and workers that have been hurt by loss of defense contracts.

Which approach is likely to prevail? Will the Government commit massive resources to cushion the conversion process for defense-related industries even though it previously made little effort to provide cushions for such declining sectors of the economy as the oil, automotive and steel industries? Can the Government's current, small-scale policy of intervention be effective? To put such questions into proper perspective it is important first to address several common misconceptions about the ways in which defense spending cuts are affecting the nation's economy.

Common Misconceptions

Defense spending is declining at an unprecedented rate. The truth is that much sharper reductions in defense spending levels occurred after Korea and Vietnam (see Neu and Kennedy, 1993; Dertouzos and Dardia, 1993). Figure 1 shows how the declines from peak defense spending levels as a

*Since August 1994, Research and Acquisitions, Federal Aviation Administration

DEFENSE CONVERSION

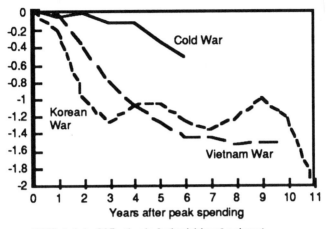

Figure 1. Post war reductions in real defense outlays (Neu and Kennedy, 1993).

percent of the U.S. GNP (or GDP) after the Cold War compare with the declines following the Korean War and Vietnam. Clearly, the current decline is not half as severe as those the nation experienced in the 1950s and the 1970s.

The decline of defense-related industries is a broad national problem. In fact, the problem is best characterized as local, not national (Defense Conversion Commission, 1992; Dertouzos and Dardia, 1993). While it is true that practically every part of the country has suffered some loss of defense-related work, only a few areas have experienced severe impacts. Table 1 shows that California was affected much more dramatically than the other states, suffering almost one-fifth of all the job losses resulting from the defense drawdown (Defense Conversion Commission, 1992). Losses in the great majority of states were minimal. Moreover, an examination of local economic data reveals that California did not suffer serious job attrition statewide. Figure 2, for example, shows that the impact of reduced aerospace work was far greater in the city of Los Angeles than in other parts of the state (Dertouzos and Dardia, 1993).

In that sense, the decline of defense-related industries parallels the earlier decline of the automotive industry. While every section of the country might have been affected by the automakers' difficulties, severe economic disruption was limited almost entirely to the State of Michigan. And in

Table 1. States with the Largest Estimated Number of Private-Sector Job Losses Due to the Defense Drawdown, 1991 to 1997.

State	Thousands of Jobs Lost	Jobs Lost as a Percentage of Total Jobs Lost Nationwide
California	178	19
New York	62	6
Texas	56	6
Virginia	47	5
Massachusetts	46	5
Pennsylvania	38	4
Ohio	38	4
Florida	38	4
Connecticut	37	4
New Jersey	30	3
Total for Top 10	570	60
Total for Job Losses	958	100

Source: Logistics Management Institute, Impacts of Defense Spending Cuts on Industry Sectors, Occupational Groups, and Localities. January 1993.
Note: Job losses represent one-time dislocations and do not reflect the economy's ability to absorb dislocated workers.

Michigan the problem was localized even more: the brunt of the impact was borne by the city of Detroit. Those who consider the economic effects of the defense drawdown to be a national problem do so only because the defense industry has been funded by Congress from the national coffers—not because of any evidence that the cutbacks have caused unusual dislocations nationwide.

Cuts in defense spending are hurting small firms at least as much as they are hurting large ones. The fact is that large firms have borne a far greater share of the burden. Figure 3 shows that the job loss problem as a result of defense cuts has been confined mainly to companies that employ more than

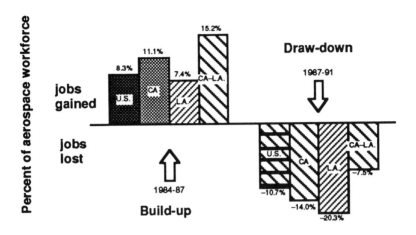

Figure 2. Aerospace has done poorly in Los Angeles.

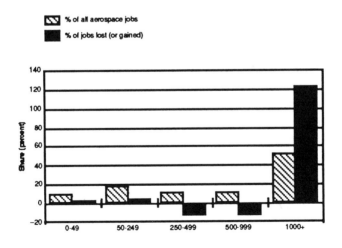

Figure 3. Share of jobs and losses, by firm size.

1000 workers (Dertouzos and Dardia, 1993). Firms employing between 250 and 1000 workers actually increased their employment levels during the 1987 to 1991 period covered by the study. Of the smaller firms, only those with fewer than 50 employees (a tiny percentage of the total picture) showed significant losses. The fear that defense cuts would cause large firms to absorb all of the remaining defense-related work and jettison their smaller subcontractors has not been realized. Yet, although the overwhelming majority of laid-off workers were released by large companies, the focus of federal defense conversion assistance thus far has been on aid to small firms and universities.

Many kinds of industries have been hurt by the defense drawdown. Actually, cutbacks in defense procurements have had the greatest effect on firms lying in a narrow band of the national industrial spectrum. Table 2 shows the four sectors of industry that rely heavily on defense contracts: missiles and space, aircraft, communications, and instruments. Table 3 lists the top 25 Defense Research and Development Test & Evaluation (RDT&E) contractors in 1992. Contractors representing 77 percent of the RDT&E total do most of their work with missiles and space, aircraft, and communications—a clear indication of where the effect of the cutbacks has been concentrated.

The decline of Research and Development activity is one of the most dramatic consequences of the defense drawdown. The facts do not support such a conclusion. Figure 4 shows that R&D spending has been holding at about 10 to 13 percent of the total defense outlay for over 20 years. It is true that the absolute value of the defense budget is declining and that even if the R&D percentage stays constant, the total R&D outlay is being reduced.

Table 2. Percentage of aerospace industries that are heavily defense-dependent (various estimates) (Dertouzos and Dardia, 1993)

Industry (SIC)	Congressional Budget Office (United States)	Department of Commerce (United States)	Data Resources, Inc. (California)
Missiles and space (376)	84%	90%	81%
Aircraft (372)	40-43%	43-46%	41%
Communications (366)	42%	36%	34%
Instruments (381-382)	18%	—	17%

RAND M/R-179-RC, 1993

Table 3. Top 25 DoD RDT&E Contractors

Firm	Primary Product/Location	FY 92 Award ($ millions)
1. Martin Marietta Corp.	Missiles/Colorado	1,600
2. Lockheed Aero Sys. Co.	Aircraft/Georgia & California	1,270
3. General Electric Co.	Diversified/North East U.S.	917
4. Hughes Aircraft Co.	Missiles Elect/California	880
5. McDonnell Douglas Co.	Aircraft/Calif & Missouri	829
6. Foundation Health Co.	Health/California	761
7. Grumman Aerospace Co.	Aircraft&Elect/New York	599
8. TRW, Inc.	Satellites/California	554
9. Loral Vought Systems	Missiles&Elect./Texas	533
10. General Dynamics Co.	Aircraft&Missiles/Cal&Texas	470
11. Boeing Skorsky	Helicopters/Penn.	457
12. United Tech. Co.	A/C Engines&Rockets/Conn.	420
13. Johns Hopkins Univ.	Navy Research/Maryland	405
14. Rockwell Inter. Co.	Diversified/Calif&Iowa	399
15. Mass. Inst. Tech.	Radar/Mass.	386
16. Westinghouse Elect.	Electronics/Penn.&Maryland	380
17. Raytheon Co.	Missiles&Elect./Mass.	354
18. McDonnell Doug. Space	Space Launch/Calif.	340
19. Aerospace Corp.	Space Systems/Calif.	253
20. AT&T Co.	Communications/N. Carolina	244
21. IBM Corp.	Computers/Virginia&NY&Col&Mary.	241
22. Mitre Corp.	Communications/Mass.&Virginia	241
23. Teledyne Ind. Inc.	Diversified/Mich&Alab&Calif.	239
24. SAIC Corp	Diversified/Calif&Virginia	229
25. Lockheed Mis&Space	Missiles&Space/Calif.	204
	TOTAL (%)	**$13,205** **(77%)**
TOP 500 LARGE FIRM RDT&E TOTAL		**$17,151**

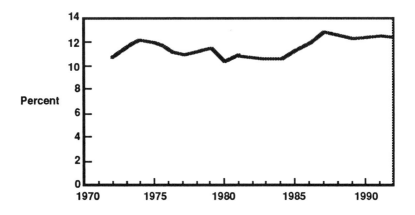

Figure 4. R&D as percentage of defense outlays.

Despite such shrinkage, however, the rate of decline in R&D activity does not come close to matching the decline in production accounts, and the overwhelming majority of workers laid off due to defense cuts have been in production, not R&D. Figure 5 shows that procurement has had a cyclical history of funding—currently in steep decline—during a period when the DoD total minus procurement has remained steady (personal communication, 20 January 1994, Kevin Lewis, RAND, Santa Monica, California).

The available evidence suggests that the present decline will not be followed by a return of growth: the future of procurement will no longer be cyclical, but will resemble a steady-state production model. Figure 6 sheds additional light on the problem, illustrating the dramatic decrease in active military aircraft production lines in recent years. The government, however, has so far provided significant assistance only to R&D activity through the ARPA Technology Reinvestment Project (TRP) (Drezner et al., 1992). Obviously, this aid will have little near-term influence on production employees' jobs.

In short, the current defense drawdown is not a unique development: in recent history, the United States has experienced reductions in defense spending that were far more drastic than the one taking place today. Furthermore, the problem can be considered severe only in several local economies and in a narrow sector of industry. Within that industrial sector, the drawdown has affected large firms much more significantly than it has affected

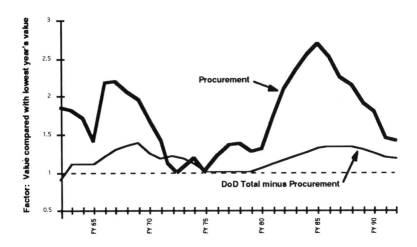

Figure 5. Procurement volatility (Personal communication, 20 January 1994, Kevin Lewis, RAND, Santa Monica, California).

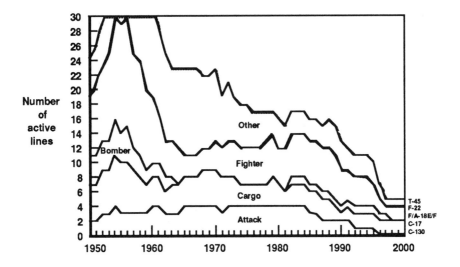

Figure 6. Active military aircraft production lines (Drezner et al., 1992).

small firms. And of the workers and firms experiencing economic dislocation and needing assistance, many more are involved in production than in R&D.

This picture, which suggests that the nation is not suffering from an acute economic crisis or from a severe disruption of defense-related R&D activity as a result of reductions in defense budgets, should allow policy makers to examine their options toward defense conversion in a dispassionate spirit. The primary question to be asked is not what sorts of intervention need to be put into place as soon as possible, but which of the two courses—intervention or non-intervention—is likely to bring about the most desirable results.

The Limited Intervention Option

The conversion option most discussed by Congress and apparently favored by the current administration is based on a notion of limited intervention. Its proponents envision using a relatively small amount of DoD RDT&E funding to encourage existing defense contractors to use or develop "dual-use technology." These contractors would then be able to expand their customer base into the broader areas of non-defense markets and to vigorously compete on the world stage, thereby hopefully increasing our national balance of trade in high-technology products.

This policy option seems to have many attractive features. Ideally, it would take maximum advantage of the enormous investment taxpayers have made in establishing research and production facilities, administrative structures, and various other defense-related support systems over the past 40 years. In addition, most of the research, design engineering, and production workers employed by defense contractors would simply be able to redirect their efforts toward civilian products. As a result, painful dislocations of workers and families would be avoided.

Another frequently mentioned benefit of intervention is that it would make the defense industry more responsive in case the need for a new military buildup arises. Many policy makers worry that the world is not as peaceful as we would like to believe and that either the instabilities caused by the demise of the Cold War or by a resurgent, nationalistic Russia may require such a buildup in the coming years. Proponents of intervention suggest that retaining the existing industrial teams may allow a reconstitution of an expanded defense development and production capability with minimum time delays and at minimum startup costs.

Prognosis

Many experts familiar with the government's favored approach, and with the history of previous conversion efforts, doubt that the proposed benefits can be realized: in the words of Norm Augustine, president and CEO of Martin Marietta Corporation, "defense conversion is an activity that has been unblemished by success." During the defense downturn of the early 1970s, many defense firms invested millions of dollars into civilian commercial ventures—a massive attempt at conversion that was almost universally viewed as a failure. Many communities remember the fragile Grumman "busses."

In my experience, these attempts at conversion were failures not because of engineering or production labor problems but because of problems in management style, procedures and experience. Both senior and middle management in defense firms have developed a style coupled to their single client's demands. The DoD, until recent years, consistently emphasized pushing the edge of the performance envelope and allowed production costs to grow and development time to slip in order to field a superior technical device sometime in the future—a device that would counter a postulated technically enhanced threat. Furthermore, contract negotiations with the government and constant audits by the Defense Contracting Audit Agency (DCAA) have led to extremely complicated and costly internal management systems that have become an inseparable part of a defense contractor's way of doing business. Given these realities, it may be easier to disband a company and start over again in the commercial world, than to try to change entrenched internal organizations and systems or to set up separate profit and cost centers. Even the simple concepts of profit and desirable profit margins are very different in the defense industry than they are in the world of commercial industry. For the defense business, profit is a negotiated quantity— typically between five and ten percent. In the commercial world, the profit is the difference between price and cost—the bigger the better.

In reflecting upon the defense conversion efforts of the 1970s, it could be argued that these efforts do not offer examples relevant to current policy because they were funded without government aid. Neither direct government support for conversion nor government advice and policy played any role in this earlier effort. However, in 1972 the Cold War had not yet abated and such assistance was considered unnecessary mainly because the government still saw the Soviet Union as an omnipresent threat and believed that the defense industry workload would ultimately pick up (as it did, see Figure 5). Today, by contrast, few observers of the international security situation and of the U.S.

budget envision a return to a Cold War situation. Furthermore, many conclude that the nature of international conflicts and the highly lethal nature of current and future weapons will never require a defense industry of the magnitude needed during WWII or the Cold War.

In my view, government aid is unlikely to make the 1990s conversion effort any more successful than the 1970s effort was. In theory, explicitly budgeted funds and expert advice would be very helpful. In practice, however, the program cannot expect to get either the funds or the advice that it needs. To date, the amount of funding the DoD has been able to devote to conversion efforts is dwarfed by the magnitude of funds that are expended in the commercial world for research, development and new products introduction. A limited program of government assistance (i.e., approximately \$500M/yr spread over many industries) will make no significant impact on the conversion process. Furthermore, there is no reason to believe that government has much expertise to dispense to defense-related industries that need good advice about what new directions to take and how to take them. Congress has been very thorough in closing the swinging door so that individuals with commercial industry experience and interests cannot come into the federal government without severe restrictions on their future employment options. Very few of the managers at ARPA, for example, one of the leading agencies empowered to invest DoD government funds to aid the conversion, have a solid background of expertise and success in the commercial marketplace.[1]

Finally, the pro-active conversion approach taken by the government thus far is moving far too slowly and focusing primarily on organizations outside the mainstream of defense-related activity. A review of the ARPA TRP reveals that it took almost a year to allocate the first \$206 million—with an undetermined degree of cost sharing (out of \$500 million allocated by Congress) to 27 consortia. Surprisingly, only a small number of the firms listed in Table 3 are involved in these consortia. Thus, defense contractors that account for almost 77 percent of the DoD RDT&E spending are only minor participants in the TRP technology conversion effort that has been attempted thus far. It should come as no surprise, therefore, that 88 percent of business

---

[1]On the other hand, the National Institute of Science and Technology (NIST) has an Advanced Technology Program funding process that emulates a commercial venture capital approach and may be more successful than the ARPA approach. NIST does not see themselves as a defense conversion activity, however.

executives surveyed at the Los Angeles-based Economic Roundtable study felt that government assistance efforts to date have been ineffective.[2]

The Non-Intervention Option: Consolidating and Liquidating Defense Contractors

The non-intervention option acknowledges that there is significant overcapacity in the defense industry. This overcapacity arises not only because of the historical change in the national security environment but also because of a change in the way that wars are concluded. Many observers argue that wars of attrition (i.e., the American Civil War, WWI, WWII) are a thing of the past. For them, modern warfare is exemplified by Operation Desert Storm in the Persian Gulf. The high technology weapons and the high level of training and professionalism required to operate these weapons systems lead to relatively short conflicts characterized by highly lethal equipment and low numbers of casualties (it should be noted, however, that another Korean war or a regional war in which several nuclear weapons were employed would certainly incur high civilian and military casualties).

Under this somewhat optimistic scenario, relatively few new systems need to be developed and major platform production runs (of aircraft, ships, tanks) will most likely number in the hundreds rather than in the thousands, while smart weapon production runs are expected to number in the thousands rather than the hundreds of thousands. This compact defense market will be handled by a small number of firms, and the choice for defense contractors at this point is whether to find a place in the new market niche or to liquidate their defense operations and turn to the civilian sector. In the present situation, many DoD industry leaders recognize that they must be either "buyers" or "sellers." They must choose between taking steps to consolidate their defense market position by acquiring the research and production capabilities of other defense contractors, or to sell off their own capabilities to those who wish to remain in defense-related fields.

One of the main problems of this option is that large numbers of highly educated and productive workers and their families are being dislocated. Many of the jobs held by these people are concentrated in a relatively small number of metropolitan areas that wind up with disproportionately high unemployment rates. Affected workers in such areas often have to go through an expensive

---

[2]Los Angeles Times, February 9, 1994.

and difficult process of relocation which, in terms of the nation's economy, translates into an unwelcome loss of productivity.

A second problem with the non-intervention option is that it may lead to the development of monopolies in the defense sector. As market forces provide clear economic incentives for strong firms to merge and weaker ones to die, fewer and fewer firms will gain larger shares of DoD business. Without competition within the defense industry, the DoD may find itself unable to maintain the necessary levels of quality and cost control. To date, the government has shown only limited interest in this problem, taking little anti-trust action to slow what has become an accelerating merger frenzy. Table 4 shows the major defense-related mergers or acquisitions that have taken place since 1990.

Prognosis

Based upon these trends, I would stipulate that defense conversion is already well underway through liquidations and consolidation within the industry. The intervention option, carried out in the slow and deliberate pace that the government reinvestment process requires, is simply too cumbersome

Table 4. Defense Firm Mergers Since 1992

Business	Buyer	Seller	Year	Price($M)
Space Systems Div	Martin Marietta	General Dynamics	1993/pend	209
Aircraft Simulators	Thomson-CSF	Hughes Aircraft	1993/pend	ND
Rosemont Aerospace	BF Goodrich	Emerson Electric	1993/pend	300
Federal Systems Div.	Loral	IBM	1993/pend	1,575
Aircraft Div	Lockheed	General Dynamics	1993	1,525
GE Aerospace	Martin Marietta	General Electric	1992	3,050
Missile Div	Hughes	General Dynamics	1992	484
Missile Div	Loral	LTV	1992	261
Ford Aerospace	Loral	General Dynamics	1990	750

to be of much help. Large defense firms have very high cash flow requirements, and savvy industry managers know that the race for survival will go to the swift. The first to consolidate with the best residual defense-related companies will be able to dominate their portion of the market in the future. Those opting to stay in the defense business believe that while procurement will be cut back severely, it will not go down to zero. Recent evidence suggests that there is strong resistance to dropping the DoD budget below the $200 billion (1994 dollars) level. It seems, therefore, that for the "buyers" there is good reason for optimism: the foreseeable future will still provide an excellent market for a smaller and leaner defense industry.

Where Government Intervention Can Help

This new version of the industry is already forming—and it is doing so without the intervention of government planners whose cautious and limited response seems to be a day late and a dollar short. Where the government can and should intervene is in the consolidation process. On the one hand, it should remove restrictions and impediments to consolidation, thereby helping the industry realign itself as swiftly and efficiently as possible. On the other hand, the government should monitor and inhibit those consolidations that might lead to monopolies so that it can ensure that adequate competition for defense services is maintained.

It remains to be seen what sorts of program ARPA and other government agencies will develop to help conversion. Changes in such seemingly nonrelated areas as environmental law, for example, would be extremely useful; however, as currently written, the stipulations of the Superfund make it practically impossible for many defense manufacturing firms to estimate their liabilities and net worth. Without such estimates, liquidation and consolidation efforts become unmanageable.

Another helpful step would be to liberalize trade policy and foreign military sales restrictions in the aerospace industry along the lines of the liberalization that is currently taking place in the electronics and computer industries. Such loosening of restrictions and reforms in liability law would be especially helpful to manufacturers in the aircraft industry, allowing them to compete more fully in a world market that is becoming more competitive every year.

Finally, government retraining efforts for both blue collar and white collar workers need to be targeted more effectively than they have been. Rather than funding retraining efforts all across the country, especially in communities which have barely felt the effects of the defense drawdown, government programs should concentrate on the few localities that have been hardest hit. Furthermore, retraining subsidies for laid-off defense workers would have more practical value if they were provided to employers who hire such workers. Employers would have a greater incentive to take on former defense workers if the costs of training them were offset. And since the subsidized training would be directly job-related, the effectiveness of the program would be almost guaranteed. Certainly, such an approach would have a much better chance of reemployment success than current government or community college retraining programs that are often poorly directed and have not proven their worth to date.

There is no doubt that well-aimed and timely government intervention could ease the conversion process somewhat. However, it seems very likely that the conversion process will be finished before many government programs can come into play. Firms and individuals hurt by defense cutbacks need to act quickly to assure their economic survival. They would be happy to receive government assistance, but most of them understand that waiting for such assistance to arrive is probably not the wisest approach.

References

Defense Conversion Commission, 1992: *Adjusting to the Drawdown.* Report, U.S. Government Printing Office.

Dertouzos, J. N. and M. Dardia, 1993: *Defense Spending, Aerospace, and the California Economy.* MR-179-RC, RAND, Santa Monica, California.

Drezner, J. A. et al., 1992: *Maintaining Future Military Aircraft Design Capability.* R-4199-AF, RAND, Santa Monica, California.

Logistics Management Institute, 1993: *Impacts of Defense Spending Cuts on Industry Sectors, Occupational Groups, and Localities.*

Neu, C. R. and M. P. Kennedy, 1993: *Do we need special federal programs to aid defense conversion?* IP-104, RAND, Santa Monica, California.

CHAPTER 3

Defense Conversion: An Operations Analysis Approach

Alex E.S. Green
Departments of Mechanical Engineering
and Nuclear Engineering Sciences
University of Florida
Gainesville, Florida

Operations Analysis

The recent publication of a summary of my operations analysis studies with the 20th Bomber Command in the China-Burma-India theater in World War II (Green, 1993) has led me to consider the role that operations analysis might serve in solving current national problems, in particular the problem of defense conversion. Operational analysis or operations research originated just prior to World War II (Miser, 1980; McCloskey, 1987) when the British recognized that operational aspects of a national defense problem, as opposed to the purely technical aspects, were often paramount in the solution of the problem. The success of the partnership between scientists and operating forces, as exemplified in the Battle of Britain, prompted the spread of operational research to other British Commands and services. By late 1942 the U.S. Navy and the Army Air Corps began forming operations research or operation analysis teams to address technical problems arising in combat theaters that were beyond the training of personnel normally available in the military command.

Over the past half century, operations research or operations analysis (or systems analysis) has developed a substantial body of theory and applications. Miser (1980) noted that "its current strength prompts it to attack difficult large-scale problems while challenging the other relevant sciences to unite, not only with each other and operations and systems research but also with society, to deal with some of the most widespread and important problems of our time."

Operations Analysis (OA) has, in effect, undergone a **defense conversion** into forms variously called "Operations Research," "Management Science," "Systems Analysis," "Systems Engineering" or "Risk Analysis." These disciplines provide approaches to the solution of complex problems that are often beyond the capabilities of any individual. The pattern developed in WWII Operations Analysis was to first identify the unanticipated need or needs that arose in a combat problem. The solution usually entailed dissecting the problem into its quantitative components and formulating various technical options that help carry out the assignment of the command. Finally an optimum solution or combination of component solutions was formulated which, when endorsed by the Commanding Officer, was quickly implemented. Of necessity, the combat operations analyst did what was needed to solve combat problems with what we had available. However, apart from the intense pace and life-and-death stakes, many aspects of WWII OA are still represented in current manifestations of operations or systems analysis.

In his recent book, Sage (1992) describes systems engineering "as a management technology to assist and support policy making, planning, decision making and associated resource allocation or action deployment. It accomplishes this through quantitative and qualitative formulation, analyses and interpretation of the impacts of action alternatives with references to the user's needs, values, and institutional perspectives."

The development of the computer has had a tremendous impact on current conversions of WWII Operations Analysis and its applications in the civilian sector (Murphy et al., 1993).

An Operations Analyst View of Defense Conversion

Some of the thoughts reflected in this Defense Conversion (DC) study go back to my service with the 20th Army Air Force (AAF) as an operations analyst during the last year of World War II. Several of my operation analyses led to conclusions that may be timely today. My first study, an analysis of B-29 losses for the first 25 combat missions of the 20th Bomber Command in the China-Burma-India theater (Green, 1993), showed that the actual combat risks to fighter attacks were greatest in frontal attacks. This analysis and the recommendation for formation change, endorsed by the gunnery and intelligence officers, were accepted and implemented by General LeMay with positive results. The combat analysis gave results directly opposite the risk estimates predicted by a million dollar stateside simulation study. The relevance today is that *costly studies sometimes give wrong answers.*

My second lesson came as a result of my participation on March 12, 1945 in a B-29 reconnaissance flight that discovered the previously "lost" Japanese Fleet in the Kure anchorage off Hiroshima (Green, 1993). The fact that no Japanese fighter attacked us or anti-aircraft guns fired at us in 3 hours over Japan and about 12 hours over occupied China suggested that the tide of battle had already turned dramatically in our favor 5 months before the Hiroshima bomb was dropped. Later photo assessments showed over 70 warships anchored in Kure Anchorage and nearby Hiroshima Bay, a formidable naval force, but effectively immobilized for lack of oil.

My third experience concerns the Force and Bomb Load Computer I developed in response to the need to speed up mission requirement calculations. By May 1945 we had exhausted all the large Japanese target cities (except those saved for our atomic bombs) and were beginning to dispatch 4 or 8 small missions each day instead of the one or two large missions dispatched earlier. The computer enabled us to calculate the requirements of 8 small missions in the time that was previously needed to calculate the requirements for one large mission (Green, 1994).

The fourth experience relates to my assignment in July of 1945 to carry out the operational calculations for the new SHORAN bombing system. This system would enable the B-29 fleet to give close protective support to the planned Kyushu beachhead (Green, 1994). Then "Little Boy," the U-235 bomb, was dropped on Hiroshima on August 6 and "Fat Man," the Pu-239 bomb, was dropped on Nagasaki on August 9. Japan surrendered on August 15th, and our invasion of Japan was canceled. In view of my invasion assignment, I have pondered long and often on the questions: "Was the Bomb needed?" and "What if we didn't have the Bomb?"

There are at least four assessments on these issues:

(1) The nuclear bombings of Hiroshima and Nagasaki were needed to convince the Japanese to surrender and *save a million American lives*, the conventional assessment.

(2) The Hiroshima bomb was necessary to achieve surrender, but not the Nagasaki since the short time interval did not allow the Japanese to fully react to the demonstration of the Hiroshima bomb.

(3) The nuclear bombs were not needed to bring about the surrender of Japan but were dropped mainly as diplomatic leverage on the Soviet Union to encourage better behavior in Eastern Europe (Alperowitz, 1965, 1989; Walker, 1990).

(4) The bombs were not needed to induce surrender by the Japanese before the planned invasion of Kyushu in November 1945. Dropping the two nuclear bombs and in the next week effectively dropping the two words *"unconditional surrender,"* provided two face-saving reasons for the Japanese to surrender. This *saved a million Japanese lives* (Green, 1994). Furthermore the quick surrender spared the Japanese from much more extensive confrontations with Stalin and the Soviets.

This fourth view is my considered assessment based on my varied operations analyses while with the 20th AAF (Green, 1944–1945) and some facts that became general knowledge after WWII. By August 1945 the 20th AAF B-29 bomber fleet in the Mariannas, 1500 miles from Japan, had reached a peak of destruction/loss efficiency. The mighty 8th AAF had almost completed its transfer from Europe to Okinawa, only 400 miles from southern Japan. The U.S. Navy, with the greatest battle fleet ever assembled, was launching strikes on all parts of Japan with negligible opposition. The Soviet Union, by agreement at Yalta, had invaded Japanese occupied Manchuria and Korea with a massive force of over 1.5 million men, 5500 tanks, 26,000 artillery pieces and 3800 warplanes (Lensen, 1972). Any comprehensive operational analysis that realistically considers the combined conventional destructive capabilities of these forces during August, September and October inescapably leads to the conclusion that Japan would have been a wasteland in another month or two.

Relevance to Defense Conversion

The relevance of the above assessments to DC is multifold. Nuclear weapons, as symbolized by "Hiroshima", escalated our Cold War with the former Soviet Union (F.S.U.) to exceedingly costly levels and under the MAD (mutually assured destruction) philosophy reached a capability probably many times more than that needed to destroy human civilization. The expenditure of resources on high technology military activities as well as on surrogate military activities (space shots, big accelerators, big science, etc.) during five decades of Hot and Cold Wars can, in large measure, explain the demise of the Soviet Union and the disastrous economic conditions which now prevail in the F.S.U. These costs also, in significant part, underlie problems with the U.S. economy. In addition, the image of Hiroshima has become a major obstacle in the U.S.A. to the revival of the United States nuclear reactor industry and the solution of a number of current global and national problems such as Climate Change (Green, 1980, 1989).

When, in the summer of 1991, I was invited to present papers on "Waste to Energy" and on "Alternate Fuels" at a conference on Climate Change at Los Alamos National Laboratory (LANL), in October (Rosen and Glasser, 1991), my thoughts went back to (1) probing further into purposes of "Hiroshima" and "Nagasaki," (2) understanding their relationships to the origin and intensity of the Cold War and (3) using such an improved understanding to project an improved path for "Greenhouse Mitigation" (Green, 1989). Then, in an uninvited presentation on "Hiroshima and the Climate Change Problem," I remarked to the assembled conference that I flew by Hiroshima 5 months before the Los Alamos bomb was dropped and that I didn't think it was needed. My point mainly was that the 20th AAF, the 8th AAF, the U.S. Navy and the Soviets were just about to accelerate the destruction of Japan and its military forces. Thus their surrender would have been forthcoming shortly anyway, particularly when we relaxed the words "unconditional surrender" as we did before August 15. Unfortunately the "bomb" has caused a bad public perception of nuclear energy, which is an important option for greenhouse mitigation.

When I returned home and intensified my examination of historical sources, the technical literature and my own records, the problems listed in Table 1 became all consuming. This led me to consider concepts for irreversibly converting nuclear "weapons to inherently safe reactors" (Green 1992). Such nuclear weapons to energy concepts will be discussed in depth in four chapters of this book (Green; Landis; Panofsky; and MINATOM). Let us therefore turn our attention to non-nuclear components of a general defense conversion program.

A General Defense Conversion Program

The general DC program in the U.S.A. has been getting under way slowly and appears to be developing primarily on a "politics as usual" or preservation of special interest basis. A sound general Defense Conversion program would preferentially help the U.S.A. and F.S.U. at this time by restoring some of the industrial and economic vitality needed to be major players on the world stage. As Chairman of the Committee for Academic-Industrial Research (CAIR) of the Fuels and Combustion Technology (FACT) Division of the American Society of Mechanical Engineers (ASME), the author initiated a "Swords to Plowshares" session for a meeting of the International

Table 1. Major Problems (1991)

---

(1) the tremendous threat posed by 50,000 "Hiroshimas" scattered around the globe
(2) the rapid proliferation of nuclear weapons and nuclear weapons-making capability
(3) the United States sell-off of its nuclear industry while Japan, Germany, France, and other countries are forging ahead with nuclear energy
(4) our mounting trade and budget deficits and our competitiveness problems
(5) the need for nuclear energy as a component of the climate change solution
(6) the large anti-nuclear movement in the U.S.A.
(7) the U.S.S.R. economic problems threatening its democratization
(8) many Chernobyl-type reactors in the Soviet Union and in Eastern Europe
(9) the global population bomb
(10) People, Economic, Environmental, Energy and Defense problems of U.S.A.

Joint Power Generation Conference (IJPCG) held in Atlanta in October 1992. This session was very stimulating and led to a consensus that there should be a follow-up. In response to this encouragement the author initiated a "Spears to Pruning Hooks" shirt-sleeve session for the meeting of the IJPCG held in Kansas City, Missouri on October 18, 1993. This was followed up by a conference entitled "Nation Shall Not Lift Up Sword Against Nation" held in Orlando, Florida in February 1994. Hopefully someday we can hold a conference involving all countries on the theme "Neither shall they experience war anymore." All four titles would complete the essence of the biblical quotation from Isaiah on seeking peace between nations.

From an operations analysis standpoint Defense Conversion can be viewed simply as an intense form of recycling, a context in fitting with the emerging environmental era. In this recycling context it is useful to categorize various types of value recovery methods (VRM) as listed in Table 2.

All value recovery methods should include "defense externalities" in economic analyses. Thus if the VRM fosters reduction in future military threat potential, a large savings can be accrued independent of the immediate economic competitiveness of the recycled product. This is an advanced way of including a societal cost not directly reflected in the price of the product. Thus a tax credit or subsidy might be given if the VRM has a high military

Table 2. Value Recovery Methods

VRM1   Direct use, e.g., a military transportation vehicle used as a civilian truck.

VRM2   Retrofitting before use. Here specific hardware components are re-engineered and modified to facilitate peacetime application. For example, an improved gearbox is installed in a military tank which is de-armed and converted into a bulldozer. The change insures longer life in the peacetime application.

VRM3   Use of a major component, e.g., an aircraft jet engine is used in a combined cycle electricity generator or cogeneration system directly or after some retrofitting.

VRM4   Recovery of critical materials, e.g., military components are melted down for civilian application, e.g., use of titanium for high performance valves.

VRM5   Use of military production facilities, e.g., the production facility is used for needed civilian products.

VRM6   Retraining of design and construction engineers, e.g., "people value" is recovered by a retraining program that does not waste skills and prior training of military hardware engineers.

VRM7   Dual Use Factories, e.g., production facilities and management, technical and production personnel change some of the military production facilities to the production of civilian products compatible with the factories' technology, e.g., military jet engine production changed to commercial jet engine production.

VRM8   Dual Use of Military. Here "people value" is recovered or preserved by broadening the role of the military to serve a peacetime objective. An example is the use of military personnel to help in natural disasters (Hurricane Andrew!) or to solve urgent social problems, e.g., breakdown of inner city structure.

VRM9   Weapons Laboratory Technology Initiatives. Defense motivated technology development transferred to the civilian sector or research evolving from a military development is directed towards a future peacetime application.

---

threat reduction benefit. Such a structural breakdown of needs by objective VRMs should help depoliticize conversion efforts and thus address the problems of the nation as a whole.

It should be obvious that the times for the different VRMs differ markedly. Obviously, VRM1 Direct Use has immediate potential and VRM 2 has near-term potential. In the U.S.A., however, these VRMs might interfere with the market recovery of our auto industry.

On the other hand, in the F.S.U. the privatization or retrofitting for privatization of military transport vehicles or armed vehicles should help in the process of establishing a market economy. Value Recovery Methods 6, 7 and 9 will only be helpful on longer time scales. VRM 8 could minimize dislocations associated with the reduction of military manpower.

The organizational breakdown of our defense and space establishments (i.e., Army, Marines, Navy, Air Force, NASA, etc.) provides another useful classification system. Thus the idea is to assess hardware, facilities or manpower no longer needed for defense or surrogate defense purposes to determine what is available for recycling and how such resources can best be redirected to solve serious national problems. It is *guesstimated* roughly that the U.S.A. might recover $100 billion in value out of a present defense complex worth about $1 trillion, a cumulative Cold War and WWII military expenditure of about $10 trillion, a national debt of about $5 trillion, a gross national product (GNP) of $6 trillion, and a net national worth of about $50 trillion.

From the standpoint of defense industries, the best conversion products are those that use available defense technologies or technological skills. However, from the national standpoint, alternative products that meet major needs or solve major problems may be more important. The Operations Analysis (OA) approach to Defense Conversion (DC) uses major national needs as the driver rather than product characteristics. A list of severe problems facing the U.S.A. today is given in Table 3.

An OA approach to developing a national DC program would first quantify these problems to determine the best use of the potentially available resources arising by virtue of the end of the Cold War. When quantitative considerations are applied it would appear that solutions of our major national problems will require some $1000 billion-dollar programs. However, prudent estimates of cumulative defense conversion resources are at the $100 billion level and annual resources at the $10 billion level. The question thus becomes: can we apply such "peace dividends" without dismantling essential defense capabilities.

Among the people problems, health costs, which are now approaching $1000 billion, are gaining recognition as a major national problem in the U.S.A. At the same time, while satisfying the need for better health care and better housing for the poor, the handicapped and the elderly could increase our staggering health costs. A preliminary analysis in 1991 led to these considerations that are now major concerns of lawmakers. Final action will probably come out of the political approach rather than an operational analysis approach.

Table 3. Major National Problems

PEOPLE	1. Lack of good jobs, 2. Health care costs, 3. No health insurance, 4. Poverty, 5. Drugs and crime, 6. Poor education, 7. Gun proliferation, 8. Quality of life of the elderly.
ECONOMIC	1. National debt, 2. Cumulative debt, 3. Trade deficit, 4. Competitiveness, 5. Export barriers, 6. Resource exhaustion, 7. Decay of infrastructure.
ENVIRONMENTAL	1. Air pollution, 2. Toxics, 3. Acid rain, 4. Haze, 5. Ozone depletion, 6. Climate change, 7. Biological water pollution, 8. Water toxics, 9. Water salinization, 10. Waste disposal, 11. Toxic chemicals .
ENERGY	1. Security, 2. Transportation fuels, 3. Oil and gas exhaustion, 4. Nuclear waste
DEFENSE	1. Regional conflicts, 2. F.S.U. instability, 3. Nuclear proliferation, 4. Declining industries, 5. Over-expansion, 6. Over-extension of forces.

There is, of course, a difference in the needs of the U.S.A., where the civilian product industries and environmental industries are very well developed, and Russia and Ukraine where these areas are just gaining attention. Accordingly, problem priorities and the development of specific defense conversion programs will, of necessity, be different.

Potential Defense Conversion Programs

Clarification of the OA approach as first developed in World War II (solve problems in consideration of national objectives using what you have!) to DC might best be given in terms of specific examples. Table 4, compiled by focusing on Table 3 and by using suggestions in other studies (Renner, 1990, 1993; Folta, 1992; Bischak, 1991), gives titles of dual- or multiple-objective programs that should assist in the solution of national problems, using resources released by the ending of the Cold War. Cooperation with Russia and other F.S.U. countries to the point that they have successfully made transitions to democracies should help insure that the Cold War does not resume. At the same time these solutions should help rebuild the industrial base needed for both peacetime competitiveness and defense capabilities.

Table 4. Programs To Solve National Problems

1. Aerospace Technology to Affordable Senior Homes (ATASH)

2. Aerospace Technology to Homes for Handicapped or disabled (AT-HH)

3. Aerospace Technology to Mass Produced Prisons

4. Aerospace Technology to Light Weight Fuel Efficient Vehicles (AT-EV)

5. Aerospace Technology to Mass Transportation (AT-MT)

6. Aerospace Technology to Renewable Energy (Solar and Wind) (AT-RE)

7. Jet Engine Technology to Combined Cycle and Cogeneration Electric Generators for Electric Power Generation (JE-PG)

8. Biological and Chemical Warfare Facilities converted to Medical Drugs, and Immunization Shots Production (BC-MD)

9. Biological Warfare Facilities to Ethanol Production (BW-EP)

10. Chemical and Biological Warfare to Environmental Restoration (CB-ER)

11. Military materials to Benign Materials Production (MM-BM)

12. Military Engineers to Highway Infrastructure (ME-HI)

13. Military and National Guard to Disaster Relief (MNSH-DR)

14. Military Engineers to Decayed City Infrastructure (ME-CI)

15. Military Officers to Science Education (MO-SE)

16. Military to Civilian Fire Protection and Fire Suppressants (M-CFP)

17. Military Transport Systems to Commercial Transport (MT-CT)

18. Military Desalinization and Water Purification to Civilian Needs (DWP-C)

19. Optoelectronics to Home Security and Fire Protection (OE-HS)

20. Optoelectronics to Anthropogenic Emissions Control (O-AEC)

21. Cannon and Armor to Nuclear Waste Containment (C-NWC)

22. Weapons to Inherently Safe Nuclear Reactors (W-ISR)

23. U.S.A. Big Science to International Science for Mankind (BS-IS)

24. Defense Advanced Research to Civilian (DAR-C)

25. Retraining Programs for Defense Conversion (RP-DC)

Table 5 gives an expanded description of Program 1, ATASH. It illustrates the type of multiple purpose programs needed now to mitigate problems of aerospace decline, aerospace worker job loss, and military base closings, while addressing the national needs to improve and reduce the cost of the Health care of seniors, to provide low-cost housing, to improve the quality of life of seniors, and to lower crime threats and possibly to reduce the growth of entitlements. Our approach follows a contingency study "A Module for National Survival" initiated by the author in 1961 (Green et al., 1961). This was a period of severe Cold War tension, when substantial federal support was

Table 5. Program 1: Aerospace Technology to Affordable Senior Homes (ATASH)

Phase 1 Preliminary design of manufactured homes and communities using advances in aerospace technology to meet the needs of seniors and to be capable of handling severe environmental conditions (hurricanes!) using closed military bases.

Phase 2 Preliminary design of machinery for the mass production of ATASH units and the installation of community infrastructure.

Phase 3 Final design and hand construction of a few basic ATASH units.

Phase 4 Final design and construction of prototype machinery for mass production of ATASH units and elderly-qualified equipment.

Phase 5 Production of specialized machinery and adaptors for fabricating ATASH units. It is estimated that 500 or more units would be required to meet national needs and that this production technology would be suited for airframe firms.

Phase 6 Large Scale Production of ATASH units for communities across the country using machinery produced in Phase 5. Factories for this production should be distributed widely throughout the U.S.A. with concentrations near retirement centers.

Phase 7 Assembly of ATASH units, initially on closed military bases, (e.g., Homestead or McCoy Air Bases). For crime protection, these might be developed as gated communities. Central preventative health care services should be arranged.

Phase 8 Adapt the above for elderly homes in smaller communities and for elderly day care centers to lower elderly Health care costs and improve the quality of life for seniors living in their hometown.

---

devoted to research, development, and demonstration (RD&D) on active ballistic missile defense (ABMD). From extensive involvements in such studies it became clear to the authors that these investments made no sense unless they were backed up by a passive defense system in the form of shelters. The authors of this study, which was supported by Convair, General Dynamics, then one of the world's largest defense companies, sought a commercially marketable dual-use product. Their analysis and general approach had many features that could be used in a program to use aerospace technology to develop affordable senior homes (ATASH).

Several features of the "Survival Module" (SM) program are parallel to the proposed ATASH project: (1) We also started with aerospace technology which is now under triple stress from the decline of military orders, the decline of commercial orders and industrial competition subsidized by the European Economic Community; (2) We are seeking a product or products that address the daily needs of people, in this case, seniors, a growing segment of our population and health care costs; (3) We develop an alternative manufacturing technology for aerospace firms without their involvement in mass production problems.

The ATASH program would also be carried out in phases and be initiated with government program funds for Defense Conversion, Economic Stimulation, or Health Care. However, privatization should follow naturally as the program matures. By focusing on the special needs of senior citizens and the lowering of health care costs, the private housing industry should be helpful and cooperative.

JE-PG, A Second Program Illustration

Program 7 of Table 4, the use of aeroderivative gas turbines (AGT) for power and heat generation, can serve as a second and more natural example of defense conversion by an important segment of the aerospace industry. Aeroderivative gas turbines in combined cycle systems in which the exhaust heat is converted to steam that drives a steam turbine are now the highest efficiency and lowest capital cost electrical generation systems. Conversion efficiencies (fuel to electricity) exceeding 50 percent are being achieved as compared to 33 percent for conventional boiler-steam turbine systems. As higher turbine inlet temperatures are achieved in advanced military and commercial jet engines even higher efficiencies will be achieved (Langston, 1994). Most additions to electrical networks in Asia, Europe and North

America are now being made as combined cycle systems fired with natural gas or oil.

Even greater use of fuel energy is attained in cogeneration systems in which an AGT turns an electrical generator and the exhaust heat is delivered as steam or hot water to a nearby community, institution or industry. Most new installations use natural gas, which at this time is widely available in the U.S.A. and the F.S.U. In the future, however, gas produced from solid fuels, coal, biomass and municipal solid waste (MSW) could also provide the fuel input to AGTs. Thus Integrated Gasifier Combined Cycle (IGCC) systems with biomass or MSW as the fuel could proceed like a Coal Gasifier Combined Cycle system, one of the most promising developments of the Department of Energy's 6 billion dollar Clean Coal Technology program. Not only are AGT generators attractive because of their efficiency but they also have the potential to drastically reduce SOx and NOx emissions.

It is encouraging that the Environmental Protection Agency, Battelle Corp., and United Technologies, Inc. have completed the engineering analyses for a seven-year project to help the Russian Academy of Sciences develop an IGCC plant. Construction on the Russian IGCC could begin almost immediately after the feasibility study is completed (C&ST 1994).

AGTs are also under consideration as replacement power for plutonium producing reactors in Russia. A U.S. Delegation recently conducted a fact finding mission aimed at the earliest possible shut-down of the plutonium production reactors at Krasnoyarsk-26 and Tomsk-7. Since these reactors currently provide heat and power locally, the Delegation identified alternate high efficiency energy supplies. AGTs figured prominently in their considerations, although their use will probably come in later phases of the program after gas pipelines become available and Russian-built AGTs have passed demonstration tests. The Delegation concluded that a feasibility study is required that would lead to a "bankable" feasibility study serving to attract international financing (DOE, 1994).

Other Programs, Approaches and Conclusions

Another quantitative approach to the national defense conversion identifies critical technologies in which the United States is now weak, is losing badly or has lost. Then, programs that would rebuild or build up these technologies would receive priority among proposed defense conversion programs. Lists of weak or lost critical technologies have been identified (Council on Competitiveness, 1991; National Science Board, 1992). We must, however, recognize that competition in the industrial marketplace can impose more rigorous demands on technology than military requirements (Inman and Burton, Jr.,1992; Borrus and Zysman, 1992). Consumer electronics is an example of a lost American technology that has important defense implications. Furthermore, success in competing in consumer products helps generate capital for many types of technology investments. Thus the operations analysis approach, which is driven by national needs, at the same time should help strengthen our defense competitiveness.

Finally, if the Cold War stays cold, environmental concerns will receive greater attention in world affairs and will accelerate the demand for "Green Products" (products whose manufacture, use and disposal place a reduced burden on the environment). Intense competition in marketing of "Green Technologies" will undoubtedly develop. Hopefully we will not be late in recognizing this trend as we were in the case of Total Quality Management, an important factor in the decline of our competitiveness with respect to Japan and Germany.

Table 3 divides environmental problems into threats to our air, our water or our land with the most complex threats posed to the atmosphere. Figure 1 presents an overview of anthropogenic problems due to emissions to the atmosphere from transportation, industry, utilities, commerce, residences, landfills, incinerators and agriculture (Green, 1990). Conversions from Defense Technologies to "Green Technologies" could best be carried out with the help of operations analyses of both areas and the development of dual- or multiple-purpose programs. If this form of defense conversion is applied to the restoration of environmental quality and industrial competitiveness it would provide a challenging domain for cooperation between the U.S.A. and the F.S.U. that would enable both to benefit from *peace dividends*.

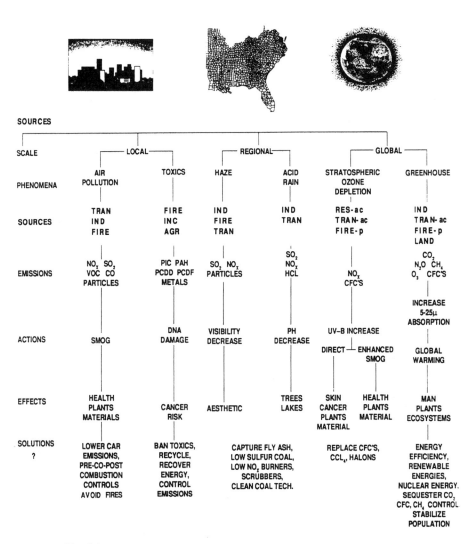

Figure 1.   Anthropogenic emission problems from various sources and potential solutions (adapted from Green, 1990).

References

Alperowitz, G., 1965: *Atomic Diplomacy, Hiroshima and Potsdam,* Simon and Shuster, New York; and *Atomic Diplomacy expanded and updated,* Viking, New York, 1985.

Alperowitz, G., 1989: Why the United States Dropped the Bomb, *Technology Review,* 26, (Aug./Sept.) 24-34.

Bischak, G.A., 1991: *Towards a Peace Economy in the United States,* St. Martin's Press, New York.

Borrus, M. and J. Zysman, 1992: Industrial Competitiveness and National Security, in *Rethinking America's Security*, G. Allison and G. Treverton, The American Assembly, Norton, New York.

CS&T, 1994: Work Progresses on Joint IGCC, *Coal and Synfuels Technology,* September 12, 1994.

Council on Competitiveness, 1991: *Gaining New Ground, Technology Priorities for America's Future,* Washington, DC.

DOE, 1994: Replacement Power Fact Finding Mission for Plutonium Producing Reactors, June 7-16, 1994, U.S. Delegation to Tomsk and Krasnoyarsk-26 Department of Energy, Washington, DC.

Folta, P. H., 1992: From Swords To Plowshares? *Defense Industry Reform in the PRC,* Westview Press, Boulder, Colorado.

Green, A.E.S., 1944-1945: Eleven operations analysis reports issued overseas by 20th AAF on combat losses, gunnery, formation defense, and slide rules for identifying ships flight engineering, force estimation, offset bombing, bomb plotting, and SHORAN, Air Force Archives, Maxwell, Alabama.

Green, A., E.J. Philbin, and A. Vampola, 1961: A Module For National Survival, *Engineering Research Report,* EER-SD-121, Convair Division, General Dynamics, San Diego, California, June.

Green, A.E.S., ed.,1980: *Coal Burning Issues,* Chapter 1. Introduction and Summary by Interdisciplinary Center for Aeronomy and Other Atmospheric Sciences, University Presses of Florida, Gainesville, Florida, 1-32.

Green, A., ed., 1989: *Greenhouse Mitigation, FACT*, 7, Published by ASME, New York.

Green, A., 1990: Preface in Advances in Solid Fuel Technologies, *FACT,* 9, A. Green and W. Lear, eds., Published by ASME, New York.

Green, A., 1992: Peacetime Application of Weapon Grade Fuel, short synopses by Jason Makansi in *Common Sense* (February) and *Power* (March).

Green, A., 1993: Finding the Japanese Fleet in March 1945, *INTERFACE*, an international Journal of The Institute of Management Science and Operations Research Society of America.

Green, A., 1994: An Operations Analyst with the 21st Bomber Command, in *Alex Green Festschrift,* A. Deepak Publishing, Hampton, Virginia, 1-15.

Inman, B. R., and D.F. Burton, Jr., 1992: Technology and U.S. National Security, in *Rethinking America's Security,* G. Allison and G. Treverton, The American Assembly, Norton, New York.

Langston, L., 1994: Combined Cycle Power Plants: A Primer for Engineers and Others, *Global Gas Turbine News,* 24-25.

Lensen, G.A., 1972: *The Strange Neutrality*, The Diplomatic Press, Tallahassee, Florida.

McCloskey, J.F., 1987: U.S. Operations Research on World War II, *Operations Research,* 35, No. 6, November-December, 920.

Miser, H.J., 1980: Operations Research and Systems Analysis, *Science,* 209, 139-146.

Murphy, F.H., et al., 1993: Perspectives on Management Science/Operations Research, *INTERFACE,* 23:5 September-October, 1-46.

National Science Board, 1992: The Competitive Strength of U.S. Industrial Science and Renner, M. 1990, Swords Into Plowshares: Converting to a Peace Economy, *World Watch Paper 96.*

Renner, M., 1993: Preparing for Peace, *State of the World 1993,* L.R. Brown, ed., W.W. Norton, New York, 139 (Chapter 8).

Rosen, L., and R. Glasser, 1991: *Proceedings of the Conference on Global Climate Change,* held at Los Alamos National Laboratory, October 21-24, American Institute of Physics, New York.

Sage, A.P., 1992: *Systems Engineering,* Wiley Series in Systems Engineering, John Wiley and Sons, New York.

Walker, J.S., 1990: The Decision to Use the Bomb, *Diplomatic History,* 14 (1) 110-111.

CHAPTER 4

Defense Conversion Techniques in the Mid-1990s

Erick G. Highum
Department of Political Science
Florida State University
Tallahassee, Florida.

Introduction

Converting United States military industry workers and U.S. military personnel to commercial industries is one of the most important opportunities for the U.S. Government in this post Cold-War era of reduced military spending. Displaced military sector employees have skills and educational training that can aid in the economic recovery. Arguments about the detrimental effect that military expenditures have on productive investment in an economy and society have a rich historical heritage. Ricardo states that any taxes that are used by a state to support war are monies that are drained from the productive industry of that state. If a state borrows twenty million to spend for a war, then it is "twenty millions which are withdrawn from the productive capital of the nation" (Ricardo, 1819, 160-161).

This view is relevant today, especially when considering the vast amount of public expenditures by the U.S. Government on military power in the post-World War II era. Modern defense conversionists are questioning current military expenditure levels, as well as the assumption that such expenditures can continue to be justified for national security reasons. This paper assumes that "national security" involves many arenas—military, economic and ecological. Defense conversion is an ongoing process of moving managers, executives, engineers, other military industry workers and U.S. military personnel into commercial free-market enterprises in Russia, the United States and many other countries. It is very important that former military workers have the opportunity to work on promising future industries in this post-Cold War era.

These industries could include alternative energies technologies, transportation alternatives such as magnetic levitation vehicles, and electric vehicles, recycling, environmental clean-up of military bases, energy conservation techniques, and improvements of infrastructure. What is primarily needed in all of the states in the international systems that undertake conversion is a coordinated strategy between military industries, national governments, and the public. The public must be educated to know that defense conversion can offer economic growth and environmental protection as well as the opportunity for engineers and scientists to work on answers to today's leading environmental problems, such as ozone layer depletion, greenhouse gas emissions, and radioactive and toxic wastes safe-storage. These are problems that engineers, scientists, and support staff could help overcome for the benefit of the United States and other parts of the Earth.

Transferability

A 1978 study entitled "Creating Solar Jobs, Options for Military Workers and Communities," by Robert DeGrasse, Jr. et al. (1978) found a positive outlook for transferring military personnel at Lockheed Missiles and Space Company to the solar energy sector. The study was limited to operatives, skilled labor and technicians. It did not include 2500 jobs in clerical/administrative support as well as engineers and managers at Lockheed. Transferring clerical and administrative support workers from Lockheed to various solar sectors was easily done. Most of these types of jobs were directly transferable. The results of this study show that engineers and managers are the most difficult of all military sector workers to re-employ in commercial sectors of the economy. The authors found that engineers in military industries are exposed to a heavier concentration of scientific and technical skills than their counterparts in other industries. The report found that managers and engineers must undergo a reorientation to the civilian marketplace since military applications use very specific designs in order to meet the necessary military requirements.

There are two principal reasons why engineers have a more difficult time transferring their particular skills to nonmilitary industries: (1) military engineers work in a very specialized area and they design systems that do not have direct counterparts in civilian industries and (2) there are a larger percentage of engineers in production personnel in military industries than in commercial industries (Degrasse et al., 1978). The very nature of the commercial market requires a lower number of engineers than that required by military industry. This is especially true in the 1990s since many more engineers were required by military industries during the arms build-up of the 1980s. Although this study was done in 1978, the findings are still relevant today. The report found that engineers have the hardest time of all categories of workers when trying to transfer their particular skills to civilian industry. The engineers must therefore adapt to the downsizing of military industry and retrain themselves for employment in future industries. These displaced military workers represent the finest intellectual power this nation has to offer any commercial sector development. Governments truly interested in spurring economic growth ought to combine investment in conversion areas with this ability.

Government's Role

Government funding of conversion technologies is extremely important to its success. The funding of the military sector in the United States points out the large influence the military has as a force in the economy. This funding of the military also exemplifies the potential that conversion technologies have to spur growth in the United States. Investment capital cannot be divorced from government spending regarding conversion technologies—they are one force in the economy.

The culture of defense procurement procedures and the climate of project investment are different in the military sector than in the free market. Therefore, successful conversion will require retraining military workers on all levels, especially regarding new administrative procedures and engineering projects. It is argued by some theorists that the record of large-scale military conversion is "unblemished by success" except for the examples of the reconstruction of post World War II West Germany and Japan (Adelman and Augustine, 1992). They suggest that the problems associated with conversion efforts in the former Soviet bloc states are nearly insurmountable such that "true economic conversion is readily dismissed as impossible or at least impractical." According to Adelman and Augustine, the same criticism can be directed at conversion efforts in the United States. In a 1992 Foreign Affairs article, they argued that research has been unable to identify a successful product in the commercial sector of the economy of the U.S. that was developed through a military-to-civilian approach, and that "as of 1990 there are very few concrete examples of actual conversion."

I will show examples of successful defense conversion in the United States using technologies that have been developed by military research laboratories and transferred, or have the potential to be transferred, into commercial sectors of the U.S. economy. The potential for future conversion is also to be seen in recent agreements such as that made by the Clinton Administration to allow private companies to market spy satellite technology to worldwide commercial customers, including environmental organizations and multinational corporations.

The Clinton Administration has allocated at least $140 million of fiscal year 1994 funds for the February 1994 Technology Reinvestment Project Awards. These awards focus on developing technologies for application in the commercial sectors involving electronics design and manufacturing, environmentally sensitive emissions control technologies, information systems infrastructure, health care, shipbuilding robotics, electric vehicles, electric transportation systems, and aeronautical technologies.

Additionally, Congress funded conversion in the 1994 Defense Authorization Act. In order to fulfill the goals of the Defense Conversion, Reinvestment, and Transition Act of 1992, the 1994 Defense Authorization Act authorized that the sum of $2,735 million be allocated for funding defense conversion, reinvestment, and transition assistance programs for 1994. Technology focus areas include ocean thermal energy conservation; advanced antenna technology; advanced wind power systems; automated manufacturing technology for composites; processing technologies; noncooled, pyroelectric thermal imaging systems; marine biotechnology; direct satellite radio broadcasting; solar furnace environmental remediation technologies; photovoltaic energy storage systems; robotic excavation and tunneling technologies; earthquake-resistant bridge composites; and advanced automatic train control systems (U.S. Congress, 1994).

Fifteen million dollars of this authorization is allocated for retraining military personnel for careers in the delivery of health care and law enforcement. Additional aspects of this funding include $575 million for defense technology reinvestment programs, with $105 million being allocated for dual-use critical technology partnerships, $85 million for defense regional technology alliances, $35 million for commercial-military integration partnerships, $50 million for manufacturing extension programs, $50 million for dual-use extension programs, $30 million for advanced manufacturing technology partnerships, and $20 million for supporting activities of manufacturing experts at major universities and institutes of technology.

Adelman and Augustine (1992) were probably correct in their assessment of economic conversion in the United States; however, the funding of technology transfers are proving that pockets of successful economic conversion are occurring in the mid-1990s led by governmental efforts. These efforts are a significant step forward towards realizing the potential markets for military technologies and economic conversion. The political will to convert is crucial if conversion is to be taken seriously by national policy-makers to a point where it can occur on a massive scale like that in post-World War II West Germany and Japan.

Individual Examples

On the individual level, former military engineers have succeeded in transferring their skills and know-how from military work to civilian markets. For instance, electrical engineers are moving from working on designing flight simulators for military use to designing video games in a commercial market (Daly, 1994). Other engineers have transferred their skills of designing military hardware systems to the health care field, providing analysis on the risks and benefits of using different health care technologies when treating various forms of cancers and other diseases (Perry, 1992). Former military engineers have already transferred their skills to commercial areas in the economy that include designing computer programming, basic research in computing and communications, consulting for utilities and governments, solar cell research and development, medical electronics, radiation therapy technologies and other aspects of the health care industry, and computer software development.

Engineers have been successful in finding new areas of employment because they were able to overcome problems from those facing managers and executives. Before managers and executives can successfully convert, they must change their mind-set and be educated on aspects of the free-market system. For the majority of managers are only familiar with "military hardware and government customers" and therefore are not equipped for the demands of the marketplace (Daly, 1994). The conversion of hardware-related aspects of military industries (engineers and technology transfers) has shown itself to be more successful than the rather elusive conversion of administration-related aspects of military industries (executives and managers).

Cooperative Research and Development Agreements (CRDAs)

The use of Cooperative Research and Development Agreements (CRDAs) between military research and development activities and U.S. industry is one way for technology transfers to occur. Under CRDAs, the Army, the Navy, or any branch of the armed services and industry are able to contribute resources such as personnel, services, and property to the cooperative effort. The funding is provided by industry alone. Since the government does not provide funding for services and products, the CRDA is not a procurement, and these agreements are not constrained by the procurement process. The intellectual property created under the CRDA can be used exclusively by the particular company involved in order to develop commercial products. However, the government agency does retain a license to use these technologies for military applications (Stern, 1994).

Army CRDAs and Potential Commercialized Technologies

(1) The U.S. Army Research Laboratory's Electronics and Power Sources Directorate (EPSD), Fort Monmouth, N.J., was involved in several CRDAs with Martin Marietta and Trontech, Inc.. The first provided novel permanent magnet structure designs to Martin Marietta that have resulted in several permanent magnetic structures that improve the performance, reliability and cost of microwave/millimeterwave sources. The second involved commercial applications of new oscillator/amplifier components, circuits and subassemblies that improve frequency spectral purity for use in extending cable TV service to high-density urban areas and by the cellular phone industry (Stern, 1994).

(2) Another Army CRDA under way involves the Office of the Surgeon General and Land O'Lakes Procor Technologies (now Advanced Food Science, Inc) and seeks to develop a ration system for use by patients that are unable to eat solid foods. Thirty-six products have been developed so far, representing meat, vegetables, starches, desserts, and liquid beverages. The commercial applications include consumption by dental patients, cancer patients, and patients who cannot eat solid foods. This food technology was adopted by Department of Defense hospital feeding systems in 1993 (U.S. Department of the Army, 1994).

Navy Commercialized Technologies

(1) Commercial applications of the Global Positioning System lie in its ability to navigate ships, aircraft and vehicles. Such navigational tools can reduce delivery and emergency response time as well as help the airline and shipping industries resolve problems associated with errors in navigation. (U.S. Department of the Navy, 1993.)

(2) Naval Research Laboratory work with firefighting foams has led to the development of NRL patented Aqueous Film-Forming Foam now being used on all United States Navy aircraft carriers, in many major airports, refineries and other industries where costly fuel fires are likely to occur, thereby improving public safety.

(3) NRL has also developed fluorinated polymers or fluoropolymers that have great potential for commercial markets. They were being used as "coatings to surfaces to provide protection from corrosion" in the interior of Department of Defense fuel storage tanks. They can be used in aircraft, boats, farm equipment, food storage facilities and motor vehicles. Reducing corrosion in these types of products will improve public transportation and food safety.

(4) The Navy's laboratory system has developed a technology for application in the commercial shipping industry called the small waterplane area twin-hull ship. The technology allows displacement ships to be built with open ocean seaway performance characteristics superior to those of larger conventional ships.

(5) Many U.S. car models now use technology achievements in propeller (fan) quieting from research by the Navy in the 1980s. Foreign commercialization has not yet taken place for these quiet fan technologies. (U.S. Department of the Navy, 1993.)

Air Force Commercialized Technologies

(1) The integrated High Performance Turbine Engine Technology, managed by the Wright Laboratory's Areo Propulsion and Power Directorate, is a joint effort by many engine propulsion companies. This technology will improve propulsion engine capabilities in fuel consumption, maintenance and performance, cost, and reliability. This program includes digital electronic engines controls, thermal barrier coatings, single crystal airfoils and swept compressor aerodynamics that have already been transferred by the U.S. Government for use in commercial engines.

(2) The High Density Interconnect Failure Mechanism Project is a joint effort between the Air Force's Rome Laboratory and General Electric (GE) to identify failure mechanisms in the packaging and interconnects used in high-density microelectronic devices. This project will assist industry as it attempts to produce microelectronic devices for both military and commercial applications that have a higher reliability and a high density. Texas Instruments is nearing completion of a factory that will mass-produce modules for military and commercial applications using these new packaging technologies.

(3) A technology being developed through a joint effort with the Air Force's Phillips Laboratory, IBM and Honeywell are radiation hardened electronics. This technology would benefit military and long-life commercial satellites operating in the Earth's radiation belts. These electronics would also provide sensing and monitoring hardware that can be used by nuclear power plants and hazardous waste sites (U.S. Department of the Air Force, 1994.)

Conclusion: Potential For Conversion

Historically, satellite-imaging systems have been used by the intelligence community for espionage activities. It is hoped that commercial applications of this technology will include scientific research on the environment, mapping for geological survey purposes, and oil and mining exploration. Currently, the most powerful satellite-imaging systems of Spot Image, a French based company, can depict photographs of small objects approximately 10 yards in diameter on the Earth's surface from as many as 22,000 miles above the Earth (Andrews, 1994). Lockheed, Orbital Sciences Corporation and other firms have been seeking permission to make commercial use of satellite-imaging systems technologies that are anticipated to have the ability to focus on surface objects as small as one square yard. This will greatly enhance the capability of satellite imaging systems to photograph valuable and scarce resources.

Conversion efforts need to be coupled to some of the most pressing social, economic, and environmental problems in the United States. Conversion programs continue to make up a small percentage of the total defense budget despite their potential economic and military benefits. The perceived military threat to the United States since the end of the Cold War has arguably been reduced. Conversion efforts have the potential for ameliorating large-scale social, economic, and environmental threats to U.S. national security if the U.S. political leadership has the will to appropriate more dollars for conversion.

References

Adelman, Kenneth L., and Norman R. Augustine, 1992: Defense Conversion: Bulldozing the Management, Foreign Affairs, Spring: 26-47.

Andrews, Edmund L., 1994: U.S. to Allow Sale of the Technology for Spy Satellites, The New York Times, March 11, A1, C5.

Daly, Les, 1994: But Can They Make Cars?, The New York Times Magazine, January 30, 26-27.

DeGrasse, Robert, et al., 1978: Creating Solar Jobs: Options for Military Workers and Communities. Mid-Peninsula Conversion Project, Mountain View, California, 135 pp.

Perry, Telka S., 1992: Engineers in Profile, *Institute of Electrical and Electronics Engineers, Inc. Spectrum*, December, 29-36.

Ricardo, David, 1819: *The Principles of Political Economy and Taxation.* Jacob Gideon, Jr., Washington City, 448 pp.

Stern, R,, 1994: Fact Sheets on Technology Transfers. U.S. Army Office of Research and Technology Applications, 3.

U.S. Congress. House, 1994: National Defense Authorization Act 103rd Congress, 1st Session, H.R. 2401, 474-475.

U.S. Department of the Air Force, 1993: Technology Transfer Report. Wright-Patterson Air Force Base, OH: U.S. Department of the Air Force, Headquarters Air Force Materiel Command, 5-19.

U.S. Department of the Army, 1993: Dual-Use Technologies, Military and Commercial Applications. U.S. Army Natick Research, Development and Engineering Center, U.S. Department of the Army, Natick, Massachusetts, 1-41.

U.S. Department of the Navy, 1993: Domestic Technology Transfer Report. Office of the Chief of Naval Research, U.S. Department of the Navy, Washington, D.C, 145-148.

CHAPTER 5

Military-Industrial Complex of Russia and the Conversion-Related Problems

Victor V. Chernyy
Former Senior Staff of the U.S.S.R./Russian Embassy in Washington

Valeri V. Semin
Consul (Scientific Affairs), Consulate General of Russia in San Francisco, U.S.A.

Russia and the Former Soviet Union

The Russian Federation (R.F.) has inherited about 60 percent of the U.S.S.R.'s gross national product (GNP) and population. As an integral part of this asset the country has got the biggest share of the military-industrial complex. Today this sector of Russia's economy comprises more than 1700 enterprises, employing about 6 million workers (Glukhih, 1993). This is the elite of the Russian workers and researchers, operating in the best equipped R&D and industrial facilities. Among the former Soviet Republics, Russia emerged as the only one capable of independently producing essentially all types of weapons systems that were developed in the U.S.S.R. Despite the hardships associated with the transition period, the Russian military-industrial complex continues developing and producing high-class modern weapons, such as jet fighters, tanks, rocket systems, submarines, etc. The Russian defense industry is working on the development of advanced systems, such as command and control, electronic warfare and stealth technology. According to Mr. A. Kokoshin, First Deputy Defense Minister, these technologies will be key areas for future procurements in Russia (Jane's, 1994b).

Development of the potential capability of producing modern weapons in big quantities required the mobilization of enormous human, intellectual and material resources. The regional approach used for achieving this goal led to a high concentration of the defense-related R&D and industrial facilities in certain areas. As a result, mammoth complexes were formed, embracing whole cities and sometimes regions where up to 75 percent of enterprises worked for defense. Nuclear cities "Arzamas-16" and "Cheljabinsk-80", the major military shipyards in Severodvinsk and Nizhnij Novgorod, missiles production centers in Leninsk and Votkinsk, industrial centers Moscow, St. Petersburg, Perm, Ekaterinburg, Izhevsk, Omsk, Krasnojarsk, Novosibirsk, North Caucasian and Volga regions are examples of this type of complex. More than 70 cities in the Russian Federation have a major part of their local economies driven by arms orders (ITAR-TASS, 1994b).

Organizationally, the U.S.S.R. military-industrial complex was managed by nine All-Union Ministries. To coordinate activities of defense industries in the Russian Federation the Committee of the Russian Federation on Defense Industries was established.

The main structural unit of the defense industry is a scientific/production association (SPA). Comprised of design bureaus, various production, test and transportation facilities, the SPA represents a relatively autonomous organizational structure, specializing in R&D and production of certain types of weapons systems. SPA "Energija," "Molnija," and "Kvant" that became the leading developers and producers of missile technologies are examples. They depend, though, on the supply of raw materials and components from other industries and have to maintain economic ties with plants all over the country.

Without exaggeration, the Russian military-industrial complex can be characterized as the core prime-mover of the scientific and technological development of the country. According to various estimates, the former Soviet Union had a larger number of scientists and engineers than any other country in the world—more than half a million—involved in defense and defense-related activities. Table 1 shows the number of people involved in defense-related R&D (as of January 1, 1991) (Russian Science, 1992).

This table illustrates the correlation of scientists and engineers involved in the defense R&D in the Soviet Union and the Russian Federation. However, it does not depict all fields of military-related R&D. A lot of projects were carried out by civilian establishments whose work supplemented activities of the defense SPA's design bureaus. Financing of these projects was channeled through appropriations for civil scientific purposes. All in all, defense and defense-related projects accounted for up to 50 percent of the scientific budget. The fact that the major part of the Soviet science, with a budget equal to 6 percent of national income, was working for defense shows the high degree of militarization of the Soviet R&D.

Table 1. People involved in defense related R&D (as of January 1, 1991; in thousands) (Russian Science Today and Tomorrow, 1992)

Sciences and Specialities	F.S.U.	Russia	Russian Shares %
Overall number of scientists (1990 average)	4031	2854	70.8
Holders of higher education degree, total	1632.9	1090.8	66.8
Including those involved in such areas vital for defense fields as:			
physics	66.4	41.8	62.9
chemistry	58.4	38.2	65.4
engineering	99.2	59.7	60.2
construction materials application in engineering	29.5	16.2	54.8
aviation and space missiles technology	22.5	20.4	90.5
shipbuilding	23.8	17.4	73.1
electrical engineering	43.1	27.7	64.4
toolmaking	59.8	42.9	71.8
radio-engineering	100.5	78.6	78.2
computers	166.0	112.2	67.6
electronics	25.6	18.9	74.0
energetics	25.6	15.8	61.9
Total	720.4	489. 8	68.0

Unfortunately since non-military items were merely by-products and there was no real competition in the country, producers usually did not bother themselves much with the quality of consumer goods and they were considerably lower than world standards. However, the prices of their products were significantly cheaper as compared to imported goods. Since domestic products were more affordable for the local population, the military-industrial complex played an important role in supplying consumer goods and maintaining socio-economic stability.

The above shows that Russia inherited from the Former Soviet Union (F.S.U.) the intellectual and technological/industrial potential that the country needed and could be proud of. The future of this potential in Russia was seen by many through the "glasses" of the conversion process. Despite the fact that this word was widely used in the country, its specific meaning was far from being clearly understood by the Russian general public. A lot of people were inclined to use a simplistic approach regarding the defense conversion. In their opinion, it was rather easy to switch from military to civilian production. According to various estimates, defense industry production accounts for about 40 percent of the country's gross production of civilian products. Many key consumer goods are made exclusively by defense plants. Table 2 shows percentages of some civilian products made by defense plants.

The aerospace industry was named as the one which seemed the most easy to convert. Statements like this sometimes were made even by some highly educated people. Apparently, that could not be the case as production of civilian planes had completely different parameters and specifications. Military planes are made on the basis of principally different technologies and electronic equipment. To change this a producer has to restructure the whole production line and cooperative ties with hundreds of components suppliers. Nonetheless, the conversion is possible and needed, but it has to be done carefully, in a manner which would allow the preservation of this valuable national asset. An uncontrolled break-up of the defense complex would mean an irrevocable loss of highly skilled manpower in the Russian economy and could have a very negative effect on the future industrial and economic development of the country. In all appearances the defense conversion will be a long process and hard to implement. In any event one has to be prudent in what is cut back and prudent in what is encouraged to stay alive in terms of both defense needs and domestic technology needs.

Table 2. Percentages of some civilian products made by defense plants

Products	Volume %
Film camera	100
Photo cameras	100
TV-sets	100
Sewing machines	100
Bicycles	100
Washing machines	80
Refrigerators	80

The Russian aerospace industry can serve as a good example of controlled conversion for the benefit of civilian and defense needs. Despite economic chaos and political upheavals, Russia's aerospace industry is not as depressed as it might be. To keep the industry afloat the Russian Government developed and approved "The Program of Development of Civil Aviation up to the Year 2000." In doing that the Government believed that civil aviation is an important transportation means that plays a vital role in the economic and social development of a modern nation. That is why the country is interested in the solution of the following tasks regarding development of the national civil aviation:

– to provide passenger transportation services;
– to provide cargo transportation and other air services;
– to maintain air carriers at the modern technological level.

The Program includes measures aimed at the achievement of these goals. Among other things it visualizes development by the year 2000 of a new generation of planes and helicopters corresponding to the highest international standards, including the following parameters:

– level of fuel consumption effectiveness for all airliners:14–18 g/pass.km; for local routes: 15–25 g/pass-km depending on their capacity; helicopters: 0.5–0.7 kg/t-km;
– full correspondence to the international standards in terms of comfort, flight and environmental safety;
– yearly flight hours capacity, for airliners: 3500–5000 hours; for local flights: 2400–3000 hours; for helicopters: 1800–2400 hours.

Russia's aerospace industry is one of the world's major producers of planes. That is why the Government prioritizes development of this high-tech and intellectual industry with a high average production cost. For example, if the cost of 1 kg of aerospace product is equal to $1000, then the cost of a kilo of electronic home appliances is $100, and that of an automobile—$20.

The Government of Russia also took into account the fact that the demand in new planes in the near future will go up as there are many planes (from 1145 to 1400) that by 2000 will be subject to discard. At the same time, civil aviation will be playing a more important role in the economic development of a new Russia, in maintaining its transportation links with former Soviet Republics and foreign countries.

The Program provides for the development and production of modern, comfortable and fuel consumption effective airliners, such as the IL-96-300, a plane for local flights, the IL-114, a medium-range plane (TU-204) and short-distance planes TU-334 and AN-338 as well as a cargo-passenger plane, the AN-74. A multipurpose amphibious plane will be developed within the conversion program. In the Program there are also plans regarding the launch into serial production of highly effective, multifunctional helicopters (i.e., MI-38, KA-62) and others made on the basis of advanced technologies.

Russians call this document a recovery program that was designed to not only assist the aerospace industry to survive but to be a prime mover of the country's technological progress. Having that in mind, the Russian Federation Ministry of Industry is financing research, development and engineering projects, while having at its disposal the necessary funds from the federal budget. The fact that Russia is able to increase central funding for its civil aviation program shows that in spite of the whole disarray in the economy there is still money available. The great benefit of the plan is that it tells industry what products are needed, as the biggest underlying problem for Russia's industry is the uncertainty that makes it difficult for design bureaus and factories to plan their human and material resources.

Despite the fact that the aerospace industry is re-orienting slowly and painfully, a sizable capacity continues to be for the development and production of fighters, bombers and missile systems. Partly, this can be explained by (1) the size of the Russian Armed Forces and (2) the recognition that the weapon systems will be needed for the export market.

Russia's nuclear industry could be another qualified candidate for the conversion. There are already programs developed with regard to destruction of nuclear weapons. Introduction of reverse technologies might be the easiest way to implement these programs. It is likely nobody can do this work better than the producers of these weapons, as they already have the necessary knowledge, skills and facilities to perform such tasks. Table 3 shows nuclear warheads that are subject to elimination (Time, 1992).

The space industry can also provide a civilian sector with valuable opportunities. A set of "peaceful" space vacuum experiments can significantly contribute to the development of metallurgy. Production of titanium and its alloys that possess a reactive capability to interact with atmospheric gases has to be carried out in a high vacuum in many stages. Fundamental research on new principles of life-support carried out in space resulted in the development of separation and substance regeneration technologies with characteristics substantially better than those developed on the ground. Introduction of these

Table 3. Nuclear Warheads that are Subject to Elimination
(in thousands)

technologies into industrial production (i.e., agriculture) can produce qualitatively new technico-economic effects in terms of environmental protection and resource savings. The Russian space industry is capable of solving the problem of establishing communication in polar regions, which cannot be provided by the satellites on geostationary orbits.

Financial Resources and Time Scale

Taking into account the size of the Russian military-industrial complex it becomes clear that the defense conversion process will be a long-term venture and require considerable financial resources. According to some estimates, some results of the conversion can only be realized in 3–7 years. Mr. M. Malei, Adviser to the President of the Russian Federation on Military Conversion, believes that the conversion will take at least fifteen years and require $150 billion (Novoye Russkoe Slovo, 1992).

Conversion-related problems are not new for Russia. Attempts to start this process were already made in 1987 when the government of the F.S.U. decided to increase production of civilian goods using capacities of the defense industry. Defense plants were ordered to develop and produce equipment for the light and food industries. The administrative measures were consistent with the principles of the command system of economic management. They imposed on defense plants production of certain items without due regard to their profile. At the same time, appropriate instructions were given concerning raw materials supply and investments to establish new facilities which were supposed to use the equipment produced by the defense plants. Funds needed for R&D were appropriated as well. The idea behind this concept implied the use of defense industry capabilities for civilian purposes without impeding their weapons production. This beginning of the conversion effort eventually resulted in a shift in the volume of the defense production in favor of civilian goods.

Developed in 1988 and slightly amended during the following years, the State Program of Conversion signified another step along this path. Prepared by the Gosplan of the U.S.S.R., this document targeted about 500 military plants with 5–6 military plants to be fully converted into non-military facilities (Christian Science Monitor, 1992). It was designed to encourage civilian production, including consumer goods and equipment for light and food industries. Specifically, it stipulated launching the production of 120 new civilian items. Having in mind first of all shipyards and plane assembly plants, it was suggested that plants should immediately start producing civilian items if substantial investments were not involved. This program, however, did not bring about expected results in terms of significant increase in the production of civilian items. The defense plants succeeded in producing only 23 new items. The plan was eventually shelved. Its failure, according to the Russian Government officials, could be explained by various reasons. First of all the substantial technological superiority of defense industries (they are 10–15 years ahead of civilian factories) versus that of civilian plants made it rather difficult for them to find appropriate partners in terms of industrial cooperation and components supply. On the other hand, enforced production of civilian items of a lower technological level created emotional problems among the workers of defense industries who were used to a privileged position and better benefits than workers of non-defense industries. Their attitude to the work began changing and some of them started looking for better options.

Without question the main reason why the State Program did not work was inadequate financial resources. Mr. Malei, the former advisor to President

Yeltsin said: The Gorbachev plan was brilliant but Mr. Gorbachev forgot to indicate sources of finance for the conversion (Izvestiya, 1990). The situation was aggravated as the country entered into a transitional period which resulted in the weakening of the central control over economic activity and, finally, disintegration of the Soviet Union. This development was a serious blow to the defense industry.

In post-Soviet Russia the conversion process took on a whole new meaning and dimension. It became more painful and difficult. Instead of proceeding with careful steps aimed at converting the military-industrial complex to civilian production, Russian defense industries were caught by what can be characterized as a "snow-slide" conversion. Some enterprises underwent conversion up to 98 percent (Commersant, 1992) and some completely stopped production of military items. Trying to control the massive budget deficit, the Russian Government began to cut defense spending. In his Press Conference on August 21, 1993, held in the Kremlin on the occasion of the first anniversary of victory of democracy in Russia, President Yeltsin recognized that in 1992 his government reduced military orders by 68 percent (TASS, 1992a). As a result, military hardware production went down sharply. Production of tanks was cut by 2.5 times, strategic missiles by 1.5 times, military aircraft by 1.4 times, and armored personnel carriers by 3.2 times (Pravda, 1992). Some industries completely lost their clientele. Especially difficult situations developed at shipyards, which suffered most since the Government failed to take any decision in respect to new naval vessels, while the building of those under construction was suspended. At the same time, the major civilian customers of the industry—the transport and fishing fleets—not having enough resources, drastically reduced purchases of civilian ships, contributing to the difficulties already experienced by about 30 shipyards, actually leaving them idle.

Those defense industries that started production of civilian items found themselves in a difficult situation as well. Not being cost-saving ventures, they produced goods at prices that were not competitive, which made their products difficult to sell. Unclaimed orders were another aggravating factor. For example, the order of the Ministry of Foreign Economic Relations accounted for up to 87.1 billion rubles (1991 prices). The Ministry paid only one-quarter of it, leaving a lot of produced military hardware unwanted. To cover their losses the defense industries put these expenses into the cost of their civilian products, thus contributing to a further increase in prices of consumer goods. Even those enterprises which could successfully operate producing consumer goods, such as TV-sets, refrigerators, radios, photo cameras, home appliances, etc., had to reduce their production due to a considerable deterioration of the general economic situation in the country. These difficulties had serious social implications for the defense industry, which began losing its labor force. In the first part of 1992 more than 170 000 workers left the industry looking for better options.

The economic decline, which became quite visible at the end of the 1980s, continued to develop in 1992. After the demise of the Soviet Union the Central Government was dissolved, resulting in the liquidation of the old economic management system. But a new one that would allow effective control of the economy was not created. At the same time the Russian Government hurriedly proceeded with the policy of radical economic reforms. Being well-intended but ill-prepared, or due to some other reasons, these reforms did not produce the desired results and intensified economic hardships in Russia. As of now the situation is still not improving very much. The economic reforms are still in their infancy. Not much progress has been made in the solution of basic questions on private property rights on land and means of production. The transportation system is dysfunctional, and law and order are not properly maintained. According to the Goskomstat of Russia, investment in the production sphere in 1992 fell down by 46 percent, compared to 1991, and the national income, by various estimates, declined by more than 20 percent.

This difficult economic situation considerably impeded the conversion process. Transforming money-losing defense industries into economically viable ventures is not possible without economic restructuring, but restructuring is facing opposition on the part of the so-called "national-patriotic" forces of Russia and on the part of the directors of defense plants who found themselves unprepared for managing their enterprises in a market economy, and in some cases are unwilling to adapt to a new situation. This, among other things, was revealed by the fact-finding missions carried out by the German Bank at some defense industries of Russia. The missions showed that the management of all enterprises are wrestling with a range of difficult issues. Many are suffering from very severe financial difficulties and have drastically reduced operations. In the last quarter of 1992 more than 400 defense industries had a 3–4 day work week, about 130 were almost at standstill, and about 20 completely idle. Nonetheless, the enterprises did not have coherent restructuring or business plans. Their legal and privatization status was not certain. The management of many of the enterprises remains fairly remote from the realities of the market economy. Their understanding of consumer markets and distribution is minimal. They have not usually analyzed their core competencies and related these to business prospects. Many conversion projects look like desperate attempts to raise cash by selling miscellaneous consumer products.

It would not be fair to say that the Russian Government completely abandoned the military-industrial complex and is doing nothing to help it. It can be heard from some quarters that, under the pressure of the defense industries lobby, the Government will not let Russia's most advanced research and manufacturing capabilities disappear and will continue fresh infusion of funds into this industry. In fact, it does so trying to save the military-industrial complex. Patriotic feelings of the Russian leadership are only a part of the reasons behind the governmental efforts in this field. Economic considerations are also involved. The Government is aware of the fact that in the highly militarized economy of the former Soviet Union the defense industry aggregated up to 56 percent of the revenues of the state budget (TASS, 1992b). To let the defense industry simply fade away meant to lose the major source of the budget financing. Under these conditions, the Government simply has no choice but to keep this sector of economy afloat, trying to encourage the defense industry to adapt to the situation. To achieve this goal the Government is pursuing vague and sometimes contradictory policies. On one hand, it tries to reduce military expenditures by cutting the defense procurement orders. On the other hand, billions of rubles are being pumped into the defense sector in the form of aid, investments or soft credits.

In 1992 Acting Premier E. Gaidar, in his speech before the Supreme Soviet, claimed that the defense industry received from the Government for conversion purposes 124 billion rubles (Christian Science Monitor, 1992). That included 77 billion rubles in long-term credits for defense plants carrying out conversion at a level greater than 15–20 percent of their production capacity. To avoid mass unemployment at defense plants, it was proposed to allocate in 1993 for conversion purposes 250 billion rubles in low-interest credits and 94 billion rubles in subsidies. It was also planned to invest into the defense sector 32.7 billion rubles (TASS, 1993b). It is generally recognized that these funds are not sufficient to stabilize the industry. Mr. V. Glukhih, Chairman of the Committee of the Russian Federation on Defense Industries stated in an interview that in 1993 at least 500 billion rubles were needed for the conversion (TASS, 1993a). To get some money, the defense industries continued producing items, including military hardware, according to state orders not supported by contracts. In 1992 they produced in this way weapons for 37 billion rubles (TASS, 1992c).

Lack of financial resources was not the only stumbling block on the way to a successful conversion. There was also no appropriate legal basis. On

March 20, 1992 the Supreme Soviet of the Russian Federation adopted the Law on Conversion of Military Industry, but that law alone did not provide a sufficient legal basis for the conversion. The legislation containing the definition of the conversion stipulated the organizational measures to be taken to proceed with this process and described activities allowed for defense industries within the framework of the conversion. That included among other things cooperation with foreign partners. But the law said nothing regarding the key question on the state weapons procurement order, saying only that weapon procurement orders will be based on the military doctrine of the Russian Federation (Rossijskaya, 1992). It is natural to assume that to be able to properly shape its defense-industrial potential, a country needs its national security concept, foreign policy doctrine, military doctrine, and law on defense. In Russia that piece of legislation did not exist. In his address to the meeting of the National Security Council on March 3, 1993 President B. Yeltsin recognized the urgency of those issues. He emphasized that Russia badly needed the military doctrine. In his opinion, further delay in formulating the foreign policy concept and the military doctrine would directly lead to destabilization of the situation in Russia (TASS, 1993c).

The New Military Doctrine

A new Military Doctrine of the Russian Federation was approved by the National Security Council on November 2, 1993 (ITAR-TASS, 1993a). The doctrine said that Russia would not treat other states as its enemies, would be using its military force for defense purposes only and would be using nuclear weapons deterrence. Under this doctrine, Russia, by 1996, should have its forces regrouped within its new borders, repatriate all units serving abroad, and continue its shift to a mixed system of recruiting both professional servicemen and conscripts. Priority will be given to development of armed forces designed to deter aggression. The document also emphasized the importance of the development of mobile forces.

Approval of the 1993 Doctrine made it possible to develop a conversion program. While visiting the 106th Paratroopers Division in Tula on November 17, 1993, President Yeltsin said that based on the new Military Doctrine the work was going forward on the development of a Program for Defense Industries that would define their activities including arms export (ITAR-TASS, 1993b). In a month's time, Mr. V. Glukhih, Chairman of the State Committee on Defense Industries stated that within the framework of the Government Conversion Program the industry began implementing 14 State

Conversion Programs with emphasis on transport, communication, medicine, fuel sector, environment and agriculture. He complained, though, that there were still not enough funds to fully implement these programs (ITAR-TASS, 1993c). Thus, deficit of funds was identified as the major stumbling block on the way to a successful conversion.

Today in Russia the following approaches have crystallized with regard to sources of financial funds needed for the conversion. First of all the Government continues its efforts to help defense industries in their conversion effort. In November 1993 President Yeltsin signed a decree to ensure that the Government and the Central Bank of Russia maintained uninterrupted financing of all government-approved conversion projects until their completion. The decree gives state contractors the right to pay in advance for a state contract to develop and produce select products with lengthy production cycles. Profit ceilings are set for military orders and enterprises having tax concessions. But real life is different and real money is difficult to get. According to Mr. V. Glukhih, the Ministry of Finance has allocated funding for only 20 percent of the annual defense budget. The money released for the conversion research amounted to one-third of that sum (Jane's, 1994a). President Yeltsin, during his press-conference on June 10, 1994 in the Kremlin, said that despite the fact that the defense budget was approved, the country did not have enough resources to maintain an Army of 3 million. He suggested cutting funds planned for weapons procurement (ITAR-TASS, 1994a).

Another approach is based on the use of private capital. Some economists suggest that the Russian entrepreneurs who have accumulated substantial capital should be involved in the conversion process. According to their advice the state has to transfer its property rights to these plants into private hands. Realization of this concept, however, does not offer solutions to the overall conversion problem, as the private Russian capital is still not big enough to cover enormous needs related to the conversion process. However, some Russian defense industries are using commercial bank guarantees. In 1993 the industry repaid 400 billion rubles ($200 million) in loan credits from profits on export orders. Thus, the idea of establishing a close working relationship between defense industries and financial institutions, including commercial ones, is becoming more and more popular. Many defense industries began to realize that in order to survive in the future as private companies they have to work closely with a network of banks and investment funds that are now mushrooming all over Russia. Many are closely connected with local governments and industries, including arms producers. Newly privatized defense industries have to raise money to stay ahead technologically in order to be able to get domestic orders and to exercise highly competitive export sales. According to Mr. Valeri Novikov, Director of the Miasishcev Design Bureau, of the 2000 defense industries in Russia, up to 1500 will be privatized in 1995. The remaining 500 represent critical strategic technologies and will be state-owned (Defense News, 1994).

Another source of financing the conversion could be foreign investments. Trying to attract foreign capital the Government of Russia is working with its counterparts in other countries, looking for support of investments in Russia. A good example of this type of activity can serve as a joint Russian-American Declaration on Defense Conversion. The Declaration states that recognizing the important role of the private sector and of practical participation by business communities in the complex task of defense conversion, the United States of America and the Russian Federation are establishing a U.S.–Russian Defense Conversion Committee to facilitate conversion through expanded trade and investment (WHPR, 1992). The Defense Conversion Committee was integrated as a subcommittee into the U.S.–Russia Business Development Committee which was initiated by Presidents Yeltsin and Bush in June 1992. The purpose of the Defense Conversion Subcommittee is to facilitate the U.S. private sectors' efforts to participate in a meaningful way in Russian defense conversion initiatives. Its formation reflects the recognition by both governments that the private sector offers the best opportunity for accomplishing the complex conversion task now facing the Russian Federation. To that end, the subcommittee will pursue the following objectives:

– collect and disseminate information to the U.S. private sector on Russian defense conversion opportunities;
– identify and address U.S. and Russian obstacles to private sector participation in Russian defense conversion initiatives;
– facilitate contacts between potential business partners on Russian defense conversion projects.

The activity of the subcommittee was supplemented by efforts of the International Civil Service Corps. Using grants received from the USAID, this U.S. organization sent small teams to Kharkiv and Nizhnij Novgorod as fact-finding missions. Some U.S. private entities also took steps to find out more about Russia's defense industries. For example, Steptoe & Johnson, Booz, Allen & Hamilton, and Ameritrade visited the nuclear facility in

Chelyabinsk-70 and met with the people at the Mil Helicopter and "Vympel" plants in Moscow.

Unfortunately, despite all these efforts there are not many practical results in terms of foreign investments in the defense industries of Russia, although some contracts were signed. For example, the Moscow Khrunichev engineering plant concluded a deal with the American Motorola company to launch commercial satellites for space communication. The SPA "Energomash" signed an agreement with the American company Pratt & Whitney to provide jet engine technologies. The technology will be used for production of a principally new RD-701 engine for the U.S. and international market. The Boeing Company opened in Moscow its Technical Research Center. The U.S. Department of Defense awarded contracts to U.S. companies in the sum of $16.8 million (Rockwell, Double Cola, International American Products). Hunter Engineering Company, Inc., Riverside, California has successfully finalized a defense conversion project in Russia valued at $135 million. The project entails the design, manufacture and installation of U.S. sourced equipment for a cold rolling mill to produce aluminum sheet, foil and related flat products at the Krasnoyarsk Metallurgical Plant (KRAMZ) in Russia. According to the U.S. Export-Import Bank, the Hunter Engineering export sale to KRAMZ represents the largest defense conversion project for Russia to date, outside of oil and gas, to be financed by the Bank on behalf of an American exporter.

According to Nizhny Novgorod's Department of Conversion report marketing conversion projects to foreigners has not been overly successful because of the "kick the tires" problem. It was reported that about 150 foreign delegations had visited converting enterprises in 1993 without concluding a contract. Enterprise directors are growing increasingly frustrated with the lack of follow-through by visiting foreign business people. In general, hopes that Western investors would come to rescue the ailing defense industries of Russia have mostly been a glimmer. Partly, it happened because of the political and economic instability in Russia. To some extent mass media, including those of the United States, contributed to it excessively dramatizing the situation in Russia, painting it in gloomy, dark colors. Naturally, capital will flow to other places with much more comfortable conditions than in Russia.

This problem can partly be explained by insufficient incentives for foreign capital in Russia. Taking into account various risks for foreign investments in Russia these incentives apparently are not adequate. Besides that, there is still no proper legal basis for foreign investments in Russia, particularly in the taxation policy. Finally, existing security restrictions on both sides also impede cooperation in a defense sector.

Nevertheless, new steps have recently been taken to attract funds from foreign investors. Firstly, the conversion enterprises enjoy the tax breaks granted by the Presidential Decree of September 27, 1993 "On Improving Work with Foreign Investments." Secondly, additional possibilities are offered by the transformation of defense enterprises into joint-stock companies. Under the law, 80 percent of defense enterprises are subject to such transformation; this has already occurred in more than 30 percent of cases.

There are a number of ways for foreign investors to become involved in such defense enterprises. First of all, by acquiring a stake in their capital and buying shares, bonds, and other securities. Foreign investors may provide loans, credits, etc. On the basis of plants fully converted to civilian production, enterprises completely owned by foreign investors can be set up. The main forms of cooperation might include the establishment of joint ventures, (the "Lockheed-Khrunichev-Energia" joint venture is a very good example). Joint stock companies would manufacture civilian goods, with credits repaid with products and in the regular way marketing through foreign companies of various civilian goods produced by conversion enterprises, and exchanges of technologies, licenses, know-how, scientific and technical information.

Arms Production and Sales

Under current circumstances, in order to be able to proceed with the conversion, Russian leadership decided to look for other options. In this context the attention is focused more and more on arms sales as a promising source of hard currency needed for conversion of the military-industrial complex. This idea is not new and has for some time been a subject of debate among people involved in the defense production. Its proponents argued that not long ago—in 1989—the former Soviet Union was the major weapons exporter in the world, and they are critical about the dramatic drop in Russia's share in the arms market. Table 4 shows levels of arms exports in the world weapons market (BASIC, 1991). Table 5 illustrates Russian arms exports from 1988 to 1993.

It is no secret that hundreds of defense industries are on the verge of coming to a standstill or are out of operation. That creates high social tension in the regions and undermines stability in the country. Besides that, money is needed to maintain the Russian Armed Forces. Speaking during the Press

Table 4. Levels of Arms Exports in World Weapons Market

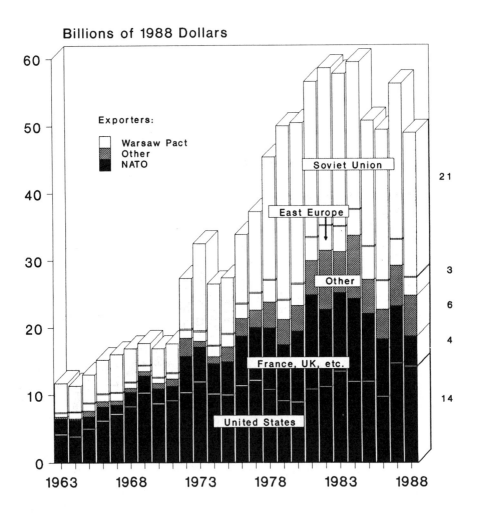

Global Arms Exporters
By Alliance

Table 5. Russian Arms Exports 1988 to 1993 (in Billion US$)

Volume /Years	1988	1989	1990	1991	1992	1993
40						
--						
30						
--						
20	21					
--						
10				7,8		
---					4,8	
0						3

Conference on July 10, 1994, President Yeltsin agreed that the military budget for 1994 could not cover all the military expenses. He suggested that the budget has to be supplemented by non-budgetary sources of finance, including arms exports (ITAR-TASS, 1994a).

Russian leadership increasingly believes that the military-industrial complex should again become an industry capable of earning money to help itself and help the country. The idea behind that is that the military-industrial complex has to produce the items it can do best, in other words it has to continue producing weapon systems competitive in the world market. Experts have estimated that demand for Russian military equipment could amount to $25–30 billion a year. Proponents of this approach consider arms exports as a great opportunity for Russia to solve simultaneously a number of political and economic issues. In terms of the internal situation, the revitalization of Russia's defense sector is a vital domestic policy concern for President B. Yeltsin.

Russian government and industry officials say that arms trade is not only an effective source of revenue, but it is also a means to conduct foreign policy. In their opinion, through arms exports Russia can regain its independence from the humiliation of Western aid as Russia could get more revenues from the sale of weapons than from Western credits that will have to be paid by the present generation's children and grandchildren. They also say that the world arms market has become a successor to the Cold War rivalry between Russia and the United States. They emphasize that seven years ago the former Soviet Union arms sales in the world market accounted for 38 percent; the U.S. 30 percent. Now Russia's share has fallen to 17 percent and the market is dominated by France, the U.K. and the U.S., whose share in the market has reached 58 percent (Jane's, 1994c).

To encourage arms exports and to recoup its position in the world arms market, Russia took a coordinated step with regard to the activities of government arms trade agencies. In January 1994, President Yeltsin signed a decree to consolidate three government agencies: Oboronexport, Spetsvnesh-technika and the General Department of Cooperation. In their place a superstructure called Rosvooruzhenie was established with offices in more than 30 countries. The new entity adopted modern Western marketing and advertising techniques. It has at its disposal color brochures, a press office and an English language magazine (Military Parade), which is printed in Italy. Russia actively participates in international armaments shows and organizes military exhibitions on its own.

In terms of marketing strategy, Russian arms traders are targeting the traditional Soviet markets, such as China, India, Syria, Iran, Kuwait, and the former Warsaw Treaty countries. They are developing new markets— Malaysia, Singapore, Thailand, Indonesia, and Brazil. To promote sales, Rosvooruzhenie uses various forms of cooperation with its customers, among them credits, joint ventures, and technical cooperation. The most popular items offered for sale are fighter aircraft (MiG-29, MiG-31, Su-27, Su-30), "Kilo" class submarines, Tarantul-III corvettes equipped with SS-N-22 "Sunburn" missiles, BMP-3 infantry combat vehicles, FROG-7 missile systems, surface-to-air missile systems (SA-10, SA-12, SA-15), manportable SAM SA-18 Igla, etc. It is expected that extremely proactive efforts of Rosvooruzhenie will result in success. According to Russia's defense experts its arms exports in 1994 could reach $3.5 billion, a $1.5 billion increase compared to 1993 (Jane's, 1994c).

With the end of the Cold War there was a unique opportunity to constrain the arms trade. It could be done in the same manner as the East-West arms race was constrained. Since most of the world's weapons sales were made by NATO and the former Warsaw Treaty States which agreed to limit their own arsenals and declared their intention to be partners in world affairs, arms trade limitations could complement the arms control agreements between the former adversaries. Unfortunately, this opportunity is not being realized. With the major arms exporters reducing their military forces, their excessive productive capacity created huge economic incentives for dumping large quantities of weapons into the world arms market. It equally applies to Russia and to the

U.S.A. Both of them became subject to temptation to earn money on the weapons surplus resulting from the Cold War. This club is now joined by the U.K., France, Germany, Italy, China, India and others. This trend will naturally lead to more severe competition and the development of new weapons systems.

Russian-American Cooperation

The above arms trade developments should not preclude Russian-American cooperation in the conversion field. Russia is still open for a mutually beneficial cooperation and could be interested in joint development of new technologies, industrial robots, engineering designs, etc. It will be in the interests of both countries to encourage the expansion of bilateral defense industrial and military contacts by addressing the full range of issues that are critically linked to the success of the conversion in Russia and the United States of America. Western assistance to conversion cannot be the panacea for Russian ills. But it can help to reduce inevitable conflicts among legitimate goals of an integrated economic policy. Medium- to long-term public assistance like the Marshall Plan would undoubtedly provide a clear positive signal for private investors.

American-Russian Partnership

The end of the Cold War paved the way for a new kind of relationship between the former adversaries. A Charter for American Russian Partnership and Friendship, which was signed during President Yeltsin's visit to Washington in June 1992, says that the United States of America and the Russian Federation share common ideals and principles. On the basis of mutual trust and respect they developed a relationship of partnership and friendship. Both sides reaffirmed their commitment to democracy, to the primacy of the rule of law and to respect human rights and fundamental freedoms. They also confirmed their resolution to settle disputes between them by peaceful means and to refrain from the threat or use of force against each other. They promised to unite their efforts toward strengthening international peace and security, preventing and settling regional conflicts and solving global problems. It is imperative that these goals be maintained as the two nations struggle with many transitional problems.

References

BASIC, 1991: Background Paper "The Arms Trade: Past Trends and Future Control," April.

Christian Science Monitor, 1992: November 27.

Commersant, 1992: June.

Defense News, 1994: October 3-9.

Glukhih, V., 1993: TASS Report, Press Conference of Chairman of the Committee of the Russian Federation on Defense Industries, January 15.

ITAR-TASS, 1993a: Report, November 3.

ITAR-TASS, 1993b: Report ,November 17.

ITAR-TASS, 1993c: Report ,December 7.

ITAR-TASS, 1994a: Report, June 10.

ITAR-TASS, 1994b: Report, July 1.

Izvestiya, 1990: August 8.

Jane's Defense Weekly, 1994: (a) May 7, (b) June 25, p. 32, (c) July 9.

Novoye Russkoe Slovo, 1992: May 11.

Pravda, 1992: June 16.

Rossijskaya Gazeta, 1992: April 27.

Russian Science Today and Tomorrow, 1992: Part 2.

TASS Report, 1992a: August 21.

TASS Report, 1992b: December 3.

TASS Report, 1992c: December 16.

TASS Report, 1993a: January 15

TASS Report, 1993b: February 26,

TASS Report, 1993c: March 3.

Time, 1992: December 7.

White House Press Release, 1992: June 17.

CHAPTER 6

Conversion of the Military-Industrial Complex of Ukraine: Problems and Solutions

V.V. Chernyy
Bureau of Defense Conversion, Technological
Industrial Development of Ukraine
Arlington, Virginia

Independence

On August 24, 1991, Verkhovna Rada, the Ukrainian Parliament, made a historic step. It overwhelmingly voted for the Act on Independence of Ukraine. Thus this second largest Soviet Republic was given the status of a sovereign state. This event signified for Ukraine the end of the whole historic era—the end of the period during which the country did not have its statehood and exercised little control over its social and economic resources. This move was widely supported by the Ukrainian people. After many years of the Soviet regime Ukrainians saw in their declaration of independence a great opportunity for themselves and their country to take control of their destiny, to become a modern and prosperous state and a recognized member of the civilized world. But the political independence of Ukraine was accompanied by enormous problems that the young independent state has had to encounter since August 24, 1991.

First of all, Ukraine had to develop genuine statehood that could ensure her sovereign status. Despite its formal independence Ukraine, like other Republics under the Soviet regime, was an integral part of a highly centralized state entity—the U.S.S.R., where Moscow monopolized the political decision-making process as well as economic planning and management. In this situation the Ukrainian authorities had nothing to do but to follow orders and instructions received from Moscow. After having declared herself independent Ukraine had to develop a new mechanism of state government, to assume a much greater responsibility for the development of internal and external policy, and to create a brand new presidency, and executive and professional legislative branches of power. Naturally, fulfillment of these tasks required appropriate expertise and skills as well as enormous organizational efforts and financial resources that Ukraine did not have.

The second group of problems was related to a rather difficult economic situation that developed in Ukraine after the declaration of independence. To become truly independent the country had to reorganize and restructure its economy, to create its own independent banking and monetary system. The economy of Ukraine was an integral part of the U.S.S.R. overall national economic structure. It was created to operate in this capacity during the Tsarist and then the Soviet Regime when nobody even thought about Ukraine as an independent political and economic entity. That is why after the independence was proclaimed Ukrainian enterprises began experiencing great difficulties; on the one hand, they lost their sources of supply of components and raw materials and, on the other hand, their customers.

The situation was considerably aggravated by difficulties associated with the transition period. Any transition from one economic system to another is often a painful, not pleasant process. In Ukraine this process was complicated due to the absence, at the level of the national leadership, of a clear vision of the economic reform process. There was no national consensus as to the nature and speed of reforms. As a result no national reform program was developed and implemented. This led to a situation in which the old system was collapsing and a new one was not being developed to replace it. The Ukrainian economy's decline continued as government mismanagement and the shock of higher priced Russian energy imports took their toll. Inflation skyrocketed up to hyperinflation levels by mid-1993 and at the end of 1993 was running at a monthly rate of 90 percent. Price rises have been spurred on by record levels of new credit issues in the second part of 1993 and a budget deficit of 30–40 percent of GDP was the highest among the newly independent states (NIS). Despite these developments the Ukrainian leadership continued using old methods of economic management. It preserved the state control over means of production, and did not stop budgetary financing of bankrupt enterprises. As a result it was not possible to restructure the Ukrainian economy with its archaic structure. Restructuring and renovation of the Ukrainian industry was vitally important as basic funds of many enterprises were cut, on the average, by a half and in some branches by 70 percent, and two thirds of capital investments required renewal. Table 1 shows the share each branch of the Ukrainian economy had of the national income.

Some Ukrainians compare the economic situation in Ukraine during its early years of independence with the Great Depression period in the

**Table 1. Shares Each Branch of The Ukrainian Economy had
in The National Income**

Branch	Percentage of National Income
Fuel and raw materials	48
Production of means of production	28
Consumer goods	24

United States in 1929–1933, that was characterized by a sharp drop in mass production and unemployment. However, one has to remember that the U.S.A. had rather developed state institutions and a political system with more than a hundred years of experience in governing the country. Indeed the "new course" policy adopted and implemented by President Roosevelt could be extremely useful for Ukraine in terms of making an effective contribution to the state regulatory practices and social reforms that would help the country's economic recovery. Unfortunately, neither the American experience nor an experience of other countries was taken into account or used by the Ukrainian leadership, and the economy plunged into more and more difficulties.

Creation of a new economic system based on a wide privatization, demonopolization, and introduction without delay of market principles into the economy could represent a major solution to economic problems of the country. Ukraine, though, made virtually no progress on economic reforms. In 1993 President Kravchuk brought in economic policy makers who largely shared his preference for slow and heavily interventionist policies, and no real reformers were left in positions of power.

The third group of problems that the independent Ukraine had to face was related to defense conversion, in a broad sense since the role that Ukraine played in maintaining the Soviet military power cannot be overestimated. This Republic hosted the best trained and equipped divisions and accounted for a substantial part of the overall Soviet military-industrial complex. All this resulted in a high level of militarization of the Ukrainian society. After the demise of the Soviet Union Ukraine realized that she did not need an excessive military capacity that became a burden and was difficult for this newly independent state to bear.

First of all Ukraine had to reduce its Armed Forces that comprised 750,000 men. Besides that Ukrainians served in other countries: in military formations of the former Soviet Union in Eastern Europe, in Baltic States, in Russia (additionally 150,000–200,000 men). The Ukrainian military thinking believes that the National Army should not exceed 200,000–220,000. Table 2 shows that Ukraine faced an enormous task in the "conversion" of her Armed Forces.

To achieve this goal it will be necessary to fulfill the following: to provide about 200,000 apartments for the demobilized persons, to organize reorientation courses for them, to create additional jobs and favorable economic conditions like private farming, business, entrepreneurship; in other words to substantially improve social and economic infrastructure as well as to develop new, more advanced elements and incorporate them into the existing socio-economic system.

Table 2. Future Reductions of the Ukrainian Military

thousands	Number of Ukrainian in the Armed Forces	Projected size of the National Army	Subject to reduction

Defense Industry

The second aspect of the conversion problem was the reorganization and reorientation of the Ukrainian defense industry. On one hand, this task represents a big problem, on the other hand its implementation provides a real opportunity for economic development and revival.

The military-industrial complex of Ukraine comprised about 700 enterprises, employing its best personnel (about 750,000 people) working on the best equipped facilities. It was capable of producing tanks, warships, tactical and strategic missiles, airplanes, power turbines for gas generators, automobiles, agricultural machinery, medical equipment, etc. In the past, Ukraine was proud of having such a potential. After she gained her independence she did not know what to do with this asset, which became a heavy and sometimes unneeded burden. For example, she did not know what to do with an aircraft carrier under construction at one of its shipyards. This project had already consumed 800 million rubles (1991 prices) and required more money to be completed. Ukraine had neither the necessary resources nor components to complete this work that was financed from the U.S.S.R. budget and supported by industries outside the country. The military-industrial complex of the former Soviet Union had an intricate setup. It was a system which comprised and depended on enterprises all over the Soviet Union. With the demise of the U.S.S.R. this structure collapsed, causing serious difficulties for defense industries in various former Soviet Republics. For example, Ukraine could not continue producing the famous T-80 tank as the needed armor, guns and machine guns in the Soviet times were supplied from Russia. Because of the lack of proper equipment Ukraine stopped producing tactical air-to-air missiles. At the shipyards there were 20 unfinished warships. It looked as if they would never be finished as more than 2500 plants throughout the former Soviet Union supplied necessary components. The Kyiv scientific/production amalgamation, named after S.P. Koroliov, was one of the best equipped plants to produce microchips needed for personal computers and other computing equipment. But those products were to be used somewhere in Russia. The enterprise actually lost its customers and plunged into crisis.

Evidently the situation was absurd and contradicted the interests of the Newly Independent States (NIS). But that was the reality. The situation was deteriorating as efforts taken by defense industries to reestablish horizontal ties with their counterparts in other NIS proved abortive.

A sharp decrease in the weapons procurement orders was another factor aggravating the situation in the military-industrial complex of Ukraine. The defense industries of the independent Ukraine did not get orders from the new

Ukrainian Army, nor were there orders from the Ministry of Defense of Russia or other NIS states. Whereas in 1991, weapons procurement orders accounted for about 160 billion rubles (in constant prices), in 1992 10 billion rubles were appropriated for spare parts and components needed by the military.

The situation that developed in the military-industrial complex of Ukraine could be characterized as a "snowslide" conversion. Obviously, the Ukrainian defense industries were not prepared for such developments and found themselves in a disastrous situation, which was aggravated by a deep general structural crisis of the national economy, the sharp drop in overall industrial output, and galloping inflation.

To make the conversion process smoother and less socially painful the Ukrainian leadership decided to proceed with a gradual transformation and restructuring of the defense industry. One of its primary goals was to maintain the technical and intellectual potential that had been accumulating in the military-industrial complex. This potential comprised thousands of highly qualified workers who, having at their disposal modern and unique equipment, were capable of fulfilling the most complicated production tasks. Simultaneously, it was necessary to define priorities of the conversion process. That effort involved analysis of emerging market, evaluation of the defense industries' capabilities to start production of civilian items without dramatic changes in their technological base, and formulation of development strategies for all sub-branches of this sector of the economy, including plans related to a technical reequipment and reconstruction of enterprises.

Along with the Armed Forces and the defense industry it was necessary to implement conversion of the whole social life. It was time to start paying rent and for services on the basis of real prices, to introduce insured medicine, and private education, while avoiding social shocks that could impede the economic development. It was necessary to find ways to reduce the use of available resources and to increase labor productivity at least by 3–5 times.

Without exaggeration it could be said that the conversion was a major national priority of Ukraine, related to its future and its economic self-reliance and prosperity.

Political Developments

Political events in Ukraine generated a growing interest of the world community to this strategic state. This interest can be explained not only as curiosity, but because of the important role of the country in Europe and beyond. Ukraine is one of the largest European states with more than a 600,000 square kilometer territory and a population of over 52 million people. She has borders with seven European states. Through the unfreezing seas, washing the territory of Ukraine, transportation routes go to the Northern Caucasus and Transcaucasus and to many foreign countries. Convenient passages in the Ukrainian Carpathian Mountains allowed the construction of railroads, roads and pipelines to Hungary, the Czech Republic, Slovakia, Romania and other countries.

It seems that God in creating Ukrainians wanted to see them happy and prosperous. He put into the womb of Ukraine immense mineral resources. Eighty minerals—practically the whole table of Mendeleev—are concentrated in numerous deposits. There are billions of metric tons of coal, oil, gas, uranium, sulphur, and iron, manganese and titanium ores, graphite and gold. Recently in Ukraine there was found the largest in the world deposit of scandium—a valuable raw material that is used as an additive to improve the quality of aluminum alloys. Use of materials containing scandium in aircraft and missile construction is extremely promising. Table 3 shows the share of mineral deposits found in Ukraine as compared to the overall natural resources of the former U.S.S.R.

Historically Ukraine's wealth was not used for the benefit of its people. Initially, the Tsarist Empire and then the Soviet Union, on the pretext of acting "in the all-state common interests," drained Ukraine's resources before going to the Urals or Siberia. Nonetheless, there are still enough natural resources in Ukraine that will last for many years ahead. A convenient territorial location of major mineral deposits—fuel, ore, non-ore and hydrominerals—permits the creation of territorial-industrial complexes of various types and specializations. Possession by Ukraine of rich mineral resources resulted in the economic

**Table 3. Share of Mineral Deposits Found in Ukraine as
Compared to the Overall Natural Resources of
the Former U.S.S.R.**

Minerals	Ukrainian share %
Iron ore	30
Manganum ore	80
Coal	30
Mineral paints	30
Kaolin	30
Ozokerite	50
Graphite	50

development of the country by creating such important branches as energy, metallurgy, chemistry, and producing building materials. Among the Newly Independent States of the former Soviet Union, Ukraine has the second largest industrial potential.

Agriculture and Food

Positive statements can also be made about Ukraine's agriculture and food industry. Favorable climate and fertile soils made it possible for the country to became a major producer of agricultural and related products. Table 4 shows the Ukrainian share of agricultural products in overall output of the former Soviet Union. Today, despite all its economic hardships, Ukraine continues to be the biggest producer of sugar and grain among the C.I.S. countries.

No doubt, Ukraine has all the necessary potential and resources to recover from the losses she suffered during the previous periods of her history and to emerge in the visible future as an important member of the community of European states and the world economic structures. Realization of these goals to a great extent depends on policies of the new Ukrainian leadership, which has to prove that it is capable not only of making political declarations and promises, but also understands the problems the country is facing and to prove that it is willing and able to solve them.

Ukraine inherited from the Soviet military-industrial complex more than 700 enterprises that accounted for 18 percent of the overall Republic's industrial output. This sector represents concentration of a considerable intellectual potential—150 R&D institutions and design bureaus employing about 1 million highly qualified specialists and scientists.

Table 4. The Ukrainian Share of Agricultural Products in Overall Output of the Former Soviet Union

Items	Ukrainian share %
Grain	22
Sugar	63
Vegetable oil	33
Meat	23
Milk	20

Having become independent, Ukraine realized that she did not need the big defense industry that had been established to satisfy all-Union needs. The Ukrainian Government began seriously thinking about the conversion and diversification of defense production. This approach was considered as a major solution to the problem. Kyiv believed that implementation of these tasks on a priority basis would not only result in the improvement of the situation in the military-industrial complex, but would help to stabilize the country's economy as a whole. Thus the military-industrial complex was supposed to help itself and help the country. However, the reality showed that due to objective and subjective factors the defense conversion was not easy to accomplish.

Some Ukrainian leaders were in favor of the so-called "Russian version" of conversion that visualized continuing production of military hardware, maintaining the military-industrial complex in the size that would allow not only satisfying needs of the national armed forces, but exporting some types of weapons to the C.I.S. countries and to the traditional Soviet arms markets. The funds received from the arms sales would be used for the conversion of defense industries and for providing social security for its workers. Being to some extent attractive, this concept, though, could hardly be implemented in Ukraine. Tough competition in the armaments market and Russia's attempts to monopolize traditional Soviet market of arms made it rather difficult if not impossible for Ukraine to sell something. Besides that, Ukraine heavily depended on Russia and other Republics in terms of components supply that accounted for 80 percent of all components used by the defense industries.

Simultaneously, a "snow slide" conversion developed in the military-industrial complex that resulted in an uncontrolled drop in the production of military items signified a complete reorientation of defense industries to a civilian production with a minimum government budgetary support. If left unaddressed this trend could cause an irreparable loss of the intellectual and technical potential of the industry as well as social tensions.

Mr. Victor Antonov was appointed first Minister of Machinebuilding, Military-Industrial Complex and Conversion of Ukraine. Having worked his whole life in the defense industry he was very much familiar with the problems of the industry. On the other hand, being an energetic person and a supporter of innovative approaches, he started active work aimed at finding solutions to the problems that the MIC of Ukraine encountered.

It is under his guidance that the Ministry of Machinebuilding, Military-Industrial Complex and Conversion of Ukraine (Minmashprom) decided to take the conversion process under control through the development of its own approach, based on program-purpose methods and state-economic regulation of the conversion. Practically since its establishment, the Minmashprom began working on the State Program of the Defense Conversion. The major goal of this document was to maintain the defense industry as the basis of the national economy and to use its capabilities for restructuring and technical reequipment of the industrial sector of the Ukrainian economy, for the development of the agriculture and processing branches. The State Program of the Defense Conversion was designed to make this process controllable, manageable and irreversible. It was also supposed to address social needs of workers of defense industries. In fact, it is on this basis the defense conversion was carried out.

By the end of 1991 the Ministry of Machinebulding identified defense-industries, enterprises, and organizations that were subject to a "deep" conversion (defense related production activities had to go down by more than 20 percent). Eventually, the list of such enterprises comprised more than 200 industries and more than 100 R&D institutions. A detailed evaluation of these entities showed that as a result of the conversion about 400,000 employees, if not helped, would lose their jobs, and the projected drop in production would be 70–80 percent.

This situation was taken seriously by the Government of Ukraine which decided to help defense industries. In early 1992 the President of Ukraine signed the order "About Urgent Measures Regarding Stabilization of Work of R&D and Industrial Enterprises of the Defense and Machinebuilding Complex of Ukraine in 1992." As a result of this measure defense industries received financial support. Thus the Government helped the entities that possessed a unique scientific and technological potential for Ukraine's survival. These included SPA "Southern Machinebuilding Plant", Design Bureau "Yuzhnoe" (Dnipropetrovsk), Aviation R&D Complex, named after Antonov (Kyiv), Production Association named after Malyshev (Kharkiv), Production Association Black Sea Shipbuilding Plant (Mykolaiv), etc.

Evaluation of capabilities of design bureaus and R&D departments of defense and engineering industries helped to develop plans and strategies for their reorientation and consolidation and made possible the establishment of specialized regional technological centers.

At the same time, the Ministry made macro analyses of the Ukrainian market to help the industries under the conversion to adapt to a new situation. Jointly, with the enterprises, the Ministry developed more than 500 special purpose comprehensive scientific/technical programs designed to convert defense industries into production of about 5,000 industrial-technical products and consumer goods. Taking into account the mobile character of the market, it was decided to build a multilevel pyramid of priorities intended to reflect potential demand on products including not only ready made items but various components, motors and spare parts.

The upper part of the pyramid contained agricultural technological complexes, food and processing equipment (48 programs), medical equipment and devices (42 programs), consumer goods and home appliances (83 programs), equipment for trade, restaurants, services (18 programs), information and communication means (77 programs), modern industrial materials (10 programs), etc. To protect the environment, a separate program designed to develop 34 environmentally safe technologies related to the disposal and utilization of industrial waste was formed .

Changing priorities when the market is saturated was planned. The enterprises that were to produce the above items were to get financing through the budget as well as beneficial treatment from banking institutions. The overall cost of the above programs (1992 prices) for the period 1992–1996 was estimated to be 1300 billion rubles.

Summing up, it is possible to say that the conversion mechanism developed in Ukraine consisted of a number of programs, multilevel independent expertise, and structures dealing with financing, credit and foreign investments.

In accordance with Minmashprom's estimate, the cost of the complex conversion programs that were instrumental in the restructuring of the military-industrial complex and the key branches of the economy could reach 550 billion rubles. The National Bank of Ukraine played a major role in providing converting defense industries with soft loans and special purpose low interest credits. These funds were provided for the development of new products and modern technologies. Fifty billion rubles were appropriated for this purposes in 1992 only.

But in Minmashprom's opinion the State Budget should not have been the only source of finance of the defense conversion projects. The Ministry's approach visualized use of diversified sources of finance including those of a non-budgetary nature such as commercial credits and foreign investments. This position corresponded to a multifaceted character of the conversion that was carried out simultaneously with the establishment of a new finance and credit system during conditions of pricing crises and a high deficit of the State Budget.

On the basis of this presumption the Ministry submitted to the Cabinet of Ministers a proposal regarding establishment of the State Fund of Assistance to Conversion. The Fund's primary goal was to provide finance for the defense conversion programs using contributions of defense industries (up to 3 percent of their product's price) and financial resources received from sales (50 percent of the sale price) of unfinished enterprises designed to produce military items. On February 22, the Cabinet of Ministers adopted a resolution regarding establishment of this Fund.

Ukraine also hoped to receive some funds for the conversion from the sale of military hardware, which became available as a result of reductions in the Armed Forces. For this purpose Minmashprom formed as its subsidiary a commercial entity (Ukrinmash) that began marketing outside Ukraine defense related equipment and arms.

At the same time, Ukraine made attempts to reestablish ties with the military-industrial complex of Russia. In January 1993, Minister Antonov and Mr. V. Glukhih, Chairman of the Committee of the Russian Federation on Defense Industries adopted a document that was called "The Decision Regarding Maintenance and Further Development of Cooperation Between the Enterprises and Organizations of the Rocket-Space Industries in Production of Special Purpose and Civilian Items." A number of agreements were signed with regard to cooperation between the defense industries in other fields. These agreements definitely reflected the intention on both sides to jointly fight the problems emerging in the defense industry after the demise of the Soviet Union. However, financial problems between Russia and Ukraine and the lack of mechanisms that would facilitate payments between industries of both states prevented these agreements from materializing.

In these conditions, Ukrainian defense industries began thinking more and more about foreign investments as a possible solution to the problem. The enterprises started developing business plans and proposals that were presented to foreign businesses. At the same time efforts were made to increase exports.

In order to stop the continuous drop in production, to maintain scientific and technical potential of the leading branches of the industry during the conversion and to increase production of necessary industrial products and consumer goods with simultaneous introduction of structural changes in the industry, the Minmashprom decided to take active steps to bring foreign investments into the country. Adopted on March 31, 1992 the Law of Ukraine "On Foreign Investments" served as a legal basis for these activities. It guarantees protection and assistance to foreign investors. Foreign investments cannot be subject to nationalization. According to the Law foreign investors are entitled to compensation for their losses. This compensation has to be quick, adequate and defined at the moment of the factual decision regarding compensation. The investment protection mechanism against bankruptcy and currency convertibility was developed as well. The Law provided a tax holiday for foreign investors in Ukraine. During a 5-year period beginning from the moment of declaration of their first profit, foreign investors shall be tax-exempt; later they shall pay only half of the taxes stipulated by the national legislation. Property rent for foreign companies shall be tax-exempt for 99 years. The political stability, absence of ethnical conflicts, and very cheap labor are other encouraging factors for investing in Ukraine.

It is necessary to say that foreign capital is needed by Ukraine not only because she has to implement the defense conversion programs but the country needs investments and credits to ensure critical imports of components and raw material and to launch production of items that are needed but are not produced locally. Ukraine considers joint ventures with western companies, including those with equity share of foreign partners up to 100 percent, as having big potential for the economic development of the country. These new companies could produce tankers with displacement up to 300,000 metric tons, cargo ships, fishing factories, floating hotels, cars and trucks, planes and many other things. All this would address social needs of Ukraine, could help the country to reorientate and restructure its machine building and defense industries and to implement the defense conversion programs. In accordance with the conversion programs in a four-year period there should be a two-fold increase in production of consumer goods: TV sets, videos, freezers, automatic washing machines, vacuum cleaners, and other home appliances.

Since 1986, more than 500 joint ventures and about a thousand foreign investors have been registered at the Ministry of Finance of Ukraine. The registration results reveal that the most active in Ukraine are American, German, Austrian, Italian, Swiss, British and French companies.

The Ivano-Frankovsk association "Karpato-pressmash" received a license from an Italian company to produce automatic washing machines. The Genichesk Engineering Plant received a license from Japan to produce sewing machines. Ukraine cooperates with Western companies in the implementation of major programs such as the development of the automobile industry, and building of passenger and cargo planes. The Kyiv SPA named after Koroliov, together with the German Company, Siemens Telecommunication, formed a joint venture and got a $600 million contract to develop together with the Ministry of Communications of Ukraine a satellite telecommunication system. The Chernigiv Devices Production Plant entered into a joint venture with AT&T to produce communication means. Table 5 shows the most active foreign countries doing business in Ukraine at the end of 1992.

Companies and individual entrepreneurs from the former COMECON countries are very active in Ukraine. Joint ventures with their participation account for one third of the overall number of the registered joint ventures in the country.

Table 5. The Most Active Foreign Countries Doing Business in Ukraine (end of 1992)

Country	Number of Joint Ventures
United States	108
Germany	83
Austria	43
Italy	35
Switzerland	31
Great Britain	26
France	16

The potential of Ukraine is far from being adequately and fully used by foreign partners. Some businessmen argue that the political and economic situation discourages doing business in the country. Others claim that Ukraine does not currently have an appropriate infrastructure for doing business, such as a developed banking system, convertibility of Ukrainian currency, communications system, private property rights and acquisition procedures.

It is not easy to argue about these claims, as the economic situation is rather difficult and market economy reforms are still in the initial stage. But this does not mean that business cannot be done in Ukraine. First of all foreign companies have to remember that the principle—first come - first served—can be applied to the Ukrainian situation. What is required for doing business in Ukraine is creativity—the unusual situation in requires innovative approaches.

In this context Ukranian-German joint ventures in Donetsk and Kharkiv with companies Varex and Kaiser, which process color metals wastes, can serve as a good example of mutually beneficial cooperation. This joint venture spent 30 percent of its profit on acquisition of the Siemens technology, equipment and components necessary for production of medical equipment.

Barter trade is another way for Ukraine to do business with Western banks and companies. Ukraine already has some experience in implementing international projects on a compensation basis (for example, the construction of the iron-ore refinery plant in Krivyj Rig; participation of the former COMECON countries in the development of the power system of Ukraine). In exchange for their technologies and equipment Western investors could get ready-made products and raw materials. For example, for cracking equipment that increases oil refining up to 85 percent Ukraine could pay with cracking products. For rolling mills to produce cold rolled steel and stainless steel Ukraine could supply appropriate products. The same system could be applied regarding plastics, agricultural machinery, fertilizers, and so on.

Ukrainian scientists have made a substantial contribution to the development of plasma and low temperatures physics, optical quantum electronics, non-linear optics, and dynamic holography. Scientists of Ukraine were the first to propose the use of chemical lasers on electrode photopassages. A substantial potential exists in applied and branch sciences in materials, physics-chemical processing, powder metallurgy, etc. Among these technologies there is a method of putting metallic covers on the surface of gem crystals and hardmelting substances, use of plasma, plasma induction and electronic ray heat for fusion of high quality steel, and gamma technology for getting construction materials of various qualities. These achievements could not help but generate an interest on the part of foreign business. One of the good examples of what foreign companies could get in Ukraine is a joint venture formed in 1993 between U.S. companies Pratt & Whitney and E.O. Paton Electric Welding Institute and the Academy of Sciences of Ukraine to explore new material applications derived from high-grade electron beam deposition processes. The processes in which electron beam guns are used to vaporize metals and ceramics into clouds that can be condensed as coatings or as tailored metal structures could eventually lead to increased ductility, high-temperature alloys, reduced cost, high-performance airfoils for gas turbine engines, and a new generation of low-cost ceramic-reinforced metal matrix composites. These processes are essentially extensions of Pratt's rapid solidifications rate work. The American company entered into a joint venture with the Ukrainian Institute because Americans did not see this technology anywhere in the world.

Projects related to the modern systems of automatic control over sophisticated devices and dynamic processes, highly effective vapor-gas devices for energy sector, pipelines and many other things can be of considerable interest for foreign partners. Ukraine needs investments and technological inputs in such fields as information systems, radioelectronics, power supply and environmentally safe technologies. Foreign partners can be compensated by getting concession rights concerning relevant enterprises that eventually might be privatized.

Today Ukraine is a member of the International Monetary Fund, International Bank for Reconstruction and Development, and European Bank for Reconstruction and Development. Naturally, taking into account its economic situation, Ukraine is actively working on having credit lines opened by these and other financial institutions, but these institutions repeatedly stated that credit is contingent upon the economic stability in the country and the status of economic reforms.

Some countries (Italy, Germany) opened credit lines for Ukraine to promote their economic interest in this country. But their credits are far from sufficient. According to the estimate of the Ministry of Economy, there are 50 units of applications for one unit of Italian credit.

Ukrainians realize that investments and credits can be obtained when well-developed investment projects exist. The Minmashprom developed special purpose branch and sub-branch programs, and enterprises formulated individual business plans—there are more than 200 of them—that can be used very helpfully by potential investors for decisions regarding various projects.

Despite the efforts of Ukraine to attract investment, it would not be fair to say that all impeding factors in this field are removed. Unfortunately, some measures taken by the Government of Ukraine made the situation even worse. On May 20, 1993 the Supreme Rada of Ukraine approved the Foreign Investment Decree that became effective beginning June 5, 1993. This Decree suspended the previous law "On Foreign Investment" and introduced significant changes to the rules of foreign investment in Ukraine. The Decree significantly increased the amount of foreign capital to be considered as "a qualified foreign investment" and introduced changes into the tax holiday structure previously afforded the foreign investor under the Ukrainian Law. There is a hope, though, that the new Ukrainian Government will take measures to create a better investment climate in Ukraine. In the meantime Ukraine's financial instability, uncertain legal environment, and underdeveloped banking system have combined to keep all but the bravest investors at bay. The U.S. business community has identified specific roadblocks which must be addressed by the new Ukrainian leadership in order to build a business climate that will be conducive to mutually beneficial long-term growth and investment. These are the following :

* Hard Currency Exchange Requirements. All exporters in Ukraine are required to sell to the Government 50 percent of the hard currency received for export at the rate fixed by the State. As a result exporters have no or minimal profit from export deals. This limit on hard-currency revenues is a stranglehold on all efforts to attract investment, earn hard currency and to develop the Ukrainian economy. Unfortunately, a new order of the President regarding currency regulation introduced very little changes in the situation.

* Export/Import Duties. Extremely high duties on both imported and exported products make it very difficult for Ukrainian companies to sell their products at a competitive price on the world market.

* Export Licences. The process and regulations regarding export licenses are rather vague. Licenses are granted for a short period of time, which makes long-term business planning impossible. These licenses are a substantial impediment for investors who need reliable and steady access to the market in order to survive.

* Margin Restrictions. The margin between a company's cost to produce a particular product and the product's final sales price is being restricted to not more than 50 percent of the production cost. There are also restrictions on what costs are allowed to be included in a company's calculation of its cost of production.

* Taxes. Ukraine has many taxes (VAT, turnover taxes, income taxes, miscellaneous local and regional taxes) that raise the cost of doing business to prohibitive levels and actually restrict potential tax revenues.

* Private Property. The privatization process is still at a very initial stage. The new Parliament made a decision to suspend the privatization program motivated by its intention to improve the process.

As a part of its efforts to help defense industries convert, the Ukrainian Government was considering assistance of foreign states. In 1992 the Ministry of Machinebuilding, Military-Industrial Complex and Conversion of Ukraine reached an agreement with a U.S. company (INTERPAR) to establish in Washington D.C. a Bureau of Defense Conversion and Technological/Industrial Development of Ukraine. The Bureau's function is to assist Ukraine in the development and implementation of a nuclear disarmament and defense conversion program beneficial to the technological and industrial development of Ukraine, to assist Ukraine in evaluating proposals from industry and institutions dealing with this these tasks, and to stimulate cooperation, investment and joint ventures with industries and institutes in Ukraine. The Bureau is working closely with the Ukrainian Government and has generated the interest of many U.S. industries in the Ukrainian military-industrial complex. However, not many projects have been realized due to the unfavorable business climate in Ukraine.

At the same time Ukraine is working with the U.S. Government to get funding for defense conversion. For this purpose, at the beginning of 1994, the American-Ukrainian Conversion Committee to develop and help realize specific projects in this field was established. However, the Ukrainian efforts to get U.S. assistance has not produce many results. Despite the fact that it was not requested by the Ukrainian side some funds were appropriated to the U.S. International Civil Service Corps that placed three of its offices in Kharkiv and then opened an office in Kyiv. An appropriation of $5 million to establish a joint venture between Khartron and Westinghouse to produce modern control systems for nuclear and conventional power stations can serve, though, as a better example of U.S. assistance to Ukraine.

The U.S. is not the only country with which Ukraine is trying to cooperate in defense conversion. Kyiv has relationships in this field with France, Germany and Japan.

In 1994 Ukraine not only celebrated the third anniversary of its independence but witnessed dramatic changes in its political, social and economic life. The Ukrainian people in a truly democratic way elected a new Parliament and Leonid Kuchma as a new President. New leaders came to the executive branch of power. Among them Mr. Valeri Shmarov, new Vice-Premier and Defense Minister and Mr. Victor Petrov, new Minister of Machinebuilding. These three Ukrainian leaders came to the political arena from the military-industrial complex. They know its problems and surely will be looking for their solutions. The new Ukrainian leadership already showed its interest in proceeding with economic stabilization and reforms. President Kuchma has promised comprehensive economic reforms. The agreement Ukraine reached with the International Monetary Fund indicates that he is prepared to live up to his promises. These developments give reason to believe in economic recovery of the country as a whole and, its defense industries would be a contributing factor to the development of the independent Ukraine.

Acknowledgment

The author expresses his appreciation to the Ministry of Machinebuilding, Military-Industrial Complex and Conversion of Ukraine and personally to Mr. V.I. Antonov for providing data necessary for writing this chapter.

CHAPTER 7

The Ukrainian Experiments

Neal B. Mitchell, Jr.
Neal Mitchell Associates
Sudbury, Massachusetts

Introduction

The economic situation in the former Soviet Union (F.S.U.) is interesting because over 75 percent of their economy was devoted to supporting the military. Large numbers of their people were in the military, and the very best and brightest of the population were directed toward the military, because this was what the government supported, and therefore, this was where the opportunities were. The Soviet Union developed a society that was built on the sword, and now everything has collapsed.

Their distribution systems are nonexistent; their manufacturing systems are inefficient and clouded by years of mismanagement at the top. In fact, the Soviet politicians were not technicians as advertised, but rather simple "party" bureaucrats. Most lacked the technical and managerial skills that were necessary to manage a large centrally controlled economy. In many cases, their approach represented the exact opposite of good systems thinking. The actions of their government usually represented random action coupled with a complete understanding and refinement of the techniques of "reverse" engineering.

The American people were told that our government had taken the necessary steps to provide some financial assistance for the disarmament of the former Soviet Union. In effect this funding would help turn the "spears to pruning hooks" by providing essential funds for this conversion. Like so many things done by our Congress, the intent was good, but the execution leaves a lot to be desired. While the Nunn-Lugar Bill represents a strong statement of support and funding one soon comes to realize that the bureaucrats have managed to create a condition where nothing can be done without violating the law as they see it.

The broader question that must be pondered is "How do you change the economic systems within the old Soviet Union, and those in the United States, away from military development programs and focus them on making more positive social contributions?" The problems in the two countries are quite similar in that since the Second World War many of the very best brains in both countries have been drawn into weapons and related occupations. This change in focus requires a paradigm shift based on policy considerations that include broader and deeper social and economic changes.

Since the end of the Cold War and the collapse of communism, we have closed military bases, slowed down (but not stopped) military purchases, and in the process we are slowly pushing people out of work and creating a situation of instability in almost every institution of our society. It is interesting that we scold the Eastern Block about their focus on industrial support and yet we continue to employ short term spending to cover up our own problems. Our need for change and rethinking are as necessary as theirs. What is our national policy for retrofitting our own society?

Because I have found a lack of direction from our government agencies, we have tried to initiate our company's activities in the C.I.S. and particularly in Ukraine without any help or interest from our government. Much of the discussion that will follow is derived from our experiences with federal agencies.

The current activities of governments and large business is briefly presented and leads one to question whether they can address the essential needs of the people. The overall bureaucracy and conservatism of large organizations often stifles the very essence of any constructive program. The key to proper solution is careful consideration and implementation of policies of both short-term and long-term activity that promote regional development that involves local people in helping themselves.

In this context a generalized systems approach is presented to illustrate that the engineering systems thinking and methodology for problem solution that was used to develop the weapons capability of both superpowers represent the type of thinking that will be required to create a reasonable program for peace. The general aspects and considerations of this overall systems study are described to illustrate the approach that was used by my small private company whose measure for success was not talk, but action.

The general theoretical systems conclusions are illustrated with an ongoing plan of action and dynamic goal definition that involves creating a program of regional economic development throughout the C.I.S. This program is designed to significantly impact a large number of people, with the ultimate goal of improving their economic capability by offering them meaningful jobs. The key to this program is the availability, without any initial costs, of advanced American housing and management technology that can be used to put a large number of people to work in a program that addresses one of the key factors necessary for social stability.

To act on defense conversion, our program of housing construction and air freight services will utilize a large number of retiring military people and provide them with jobs that benefit the general population. An integral part of this program is the creation of an air freight delivery system for housing components throughout the C.I.S. To support this delivery system, as well as the American program of developing oil resources in the C.I.S., the Ukrainian Government is now considering the transfer of one hundred IL-76 heavy cargo planes and three major strategic air bases to this new private Ukrainian air freight/housing company, where partial ownership is in the hands of Americans.

When completed, this program will represent a financial commitment from the Ukrainian Government of over 1.5 billion dollars. It will represent the World's largest program of Defense Conversion, and has the added benefit of creating a positive impact on a large segment of the Ukrainian military. The program serves to illustrate the creativity of the Ukrainian Government and their willingness to create innovative private businesses in cooperation with American companies. Programs like this generate hard currency and jobs for local people, which leads to an overall improvement in their living standards. The hard currency generated from air freight activities will permit the people and the government to address the health and food needs of their society.

The chapter further describes the other necessary elements of this capability that are being put in place to support this effort to insure overall success. It should be stressed that the entire effort is entrepreneurial, and when completed over three-quarters of the present Ukrainian Air Force will be engaged in peaceful activity that will be generating hard currency as well as helping to build their country. In addition a significant amount of "State" assets will be converted for private use in a way that improves the overall welfare of the citizenry. It is interesting to note that we could find no American Government interest or support for this program.

Description of Systems Thinking

Perhaps the way to begin a reasonable analysis of the problem is to define the process that should be used to structure a solution and then to compare this method of thinking to the activities being used in the various governments. The most comprehensive procedures for problem solution, long used by the military-industrial complex as a guide for technology development, is the "Systems Process." Perhaps the broadest definition of systems thinking is the statement by Ludwig von Bertalanffy (1968):

> "Systems theory is a broad view which far transcends the technological problems and demands, a reorientation that has become necessary in science in general and in the gamut of disciplines from physics and biology to the behavioral and social sciences and to philosophy. It is operative with varying degrees of success and exactitude in various realms, and heralds a new world-view of considerable impact."

Systems theory was greatly expanded through its extensive use in technology because of the need for development programs that were based on both long- and short-term goals. These military considerations involved the clear definition of goal statements that considered a complexity of clearly definable needs. Ashby (1962) defined this deductive methodology within the context of "machine with input." Systems Engineering uses the methodology of cybernetics, information theory, network analysis, flow and block diagrams, etc., and it is normally based on detailed mathematical support. This approach to problem solution follows rather rigorous mathematical considerations, and the results have certainly been interesting when this method has been used for the development of advanced technology.

However, these procedures must be broadened for application to the solution of real problems that involve people and time considerations. These people-related solutions must be practical and almost evolutionary so that they exhibit constant progress within an overall framework of positive goal statements. The basis for this thinking is best characterized by the open-systems model which implies the dynamic interaction of its components. This model represents a fertile working hypothesis permitting new insights, quantitative statements and experimental verification.

The necessary investigation of the problems associated with Defense Conversion not only involve considerations of the technology, but more importantly, the activity process that produces longer term patterns for economic success, positive work environments and an overall improvement in the general living conditions for people. Therefore, the very powerful, but more restricted, engineering definition must be enriched by this broader based view that encompasses life itself.

Therefore, this chapter will adopt this broader-based context for evaluation and analytical review of activity. In addition, the focus of the paper will be on real activity that implies implementation and not esoteric talk about the problem. We must always be aware of the old Kantian maxim that "experience without theory is blind, but theory without experience is mere intellectual play."

The methodology employed in this work permits the consideration of both the open-system model with its dynamic interaction of components and the cybernetic model with its feedback loops and information. Perhaps the elegance of the approach that was taken was not its strict adherence to classical methodology, but rather a willingness to permit the process to create an environment for paradigm shifts. The most exciting aspect of this approach was the willingness to let the methodology exploit the business reality to the point where the solutions would take advantage of the fact that the crisis of the situation offered the opportunity for significant change.

Virtual Reality and Reality

The recent advances in virtual reality have provided scholars with a theoretical "reality modeling tool" that can be used to explore problems in an abstract sense. This technique of non-confrontation of issues is now being practiced by governments. By dealing with the new computer ideas of "virtual reality" we can do it in a "virtual environment", and in that way we can manage success and limit failure. In a society that punishes failure, this protection is essential for bureaucratic survival.

When you try to solve real problems you must deal with reality. Reality often creates circumstances where "doing it" becomes impossible because the simple "clean" problem for theoretical analysis is usually clouded by unanticipated extraneous contaminants, and the measure of an action policy is not only its elegance in thought, but also its success in implementation. This paper discusses the application of systems thinking to the solution of national and multinational issues. It identifies the goals of the effort, the actions that have been taken, and then it explains the present progress and anticipated results. The process is somewhat inelegant because of the realities and personalities. Yet this entire program could be very interesting because of the single-mindedness of the implementation process and the commitment of the people. It is hard to even consider failure.

A Simplified Statement of the Problem

The three fundamental needs of the C.I.S. population are all missing. Food, shelter and health are the driving factors behind population stability. A non-technical description of these factors has been given by Mitchell (1992).

The situation in all the Republics of the C.I.S. can be best summed up by citing the fact that there are extreme deficiencies in the supply of food, shelter and health services. Couple these problems with a completely broken down distribution system for products and goods, rapid inflation, and an extensive concern for democratic expression. The population itself has been completely starved for any type of quantity or quality in the availability of normal consumer goods. Add to this mixture a relatively free press and extensive television coverage along with complete access to all of the Western European television broadcasts. The people in the C.I.S. are now well aware of how other people are living and that their standard of living is significantly below that of other countries.

In other words, the normal people are aware that there are extreme deficiencies in everything necessary for living and a very keen awareness that they are "behind" in almost everything. Their major pride is with their military arsenal. They do have an abundance of military hardware and a vast supply of nuclear devices. This asset draws the world's radicals in their attempt to obtain these tools of mass destruction. However, the great picture of military might painted by the western intelligence agencies is totally false, although the destructive power of the nuclear devices is still very real.

It should be pointed out that Western-led negotiations that focus only on these nuclear devices will eventually fail, because they do not consider the other necessary factors that are influencing the life of the people. Concern for controlling the destructive power of this hardware must be considered in the context of improving the overall well-being of the people. This concept seems to have eluded our governmental negotiators.

The Present Goal Situation

Invariably, the "stated" goals of everyone that I have met in the C.I.S. was the need to solve the immediate short-term problems, but to solve them in a way that permitted them to also address the longer term needs of both the people and the regions. Most of the people in the C.I.S. are prepared to work for their rewards, and few want something for nothing. The simply stated goals for most groups in the C.I.S. is their need for participation in the economic changes that must take place in their countries. They are very interested in changing their standard of living. If we choose to stop them from making these changes, or if we destroy their dignity by our demands, we can expect serious problems in the future.

Systems Solution Considerations

Given this situation, any systems solution must also consider the human variants of this problem. Churchman (1979) clarifies the fact that we can only solve the problems of hunger, shelter and health after we have solved "the problem of the insecurity of the world in the face of sanctioned warfare."

It is very exciting to speculate that "sanctioned warfare" is in abeyance during this particular window of time. Perhaps we are in a unique position to solve a wide variety of problems that have affected all countries in the world and in so doing to provide real leadership. Certainly this opportunity for significant non-military leadership exists for the first time in many lifetimes. Are we smart enough to seize this opportunity? The complexity of the problem and the solution leads many to the conclusion that the way to solve these complex interconnected problems is to break the total system into solvable components. Each of the smaller problems can then be solved, and these segmental solutions can then be integrated together to solve the larger problem. An engineer is taught that this is "the way" to solve complex engineering problems. Divide and conquer is well established as a method for winning, and it is the foundation of good engineering analysis.

In many cases in engineering people substitute analysis for design. Some carry this thinking to the limit and solve the specific problems associated with a subsystem, without the understanding that the subsystem is part of a much larger open system, where there is a dynamic interaction of components. Many times these limited solutions produce disastrous effects on the larger system.

The systems process for analysis assumes that the subsystems are components of a larger system and, therefore, decisions within a subsystem are conditioned by the considerations at broader and broader levels. Proper analysis is based on careful structuring with clear goal statements at every level of detail and constant evaluation of actions at any level of detail compared within the questioning of a larger context. This process of problem solution, although common in engineering, is quite foreign in both diplomatic and business decision making. Problem solution becomes almost impossible if one has not been taught to think correctly.

A Russian Example

Certainly the limited solutions built around a non-systems approach to problem solution can be clearly demonstrated by the recent actions of the world monetary group in their requirements to Boris Yeltsin. To deal with the problem of distribution of goods, the government of Boris Yeltsin gave the general public a large number of military trucks. It seemed that in Moscow, everyone had their own military truck. Things started to "move" throughout the country as adequate transportation stimulated a wide variety of companion economic activities. Simple people, with their personal military truck, were participating in the economy as individual suppliers of service. What a great example of problem-solving and the benefits of a free enterprise system.

Then the economists showed up with their requirements to bring the entire Russian system into conformance with world pricing. This economic requirement was applied "cold turkey" to the economy with the admonition that deviation would result in the loss of Western support. This required the elimination of state-supported services and subsidies. As part of this program the money men demanded that Yeltsin bring the price of gasoline into compliance with the prices of the Western countries. When he resisted with only a partial price increase, the money people punished him by reducing their economic support.

The effect of the price increase in Russia was much more devastating. Every sidewalk in Moscow now has its "ornament", which is a nonfunctioning, gas inefficient military truck. This new trucking distribution system was working on the very margin of the economy, and it died with the smallest change.

The macroeconomists were very effective in mandating policies that were responsible for putting the economy back where it started. No one can criticize Yeltsin for what he did, and in the larger picture no one can criticize the economists for forcing a reduction in price support. However, within the overall economic system these decisions were disastrous. It is even more interesting that the decision by outsiders has served to stifle the very thing that they were trying to create.

Defining the Analysis Process

The problem definition usually starts with an identification of goals and objectives of the effort. Defense development procedures usually assume that the problem can be expressed in a Work Breakdown Structure (WBS). I have found it productive to define problems in this way and then break down the Goal Statements so that they are at every level of the WBS. This process insures that the "testing" of decision making at each level of problem solution is consistent with the overall goals of the problem.

The key to any WBS is the careful breaking down of tasks from the macro to the micro levels of detail. Then the solution of each subsystem or micro aspect of the problem can be considered within the context of the overall system. Certainly this process has been effective in the development of military hardware.

One of our consulting contracts involved the development of a new missile for NATO. The program was being developed by a Norwegian company who delivered the missile, only to have it fail on every test. It seems that the design carefully stated the present Soviet capability at the start of the design process, and by the time the missile was ready for test the Soviets had made enough improvements to their systems that the NATO solution was ineffective. Our clients were interested in developing a process of analysis that constantly updated their requirements and goals within the overall requirements of the problem. The dynamic goal structure that we developed resulted in competitive considerations that significantly impacted the basic development process. We must utilize similar procedures for solving civilian problems.

In general the multiple level goal structure is then followed by a careful statement of procedures for cyclic modification so that the process becomes a dynamic process of changing goals with time. This process for problem solution means many things to many people. Without a proper Goal Statement, before you start, you will not know when you reach a reasonable conclusion. However, this Goal Statement should be changing on an ongoing basis so that the feedback loop of reality constantly impacts the development and solution process. It is interesting that education focuses on fixed goals, static solutions and "correct answers." In fact there is no correct answer; nothing is constant, and all solutions of value are constantly changing and adapting to the specific conditions that impact them.

We have been very effective in this development process by creating multiple solution teams who work on the problem and multiple management teams who constantly change the environment for evaluation. This interrelated analysis and design process annoys most engineers who complain that if desires are kept constant then it will be possible to meet them. In fact it is not the answer that is important as much as it is the understanding that the changes in requirements create a zone of change that helps to suggest the future. In fact, it is in the management of this process that the comprehension of this change creates the framework for real innovation. Significant technical advances come from these insights derived from patterns of activity that suggest future positioning.

This process must be applied to the solution to problems in the C.I.S. because suggested activity must complement all groups. What we do must be consistent with what we want and what they want, and these considerations should cover both long- and short-term goals. More importantly the process is ongoing, requiring the continuing effort and updating of information. Change is a necessity and the management of this change is the problem that must be mastered if we expect to achieve meaningful success.

Background

It is interesting to contrast my experiences in using an engineering approach with the conventional diplomatic approach. It seems that the American diplomatic approach is based on first setting our goals and then structuring the negotiations so that all others agree to conform to our preset goals. This is very much the way ideas are presented in a court case, where the arguments are presented in a way that convinces everyone else that you have the only solution and that you are correct.

The engineering systems approach is to first listen to all relevant problems and concerns, help people define their goals, and then participate in a dialogue that explores the limits of this thinking. This process is used to define an environment and a general goal structure for more intense discussion. Success is dependent on the active solicitation of other views and the aggressive "testing" of ideas. The process requires leadership and candor because these discussions often get "out of control," as does any good discussion of product development involving R&D groups here in the United States. The testing of what you want, and what you can get, using the reality of the situation is a critical part of this process, and it requires patience and time for proper development.

The development of goal structures carries with it the requirement to have all participants define and then justify their goals within the context of the overall Goal Structure. It should be pointed out that my friends in the C.I.S. found this as strange as did similar friends in the West. However, this dialogue was always based on patience and probing so that all aspects of the considerations and concerns are fully explored. Of course this process leads to some interesting and often fascinating insights.

My study of this problem is based more on my engineering experience with analysis and interpretation, rather than the more formal diplomatic procedures that are being used by our bureaucrats. My studies took place over several years and multiple trips to the C.I.S. Each time I talked to people, listened to what they had to say, tested new ideas on them, observed conditions within the context of my developing structure, and then engaged in dialogue with them that was designed to probe the thinking of my hosts in an effort to let them better define their needs and goals. The framework that was developed has been structured within our Work Breakdown Structure (WBS) for our own development process. We have created a team that constantly tests this structure and changes the goals at all levels as our understanding increases. The result is a dynamic goal structure that carefully reflects everyone's considerations so that segmental solutions are fit in as a part of an overall solution process. The result is an activity program with multiple interrelated parts that are both dependent and independent in their eventual execution.

The most important conclusion that we can report is that the goal structure and "critical needs" that we began with have changed. What people said they wanted and what they really wanted were quite different. Anyone who has worked in system development has experienced this phenomenon, so the changing nature of our information was not a concern. Things changed as the problem became more defined, and the change continues as the solutions start to be implemented. We assumed the responsibility for managing this change, and it is interesting that our friends in the C.I.S. were less frightened by this ongoing change than the Americans that we were dealing with. The constant American request has been to "freeze" things so that the "business and financial people" could get a handle on the evaluation process for a solution. However, the key to proper management is to understand the process of change and to manage it by making decisions within the context of a constantly changing environment. The best description that I have seen with respect to dealing in the C.I.S. was provided by Deloitte Touche Tohmatsu International in their "white paper" entitled "Successfully Managing Investments in Russia." This comment is made with respect to the required qualifications of a manager that must deal with a venture in the C.I.S.

"Given the above context, the choice of the Western manager is fundamental. Only people who have demonstrated the ability to perform in unstructured situations and an undefined legal environment and without the usual corporate support should be chosen. Experience abroad in a highly political context is recommended, as most business contacts in Russia are political contacts. Technocratic profiles should be avoided to the benefit of people with well developed interpersonal skills and the ability of building work relationships through personal contacts, most often in informal environments."

My experience is that technical skills are also essential for any manager. One of the very important qualifications in dealing with technical people is technical competence. The people that usually do the talking in the C.I.S. for American companies are usually business oriented, and they usually lack technical skills. However, technical skills combined with business understanding seem essential for building the proper personal contacts with the people that actually do the work. Without this relationship, long-term business possibilities are limited.

Our Information Structuring Process

Once the goal was properly defined by the other side, and in their terms, it then became necessary to figure out how to comply with their goals while utilizing all available capabilities on both sides. The measure of success for these solutions was that they had to meet the goals of all parties, which meant that we had to also structure our own goals. I have always felt that it was important to explain and justify our thinking to them before we proceeded. A one-sided solution was not acceptable, and a solution to meet their needs and not ours was equally foolish. For a solution to be reasonable and acceptable, it must meet the goals of everyone. More importantly, these goals were normally broken into long- and short-term goals, which any proposed solution then had to address and resolve.

Perhaps the diplomatic thinking fails in this kind of problem analysis because it follows the normal "legal brief" approach. This process only requires an expression of the views from one side, and this is usually done in the context of an adversarial environment. In contrast, the engineering systems approach is dependent on careful identification of all aspects of the problem and a resolution that meets the needs of all sides. My assumption is that more people with engineering training should be structuring and negotiating the arrangements that are being made by and for our country.

At a lunch with my Ukrainian partners in the air freight business, the discussions were rich and animated, the food was good, the conversation rich, and the vodka plentiful. As we discussed long-term plans and goals we fell to reminiscing about the differences between our two countries. The intensity of our argument increased till eventually we were raising our voices in an attempt to win the argument over which government had been more successful in poisoning the minds of its people against the other people.

Using military people in a civilian operation would permit three quarters of the Ukrainian Air Force be retired and moved to the civilian sector. These people needed jobs, medical facilities, housing and food if they were to survive. Aren't these the things that we should be providing for in our overall problem goal statement? It should also be obvious that these factors require talent as well as money because a completely new business infrastructure must be put in place.

The economy is shattered, the living conditions minimal, and both food and health services are in short supply. They think that their military is special, and they wonder how to salvage at least some of this investment. They are concerned that the best and the brightest of their society will be without work if they shut down both their military and their Defense Industry. They estimate that almost 75 percent of their production was military focused and that the complete termination of these interests will create a social disaster. How can anyone disagree?

I found it interesting that the real needs of the old Soviet society were not even being addressed by the West in their programs of support for the C.I.S. More importantly, I was dismayed at the inefficient use of talent and the hardships being faced by the general population. However, with all of the rather obvious problems, it was interesting that not one person ever asked for money. I never met anyone that wanted something for nothing except in the Moscow bureaucracy. I found it interesting that these were the people that our bureaucrats sent us to work with.

Basic Conclusions for Action

Our conclusions were depressing when we considered arrangements that included large company participation in our projects. These companies were very concerned about 90-day profit statements and multiple layers of protection on their investment. They wanted to do things in the same old way they had always done them. In general they were frightened about doing anything where failure might be a possibility and where the rewards would not be immediately available. What has happened to the old entrepreneurial spirit that built America?

The Business School approach to business management seems to focus more on either "Caretaking" or "Undertaking" than on business expansion through the creation of new and better products. Obviously this is not true for all companies, but a conservative outlook and lack of creativity seem to be pervading our business decisions. Any hint of this thinking makes activity in the C.I.S. very risky. In many cases business deals that are structured with this much protection are like bank transactions that encourage failure.

It's interesting to look at the large consulting engineering firms in that they have usually wanted their contractual arrangements in the C.I.S. to mirror similar arrangements in America. The fact that the governments in the C.I.S. are broke, and the large "State" run enterprises are in disarray and poorly managed, is of little concern. Their business flexibility seems to be minimal, and because of this, their actual failures in the C.I.S. will increase.

If we couldn't count on government, or the large American companies, then what could we count on? It was obvious to us that the need for technical expertise was even more important than money, so we decided to proceed with this capability as our main offering. In addition we found that our potential partners had great theoretical capabilities, but little experience in dealing with a free market economy. They desperately needed technical help on "how to do business" and, more importantly, how to build their business and product delivery capability within a world economy.

They rebel quickly when exploited and yet they possess a great desire to participate. They understand how to share, and they are not afraid to work, but they don't understand how to get and use money. The older and more serious managers have the fear of competition, and it is obvious that they are concerned that they just might not be able to make it in a very competitive business climate. The younger people are excited because they know that the new system offers opportunity for the brightest to advance without the need to wait for their boss to die.

They obviously need to create an organizational control structure for their businesses like the Japanese did when they created MIDI. Yet, this type of central control is actively resisted based on the years of central control by the Communists. The question that needs an answer is, How could they create the opportunities that existed in the early years of the United States without centralized control?

We decided that our success was dependent on creating a program of Regional Development where the local people were participating in the increased asset value of the new industries and businesses that were being created. It was essential that the economic considerations that we made would also result in significant increases in the standard of living for the population in general. Using our initial considerations of food, health, and shelter, we chose to focus on shelter. We had the available technology and everywhere we went we found that people wanted our product. The question was how to manufacture it inexpensively and how to get it to the locations where it was needed.

It was obvious that adequate food was being grown, but that most of it rotted in the fields because the distribution system was non-existent. We could not see how we could impact this distribution system without a program that would develop hard currency funding from activities from outside of the country.

Soviet medicine is often quite good, but woefully behind the times in terms of necessary drugs and equipment. It was obvious that it would take a lot of money to remedy this problem, and more importantly this entire system was not and could not be self-supporting at this time.

Every program with which we have been involved included considerations of food, health and shelter as basic ingredients. We have always considered the idea of Defense Conversion within the framework of programs that addressed these factors as a supporting element and always with the idea that Defense Conversion was not the central issue. Perhaps that is why we are being successful.

Our Action Program

We had initially traveled around the C.I.S. to talk about our housing technology. Our one- to five-story building system utilized a single column for all building heights and a unique panel system that employed the use of lost forms to create a cast in place of a concrete frame (Mitchell, 1992). The key to this technology was the use of minimally skilled labor and advanced management control systems in the construction of low-rise to mid-rise dwelling units. The technology permitted rapid construction times, minimal costs and high quality finishes.

The refinement of this technology for self-help construction had been initiated during a contract awarded by the U.S. Defense Department (1970) for the construction of refugee housing in Vietnam. The de-industrialization of a previous design by the author permitted our company to explore and test the fabrication, erection and management procedures necessary for this type of construction. Over the years this technology has been improved and refined to its present state.

The key to the use of this technology in the C.I.S. was that it permitted retired military personnel to be put to work with high productivity after a very short training period. The systems process that we have developed extends from design through component fabrication and on to the completion of construction. This integrated building system was "packaged" so that it could be totally transferred to our partners in the C.I.S. The technology included a program of industrial management and control systems that had been coupled with a business support structure that included support for sales and marketing. This entire package was made a part of our technical offerings to potential partners in the C.I.S.

Everyone we met in the C.I.S. was excited about what we had to offer, and our ability to interest potential partners was almost embarrassing. The only problem that we encountered was that their civilian and military organizations were without funding. Tanks, planes, bombs, and guns were all available in ample supplies, but not money. In addition, there is no housing mortgage system in the C.I.S., and the normal bank interest is 40 percent per month. Local funds were not available for long-term investment because short-term investments were producing such a favorable return. International funding is also focused on activities that would produce high returns in short time periods. Housing is a long term effort.

Everywhere we went we received orders for our housing. Insulated, well-designed houses created great interest, but frankly anything that involves housing construction creates interest in the C.I.S. This hunger for any available living accommodations is so strong that almost anything will be accepted over the short term. However, if we build our standard "cheap" American "Builders House" in the C.I.S., we will pay dearly for this mistake over the long run.

Everywhere in the C.I.S. we have met senior officers who are retiring from the military as their military forces reorient to new conditions. We have found these people ready and willing to work, and in our discussions they have not let us forget that they want jobs, housing, food and medical support. The military was competent, organized and willing to work. This too represented a Defense Conversion consideration, and perhaps this more human approach to this problem held the key to both short- and long-term social solutions for the C.I.S. Given these considerations we concluded that our activities should focus on working with military groups throughout the C.I.S.

Our decision to move forward with our own programs in the C.I.S. was based on the fact that we could offer completely engineered building systems technology and know-how to our potential partners. In each country we were able to establish that housing was a prime need and an important consideration in every decision. Everyone wanted and needed housing, but no one had the necessary funding. Everyone we talked to gave us orders for our housing, and everyone wanted to work with us, but no one had any money. They really didn't understand all of the implications of a "Building Systems Solution," but if it provided good housing, they wanted to participate in some way.

Our approach to housing was based on the fact that their infrastructure systems (water, sewer, power, waste) would not support the American ideal of a small, privately-owned house on a quarter-acre lot. Construction and infrastructure efficiencies require the use of three- to five-story buildings. If you minimize considerations that deal with American fire and life safety codes, then you can build the five- to ten-story concrete panel buildings that are so common in the C.I.S. Bad concrete, minimal insulation, harsh winters, no maintenance and low standards of construction have produced terrible results and a general rejection of the standard state-promoted building construction programs. Without money even these minimal efforts at meeting the housing needs have slowed.

We seemed to have the ideal solution for the C.I.S. with highly insulated panels coupled with low cost and very favorable exteriors. However, as we talked with people we found that the pressing needs were blinding them to the longer range consequences. During several meetings we were able to "stop the conversation" with the suggestion that perhaps this technology should be transferred in a way that permitted it to be owned by the local groups. The discussions were interesting because they fully expected to pay for the technology even though they were unfamiliar with the process of progressive ownership. However, the discussions illustrated the fact that any program where outsiders controlled a majority interest in essential technology would in time become unacceptable.

Our discussions convinced us that we had to set up a mechanism that over time would transfer the ownership of this technology to our partners. This could not be a gift, and it could not be a rip-off because both extremes were offensive. We returned to the United States and spent a lot of time developing a transfer mechanism that didn't give away anything, and yet it would assure everyone that the technology would eventually be locally owned.

We went back and talked to our potential partners about these arrangements. In most cases we were received with amazement. We were equally as excited because it was obvious that we had solved a subset of our total problem, but without large capital infusions for startup we could not make this a reality. Although the business program for housing was financially sound, the necessary infusion of construction capital was beyond what any Western bank would consider. However, our leverage to do other types of business seemed to expand when we used this housing capability as a negotiating tool.

For example, we were able to negotiate landing rights for our supplies at a super secret Russian Navy Base with the promise that we would pay for these landings with houses. It was interesting that in discussion with the commanding General, I asked him if he would consider taking money for the landing fees. He was quick to respond "Nyet," he wanted housing for his men. The need for military housing in the C.I.S. is beyond measure. I find it interesting that the extent of this need has not been understood nor has the linkage been exploited by our political and diplomatic negotiators. We found that we were able to barter housing for almost every other commodity and resource in the C.I.S. It was interesting that quality housing had value to everyone. As our discussions continued, we were satisfied that we could deliver this commodity through local partners. By setting up component manufacture on a local basis and tying these efforts in with retired military people, we could introduce new technology with the assurance that it would be well managed and controlled. Therefore, we concluded that our housing had to be provided on an almost nonprofit basis to create jobs, minimize cost, and to maximize the impact of this activity. It became very obvious to us that if we structured the housing activities as a normal business we actually jeopardized our investment in the housing venture itself.

Our systems technology required discipline and management control as well as lots of people. Our development program in Vietnam demonstrated that we could utilize entry level skills if the necessary design and engineering had been done on the component systems. This Vietnamese program involved the construction of buildings up to four stories high using self-help construction technology coupled with an erection system that used 55-gallon barrels as the staging that permitted hand lifting and passing of concrete components for component erection. The system design permitted the erection of lightweight concrete elements within a framework of tight dimensional control, repetitive componentization and relatively complete design flexibility so that a varied urban fabric could be created. Our present designs reflect 20 years of continued development and improvements, and our computerized design capabilities represented a competitive edge that led us to believe that significant cost savings were possible.

The Germans have demonstrated that in order to make comparable headway in manufacturing operations it is necessary to create an extensive schooling system to train and create the necessary skill pool of technicians. This labor source must be well trained on the equipment that is being used, and they must have the necessary understanding of controls for both quality and accuracy. In general this effort takes many years to accomplish, and it seemed to us that the problems in the C.I.S. needed immediate attention. This more ambitious manufacturing program also requires significantly more money and support. Instead, we focused our activities on the construction business because of the ample supply of military labor and the lower entry skills that would be required.

The interesting feature about housing construction is that it is labor intensive, and with sufficient pre-engineering studies it can be designed in a way that minimizes the required skills. The military people confirmed the fact that the supply of available personnel was almost unlimited. We found the discipline to be superb, and the officers were well educated and sympathetic to our methodology. Given these positive situations we decided to form a new company with the military and to transfer our technology to it in the form of an equity investment.

However, now we had a company whose clients (the general population) could not buy our product because the general society lacked the necessary capital to support this type of building program. In addition, the idea of privatization, although common with the farms, was not permitted in the cities. How do you develop new housing areas without city cooperation for water, sewer, power and telephone? How do you create housing estates when all of the land is owned by the government?

Initial Activities in Ukraine

Our initial activities in Ukraine involved discussions with a broad spectrum of people. We tried exploring a number of business relationships, and at all times we continued to gather information on our Goal Statements for our ongoing systems study. This investigation made it very clear that any real local activity involved the creation of a Joint Venture Partnership with a local group that had some political power and some local presence.

We were being introduced to potential partners by a group that had an Intellectual Foundation and a Business Group. This Business Group was responsible for activities that would generate revenue that in turn would be used to support the broader activities of the Foundation. After several unsatisfactory preliminary relationships, we convinced our friends in the Business Diaspora Ukraine to join with us in a Joint Venture Agreement to commercialize our business capabilities. **We had concluded that without a local business**

partner, any venture will eventually fail. The relationship with the military group was just not enough for long-term success.

In structuring our Agreements, we explored different distributions of both investment and profits. It was interesting to watch the faces of our potential partners. They laughed with us, smiled when required, but became obviously somber when they thought they were not getting a good deal. This became more difficult when it became obvious to us that they didn't know what a good deal was. The type of elegant business structure that would have received great praise in an American boardroom brought icy silence in Kiev.

This approach to business has produced many interesting incidents which, added together, became the basis of our evolving business plan that includes a significant amount of Defense Conversion. Our activities involve finance and technical support in these conversion activities, and in all cases our proposals include considerations of food, shelter and health. A description of some of our activities will be presented to illustrate the interconnection of activities and objectives and the unifying effects of our business development program.

Housing Development Activities

In an effort to create a hard currency base for our housing business we decided to develop a Diplomatic Village in Kiev. Over 125 countries now recognize Ukraine, and the country is without housing or Embassy facilities to meet the needs of the diplomatic representatives. In discussions with city leaders they provided us with 600 acres of land to lease on the Dneiper River, along with the request that we develop a reasonable development plan to solve this critical national problem.

We prepared the program for embassy buildings, office buildings, hotels, housing, shops and commercial spaces, schools, medical facilities and recreation facilities for the diplomats. The entire program represented a 4-year construction program with an investment of over $950 million dollars. The embassy buildings themselves were divided into three "prototype" sizes. The larger embassies would be built by countries that wanted these buildings to represent an image statement for their country. These large embassies could also have private Ambassador residences. The medium-sized and small Embassy buildings included the Ambassador's residence apartments in the Embassy buildings.

These small and medium-sized embassies utilized our building system so that this project could immediately employ our retired military partners. In addition this project required over 3,500 housing units for embassy staff. These three-, four-, and five-story apartment buildings also utilized our "Building System" technology. The construction was based on leased space to each Government and the construction program itself was designed to insure a 4-year-long hard currency program of construction.

We put together the necessary detailed designs for all buildings and then developed a funding program based on offering multi-year leases to each country. This program permitted us to utilize the credits of the countries leasing the buildings so that construction costs could be paid in hard currency advances based on the lease agreements and the credit of each country requiring space. This project would not require any Ukrainian Government financing or financial guarantees.

The design technology for the infrastructure utilized plastic pipes for electricity, water, and waste disposal. Because of the flat, sandy site, a vacuum waste disposal system was selected. This extensive use of plastic pipe (never before used in Ukraine) and innovative technology permitted us to design all infrastructure activities so that simple ditching machines could be used to trench to a standard 4-foot depth in the sandy soil. By distributing water, power, telephone, and waste in the plastic pipes (and at a fixed depth) we could simplify the infrastructure construction process and in doing so create a large number of jobs for the retired military. Simplified construction carried with it the ability to lower the cost and improve the quality of the construction for the diplomats.

Our goal was to create construction procedures that could be easily and rapidly accomplished by the retired military so that jobs and productivity would ease their transition to civilian life. The project permitted us to utilize the credit base of the countries that wanted to locate in Ukraine for diplomatic reasons, so the overall process seemed to benefit everyone. At the present time these diplomatic missions are occupying complete floors in hotels, which in turn has created a severe hotel room shortage in Kiev. This shortage of rooms has seriously impacted the tourist trade, so now the normal hard currency from these activities has been lost to the general population. Our development program was designed to rectify this problem, while at the same time pump significant amounts of construction money into the local economy.

We also took our designs to the oil producing regions in other parts of the C.I.S. and bartered this housing construction for oil and gas. It surprised us that this housing technology represented a readily usable commodity that had greater value than dollars. An interesting aspect of these discussions in the oil regions involved the condition that we would supply the components and also send the crews to construct the buildings. Our Ukrainian labor pool permitted us to meet this stated need of the C.I.S. oil producing areas.

It was obvious to us that the American companies that were developing these oil resources also needed housing, and local methods and construction were usually completely unsatisfactory. This need offered us hard currency arrangements as well as barter arrangements, which greatly modified our cash needs and changed our projected cash flow requirements. As these opportunities increased it became obvious to us that we needed the proper computer tools to manage the dynamics of our business. The cash needs for component manufacture and construction would be extensive, and the need for tight management and control were essential for success.

Computer Software Development

Because all of our housing activities relied on the computer, we started looking around in the architectural and engineering profession to see what capability existed. We found an almost complete wasteland of thinking and capability. The bureaucratic processes in this profession have been complete and illustrate the old adage "that power corrupts, and that absolute power insures absolute corruption."

The professions lacked understanding of the newer design methods and systems and were frankly not interested in changing their thinking. No one was using computers, and all seemed very proud of their nineteenth century approach to drawing and document production. No one could give me justification for the technical decisions that they were requiring, and yet no one was prepared to change anything. Perhaps the most serious problem arose when they displayed complete revulsion to the fact that we would even consider working with the military.

To address this local technology problem we created a joint venture for software development with a group of Ph.D.'s from the Institute of Cybernetics in Ukraine. Our initial development contracts were very successful. We utilized the C++ object-oriented language to create software packages that were in great demand in the American market. These initial contracts have permitted us to develop the new company to a level that permits it to generate maintenance funding from the American market. This team now provides us with essential computer capability for our activities in the C.I.S.

This company is now developing our multi-language information and control systems for all of our other activities. This specialized capability is essential for the development of any long-term, "world class" business activity in the C.I.S. The technology is also essential if the new companies plan to work with American companies that are trying to do business in the C.I.S. Computerization must be the backbone of any company that expects to have an ongoing manufacturing and delivery program in the C.I.S.

Perhaps the significant aspect of this relationship is that we are employing, in a joint venture partnership, key intellectual assets of Ukraine. The Institute of Cybernetics is the leading Mathematical Institute of the old Soviet Union, and its employees were instrumental in preparing the computer software for the Soviet Space Program. The transfer of these assets to a new focus on commercial activity represents a Defense Conversion program in itself.

As a result of our activities with the computer team, we have been introduced to a number of other people in the Institute who have developed new technology and who are interested in proper commercialization. These opportunities are interesting because offers to share technology are not common in the C.I.S. In many instances we have seen people try to conceal the obvious technical facts because they are afraid of everyone, and their intelligence system has made them well aware how easy it is to steal ideas. Therefore, we are quite honored at these opportunities because they involve sharing ideas and working together for proper commercialization.

It seems that the opportunities and ideas are endless, but in each case we have found that the researchers have no idea about investment, commercialization or value. Because of this they are hesitant about discussing their ideas. They usually have no idea if they are being taken advantage of and as a result they are easily frightened. Perhaps our track record and our fairness in our other business dealings is the key to these ongoing opportunities.

It is obvious to us that these conversions of military hardware development programs represent Defense Conversion opportunities, but in our opinion they are each commercially viable. They should stand on their own without interference or sponsorship from governments. In addition they represent small entrepreneurial ventures where their connection with small American companies could represent mutual benefits. We believe that these opportunities for mutual cooperation between small companies in both countries will represent positive business activity and an opportunity for small active companies from both countries to get to market with good ideas. Why doesn't our Government support efforts like this?

Programs of technical information, trade and idea development are the key to creating understanding, and the proper type of business transactions are essential for success. Cooperative development and commercialization are essential if we expect to create a broad-based development program that is of benefit to both countries. Certainly America is well respected around the world for its ability to incubate small companies with creative programs of support. This opportunity in the C.I.S. would seem to offer the American Government creative new ways to stimulate business and commercialization between the two countries that would also create benefits for the small companies in our country.

Air Freight Company

The need to deliver equipment to the American oil companies that were helping the various Republics commercialize on their natural resources has been an important consideration of our Government. Major development of these resources would require proper transport of equipment, supplies and provisions to these remote sites. Normal road, water and train distribution of goods within the C.I.S. is anything but safe and timely.

In support of this program we have become partners in a private Ukrainian company that was formed by retired military officers. These officers had converted four IL-76 airplanes from the military to civilian use. After extensive discussions, we developed a Business Plan for a new company called Busol Air Bridge (BAB). This company has now requested the transfer of one hundred IL-76 airplanes and three strategic military airfields to meet a plan of expansion and investment from America.

These strategic bomber bases are located at Uzin, at Bella Tsarka and at Nicholayev. The one at Nicholayev is adjacent to port facilities, permitting intermodal goods transfer from ship to air. The base at Bella Tsarka has the largest airplane repair facility in the old Soviet Union, and the facility at Uzin is close to Kiev and the air lanes from the West. Each of these bases has associated housing and commercial facilities like a bakery, clinic, stores and restaurants. Each base has over 1000 employees who maintain all aspects of these facilities. These bases constitute the facilities of the old Soviet Southern Bomber Command.

For planning purposes, we were advised that all of these employees would move from the Ukrainian Government payroll to ours once the transfer of these bases had been completed. In addition, all pilots, crews and repair teams would also be on our payroll. Our manager in BAB was a retired General from the Ukrainian Air Force. He had been the commander of the central command and facility at Uzin. The key managers, pilots, crews and support people in BAB were former officers from the Ukrainian Air Force. We are expected to provide the commercial systems, the economic training, and the financing for this program. Of course, this transfer carries with it maintenance of the equipment, so the repair and maintenance costs will be transferred from the government to us once this transfer is complete.

Our business plan projects a cash need of about eight million dollars worth of equity and about thirty million dollars worth of debt for a business that would be generating 100 million dollars worth of revenues in the first year. We have been able to secure commitments for both the debt and the equity investment financing from American and overseas sources. We are now waiting for the transfer of the assets so that we can complete the necessary arrangements for this company to begin widespread operations.

In support of this effort we have been able to get commitments to land and transfer goods in Turkey, Lebanon, Israel and Oman. Each of these countries has specific connections with the various oil regions in the C.I.S. and with the American oil companies. Business and government groups in each country are interested in the trading potential of this venture, and each country is assuming some additional financial participation in this venture. This ability to support with freight, housing and reprovisioning services by air permits this new Ukrainian company to offer unique benefits to its potential American oil company customers as well as to businesses in other countries.

The ability of these freight airplanes to fly equipment, housing components, food, and crews insures the fact that this new company can serve as a "supply bridge" for the development of the various resources of the C.I.S. Discussions are underway with gold mining companies, diamond miners, and even lumber producers for extensions of our freight service. In every case this includes our housing and building capability. Success is almost guaranteed because of the needs for this service and the present conditions in the C.I.S.

The local Mafia is in strong control of the major cities and commercial centers. They extract their tolls from all goods that pass through the ports or the city gates. In many cases people are losing as much as 40 percent of their goods in the unloading-loading operations during transport changes. Trains must now carry armed guards with heavy weapons for defense because of train robberies and the general lack of law and order that pervades the countryside. In many ways this can be compared to the American West in the 1800s. It will change with time.

Our proposed air freight company would resolve the problems of delivery by flying to old Soviet military bases. For strategic reasons these bases are adjacent to natural resources, and their use can be assured through the relationships of our (former) military partners. We have negotiated landing rights for housing construction at these bases, and in every case this has proven to be more valuable to us than money. This ability to deliver secure cargo reduces insurance costs and increases our competitiveness.

Summary and Conclusions

This chapter was initially based on the premise that American foreign policy should be directed at helping to produce social stability in the various Republics of the C.I.S. if defense conversion is to be successful. This social stability requires that any programs of mutual support address the pressing deficiencies in shelter, food and medical needs of the general population. Each of these essential needs for basic living have been badly serviced by the previous governmental system, and can now be considered to be in a very serious condition of disarray. Because of the breakdown of the previous system, these human needs are now spiraling out of control, and they are creating a situation where the resulting chaos of human needs will impact and nullify any other action that is being taken in or with these societies.

This chapter shows that to operate successfully, Western companies working in the C.I.S. should:

(1) Not assume that you can set up consulting contracts that mirror the contracts set up with the U.S. Government.

(2) Expect to find that the C.I.S. governments are broke and that the state run enterprises are in disarray and poorly managed.

(3) Be prepared to be extremely flexible and imaginative in business matters. The U.S. model will fail in the C.I.S.

(4) Expect a desire for technical help on how to do business and deliver products. Their theoretical capabilities are excellent.

The best conclusion that can be drawn from our entrepreneurial experience is that it is very difficult to initiate long-term relationships for business action in countries of the C.I.S. Most people in the C.I.S. don't trust anyone, and after the long years of state control, secret police, and the absence of personal rights these feelings are ingrained into an entire population. The sophistication needed for the mechanics of business is often lacking, creating a serious situation for ongoing business development and management.

As we explored opportunities in the C.I.S. it quickly became obvious that the industry, and in fact the society, was built around their military industrial complex. Add to this situation a failed economic system that focused its very best talent and assets on the military. Almost anything that we looked at or talked about had been a part of the military. Therefore, almost everything that we considered doing involved Defense Conversion.

This economic base must be turned around into a more productive economic system that benefits the entire population. How do you reorient minds and capabilities to private ownership and ongoing jobs that will permit people to participate in improving their own conditions? How do you change a system and the people that have learned to survive in that system? How do you create a paradigm shift during which the general population experiences hope that their economic condition will improve? These considerations and actions represented a massive undertaking requiring both talent and money.

In Ukraine the discussions with the military have been business-like and very direct. They are aware that our proposal means jobs and economic benefits, and that if properly developed, it represents the utilization of assets that would only decay rapidly if they were left to stand unused. These discussions were conducted by engineers who are trying to make rational and logical judgments for ongoing activities. Certainly before everything is finalized the final political evaluation must take place. American ownership in a company that controls State assets is certainly a very big step for any government to take.

A significant number of military assets are being considered in this proposed Defense Conversion. This conversion must be done by one government and then supported by the other. Governments are the only entities that control this scale of assets and funding. The foreign exchange conditions in most of the C.I.S. Governments are limited. During this crisis of economic reorientation these governments are experiencing serious problems with respect to their required debt repayment and their need for new investment. Investment from the West usually carries conditions that are onerous as well as limiting. It is certainly time for new thinking, new programs and clearer policy. We will never again have this opportunity to restructure the world and refocus the future.

The real talent necessary to do this job requires a partnership of American and C.I.S. entrepreneurs who are committed to long-term action and who will be supported by their governments. I suspect that relationships with the military will be essential because this is the only group with the required discipline for short-term progress. This group also contains a needed reservoir of talent. The civilian bureaucracies of the C.I.S. are modeled on the old system of "do nothing," and the political volatility is such that the person you meet in a ministry during one month will be gone the next. The only real stability in both action and thought is the military. However, some serious and senior managers from their defense industries are gravitating toward government service and their cooperation could be the basis for success.

In our case it is creative people and a very aware Government in Ukraine that have made our progress even possible from a "talking point of view." Americans also face a problem of military conversion, but it seems to me that this is being approached in an unstructured way, with localized solutions and band-aid remedies. This can only produce long-term failure in our country. I hope we don't continue to permit this sloppy thinking in our dealings with the C.I.S.

The resolution of Defense Conversion will take courage, creativity, and commitment. The crisis is severe enough in the C.I.S. to demand action. The question is, Will they be able to select proper programs for support, and will the managers of these programs have the necessary skill for proper implementation of these programs? One can only hope that this process will be self-regulating and that proper development will insure the fact that these creative solutions will help to create the paradigm shift that will be needed for overall success.

I can't help but be distressed that our government is not proceeding with a more positive program. Perhaps it would be wiser for them to disband everything and not meddle anymore than they already have. Certainly the conversion of weapons is a State to State program that requires both trust and mutual guarantees. However, it is very obvious that the major skill of any Government is in spending money and not making it. Defense Conversion can succeed as a private exercise, but never as a totally Government initiative. The real essence of Defense Conversion is that it can create large-scale opportunities for regional development so that the conversions themselves are considered within a changing social and economic fabric and not as individual vignettes. How well we do will directly impact the lives of our children and grandchildren. We can't afford to fail.

Perhaps it is time to reflect on the Winston Churchill admonition in his 1935 speech before the House of Commons:

"When the situation was manageable it was neglected, and now that it is thoroughly out of hand, we apply too late the remedies which then might have effected a cure."

References

Ashby, W.R., 1962: "Principles of the Self-Organizing System," in *Principles of Self-Organization*, H. Von Foerster and G.W. Zopf, Jr., eds., Pergamon Press, New York.

Bertalanffy, L. von, 1968: General System Theory, George Braziller, New York. (Third Printing, 1972)

Churchman, C.W., 1979: *The Systems Approach*, Dell Publishing Co., New York.

Defense Department, 1970: Shelter Technology - Contract N-62464-70-C-0018-P001.

Mitchell, N.B., Jr., 1992: The 1992 Distinguished Rinker Lecture, "Industrialized Shelter Technology," published by the University of Florida, M.E. Rinker School of Building Construction, Gainesville, Florida.

CHAPTER 8

The Middle Ultraviolet (MUV)

Alex E. S. Green
Departments of Mechanical Engineering and
Nuclear Engineering Sciences
University of Florida
Gainesville Florida

Introduction—A Satellite Surveillance System

In 1962, the Space Science Laboratory of General Dynamics Convair undertook a multidisciplinary analysis of a satellite system for the surveillance of hostile rocket launchings (Green, 1962). The work made use of the special features of the middle ultraviolet (MUV) defined as the 340–170 nanometer spectral region. We opened the work with a treatment of the gas dynamics of rocket exhaust plumes that was followed by a description of the emission properties of rocket plumes, flames and flares and a survey of laboratory flame observations in the MUV. Next we discussed the distribution of ozone and its variations with altitude as observed in early balloon and rocketborne experiments. The absorbing properties of stratospheric ozone largely dominate the potential space applications of the MUV spectral region. We next calculated the transmission of MUV radiation through atmospheric gases in relation to the ozone distribution to arrive at an approximate analytical expression for transmission as a function of height and slant angle. Knowing approximate source strengths and atmospheric attenuations we could calculate the possible signal strengths reaching a satellite detection system.

To estimate the background radiation we used measurements of the MUV radiations of the Sun obtained in our space program and calculated the scattered irradiance from the air above the ozone layer. Essentially, we estimated the Earth's apparent albedo in the MUV as determined largely by the characteristic MUV transmission of the ozone layer and Rayleigh scattering by atoms and molecules in or above the ozone layer. We followed this with a discussion of auroral, airglow and other possible sources of interfering MUV radiation originating above the ozone layer that could be mistaken for rocket launches.

The upper atmosphere is a storage bank of chemical energy which is optically pumped by the sun and also pumped by incoming solar particle radiation. This energy may be transformed by various chemical processes into emissions of the atmosphere in the MUV. Certain atomic and molecular species play particularly important roles in the space involvements of the MUV. We collected the properties of the principal emitters and absorbers in the MUV and followed this with a survey of the state of the art of detection in the MUV. Even in 1962 it was clear that signal-to-noise problems would determine the application limits of an MUV surveillance system and data storage and processing techniques.

The systems analysis undertaken by the Convair group revealed that the MUV appeared to be a fruitful region for a number of space surveillance applications. The Convair report, "The Middle Ultraviolet and Its Space Applications (MUVSA)," was a collection of manuscripts containing scientific information and analyses issued for the purpose of discussions between Convair and the Aerospace Corporation and with other Department of Defense agencies. Table 1 is the Table of Contents of the MUVSA report.

Unfortunately, 1962–63 was a period of organizational instability at Convair, *not due to government cutbacks*, but rather the large financial loss associated with Convair's 880–990 commercial transport program. During this period several scientists in DoD agencies who had read this report encouraged the author to expand it and issue it as a monograph on the MUV spectral region. I was able to do this after I returned to academic work in Florida in fall 1963 when I received a publishing contract from Wiley. With the help of chapters by R. Tousey of the Naval Research Laboratory, C. Barth, then of the Jet Propulsion Laboratory, K.L. Hallane, J. Hennes and L. Dunkelman of NASA Goddard Space Flight Center, and chapters derived from the Convair report we assembled the monograph "The Middle Ultraviolet, Its Science and Technology (MUVST)" (Green, 1966). Its purpose was to bring together the scientific information on solar, atmospheric, aeronomical, atomic and molecular physics related to the middle ultraviolet and to serve as a guide to the intensive pursuit of advanced studies in this spectral region. Table 2 is the table of contents of this book. The selection of topics chosen in this work was strongly influenced

Table 1. Contents of *The Middle Ultraviolet and its Space Applications* (MUVSA)

1.	Introduction	*A.E.S. Green*
2.	Gasdynamics of a Rocket Exhaust Plume	*H. Yoshihara*
3.	Middle U.V. Radiation from Flames	*A. Berlad/S. Kaye*
4.	Atmospheric Ozone	*M. Griggs*
5.	The Attenuation of Optical Radiation	*A.E.S. Green*
6.	Absorption by Ozone and the Earth's Albedo in the Ultraviolet	*A.E.S. Green*
7.	The Sun and Its Radiation	*A.E.S. Green*
8.	The Aurora	*A.E.S. Green*
9.	Light Observed in Wake of Rockets During Unpowered Flight	*C.E. McIlwain*
10.	Atmospheric Processes	*B.F. Gray*
11.	Atomic and Molecular Properties	*A.E.S. Green/L. Nugent B.F. Gray/H. Papazian W. Malkmus*
12.	Atomic and Molecular and Selected Radiative Processes	*R. Marriott/L. Marino*
13.	Detection of Middle Ultraviolet Radiation	*J.R. Nelson*
14.	Spatial Filtering	*W. Montgomery/F. Broome*
15.	Future Field Measurements on Targets and Background	*C. Ferriso*
16.	Summary	*A.E.S. Green*
Appended: N.B.S. Circular 541		*A.M. Bass/H.P. Broida*

Table 2. Contents of *The Middle Ultraviolet, Its Science and Technology*
(MUVST)

by a broader study, "Atomic and Space Physics," published by the author and a colleague (Green and Wyatt, 1965).

The 340–170 nm wavelength region was chosen since this is the spectral region excluded from ground-based observation by the opacity of the atmospheric molecules ozone (O_3) and oxygen (O_2). Ozone is a strong absorber from 300 to 220 nm, and molecular oxygen is a strong absorber from 220 to 170 nm. The spectral region, when looking outward from altitudes up to about 50 km, from 340 to 170 nm (3.65–7.30 eV) spans one octave just as does the "classical" 760 to 380 nm region of vision and optical astronomy.

In addition to the contribution on major topics by the leading outside authorities, several specialized chapters by members of the Aeronomy Group at the University of Florida (UF) were developed to fill important gaps. These included the application of the middle ultraviolet to remote sensing of air pollutants (Green et al., 1966). Figure 1 illustrates the absorption coefficients of NO_2, NH_3, O_3, SO_2 and H_2O in the 180 nm to 330 nm region assembled in MUVST. Figure 2 illustrates an early University of Florida apparatus for the remote sensing of ambient air pollutants. The system used a correlation

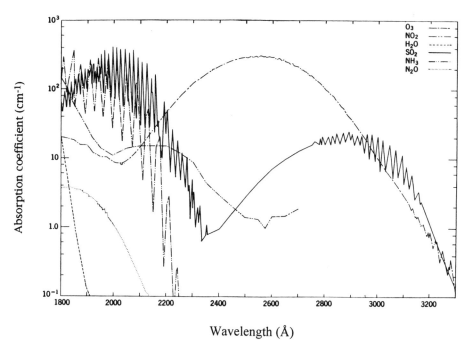

Figure 1. Absorption Coefficients (adapted from Green et al., 1966).

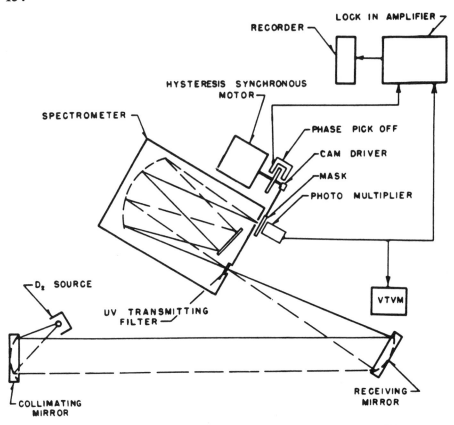

Figure 2. University of Florida Long Path Remote Sensing System (Kaye, 1967).

technique that took advantage of the oscillatory nature of the SO_2 absorption coefficients in the 300 nm neighborhood (see Fig. 1). Measurements over a 150-m path in Jacksonville, Florida gave average SO_2 concentrations of 45 ppb (Kaye, 1967).

While there was some interest in this technique or in variations of it during the late '60s, the prevailing method of ambient monitoring, encouraged by environmental regulators in this country was the in situ pollutant monitor. In these instruments, air is drawn into a monitor for a specific gas and a comparative spectral analysis is made using a reference spectrum of the molecular pollutant of interest.

Interest in the middle ultraviolet was very low in 1966 when the MUVST was published. Most of the new studies from rockets and spacecraft focused on the far and extreme UV. However, potential stratospheric ozone depletion due to nitric oxide emissions of commercial supersonic transport fleet flying in the stratosphere and the consequent increase of ultraviolet radiation reaching the ground became a public policy issue a few years later (Johnston, 1971). The $50 million Climatic Impact Assessment Program (CIAP) managed by the U.S. Department of Transportation gave considerable impetus to middle ultraviolet studies. This program generated five volumes of technical material totaling some 5000 pages (Grobecker, 1975).

Just as the CIAP study was completed the potential impact of freons and other halogenated hydrocarbons upon the ozone layer became an environmental concern. This was initiated by the pioneering works of Stolarski and Cicerone (1974) on the catalytic destruction of stratospheric ozone by chlorine, and Molina and Rowland (1974) on freons as a source of stratospheric chlorine.

At the University of Florida the author continued in a variety of studies that were derivatives of his defense and space work at Convair. On behalf of the Air Pollution Control Association (APCA), now the Air and Waste Management Association (AWMA), he prepared and presented a short course and educational materials on "Remote Sensing of Air Pollutants" (Green, 1972). The original references from this early survey of remote sensing of air pollutants included Bartle et al. (1970); Goody (1964); Green (1964); Green et al. (1971a, 1971b, 1972); Griggs et al. (1970); Ludwig et al. 1968, 1971); McClintock et al. 1970); Nader (1971, 1972); National Academy of Sciences (1969); University of Michigan (1971); U.S. Department of Interior (1972); Valley (1965). Ludwig, Bartle and Griggs were from the same Convair laboratory, and their pioneering work on remote sensing of air pollutants in the infrared also had its roots in military-space application studies.

Since 1970, the science and technology related to stratospheric ozone issues has literally exploded and moved into the international policy arena. With the Montreal Protocol now banning many halogenated compounds used in refrigerants, propellants, solvents, fire suppressants, etc., this explosion now impacts many aspects of our daily life and is having a major impact on our industries. Environmental measurements represent a particularly fruitful opportunity for the conversion of military and space technology into civilian applications. Since MUV techniques are largely an extension of visible spectroscopic techniques, we will refer to both via the acronym MUVV.

MUVV Spectroscopy

Middle ultraviolet-visible (MUVV) spectroscopy has benefitted significantly by the demands of military and space systems. Table 3 shows major instrumental categories that have been used in measuring the exhaust products of stationary combustors, in remote or direct spectral analyses of gases from stationary combustors, and sampling and remote analyses of exhaust products of moving combustors, in fire suppressant studies and in other studies motivated by environmental concerns (Miller and Green, 1994).

MUVV spectroscopy has historically led to the development of some of the most sensitive chemical analysis techniques along with the quantum theory of light and atomic and molecular structure. When applied in our military and space program (Green, 1962, 1966; Green and Wyatt, 1965) MUVV spectroscopy led to the recognition and quantification of the stratospheric ozone depletion problem which became generally recognized in the mid 1980s.

A scanning spectrometer with a photomultiplier tube detector is particularly useful in MUVV spectroscopy when the source is weak and the signals reaching the detector at all wavelengths are steady. A spectrographic system gathers all wavelengths at the same time and is particularly useful for studies when time variations of the signal would confuse the time dimension used in scanning. Linear photodiode arrays were introduced about 25 years ago

Table 3. Spectroscopic Approaches for Combustion Product Analysis (adapted from Miller and Green, 1994)

Technologies	Species	Recommended Instrumentation
OPTICAL SPECTROSCOPY		
UV-VIS	Free Radicals, Molecules Atomic Species, Metals	MUVV
Infrared	IR Active Hetero- nuclear Molecules	FTIR
Fluorescence	Free Radicals	Laser Induced Fluor.
Raman	IR Active Molecules, Homonuclear Molecules	FT Raman/CARS

to serve as multichannel detectors permitting the functions of a scanning spectrometer to be combined with those of a spectrograph. Development of two dimensional photodiode arrays and charge coupled devices in connection with video recording devices and a variety of space and military applications has opened up new vistas in MUVV spectroscopy, some of which are just being exploited in applied studies.

Early efforts at MUVV spectroscopic measurements of air pollutant concentration made use of correlation (Kaye, 1967) and second derivative techniques (Williams and Hager, 1970) to improve signal-to-noise levels. However, the wedding of the modern fast personal computer (PC) with the spectrograph has finally helped commercialize remote sensing of air pollutants.

Recent MUVV Air Quality Monitors

While air quality monitoring by MUVV had an early start in the U.S.A., its first large-scale commercial realization has been mainly achieved abroad with the Opsis system marketed by ABB (Hallstadius et al., 1991). The Differential Optical Absorption System (DOAS), developed mainly in West Germany and Sweden, makes use of a broadband light source, e.g., a high pressure xenon lamp or a halogen lamp. This light is collimated by a parabolic mirror to a narrow beam, which passes through the atmosphere over a path of several hundred meters to several kilometers. At the end of this absorption path the light is captured again and focused onto the end of an optical fiber that transmits it to the opto-analysis unit.

The analyzer is basically a computerized spectrometer. In the computer the atmospheric spectrum is compared with a library of pre-recorded absorption spectra. By these means a number of different species in the atmosphere can simultaneously be determined and calculated (Hallstadius, 1993). Table 4 gives detection limits in the UV of an Opsis system for a number of atmospheric pollutants or toxics (Spellicy, private communication).

Only those gases having unique narrowband absorption spectra in the UV or visible wavelength ranges can be detected with the DOAS technique. On the other hand, as the light absorption is connected with electronic transitions in the molecules, the sensitivity is high. The detection limits for most compounds are therefore in the ppb-range, averaged over a 500 meter monitoring path.

A great number of Opsis DOAS urban air monitoring stations are currently in use in Europe. In Switzerland, Italy, Great Britain and Sweden the open path technology has been well established for several years. In countries

Table 4. Detection Limits UV System (R.L. Spellicy, Private Communication)

Substance	ppm.m	Substance	ppm.m
methane	55	ammonia	1.1
monochloride benzene	1.5	1,2,3 trimethyl benzene	1.5
nitric oxide	0.8	1,2,4 trimethyl benzene	1.5
nitrogen dioxide	0.25	1,3,5 trimethyl benzene	1.5
nitrogen trioxide	0.02	benzene	0.82
nitrous acid	0.55	carbon disulfide	0.15
o-xylene	3.85	chlorine	22
ozone	0.8	chlorine dioxide	0.55
p-xylene	0.82	dichloride benzene	1.5
phenol	0.8	ethyl benzene	1.5
styrene	0.8	formaldehyde	0.25
sulfur dioxide	0.16	fosgene	27
toluene	0.82	hydrochloric acid	55
xylene	0.56	m-xylene	0.82

that have an existing air monitoring network based on conventional in situ analyzers, for instance Germany, the acceptance of the open path technology has been slower.

In the 1990 Clean Air Act amendments, 189 toxics have been identified to come under regulations in the 1990s. Stimulated by these forthcoming regulations, it might be expected that measurement of concentrations based upon middle ultraviolet-visible spectroscopy will reemerge on the air quality monitoring scene in the United States.

Multichannel MUVV Spectroscopy and Fire

In multichannel MUVV spectroscopy, the grating is fixed, and a linear array of detectors, each viewing a different wavelength, is at the exit aperture.

Two main array types are used: silicon photodiode arrays (PDAs), a linear array of individual photodiodes fabricated using integrated circuit technology, and charge coupled devices (CCD), a two-dimensional array of photosensors, which, like the PDA, comes in a semiconductor "chip" package. A typical spectroscopic CCD layout is a two-dimensional array of 1024 by 256 elements with each element 27 mm square. Unlike the PDA there are no electronic switches to access each element. Instead, the signal is shifted down sequentially and across to the output node. The most important benefit of this readout method is that the associated readout noise is very low, particularly if the CCD is cooled, giving the CCD approximately 100 times the sensitivity of a PDA. The great advantage of such a multichannel detection system is that these signals can be processed by recent personal computers (PC) so that some of the signal-to-noise enhancing techniques previously carried out by mechanical or optical tricks can now be carried out more powerfully by PCs.

Metals, such as sodium, lead and other strong emitters, if present in the fuel, can be observed in the emissions of the flame itself. The strongest atomic spectral line intensities in the MUVV spectral region have been compiled by the National Institute of Standards and Technology (formerly NBS) (Meggers et al., 1961). The highly toxic metals Cd, Hg, Mn and Pb are represented by strong lines in the 229–283-nm range. With the help of a continuum light source with strong MUV intensities such as a high pressure xenon arc or a deuterium lamp (Koller, 1965), we might also use the same spectral system to study absorption by stack gases or the air in a polluted region.

The immediate and fast time information gained with respect to specific species emitted by combustors or fires could be a major advantage of multichannel MUVV spectroscopy. Metallic toxic species such as mercury, lead, cadmium, manganese, and others are now of great importance in relationship to coal-based utilities, waste-to-energy plants, and other industrial sources of emissions or residues to be disposed of in landfills (Phillips, 1983; Williams and Green, 1994). These metals are strong emitters or absorbers of middle ultraviolet light.

MUVV spectroscopy can be useful to differentiate many organic and halogenated organic combustion products, and for an overall assessment of pollutant and toxic species from combustion. Of particular importance are the strong intensities of the spectra of C, H and O containing molecules and free radicals represented in electronic emissions of flames. The free radicals, while in very minute concentrations, play major roles in the chain reactions that propagate flames (Berlad, 1966; Glassman, 1977; Vaidya et al., 1982; Pamidimukkala et al., 1983; Horvath et al., 1984). Table 5 gives a listing of the band heads of C, H and O containing free radicals and molecules in the 500 to 200 nm spectral region selected from the tabulation of Pearse and Gaydon (1976). Table 6 lists band heads of halogenated molecules that might be expected as a result of flame-halon interactions.

The fact that free radicals tend to be strongly represented in electronic emissions of flames (Gaydon, 1957) should be very advantageous in fire and fire suppressant studies. Figure 3 illustrates the type of data possible using current multichannel MUVV spectroscopy in which an 1/8-meter spectrograph is used in conjunction with a 400-line/mm grating to cover the 200- to 800-nm emissions of a premixed propane flame. The diagram clearly shows the emissions of free radicals and other molecular species. Figure 4 shows the spectra of the same flame when a 1200-line/mm grating is used to give better resolution in the MUV.

Table 5. Selected Hydrocarbon Emissions in UVV Spectral Range

λ (nm)	Appear	Molec.	System	λ (nm)	Appear	Molec.	System
473.0	R	OH	Schuler-V	311.9	M	C3H3	
433.7	R	OH	Schuler-V	311.5	R	CH3	
424.5	M	CH2O	Cool flame	306.4	R,DCD,wv	OH	
423.0	M	CH2O	Cool flame	298.7	R	C2	Fox-H.
412.1	R	CH2O	Cool flame	297.7		CO	
410.2	V	C2	Desl.-d	293.1	R	CH2O	
405.0	R	C3	Comet	285.5	R	C2	Fox
402.5	R	CH		283.9	R	CH2O	
395.2		CH2O		281.1	R,DCD,wv	OH	
389.3		CO		273.9		C6H6	
387.1	R, D	CH		268.3	R	OH	U-V
385.2	R, D	CH		267.9		C6H6	
367.1		O2	Des.-d	260.0	R	OH	U-V
362.7	R,D	CH		259.7		CO	
350.1	R	CHO		258.9		C6H6	
337.6	R	CHO		254.5	R	OH	U-V
332.5		N2		249.2		CO	
330.5		CO		246.3		CO	
321.1		O2		244.8		N2	
318.6	R	CHO		231.3	O	C2	Mulliken
316.4	R	CH2O		216.4	M	CH3	
314.4		CH		215.8	M	CH3	
				214.3	V	C2	Fre

Remarks in appearance column: R - degraded to longer wavelengths; V - degraded to shorter wavelengths; D - double head; DCD - double head, each component a close double; L - Narrow band resembling an atomic line; M - maximum of a headless band; O - origin of a band; wv - accompanied by weaker head to shorter wavelengths.

Table 6. Emissions from Halogenated Compounds in UVV Spectral Range

λ (nm)	Appear	Molecule	λ (nm)	Appear	Molecule
476.1	R	ClF	278.8	V	CCl
439.8	R	BrO	278.2	V	CCl
438.5	V	CCl	277.8	V	CCl
432.4	L	CCl	255.8	V,DCD	CF
397.3	R	ClO2	251.9	R	CF2
324.8	R	BrO	248.8	R	CF2
320.8	R	BrO	247.9	V,DCD	CF
311.1	M	Br2	240.4	V,DCD	CF
305.2	V, D	CBr	236.8	R	CCl
301.5	M	CBr	207.6	R,DCD	CF

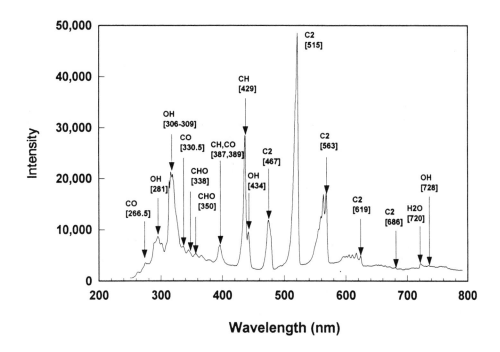

Figure 3. MUVV spectra of a premixed propane flame.

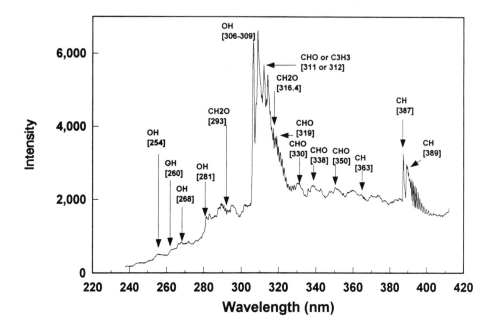

Figure 4. MUV spectra of a premixed propane flame.

In smoky fires such as those that arise from diffusion flames, the strong Planck continuum in the visible and infrared tends to overwhelm free radical and molecular features. Since the blackbody spectrum falls off rapidly at shorter wavelengths this problem is mitigated in the MUV. However, the spectrograph and the external optics must be chosen carefully to minimize stray visible light reaching the MUV channels. Figure 5 shows the MUVV spectra of a propane diffusion flame without and with added halon 1211 and 1301. The soot, due to lack of oxygen, causes a large Planck continuum that is substantially enhanced by the addition of these suppressants. While there is little evidence of molecular features in these spectra, it is possible to see some of them by focusing on the MUV and using stray light suppression techniques. Figure 6 shows the same three flames as in Figure 5, but in the MUV. A $NiSO_4$ blocking filter is used to lower the stray visible light that would otherwise get into MUV channels.

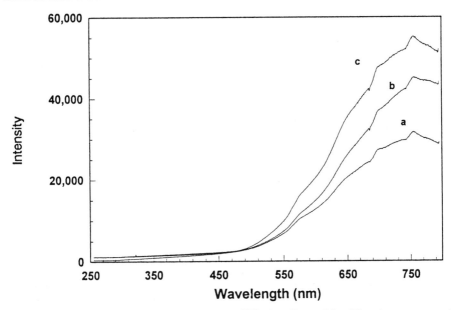

Figure 5. MUVV spectra from a propane diffusion flame (a) without suppressant and (b) with Halon 1211 added (c) with Halon 1301 added (from Green et al., 1994).

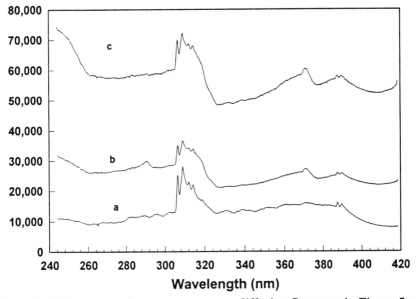

Figure 6. MUV spectra from same propane diffusion flames as in Figure 5 with a Schott-NiSO$_4$ filter.

The MUVV spectrum of a methanol pan fire shows molecular features that are washed out as halon 1211 is added. Then a broad visible and near infrared Planck continua appears that increases in magnitude with added 1211 concentrations. On the other hand preliminary MUV spectra show the strong OH peak near 306 nm that decreases with increasing 1211 concentrations. This might be due to free radical scavenging by halons. However other possible explanations based upon thermal mechanisms are possible.

MUVV spectra of oil fires show more visible continua than do methanol or other oxygenated fuel fires and little evidence of molecular features. Here too, however, it is possible to observe free radicals in the MUV by careful avoidance of stray light and by computer management of the data.

UV Global Space Weather Systems

A recent monograph, "Atmospheric Ultraviolet Remote Sensing" by Huffman (1992a, 1992b) of Phillips Laboratory, Hanscom Air Force Base, Massachusetts, reflects further examples of ultraviolet defense conversion. The book covers a broader wavelength range and uses NUV (near UV) to cover 400–300 nm, MUV to cover 300–200 nm, FUV (far UV) to cover 200–100 nm, VUV (vacuum UV) to cover 200 nm to 10 nm EUV or XUV (extreme UV) to cover 100–10 nm, and Soft X-ray to cover 10–1 nm. The book's concerns extend beyond stratospheric ozone questions into ionospheric and thermospheric aeronomical phenomena. The recent review "The New Ultraviolet: Global Space Weather Systems" (Bohlin et al.,1990) calls attention to new applications of ultraviolet sensors to remote sensing of the ionosphere and thermosphere from satellites. These aeronomical phenomena, explored first in defense contexts, now impact daily life through radio propagation. Huffman notes it is likely that in the future most UV space sensors will utilize the stars and possibly the sun (in the 200–400 nm region of the UV) as standard sources for in-flight calibration. This trend is greatly aided by the improved knowledge of stellar intensities most recently made by the International Ultraviolet Explorer satellite program. Sets of standard, non-variable stars are being used for the Hubble Space Telescope (Hufford, 1993).

Summary, Discussion and Conclusion

MUV spectroscopy, applied in past military and space programs (Green, 1962; Green et al., 1966; Green and Wyatt, 1965), eventually led to the recognition and quantification of the stratospheric ozone depletion problem (Grobecker, 1975). The ozone depletion potential of halon fire suppressants is the major reason alternatives are now actively being sought. Since MUV spectroscopy of fires can contribute to the selection of alternatives it would seem that we have come full circle.

We have indicated how a feasibility analysis of a military satellite system for detecting hostile rocket launches became a program of research and development on environmental applications of the middle ultraviolet. The scientific studies evolving from this original effort range far wider than the MUV optical studies directly cited (Deepak et al., 1971; Olivero et al., 1972; Sawada et al., 1973; Sawada et al., 1974; Chai and Green, 1976; McPeters and Green, 1976; Green, 1981, 1982; Saunders et al., 1984; Baker et al., 1980; Jackman et al., 1977). Indeed, work initiated originally to estimate interfering backgrounds led to scientific studies of auroral and airglow phenomena (Stolarski and Green, 1967; Prasad and Green, 1971). Our approach made a detailed treatment of the radiation physics of water and other substances possible (Green et al., 1971b; Olivero et al., 1972).

The fact that free radicals chemistry is important in combustion is widely known in military application of MUV. This chemistry is also very important in halon fire suppression. It would seem fitting if MUV techniques could now contribute to an improved understanding of fire suppression mechanisms and assist significantly in the selection of alternatives to halon. The eventual possibility of using MUV spectrography to diagnose the principal fuels in a fire and to use the most appropriate suppressant might also be pursued. In view of the defense origin of the University of Florida MUV program, our efforts to use MUV techniques in fire suppression R&D are a good example of defense conversion.

With the help of a continuum light source with strong MUV intensities such as a high pressure xenon arc or a deuterium lamp, multichannel MUVV spectral systems can be used to study absorption by the gases exiting a flame. This could give an immediate indication of the product gases generated in the fuel-suppressant fire chemistry.

There are other possible applications of these techniques to environmental problems. Whereas the Opsis system uses a scanning spectrometer, a MUV spectrograph-CCD detector-computer system should be advantageous if signals vary rapidly with time. Possible examples include on-line MUV monitoring of incinerator emissions exiting a chimney to determine whether a batch of waste containing toxic generating substances has entered the input. Long-path monitoring of ambient toxics active below 290 nm might also be feasible if instrumental straylight can be minimized, since the stratospheric ozone layer will exclude solar UV. With the help of fiber optics to convey emissions from a hostile environment to the MUV spectrography-computer system in a friendly environment, on-line monitoring of boiler flames, jet combustor flames, and even internal combustion flames might be possible as extensions of measurements illustrated in Figures 3–6.

While this chapter has focused on the University of Florida MUV program, it should be viewed as illustrative of many other cases where intensive studies of high technology military problems expose topics whose science had become stagnant or whose applications have been overlooked.

It is ironic that despite the tremendous head start the United States had from its military and (surrogate military) space program in remote sensing of air pollution, both in the middle ultraviolet and the infrared, the largest commercial applications of these technologies are now centered abroad. One might speculate as to how this came about with the hopes of preserving our technological competitive edge when we have it in the future. From personal observations and involvements the author notes that regulatory pressures in the U.S.A. tended to freeze upon conventional pollutant measurement methods and that promising longer term and more powerful methods had little encouragement from our environmental regulation establishment. In addition our national laboratories were rather slow to become scientifically involved with global environmental topics such as ozone depletion or climate change (Van Hook et al., 1989; Rosen and Glasser, 1991). Furthermore, security concerns probably also impeded our commercial use of technologies evolving from our defense program. Now that the Cold War is over we must recognize these problems and proceed in an organized operations analysis way to maximize competitive advantages that might derive from our continued defense and space programs. How best to do this while maintaining the momentum towards global peace, of course, is a major question addressed by this book on Defense Conversion.

Acknowledgments

The author would like to acknowledge the contributions of Mr. Dale Walter, Dr. Juan Vitali, Dr. Theresa Miller to acquiring Figures 3–8. Discussions with Drs. Richard Schneider, James Winefordner, Ben Smith and David Williams were helpful in the development of the MUVV spectroscopy section. Thanks are also due to Dr. Charles J. Kibert and Applied Research Associates, Inc. for partial support of this work.

References

Baker, K.S., R.D. Smith, and A.E.S. Green, 1980: Middle Ultraviolet radiation reaching the ocean surface, *Photochem. Photobiol.* 32, 367-374.

Bartle, E.R., M. Griggs, and C.B. Ludwig, 1970: Global Surveillance of Air Pollution, Second International Clean Air Congress of the International Union of Air Pollution Assoc., Washington, DC.

Berlad, A.L., 1966: Radiation from Flames and Chemical Perturbations of the Atmosphere, *The Middle Ultraviolet: Its Science and Technology,* A. Green, ed., John Wiley and Sons, Inc., New York.

Bohlin, R., A. Harris, A. Holm, and C. Gry, 1990: The Ultraviolet Calibration of the Hubble Space Telescope IV, *Astraphys. J. suppl.* 73, 413-439.

Brinkman, R.T., J. Dowling, Jr., A.E.S. Green, and A.T. Jusick, 1966: *The Middle Ultraviolet: Its Science and Technology,* A. Green, ed., John Wiley and Sons, Inc.

Chai, A.T., and A.E.S. Green, 1976: Measurement of the Ratio of Diffuse to Direct Solar Irradiances in the Middle Ultraviolet, *Appl. Opt.,* 15, 1182-1187.

Deepak, A., B.J. Lipofsky, and A.E.S. Green, 1971: Interpretation of the Sun's Aureole Based on Atmospheric Aerosol Models, *Appl. Opt.,* 10, No. 6, 1263-1279.

Gaydon, A.G., 1957: *The Spectroscopy of Flames,* John Wiley & Sons, Inc., New York.

Glassman, I., 1977: *Combustion,* Academic Press, New York.

Goody, R.M., 1964: *Atmospheric Radiation, I Theoretical Basis,* Harvard University, Oxford University Press, London.

Green, A.E.S., ed.,1962: *The Middle Ultraviolet and Its Space Applications,* ERR-AN-185 Convair General Dynamics.

Green, A.E.S., 1964: Attenuation by Ozone and the Earth's Albedo in the Middle Ultraviolet, *Applied Optics*, 3, No. 2, 203-208.

Green, A.E.S., ed., 1966: *The Middle Ultraviolet: Its Science and Technology (MUVST).*, John Wiley and Sons, Inc, New York, 390 pp.

Green, A.E.S., and P.J. Wyatt, 1965: *Atomic and Space Physics*, Addison-Wesley Publishing Company, Inc., Reading, Massachusetts.

Green, A.E.S., 1972: Remote Sensing of Air Pollutants, Sound Cassette, References and Visual materials distributed by the Air Pollution Control Association.

Green, A.E.S., 1981: Multiwavelength determination of total ozone and ultraviolet irradiance, Proceedings of the NATO Conference on the Role of Solar Ultraviolet, J. Calkins, ed. (Copenhagen, Denmark, July 28-31, 1980) Plenum Press, New York, 109-120.

Green, A.E.S., 1982: The Penetration of ultraviolet radiation to the ground, *Proceedings of the International Workshop on the Effects of Ultraviolet Radiation on Plants*, L.O. Bjorn and J.F. Bornman, eds., Delhi, India.

Green, A.E.S., D.T. Williams, R.S. Sholtes, and J. Dowling, Jr, 1966: The Middle Ultraviolet and Air Pollution, *The Middle Ultraviolet : Its Science and Technology,* A. Green, ed., John Wiley and Sons, Inc., New York.

Green, A.E.S., A. Deepak, and B.J. Lipofsky, 1971a: Interpretation of the Sun's Aureole Based on Atmospheric Aerosol Models, *Appl. Opt.,* 10, No. 6, 1263-1279.

Green, A.E.S., J. J. Olivero, and R. W. Stagat, 1971b: "Microdosimetry of Low Energy Electrons," presented at Lucas Heights, Australia, published in *Biophysical Aspects of Radiation Quality*, IAEC, Vienna, 79-97.

Green, A.E.S., G.D. Ward, T. Sawada, R.S. Sholtes, J.M. Schwartz, A. Deepak, D. Eisenhart, R.D. McPeters, and D.B. Reller, 1972: Light Scattering and the Size-Altitude Distribution of Atmospheric Aerosols, *Journal of Colloid and Interface Science,* 39, No.3, 520-535.

Griggs, M., C.B. Ludwig, and M.L. Streiff, 1970: Remote Sensing of Air Pollution in Urban Atmospheres, Second International Clean Air Congress of the International Union of Air Pollution Prevention Assoc., Washington, DC.

Grobecker, A., ed., 1975: Climatic Impact Assessment Program, Vols. 1-6, Published by the Institute of Defense Analysis for the Department of Transportation, Arlington, Virginia, September.

Hallstadius, H., L. Urieus, and S. Wallin, 1991: A system for evaluation of trace gas concentration in the atmosphere based on the Differential Optical Absorption, SPIE Vol.1433, Measurement of Atmospheric Gases.

Hallstadius, H., 1993: Monitoring of Air Quality in Urban Areas in Europe by Long-Path UV-D0AS Technique.

Horvath, J.J., K.M. Pamidimukkala, W.B. Person, and A.E.S. Green, 1984: Spectroscopic Observations of Methane-Pulverized Coal Flames, *J.Q.S.T.R.*, 31, No. 3-A.

Huffman, R.E., 1992a: *Atmospheric Ultraviolet Remote Sensing,* Academic Press, Inc., Harcourt Brace Jovanovich Publishers, Orlando, Florida, 319 pp.

Huffman, R.E., 1992b: The New Ultraviolet: Global Space Weather Systems, SPIE Vol. 1764, *Ultraviolet Technology.*

Hufford, D., 1993: *Ultraviolet Index Meeting Agenda,* published by EPA, Nov. 18.

Jackman, C.H., R.H. Garvey, and A.E.S. Green, 1977: Electron Impact on Atmospheric Gases, II, Yield Spectra, *J. Geophys. Res.,* 82, 32, 5081-5111.

Johnston, H., 1971: Reduction of stratospheric ozone by nitrogen oxide catalysts from supersonic transport exhaust, *Science*, 173, 517.

Kaye, R., 1967: Measurement of SO_2 in Jacksonville, FL by long path spectroscopy, *Applied Optics,* 6, No. 4, 776-777.

Koller, L.R., 1965: *Ultraviolet Radiation*, John Wiley and Sons, New York.

Ludwig, C.B., R. Bartle, and M. Griggs, 1968: Study of Air Pollutant Detection By Remote Sensors, NASA Contract Report, NASA CR-1380, General Dynamics Corporation, San Diego, California.

Ludwig, C.B., R. Bartle, and M. Griggs, 1971: Remote Measurement of Pollution, NASA Special Publication, NASA SP-285, U.S. Department of Commerce, National Technical Information Service, Springfield, Virginia.

McClintock, M., T.A. Hariharan, and A. McLellan IV, 1970: Studies on Techniques For Satellite Surveillance of Global Atmospheric Pollution, A Report to the National Air Pollution Control Administration, The University of Wisconsin.

McPeters, R.D., and A.E.S. Green, 1976: Photographic aureole measurements and the validity of aerosol single scattering, *Appl. Opt.*, 15, 2457-2463.

Meggers, W.F., C.H. Corliss, and B.F. Scribner, 1961: Tables of Spectral Line Intensities, National Bureau of Standards, Monograph 32, Part II, Washington, DC.

Miller, T.L. and A.E.S. Green, 1994: A Survey of Techniques for Fire Suppressant Studies, report prepared for Wright Laboratory, Tyndall AFB, FL and published in condensed form in the 5th Halon Conference Proceedings, May 5, Albuquerque, New Mexico.

Molina, M.J. and F.S. Rowland, 1974: Stratosphere sink for chloroflouromethanes, chlorine atom catalyzed destruction of ozone, *Nature*, 249:810-812.

Nader, J.S., 1971: The Status of Remote Detection and Measurement of Gaseous and Particulate Emissions from Stationary Sources, National Environmental Research Center, Research Triangle Park, North Carolina.

Nader, J.S., 1972: Developments in Sampling and Analysis Instrumentation for Stationary Sources, Environmental Protection Agency, National Environmental Research Center, Research Triangle Park, North Carolina.

National Academy of Sciences, 1969: Atmospheric Exploration by Remote Probes, Summary and Recommendations, Final Report on Remote Atmospheric Probing to the Committee on Atmospheric Sciences, National Research Council.

Olivero, J.J., R.W. Stagat, and A.E.S. Green, 1972: Electron Deposition in Water Vapor, with Atmospheric Applications, *J. Geophys. Res.* 77, 25, 4797-4811.

Pamidimukkala, K.M., P.F. Schippnick, D.B. Vaidya, and A.E.S. Green, 1983: "Ultraviolet OH Emissions in H2-Air Diffusion Flames."*JANAF 14th Plume Technology Meeting*, Inkyokern, California, Nov. 15-17.

Pearse, R.W.B. and A.G. Gaydon, 1976: *The Identification of Molecular Species*, Chapman and Hall, London.

Phillips, R., 1983: *Sources and Applications of Ultraviolet Radiation,* Academic Press, New York.

Prasad, S.S. and A.E.S. Green, 1971: Ultraviolet Emissions from Atomic Nitrogen in the Aurora, *J. Geophys. Res.*, 76, #10, 2419-2428.

Rosen, L. and R. Glasser, 1991: *Proceedings of the Conference on Global Climate Change*, American Institute of Physics, New York.

Saunders, R., H. Kostkowski, A. Green, J. Ward, and C. Popenoe, 1984: High precision atmospheric ozone measurements using wavelengths between 290 and 305 nm, *J. Geophys. Res.* 89, D4, 5215-5226.

Sawada, T., B.C. Edgar, M.A. Uman, and A.E.S. Green, 1973: Production of Carbon Monoxide by Charged Particle Deposition, *J. of Geophys. Res.,* 78, 24, 5284-5291.

Sawada, T., E.P. Shettle, and A.E.S. Green, 1974: The Middle Ultraviolet Reaching the Ground, *Photochem. and Photobiol.,* 19, 251-259.

Stolarski, R.S., and A.E.S. Green, 1967: Calculations of Auroral Intensities from Electron Impact, *J. Geophys. Res.,* 72, 3967-3974.

Stolarski, R.S. and R.J. Cicerone, 1974: Stratospheric chlorine a possible sink for ozone, *J. Chem.* 52, 1610-1614.

United States Department of the Interior, 1972: How to Get Started in Remote Sensing, Earth Resources Observation Systems Program.

University of Michigan, 1971: Seventh International Symposium on Remote Sensing of Environment, Center for Remote Sensing Information.

Vaidya, D.B., J.J. Horvath, and A.E.S. Green, 1982: Remote Temperature Measurements in Gas and Gas-Coal Flames Using the OH (0,0) Middle-UV Band, *Appl. Opt.,* 21, 3357.

Valley, S.L., Scientific ed., 1965: Handbook of Geophysics and Space Environments, Air Force Cambridge Research Laboratories, McGraw-Hill Book Company, Inc., New York.

Van Hook, R., P. Fairchild, W. Fulkerson, A.M. Perry, J.D. Regan, and G.E. Taylor, 1989: Environmental, Health, and CFC ORNL, Center for Global Environmental Studies, Oak Ridge, Tennessee.

Williams, D.T. and A.E.S. Green, 1994: A New Continuum-Source Atomic Absorption Apparatus, Rev. Sci. Inst., 65 (11), 3339-3343.

Williams, D. T. and R. N. Hager, 1970: The Derivative Spectrometer, *Appl. Opt.* 9, 1597-1605.

CHAPTER 9

Laser Remote Sensing and Defense Conversion

Vladimir E. Zuev
Institute of Atmospheric Optics
Tomsk, Russia

Introduction

The unique characteristics of laser radiation are being used extensively for military as well as nonmilitary applications. A typical example of "dual use" of lasers is atmospheric sounding, whose data can be applied to help direct gunfire as well as for meteorology and an assessment of the ecological condition of the atmosphere. In this connection it is clear that the use of lasers for remote sensing of the atmosphere should present no problems for defense conversion.

In the former Soviet Union, remote sensing of the atmosphere has been developed mainly at the Institute of Atmospheric Optics Siberian Branch of the U.S.S.R. Academy of Sciences (now SB of Russian Academy of Sciences). These programs encompass all the basic aspects of laser remote sensing, namely:

1. Development of sounding techniques.

2. The use of all main phenomena of interaction of laser radiation with the atmosphere.

3. The use of different lasers for remote sensing in the IR, visible and UV regions.

4. Solution of corresponding inverse problems.

5. Coverage of the maximum number of parameters being sounded.

6. Creation of surface-based, ship-, air- and space-borne lidars.

This chapter describes the most important original results of laser remote sensing of the atmosphere obtained at the Institute of Atmospheric Optics in the previous 25 years of its existence.

Basic Principles of Laser Sounding

Laser sounding is based on the principle of laser ranging, which by analogy to radar is called lidar (an abbreviation of the English words *light detection and ranging*). In a generalized sense the laser in a lidar is used as a pulse source of directed light emission. In contrast to the radio-frequency range, in the light-frequency interval all molecular and aerosol components of the atmosphere are reflectors of the ranging signal, owing to the fact that the wavelengths are short, especially those of visible and UV radiation, i.e., the atmosphere itself produces a lidar return from the entire sounding path. This makes it possible to perform laser sounding in any direction in the atmosphere.

Laser-Sounding Equation

While propagating along the atmospheric sounding path, the laser pulse undergoes absorption and scattering by molecules and aerosols of the atmosphere. The radiation fraction that has been backscattered toward the lidar system can be collected and focused with the help of a receiving telescope onto a photodetector which converts it into an electrical signal proportional to the incident light flux. In the process, the range to any scattering volume along the sounding path is uniquely determined from the time interval since the laser pulse was emitted, because light propagates with a well-known velocity. The detected signal intensity at each specific time depends both on the properties of a specific scattering volume of the atmosphere and on the characteristics of the entire sounding path, i.e., from the lidar to the scattering volume and back. The following functional relation exists between all parameters of a receiving-transmitting lidar system and the intensities of the return signal, detected from different ranges of an extended sounding path (Zuev, 1982):

$$P(r) = \eta P_o A \frac{c\tau}{2} \beta_\pi(r) \, \exp[\, -2\int_o^r \alpha(r\,')dr\,'] \qquad (1)$$

where $P(r)$ is the return power, P_0 is the initial power of the sounding pulse, A is the area of the receiving telescope, r is the range from the lidar to the atmospheric volume which is sounded, c is the speed of light, τ is the pulse width, and $\beta_\pi(r)$ is the interaction cross section in the backward direction. The exponential term characterizes the squared transmission of the atmospheric layer between the lidar and the volume which is sounded, $\alpha(r)$ is the volume extinction coefficient, and η is the calibration constant.

For the most typical situation when the phenomena of Rayleigh scattering, aerosol extinction and molecular absorption are involved in the interaction of the laser pulse with the atmosphere, we have the following relations for $\beta_\pi(r)$ and $\alpha(r)$:

$$\beta_\pi(r) = \beta_\pi^R(r) + \beta_\pi^M(r), \tag{2}$$

$$\alpha(r) = \alpha_R(r) + \alpha_M + \alpha_N(r), \tag{3}$$

where $\beta_\pi^R(r)$ and $\beta_\pi^M(r)$ are the cross sections of Rayleigh scattering and aerosol (or Mie's) scattering in the backward direction, respectively; $\alpha_R(r)$, $\alpha_M(r)$ and $\alpha_N(r)$ are the volume coefficients of Rayleigh scattering, aerosol extinction and molecular absorption, respectively.

Note that the relations (1–3) are written for one and the same wavelength of the sounding pulse. For this reason, we have dropped the wavelength symbol. Interpretation of equation (1) and its solution methods, accounting for the multiple scattering and other fundamental problems, has been treated previously (Zuev, 1982).

Mathematical Formalism and Physical Principles of Laser Analysis of Atmospheric Gases by the Differential Absorption Method

The method of differential absorption was proposed and implemented for the first time by Schotland to retrieve moisture-content profiles (Schotland, 1964). Now this method is widely accepted and realized in two ways: long-path differential absorption lidar (DIAL) and simple DIAL. In the first case the laser system makes it possible to obtain the *mean number density* of the gas which is sounded along the path from transmitter to detector. In the second case the number-density *profile* is retrieved.

The lidar methods of differential absorption make it possible to retrieve the number density profiles of a gas with a prescribed spatial resolution. In this case, aerosols and gas molecules distributed along the sounding path play the role of counter-reflectors. If the wavenumbers v_o and v_1 are close, e.g., differing by only a few or even tens of cm^{-1}, then the quantities appearing in the two sounding equations for the wavenumbers v_o and v_1 and characterizing aerosol and Rayleigh scattering may usually be regarded as identical for both wavenumbers. If, in addition, sounding is performed during a relative short time interval, when temporal variations of the cross sections of interaction of the laser radiation with the atmosphere are negligible, then one can derive the following formula for the concentration profile $N(z)$ of the gas which is sounded:

$$N(z) = \frac{1}{2\Delta\sigma(\Delta v,\, z)} \frac{d}{dz} \left[\ln \frac{P(v_1,\, z)}{P(v_o,\, z)} \right]. \tag{4}$$

Equation (4) shows that the retrieval profile $N(z)$ in a continuous form is feasible when the lidar returns are continuously recorded. However, in actual practice, the lidar returns are recorded in the form of a discrete digital data set, the data being obtained in equal time intervals, Δt, which corresponds to the spatial resolution $\Delta z = c\Delta t/2$. In this case, the following familiar equation arises for the signals detected from the atmospheric volumes at distances z and $z + \Delta z$ along the sounding path:

$$N(\bar{z}) = \frac{1}{2\Delta\sigma(\Delta v,\, \bar{z})\Delta z} \ln \left[\frac{P(v_o,\, z)\, P(v_1,\, z+\Delta z)}{P(v_o,\, z+\Delta z)\, P(v_1,\, z)} \right]. \tag{5}$$

where $\bar{z}$ indicates averaging over each spatial volume with extension Δz.

Sounding of Aerosols

With single-frequency sounding, information can be obtained about the scattering ratio R characterizing the behavior of the vertical stratification of aerosols:

$$R = \frac{\beta_{\pi}^{R}(r) + \beta_{\pi}^{M}(r)}{\beta_{\pi}^{R}(r)} . \qquad (6)$$

The vast majority of results of single-frequency sounding are represented only by profiles of the lidar ratio. In order to obtain profiles of the volume aerosol extinction coefficient, we must know the corresponding profiles of the lidar ratio

$$b(r) = \frac{\beta_{\pi}^{M}(r)}{\alpha_{M}(r)} . \qquad (7)$$

Actually, the laser sounding equation (1) consists of four unknown values: $\alpha_{R}(r)$, $\alpha_{M}(r)$, $\alpha_{N}(r)$ and β_{π}^{M} . The coefficients $\alpha_{R}(r)$ and β_{π}^{R} are taken from the standard model of the Rayleigh atmosphere.

In 1974, at the 6th International Laser Radar Conference (ILRC) in Sendai, Japan, we proposed an original method for determining $b(r)$ together with other parameters (Zuev, 1982). The vertical profiles of the lidar ratio were obtained by the simultaneous application of two lidars using ruby lasers ($\lambda = 0.6943 \ \mu m$)—one situated on the ground for sensing of the atmosphere in the vertical direction, and the other onboard an aircraft flying through the

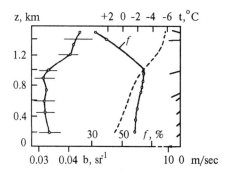

Figure 1. Height dependence of the lidar ratio (left curve), relative humidity f, temperature (dashed curve), and wind velocity vector W.

sensing zone of the first lidar at various heights. Figure 1 gives one illustration of the results obtained, clearly exhibiting the height dependence of the lidar ratio and its correlation with the relative humidity at heights from 0.2 to 1.5 km.

By multifrequency sounding, information can be obtained on important microphysical parameters of aerosols (concentration, size distribution and components of the complex refractive index of particles). In our work (Zuev and Naats, 1978) the inverse problem of determining the microstructure of atmospheric aerosols using laser sounding at several frequencies is considered. An iterative method based on Tikhonov's regularization using a smoothing constraint is described. Numerical experiments based on this method have been used for the optimization of the corresponding experiment. Some experimental determinations of altitude profiles of the backscattering coefficient using a three-frequency lidar sounding system and the corresponding inversion results for particle number density vertical profiles, and tropospheric aerosol microstructure at several altitudes, are presented.

In the monograph (Zuev and Naats, 1983) we considered systematically the methods for solving the inverse problem of lidar sensing of the atmosphere with emphasis on lidar techniques that are based on the use of light scattering by aerosols. The theory of multifrequency lidar sensing, as a new method for studying the microphysical and optical characteristics of aerosol formations, is also presented in detail. The possibilities of this theory are illustrated by the experimental results on microstructure analysis of tropospheric and low stratospheric aerosols obtained with ground-based two- and three-frequency lidars. The lidar facilities used in these experimental studies were constructed at the Institute of Atmospheric Optics.

A rigorous theory for inverting the data of polarization lidar measurements is discussed along with its application to remote measurement of the complex index of refraction of aerosol substances and the microstructure parameters of background aerosols using double-ended lidar schemes. Solutions to such important problems as the separation of contributions due to Rayleigh-molecular and Mie-aerosol light scattering from the total backscatter are obtained by using this theory. Lidar polarization measurements are shown to be useful in this case. The efficiency of the methods suggested here for interpreting the lidar polarization measurements is illustrated by experimental results on the investigation of the microphysical parameters of natural aerosols and artificial smokes using polarization nephelometers.

A brief discussion is also given of the inverse problems related to the remote sensing of profiles of such atmospheric parameters as humidity, temperature, wind velocity, and characteristics of atmosphere turbulence.

Figure 2 shows the vertical profiles of aerosol particle size distribution in the atmospheric boundary layer every 30 m at altitude. These results were obtained using our three-frequency sounding data obtained in 1975 and processed using the algorithms of the method of multifrequency laser sounding.

Below we describe the lidar used in these investigations. It is in a special section of the chapter devoted to lidars and lidar complexes developed at the Institute of Atmospheric Optics.

Sounding of Temperature

Temperature is one of the main properties of the atmosphere responsible for the processes of formation of weather and climate. In principle, laser sounding of the temperature in the troposphere, stratosphere, and mesosphere can be performed by different methods using Rayleigh scattering phenomena, purely rotational, and vibration-rotational Raman scattering. Considerable progress has been achieved during the last few years (Zuev and Zuev, 1992).

Here we consider temperature profiles obtained first with the use of purely rotational spectra of Raman scattering of N_2 and O_2 in the atmospheric boundary layer at the Institute of Atmospheric Optics (Arshinov et al., 1983).

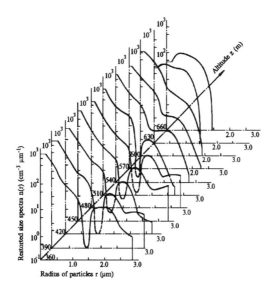

Figure 2.   Altitude dependence of aerosol size spectra.

The basis of this method is the inverse temperature dependence of line intensity of the Stokes and anti-Stokes branches of purely rotational bands of Raman spectrum of N_2 and O_2.

Omitting the mathematical formalism here, it should nevertheless be noted that a serious restriction exists on the laser pulse: namely, the power in the "wings" of the laser frequency corresponding to purely rotational lines of N_2 and O_2 must be suppressed on the order of 10^9. This difficulty was finally overcome, and resulted in Figure 3, which compares lidar-obtained temperature profiles as compared with radiosonde data.

In succeeding years a new version of the Raman lidar has been developed with additional use of the vibriation-rotational spectrum. This new system provides simultaneous profiles of temperature, humidity, and the aerosol backscatter coefficient.

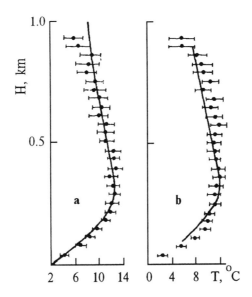

Figure 3.   Profiles of atmospheric temperature obtained with the lidar (dot) and radiosonde (solid line). The length of bars in the lidar profile denotes the calculated values of standard deviations assuming the Poisson statistics to be only a source of errors in measurements of the lidar returns.

Finally, in the last few years we have developed and successfully tested the revised version of a Raman lidar for remote monitoring of atmospheric emissions from plant stacks (Arshinov et al., 1994). As has been already mentioned, these lidars will be described in a separate section of this chapter.

Sounding of Humidity

Humidity, as well as temperature, contributes greatly to the processes of weather and climate formation. The profiles of both parameters are obtained systematically using hydrometeorological observatory networks throughout the world. As to laser sounding of humidity the DIAL technique is the most sensitive, and it has been successfully developed at the Institute of Atmospheric Optics as demonstrated by the paper presented at the 9th ILRC (Zuev et al., 1979). Using a unique lidar (to be described later), we have managed to increase the maximum sounding altitude to 17 km, and the restitution errors of the humidity profiles up to 8–10 km altitude did not exceed 20–30 percent. The maximum sounding altitudes achieved by other experimental groups has not more than 2 or 3 km.

Sounding of Wind Velocity

This quantity parameter is also recorded by conventional world observation networks. Laser sounding of wind velocity is carried out with the use of the Doppler effect or correlation analysis. The first one is of considerable current use due to the possibility of obtaining the profiles of wind velocity over much larger distances, although, since it uses lidars, it is more expensive than the second method.

Our Institute, over a long period of time, has been engaging in the development and improvement of the correlation analysis method, using all of its possible advantages. Thus, for example, introduction of spectral analysis into algorithms to process lidar returns enables one to evaluate the profiles of such turbulent characteristics as intensity of turbulence and dissipation rate of kinetic energy that make it possible to perform the monitoring of dynamics of the atmospheric boundary layer (Zuev et al., 1977).

The potential of the correlation method is illustrated by Figure 4, obtained at our Institute under two typical conditions in the lower layers of the atmosphere, with a spatial resolution of 2–3 m. From this figure we notice that both the magnitude and direction of wind velocity in the case of an arctic front are subject to significant variability in time and space, as compared to an anticyclonic situation. Beyond all doubt, the possibility of obtaining such results favors the correlation method, especially if we take into account its low price compared to the Doppler lidar with heterodyne reception.

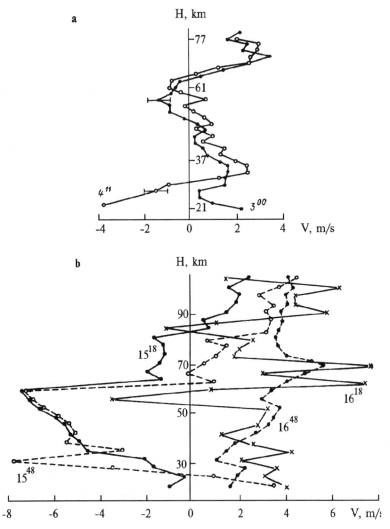

Figure 4. Vertical profiles of wind obtained using a correlation lidar under anticyclonic conditions on June 25, 1986 (a) and with arctic front on December 16, 1985 (b). Local time of measurements are shown by digits near each profile. Right parts of profiles refer to wind directions from 0° up 180°, left parts refer to those from 180° to 360°.

Sounding of Ozone

In recent years, increasing attention has been paid atmospheric ozone. The main reason for this is the very important role of the atmospheric ozone layer in radiation transfer processes and the probable anthropogenic factors affecting this layer. In addition, atmospheric ozone is one of the most active components of industrial smogs.

A network of atmospheric stations currently provides systematic data on the column density of atmospheric ozone as well as on its variations with geographical location and season. The ozone measuring instruments in current use provide information on the atmospheric ozone density profiles. However, certain important characteristics of the ozone layer behavior cannot be studied with standard techniques. These include, for example, short-term variations in the ozone profiles, horizontal inhomogeneities in its concentration and, of course, local peculiarities of the ozone content which may be caused by anthropogenic factors. These features of the atmospheric ozone distribution can be studied using the DIAL technique.

The problem of stratospheric ozone has aroused considerable interest of not only scientists, but also politicians and ordinary peoples of the planet in connection with the "ozone holes." The fact is that disappearance of the ozone layer will result in the death of most, if not all, vegetation, human and animal life on Earth. The ozone layer completely absorbs the destructive short-wave solar radiation, although its average total depth above the Earth is about several mm. For the above reason, much recently progress in the development of unique lidars and lidar complexes has recently been achieved. These lidars have been created to obtain regular vertical profiles of ozone from the ground surface up to altitudes of about 50 km. A decrease in the stratospheric ozone concentration has been recorded, where its maximum exists, as well as a simultaneous irregular increase of concentration in the troposphere and at the ground surface that immediately is a threat to human life, since ozone is toxic to man.

The Institute of Atmospheric Optics has made a significant contribution and continues contributing to the progress achieved. First and foremost, this contribution is connected with the development, creation and operation of unique lidar complexes, which makes it possible to study in detail the physico-chemical mechanism for diverse transformation of ozone when interacting with the molecules of other gases and with aerosol particles in a manner that depends on meteorological conditions and synoptic situations. Undoubtedly, the fundamental results in this field can be obtained only when it is possible to obtain simultaneous information on ozone concentration as well as on concentrations and other characteristics of all main components of the ozone cycle, including dynamics under various meteorological conditions and synoptic situations. It has been just this approach to the problem that has been carried out by the scientists of our Institute. We have obtained unique data on the interaction of aerosol particles of a volcanic cloud (Mt. Pinatubo eruption, middle of June 1991) with the ozone molecules in the stratosphere over the city of Tomsk, beginning with the appearance of clouds on July 6, 1991 up to 1994, inclusive. The possibility of simultaneous measurements of the aerosol profiles and particle size distribution as well as ozone concentration at different altitudes in the stratosphere (using six different wavelengths of the stationary unique lidar complex) will be in a later section. Repeated observation of ozone "microholes" in the stratosphere over Tomsk showed their dependence on the microphysical parameters of the particles. Simultaneously, knowledge of the latter allows one to exclude the influence of aerosols on the value of ozone concentration obtained from its sounding. Figure 5a illustrates the data from simultaneous sounding of ozone concentration and microphysical characteristics of aerosols of volcanic cloud.

From these figures we notice that, for all profiles, the scattering ratio R exceeds essentially the value of unity, thus indicating the presence of considerable aerosol content at corresponding altitudes in the stratosphere over Tomsk. On the other hand, the simultaneously obtained profiles of ozone at corresponding altitudes show the decrease of concentration due to the O_3 molecule adsorption by aerosol particles. Within three days after the appearance of the first tracks of volcanic cloud, namely, on July 9, 1991, the ozone column content decreased by a factor of two (Figure 5b). In January–February 1992, a larger decrease of ozone concentration, as well as larger values of the scattering ratio, were detected.

Lidars and Lidar Stations

For 25 years of its history the Institute of Atmospheric Optics has developed and created a whole complex of lidars and lidar stations; and a discussion of lidars could take a great deal of this chapter. We shall, therefore, restrict our consideration to the information on their applications, and a discussion of only those lidars where any original special features are presented will be considered.

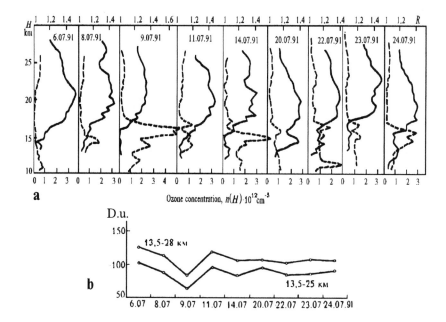

Figure 5. Vertical profiles of lidar ratio R for $\lambda = 353$ nm (dashed line) and ozone concentration (solid line) (a); temporal dependence of integral content of ozone (Dobson units) (b).

Ground-Based Stationary Lidars

1. For the two-wavelength polarization lidar for the sounding of profiles of scattering cross section, horizontal and slant visibility in the atmosphere, determination of the lower boundary and phase state of clouds, sounding of profiles of aerosol particle size distribution, and the obtaining of profiles of all four components of the Stokes parameter, we use ruby lasers ($\lambda = 0.6943$ μm) and Nd-glass lasers ($\lambda = 1.06$ μm) and, if required, their second harmonics. The receiving aperture diameter is 60 cm. The first version of this lidar was created in 1973.

2. For the Raman lidar (1980) developed for the sounding of temperature profiles in the atmospheric boundary layer by pure rotational spectra from Raman scattering of N_2 and O_2, we built and used a copper-vapor laser with average power of 10 W. The receiving aperture diameter is 40 cm.

3. For the DIAL lidar (1985) for sounding of humidity profiles, we used a special ruby laser with a spectral line purity of about 10^{-3} cm^{-1}, with stable

irradiation in the line center of water vapor absorption, as well as the second ruby laser, whose wavelength coincides with the nearest H_2O line in the atmospheric transmittance microwindow. Both lasers generate their pulses simultaneously. The receiving aperture diameter is 30 cm.

4. For the lidar station for sounding of aerosols (the scattering ratio, from 1986; particle size spectra and particle concentration, from 1992; and ozone, from 1989) we use excimer lasers: XeCl ($\lambda = 308$ nm); XeCl + Raman-cell (H_2), ($\lambda = 353$ nm); Nd:YAG ($\lambda = 1064$ nm); Nd:YAG (frequency doubled, $\lambda = 532$ nm) plus Raman-cell (H_2) ($\lambda = 683$ nm). The diameter of the receiving mirror is 100 cm.

5. A simplified block-diagram of the multiwavelength lidar station is shown in Figure 6, and the main parameters are given in Table 1. The table includes properties of the metal-vapor lasers (Cu, Au, Pb) built within our Institute.

For sounding of stratospheric ozone, we use the UV DIAL channel based on the Raman-shifted excimer XeCl laser. Other kinds of lasers are used for multifrequency aerosol sounding. For a sounding channel at the Nd:YAG laser wavelengths, the spectral selection cell consists of spectral dividing mirrors and interference filters. Collimating and focusing lenses are located together with a photomultiplier (PMT) immediately in the focal plane of the receiving mirror. Tropospheric ozone sounding in the daytime and nighttime is best made at wavelengths between 271 and 289 nm. At the other sounding lines, the optical signal is transmitted from the receiving mirror focus to systems of spectral selection, data processing, and recording.

In September 1994 NASA/Langley Research Center flew a spaceborne lidar (Lidar in Space Technology Experiment - LITE) on a space shuttle. It successfully sounded clouds, tropospheric and stratospheric aerosols, characteristics of the planetary boundary layer and the "eye" of a hurricane. The LITE mission used three wavelengths of Nd:YAG laser, namely: 1064, 532 and 355 nm.

At the Siberian Lidar Station in Tomsk it is possible to perform sounding of stratospheric aerosols at wavelengths of 353, 532 and 1064 nm. The 57° satellite orbit inclination makes it possible to encompass the Tomsk territory (56°N). Consequently, the data of ground-based sensing of the stratosphere, obtained in Tomsk, are being compared with the experimental data from LITE.

Up to now there has not been an analogous stationary lidar station, and we continue its development and improvement in different directions. Our main concern is with enhancing our ability to study the destruction mechanism of ozone molecules in the presence of other gases and aerosols, measured simultaneously.

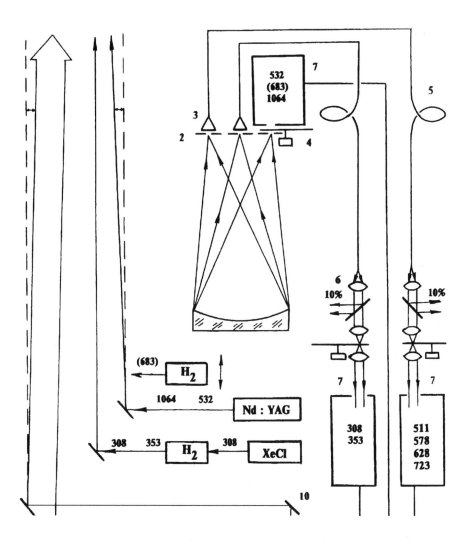

Figure 6. Block diagram of the multifrequency lidar: 2.2 m receiver mirror (1), field diaphragm (2), phocon (3), chopper (4), fiber (5), lenses (6), cell of spectral selection with PMT (7), photon counter (8), computer (9), beam-deflection mirrors (10).

Table 1. Parameters of the MultiFrequency Lidars

Sounding Parameters				
Aerosol scattering ratio				
Microstructure characteristics of aerosol				
Ozone concentration				
Range of sounding heights, km				10–35 km

Transmitter				
Laser	λ, nm	E, mJ	P_{av}, W	f, Hz
XeCl	308	50		50-100
XeCl+Raman-cell (H_2)	353	30		50-100
Nd:YAG	1064	150		10
Nd:YAG + frequency doubler	532	60		10
532 + Raman-cell (H_2)	683	30		10
Cu	511		2	$2.5 \cdot 10^3$
	578		1	
Au	628		2	$2.5 \cdot 10^3$
Pb	723		1	$2.5 \cdot 10^3$

Receiver	
Telescope diameter, m	2.2
Telescope focal length, m	10
Field of view, mrad	0.5-1

Registration	
Photon counting regime	
Spatial resolution, m	50-500
Strobe number	512
Temporal resolution, min	15-30

In addition to the described lidar station we have recently developed and created a lidar for the sounding of tropospheric ozone using a copper-vapor laser and an excimer laser with the parameters given in Table 2 (Zuev et al., 1994). For selected line pairs the ozone numerical simulation was carried out using the differential absorption method. The results are shown in Figure 7.

Table 2. Parameters of Sounding Channel of Tropospheric Ozone

	*Emitting system**			
Laser	λ, nm	E, mJ	P_{av}, W	f, Hz
Cu, doubled yellow	289		~ 0.2	$5 \cdot 10^3$
Cu, sum frequency	271		~ 0.2	$5 \cdot 10^3$
XeCl	308	50		50-100

Receiving system	
Telescope diameter, m	0.3
Telescope focal length, m	1
Field of view, mrad	0.5
Photomultiplier	PMT-130; PMT-142
Spatial resolution, m	100
Temporal resolution, min	~10

* Beam divergence   ~ 0.2 mrad

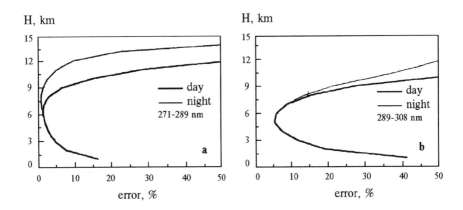

Figure 7. **The result of modeling the errors in sounding of ozone at the wavelength 271 with 289 (a) and 289 and 308 nm (b).**

Mobile Lidars

1. The first mobile lidar designed at our Institute in 1978 was an aerosol lidar of the "LOZA" type analogous to a double-wave polarization stationary aerosol lidar. The five modifications of this lidar differ from one another by constant improvement of all its components and by the increase of potential. A small-size lidar has been developed on the basis of the last (fifth) modification. Lidars of this type were repeatedly used in expeditions within the former Soviet Union and Bulgaria, and they were used to monitor air pollution in Moscow during the Olympic Games.

2. A spectrochemical lidar (1982) made it possible to generate a laser spark at various distances from the lidar by focusing a high-power CO_2- laser pulse at the wavelength of 10.6 μm and with an energy of 200–300 J. One laser spark is formed per pulse via the evaporation of aerosol particles, atomic dissociation of molecules, and/or ionization of atoms. This technique represents a high-power source of information on the element composition of aerosol particles and air molecules along the spark channel. Simultaneously, the spark generates high-power acoustic waves whose detection makes it possible to determine temperature, humidity, and wind velocity in the ambient air.

A focusing system provides laser spark ignition in the atmosphere at distances from the lidar up to 300 m. The spark channel length is usually several meters. By increasing the CO_2- laser pulse energy up to $(1-2) \times 10^3$ W, the spark channel distance can be increased to 1 km. This type of lidar may be successfully used to analyze the element composition of water, minerals and any matter in any state aggregation.

3. The Raman lidar (1986) simultaneously uses the pure rotational and vibration-rotational spectra of Raman scattering as well as the effect of resonance scattering. A copper-vapor laser of 10 W power produced at the Institute is used as a radiation source. The lidar makes it possible to obtain simultaneous information about the profiles of temperature, humidity and backscattering coefficients in the atmospheric boundary layer. This lidar was often used in complex programs for investigating the atmospheric boundary layer together with the "LOZA" lidar and other systems. Actually, this lidar is a Raman lidar for remote monitoring of atmospheric emissions from plant stacks.

This new lidar (Arshinov et al., 1992, 1994) uses a nontraditional optical arrangement. In order to bring sounding radiation from the copper-vapor laser to the lidar transmitter, we use a monofiber waveguide of fused quartz (Arshinov et al., 1992). To make the lidar receiver-transmitter more rigid and stable and, at the same time, not very heavy, we have designed a matrix optical antenna composed of seven identical parabolic mirrors. The central mirror of the matrix makes up the transmitter with the output end of the monofiber from the laser positioned at its focus. Six other mirrors work together to make a single optical receiver. This optical arrangement of the receiver allows the lidar spectrometer entrance slit to be imaged at the output ends of the receiving monofibers from each mirror of the matrix that, in turn, provides narrower instrumental contour of Raman lines isolated with the lidar spectrometer. As a result we managed to build a compact, lightweight transmitter-receiver which, at the same time, is sufficiently rigid. We also took measures to efficiently suppress the crosstalk between Raman lines and the line of unshifted scattering and blocking filter fluorescence.

This version of the Raman lidar has been tested in field measurements to monitor atmospheric emissions from stacks of electric power plants in Ulan-Ude and at a steel production plant in Novokuznetsk. An advanced version of this lidar is currently being used for ecological monitoring by the municipal authorities of the city of Khabarovsk. The diameter of each of seven mirrors is 6 cm, and it uses a copper-vapor laser with the following parameter: $\lambda = 510.6$ nm, divergence of the sounding beam is 0.3 mrad, mean power is 10 W, and pulse repetition rate is 8 kHz. The other parameters, as well as mathematical formalism and the results of numerical simulation, are found in Arshinov et al. (1992, 1994).

4. We also developed a lidar system for sounding of wind speed and direction (1983) based on the correlation analysis method. The sounding is performed when scanning radiation around the vertical axis and recording lidar returns from scattering volumes located in horizontal planes at different altitudes. The lidar was often used in different expeditions within the territory of the former Soviet Union.

5. The long-path DIAL lidar (1979) was based on a continuous wave CO_2 - laser of 10 W power. It was later modified (1985) and became a unique lidar. Its singularity is caused by the use of a nonlinear crystal $ZnGeP_2$, whose technology of production was developed at the Siberian Physico-Technical Institute of the Tomsk State University and has been improved at the Institute of Atmospheric Optics. This crystal possesses properties of harmonic generation of CO_2, CO and other lasers emitting in the wavelength range from 2 to 12 µm as well as summation and subtraction of frequencies. In our new version of this lidar we have used a CO_2 - laser, its second harmonic, and a CO laser. Using combinations of three lasers, it has been possible to obtain synthesized radiation whose frequency coincides (with the accuracy up to

10^{-3} cm^{-1}) with the center of a previously-identified absorption line of one or another gas whose concentration should be determined.

The very complicated technology of crystal growth can yield nonlinear elements with unique characteristics. We give only one example illustrating this statement. Using the best nonlinear element produced at the well-known Kurchatov Institute, our scientists have obtained second harmonic generation efficiency of 83 percent for a CO_2 laser pulse at a wavelength of 10.6 μm, with a duration of 2 ns and with peak power of 10^9 W. This demonstration was described at one of the Optical Society of America's (OSA's) topical conferences (Andreev et al., 1988). In the experiment mentioned, the crystal emitted high radiation energy and showed mechanical strength.

The developed versions of this lidar were used during many expeditions within territory of the former Soviet Union. The last version of this lidar has made it possible to determine the <u>mean</u> concentration between the lidar and the retroreflector for 20 different gases in the atmospheric ground layer, including nitric oxides, ozone, benzene, ammonia, carbon monoxide and other components of the ozone cycle. In 1993, our Institute, under the Agreement with the Korean Institute of Advanced Science and Technology (KAIST), produced and delivered a prototype of this lidar.

Laser-Receiver Lasers

This original type of lidar was based on the idea of using a laser, not only as a radiation source, but also as its receiver. In this case, according to the Kirchhoff law, the radiation and transmission line contours coincide, providing the maximal signal-to-noise ratio. On the other hand, when considering the retroreflector in the version of long-path DIAL as one of external mirrors of the resonant cavity, whose volume includes the atmosphere, we can use an idea of intracavity spectroscopy for high-power amplification of sensitivity to determine gas concentrations. As a whole, this type of lidar increases concentration sensitivity by 4 or 5 orders of magnitude. Thus the distance between the lidar and retroreflector is equivalent to tens of meters instead of, typically, several km.

We have created three types of lidars of this class operating successfully with the ruby, Ar, and CO_2 lasers. We have studied in detail their performance as a function of path length, and found them to be reliable under different meteorological conditions, when the path length did not exceed 10–150 m. Practical application of these lidars is especially promising for determining the concentrations of trace gases in the atmosphere.

Airborne and Shipborne Lidars

The first airborne single-frequency lidar was created at the Institute in 1972 for investigating clouds and aerosols. A ruby-laser was used as the radiation source. Its application for determining the value of the lidar ratio was discussed earlier.

The second version of an airborne lidar was specially created for investigating dynamic processes in clouds within their lower and in the upper boundaries. This lidar is intended for possible measurements of the depolarization of lidar returns to determine the phase state of clouds, and sounding is performed using a pulsed laser with a wavelength of 532 nm and a pulse energy of 50 mJ.

A collective series of modifications of this lidar was created to search for fish shoals in the oceans and seas using polarization effects. A small series of lidars was created, providing effective search capabilities in the daytime and at night. The same lidars are used nowadays for ecological monitoring of aerosols of industrial origin, including investigations of smoke plume transfer in the atmosphere.

Developed at the Institute, shipborne lidars are widely used for studying aerosols above the water surface as well as for detecting and identifying oil films, including their thickness and sounding of the upper water layers as well as measurements of depths of shelves. In all these cases, excimer lasers are used to provide the fluorescence generation in media.

Lasers for Lidars

Over the entire existence of the Institute of Atmospheric Optics, our scientists have been studying fundamental problems, developments and creation of metal-vapor lasers and their application in lidars and other laser systems. In a number of cases our results in this field have been obtained for the first time, including for the use in lidars. This has been already mentioned in this section.

The copper-vapor lasers in this field are very promising. Their use for pumping other lasers, being promising for lidars, is of interest. In particular, it should be noted that we first performed pumping of a very promising sapphire-titanium laser (Bartoshevich et al., 1992) and currently continue this work. Recent results in this field were presented at the 17th ILRC (Maltsev et al., 1994). In this paper, a new class of laser sources using activated crystals is proposed, which use ionized and radiation pumping, in particular, by a high energy electron beam. Also, proposed is simultaneous optical and electron beam pumping for laser generation in one crystal with wide continuous tuning wavelength range in the visible and near-IR regions of spectrum.

Omitting details of the experiment and physical interpretations of the very interesting data obtained, we present the main results of the experimental data shown in Figure 8. The space-time characteristics of the crystal radiation shortwave band (with center at 0.32 μm ... 0.4 μm) are analogous to the same characteristics for the long-wave band (with center at 0.7 μm ... 0.8 μm); that is, we deal with superluminescence in the shortwave band and, probably, with a possible UV laser source.

The totality of characteristics and regularities stated in this paper shows fundamental possibility of Ti-sapphire crystal laser creation in a continuous tuning range from 0.27 μm to 2 μm and at frequencies mixing or doubling in a wider range. In particular, some good lines for a series of components and atmospheric pollutants analysis falling in both crystal luminescence ranges are given in the upper part of Figure 8. For example, the multifrequency laser sensing of aerosols and atmospheric water vapor with the use of the H_2O

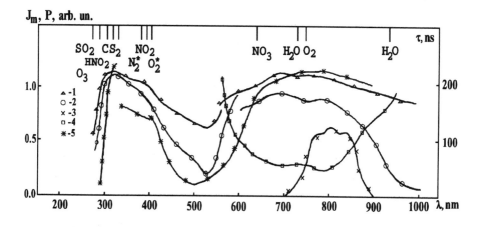

Figure 8. Spectral behaviour of luminescence intensity amplitude J_m for electron energy (1) 430 keV, (2) 600 keV, (3) time constant t_L of emission relaxation, (4) average laser power P by copper laser pumping, and (5) transparency of Al_2O_3:Ti^{3+} crystal.

resonance absorption effect centered at 0.72 and 0.94 μm, as well as monitoring the atmospheric thermodynamic parameters in the O_2 absorption band centered at 0.76 μm should be mentioned. Also, this spectral range involves resonance absorption lines of more than 10 atomic components and their ions and of excited N_2 and O_2 molecules that make this laser promising for use in sensing the upper atmosphere.

Spaceborne Lidars

We present the material of this section based on the text of the authors' invited paper at the 17th ILRC (Zuev, Zuev and Matvienko, 1994), from which it is evident that the title of this paper fully corresponds to the shortened title of this section of the chapter.

The first announcement on the NASA spaceborne lidar development program was reported at a special session of the 9th ILRC in Munich, 1979 (Harris and Greco, 1979). In recent years the corresponding ESA programs have been reported. In the former Soviet Union, and nowadays in the Russian Federation, a special program on spaceborne lidars was unavailable and remains yet to be available. On the initiative of the Institute of Atmospheric Optics and stimulated by the announcement by Dr. M.P. McCormick (NASA Langley Research Center) that scheduled in late 1987 or early 1988, launching of the first spaceborne lidar was to take place, the joint work was begun in 1986 to create the first Soviet spaceborne lidar, "BALKAN-1." The work was done on a contract with the scientific and production association (SPA) "ENERGIA" with participation of the SPA "RADIOPRIBOR." In 1989 the Institute of Atmospheric Optics sent this lidar to SPA "ENERGIA" to be installed onboard the module "SPEKTR" of the Russian orbital station "MIR." The module "SPEKTR" was scheduled to be launched in late 1992 or early 1993, but the launching did not take place up to now because of lack of funding.

We reported on the above lidar at the 15th ILRC held by the Institute of Atmospheric Optics in Tomsk, July 1990. At present the Institute of Atmospheric Optics, together with SPA "Mashinostroenie" and the Scientific Research Institute of Space Instrument Manufacture, is developing a new spaceborne lidar "BALKAN-2" to be installed at the unique space platform "ALMAZ." Simultaneously, consideration is being given to the development, creation and launching of a future spaceborne lidar, "BALKAN-3."

Lidar "BALKAN-1"

The "BALKAN-1" spaceborne lidar is briefly described in (Balin et al., 1990). Here we enumerate the problems which may be solved using the above lidar: a) identification of scattering objects like, e.g., clouds against the background from underlying surface; b) determination of the upper boundary height, and optical properties of clouds; c) investigation of the statistical structure and optical parameters of underlying surfaces, and, in particular, sea and ocean surfaces. The main specifications of the lidar are as follows: energy of frequency-doubled radiation of the Nd:YAG laser is 0.15 J per pulse; its repetition rate 0.2 Hz; receiving aperature diameter of 27 cm; transmitting beam expander aperture is 10 cm in diameter; sounding beam divergence is 30' and the receiver's field of view is 90'.

As was mentioned above, the "BALKAN-1" lidar is scheduled to be launched on board the "SPEKTR" module of the manned space station "MIR," whereas the lidars "BALKAN-2" and "BALKAN-3" are aimed at operation onboard the unique space platform "ALMAZ." For this reason we shall briefly describe below the platform "ALMAZ" and its advantages are compared with those of space station "MIR."

Space Platform "ALMAZ"

This exceptional platform was launched into orbit twice, first as a satellite "Kosmos-1870" (1987) and second as "ALMAZ-1" (1990). A number of instruments including radars, radiometers, and optoelectronic instruments were installed on board this platform; all of them are very essential and effective for remote sensing of the Earth's surface.

At present work is underway to widen the potential of the platform both with respect to improvement of its parameters and in an enlargement of the number of usable techniques, first of all, for remote sensing of the Earth's surface, including the lidar "BALKAN-2.". In this case the platform itself is known as "ALMAZ-1B" (see Figure 9) and its improved technical data are as follows:

1. Orbit: Height is 335–400 km; flight path angle is 73°.

2. Power supply unit: Average power per one revolution is 2300–3300 W; maximum power (under peak loading for 15–20 min) is 8600 W.

3. Data sampling rate: Directly at the SIR–122.8 Mbit/s; through a retranslatingsatellite–10 Mbit/s.

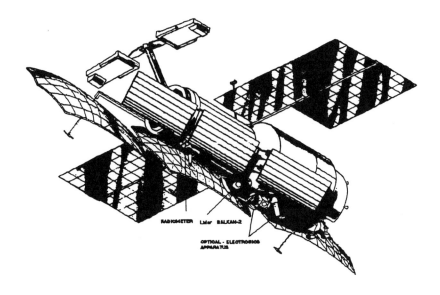

Figure 9. ALMAZ-1B Automatic Space Station.

Lidar "BALKAN-2"

The lidar "BALKAN-2" is a single-frequency lidar, which uses backscattering from the atmosphere, ocean, and from ground surface. Its main parameters are cited in Table 3. This lidar is used for many technical applications, verified by modeling and tests of lidar "BALKAN-1." This allows us to accelerate "BALKAN-2" manufacturing.   In comparison with "BALKAN-1," lidar "BALKAN-2" potentialities are extended in the following directions: pulse repetition rate is increased, scanning is created, and photon counting used for signal processing. In addition, it has the ability to analyze the polarization of lidar returns.

Suggested novelties extend significantly the sphere of problems, solved by the lidar "BALKAN-2." Atmospheric parameters measured by "BALKAN-2" are listed below:

1. Stratosphere (night side of the planet): aerosol backscatter ratio, aerosol scattering ratio, tropopause height, temperature and density profiles.

Table 3. The Main Parameters of Lidar "BALKAN-2"

Output wavelength, nm	532
Output energy, mJ	200
Laser pulse length, ns	10
Beam divergence, arc-sec	30
Repetition rate, Hz	1
Primary mirror diameter, mm	275
Field of view, arc-sec	90
Digitizing rate, MHz	50
Digitizer accuracy, bits	6
Strobe duration of photon counter, ms	2.0 ; 6.67 ; 20
Number of strobes	26
Scanning angle, degrees	±10
Power consumption, W	600
Lifetime, shots	$2 \cdot 10^5$

2. Troposphere: aerosol backscatter cross section, planetary boundary layer (PBL) height, PBL optical depth.

3. Strong ecological danger in tropo- and stratosphere (day and night sides): aerosol backscatter cross section; geographic distribution.

4. Clouds (day and night sides): top and base (for thin heights clouds); scattering cross section, phase composition; geographic distribution, albedo.

5. Ocean (day and night sides): albedo, transparency subsurface layer; height of powerful waves; depth of bottom at the sea shelf; searching of bioproductivity areas (fish shoals, plankton, etc.).

6. Surface (day and night sides): average height of the forest cover; height of the desert barkhans; precise orbit altitude.

Lidar Complex "BALKAN-3"

The lidar complex is an active optical system, which makes it possible to solve the problems of remote sensing of the Earth independently and in combination with the other systems of the station "ALMAZ-2." The multifrequency lidar "BALKAN-3" is intended for remote sensing of atmospheric parameters and different types of underlying surfaces. The lidar applications are the following: ecological monitoring; observations of natural and anthropogenic disasters; climatology; weather monitoring; and land, forest and water cadastres. The planned problems should be solved using the lidar and data processing techniques. The following parameters of the atmosphere and underlying surface are determined:

1. Altitude of the upper boundary of cloudiness and its optical density (water content) and its selection against the background of snow.

2. Vertical distribution of aerosol scattering coefficient in the atmosphere, aerosol particle size spectrum and particle mass concentration.

3. Density and phase composition of cirrus, nacreous clouds, noctilucent (including polar stratospheric) clouds.

4. Vertical distribution of ozone concentration in the atmosphere.

5. Variations of total concentration of gas molecules at orbit altitude along the flight trajectory.

6. Vertical distribution of temperature in the upper troposphere, stratosphere and mesosphere.

7. Density of the stratosphere.

8. Spectral albedo of separate parts of the Earth's surface.

9. Height of sand-hills in the desert and trees in large forest areas.

10. State of vegetation according to the peculiarities of its fluorescence.

11. Depth of shallow parts of sea shelves.

12. Height of energy-carrying waves in the sea.

13. Turbidity of the marine upper layer.

14. Chlorophyll content in the marine upper layer.

15. Presence of oil product contamination in water surface.

16. Density of the bioactive surface layer of the ocean.

Widening of the scope of potentialities of this lidar as compared with those of the "BALKAN-2" lidar is connected with the use of large number of wavelengths of a sounding emitter and with the potential increase of its energy. This is manifested in qualitative increase of the number of measured characteristics of the atmosphere, sea and dry land as well as in the increase of measurement accuracy.

Specifications of the lidar

The lidar consists of a laser multiwave transmitter based on a solid Nd:YAG laser, second-, third-, fourth-harmonic generators and a radiation frequency converter in the hydrogen cell by stimulated Raman scattering, a mirror receiving antenna, a lidar return spectral selector, polarizers, photoreceivers and lidar return detectors. The specifications of the lidar and its main parts are given in Table 4. The measured parameters and body of data are listed in Table 5.

Fundamental Problems of Laser Remote Sensing of the Atmosphere

The material given in this chapter refers mainly to the applied aspects of the program considered. Incidentally, the basis for these aspects always were the results of corresponding fundamental investigations of the Institute of Atmospheric Optics, whereas in the other Institutes of the Russian Academy of Sciences the prime object is to solve the problems of fundamental science. Taking into account the limited space of this chapter, we shall discuss only the general characteristics of the problem and provide a brief description of the main results of the most difficult and complex problem of absorption spectra of atmospheric gases without whose reliable data most problems of laser sounding of the atmosphere could not been solved.

When considering laser sounding of the atmosphere as one of the complex problems of atmospheric optics and keeping in mind that the fundamental problems of the latter, apart from the cited earlier monographs, we give here the references of the library of monographs entitled *Modern Problems of Atmospheric Optics*, consisting of eight volumes published by us between 1986 and 1992 (Zuev and Komarov, 1986; Zuev and Krekov, 1986; Zuev, Makushkin, and Ponomarev, 1987; Zuev and Kabanov, 1987; Zuev, Banakh, and Pokasov, 1988; Zuev, Zemlyanov, and Kopytin, 1987; Zuev and Naats, 1990; Zuev and Zuev, 1992).

Table 4. Specifications of the Lidar "BALKAN-3"

Parameter	Values				
Laser transmitter					
Radiation wavelength, nm	1064	532	355	266	299
Output power, J	0.15	0.35	0.2	0.15	0.15
Pulse duration, ns	3	3	3	3	3
Radiation divergence, mrad	0.25	0.20	0.20	0.20	0.25
Pulse repetition rate, Hz	< 50	< 50	< 50	< 50	< 50
Diameter of transmitting collimators, mm	120	120	120	120	120
Optical receiver					
Band width of interference filter, nm	4.0	3.0	1.5	1.0	1.0
Polarization analysis	-	+	-	-	-
Diameter of receiving telescope, mm	300	300	700	700	700
Viewing angle, mrad			0.5		
Photoreceiver					
Current mode	+	+	+	+	+
Photon counting mode	-	+	+	+	+
System of lidar return processing					
Transmission band of amplifier, MHz			40		
Amplitude resolution of A/D converter, bit			10		
Time resolution of A/D converter, ns			20		
Strobe duration, μs		2.0	6.67	20	
Number of strobes			26		
Lidar					
Power consumption, W			1500		
Weight, kg			1200		
Time for full-load condition, min			40		
Resource characteristics					
Maximum number of radiation pulses			10^8		
Time of standard operation, hours			5000		
Maximum number of lidar switching			2000		

Table 5. List of Measured Parameters and Body of Data
(parameter, indicated by *, are measured at the nightside of the Earth)

Measured parameter	Range of parameter variation	Measurement error	Space resolution vert./horiz.
Cloudiness			
Altitude of upper boundary	50...12000 m	50 m	3/320
Vertical profile of scattering coefficient	5...100 km^{-1}	20%	3/320
Atmospheric aerosol			
Altitude of upper and lower boundaries of aerosol plumes	50...5000 m	50 m	3/320
Vertical profile of scattering coefficient (mass concentration for the visible range in the lower troposphere*)	2...10 km^{-1}	30%	300/1600
	(0.5...5 mg/m^3)	40%	
Particle size spectrum in the upper troposphere and stratosphere*	0.4...1.5 mm	50%	300/1600
*Atmospheric gases**			
Atmospheric density fluctuations at orbit altitude	50%		5000/16000
Vertical profile of ozone concentration	0.3...10.0 ppm	10 60%	500
			5000/16000
Density and temperature of the air*	20...0.003 g/m^3		200
	-50°C...+5°C		2000/16000
Underlying surface			
Spectral albedo for λ=1064, 532, 355 nm	0.3...0.9	15%	-/320
Height of sandhills desert	5...50 m	0.5 m	-/320
Height of trees	5...50 m	0.5 m	-/320
Vegetative state of vegetation			
Depth of shallow carrying waves	3...30 m	0.5 m	0.5/320
Height of energy carrying waves	0.7...8 m	0.5 m	0.5/320
Extinction coefficient of the sea upper layer at λ=532 nm	0.5...0.15 m^{-1}	30%	-/320
Presence of chlorophyll in the sea upper layer above the threshold level	yes/no		-/320
Presence of oil products on the sea surface	yes/no		-/320

The title of each volume coincides with the title of the corresponding problem. The first and sixth volume of this series are published in the English language; the second and fifth ones translated into English and published by the U.S. Department of Defense. The remaining volumes were translated with our permission, in one copy of each volume, by Lawrence Livermore National Laboratory for its internal use.

As to the complexity and difficulty of the problem of spectroscopy of atmospheric gases, this problem, first of all, is connected with extremely hard requirements on the accuracy of determining parameters of individual absorption lines; namely, positions of centers, intensities, and halfwidths; and taking into account their dependence on temperature and pressure, in general, for every individual line. In this case, every vibration-rotational band of any atmospheric gas contains a large number of lines. Moreover, the isotope spectra of every gas have their own peculiarities.

As pointed out, when the first laser was created all the accumulated materials on the parameters of spectral lines, both theoretical and experimental, were unfit for practical use when estimating quantitatively the absorption of laser radiation by the atmosphere. Thus, new theories and new experimental techniques were called for to obtain the true, practically undistorted spectra; that is, the superhigh resolution spectra. At our Institute both directions, over a period of all years of its existence, have been developed successfully, and that has made it possible to obtain the original results satisfying the requirements of current practice, in particular, for a reliable quantitative analysis of laser radiation absorption by atmospheric gases for arbitrary radiation sources, direction of its propagation, and physical parameters of the atmosphere.

Owing to the long-standing cooperation of the Laboratory of Theoretical Molecular Spectroscopy of our Institute with universities in Paris, Dijon, Reims (France) and with the university in Giessen (Germany), the head of the mentioned laboratory, Prof. Tyuterev, has managed to develop the applications of his mathematical models to the creation of theoretical spectra of different atmospheric gases with the use of corresponding normalization factors obtained from the best current experiments at the Universities mentioned (according to the resolution and accuracy of determination of the spectral lines parameter). The main results in this case are given below.

A new approach is proposed to the description of intramolecular interactions based on the generalized method of effective Hamiltonians and generating functions (Tyuterev, 1992), assuming a mathematical model of behavior of quantum states of molecules and spectra of atmospheric gases in the infrared and microwave ranges. The papers present the first qualitative and quantitative explanations of the effect of anomalous variation of parameters of rotational structure of spectra of nonrigid molecules and radicals of H_2O, CH_2, HN_3, etc. when exciting deformation and inversion modes and its physical mechanisms are given (Tyuterev, 1992, Tyuterev, and Starikov, 1982).

A regularity is discovered in asymptotic behavior of rotational energies of nonrigid quasilinear systems, which qualitatively differs from a classical one and explains the experimental data on emission spectra of water vapor (Tyuterev, 1992). On the basis of the developed theoretical models, a better (by one order of magnitude) description is obtained for infrared experimental spectra of molecules with larger effects of nonrigidity. Their application makes it possible to improve the quality of extrapolation for high rotational states by 2 or 3 orders of magnitude as compared to the traditional methods (Tyuterev et al., 1994a).

The mathematical models for the solution of inverse spectroscopic problems have been developed and introduced into the practice of processing the experiment to describe the structure of multiply generate and resonance molecular states, providing fast convergence of the process of solution and its identity (Tyuterev et al., 1986). The developed theoretical models and methods are used to describe, with experimental accuracy, the complex molecular spectra disturbed by the effects of nonrigidity; and random resonances, including the spectra of water vapor (Tyuterev et al., 1994a), methane (Hilico et al., 1994), ozone (Barbe et al., 1994) and other gaseous components of the atmosphere.

In collaboration with Dijon University, the data bank has been created as well as the information system of spectroscopy of novel generation for highly symmetric molecules. The work has resulted in the creation of the bank of high-precision data using a commercial diskette (Tyuterev et al., 1994b) widely used in corresponding institutions. The other major achievement of our theoreticians is confirmed by their fundamental co-authorship in the last version of the database GEISA (Chursin et al., 1994). The joint effort of the authors from the Reims University paper presents the experimental and theoretical investigation of absolute intensities of spectral lines of ozone absorption (Barbe et al., 1994).

The following major achievement in the field of theoretical molecular spectroscopy is connected with the name of Prof. Tvorogov, Chief of the Laboratory of Statistical Optics of our Institute and founder of the original rigorous theory of continuum absorption due to the far line wings of the vibration-rotation bands of molecules of atmospheric gases. This theory has made it possible to obtain reliable quantitative data on the coefficients of continum absorption in the transmittance windows of the atmosphere in the IR spectral range. Successive statements of the theory and results of its applications are given in the monograph (Nesmelova, Tvorogov and Fomin, 1977). A summary of its mathematical bases is contained in the monograph of the author (Zuev, 1982).

Our main experimental investigations of absorption spectra of atmospheric gases have been carried out using a whole complex of the high-resolution laser spectrometers developed and created at our Institute, notably, the intracavity ones with the absorption coefficient sensitivity on the order of 10^{-9} cm^{-1}. The main results of these studies, whose leader is Prof. Sinitsa, consists of, first of all, an original detection of many thousands of absorption lines in such well understood molecules as H_2O, CO_2, HN_3, NO_x and their isotopes as well as tens of new vibration-rotation absorption bands (Bykov et al., 1992a and 1994; Sinitsa, 1992). The second large complex of experimental investigations on photoacoustic spectroscopy of atmospheric gases has been performed in recent years under leadership of Prof. Ponomarev in the field of absorption line shape (width, shifts, etc.) of different gases due to variations of pressure and temperature having direct relation to the problem of remote laser sensing along inhomogeneous atmospheric paths (Ponomarev, 1991, Lazarev and Ponomarev, 1992). The main result of these studies is the creation of a special spectroscopic data bank (Bykov et al., 1992b).

Conclusion

Taking into account the fact that in one chapter it is not practical to cover all the most important results of investigations and developments on the principal direction of studies performed at the Institute of Atmospheric Optics over 25 years of its activities, in concluding this chapter I consider it necessary to present some major achievements for this period, including their official recognition.

First of all, it should be noted that over the above period the scientists of the Institute have published more than 120 scientific monographs and more than 4000 scientific papers in the Russian and English languages; more than 5000 scientific reports have been presented at different national and international conferences; about 200 candidate and 40 doctoral theses have been defended successfully in the physical-mathematical sciences; 8 scientists from the Institute have been appointed full members of the U.S.S.R. Academy of Sciences (nowadays the Russian Academy of Sciences); 15 scientists have become state Prize Winners of the U.S.S.R. and Russia and U.S.S.R. Council of Ministers Prize Winners; one scientists was awarded the title of Hero of Socialist Labour and received the Gold Medal and Order of Lenin.

In spite of the difficult years we experienced due to the conversion, the Institute has preserved its most valuable property—its main intellectual potential and unique experimental base that has made it possible to promote the scientific-engineering cooperation between the Institute and leading firms of the former Soviet Union as well as International Associations.

References

Andreev, Yu. M., 1988: Advances in Gas Analyser Best on IR Molecular Lasers. *Proc. of 3rd Int. Conf. on Adv. Laser Science*, Atlantic City, U.S.A., 3, 193-195.

Arshinov Yu. F., S.M. Bobrovnikov, V.E. Zuev, and V.M. Mitev, 1983: Atmospheric Temperature Measurements Using Pure Rotational Raman Lidar, *Appl. Opt.*, 22, 2984-2990.

Arshinov, Yu.F., S.M. Bobrovnikov, V.K. Shumskii, A.G. Popov, and I.V. Serikov, 1992: Remote Determination of the Composition, Temperature and Velocity of Outflow of the Atmospheric Emission from Plant Stacks Using Raman-lidar, *Atm. and Ocean. Opt.*, 5, 323-328.

Arshinov, Yu., S.M. Bobrovnikov, V.K. Shumskii, and D.I. Shelefontyuk, 1994: Revised Version of a Raman Lidar for Remote Monitoring of Atmospheric Emissions from Plant Stacks. *Proc. 17th Int. Laser Radar Conf.*, Sendai, Japan, 242-244.

Balin, Yu. F. et al, 1990: Spaceborne Aerosol Lidar "BALKAN-1". *Abstracts of Papers of 15th Int. Laser Radar Conf.*, Tomsk, U.S.S.R., 12-14.

Barbe, A. et al, 1994: Experimental and Theoretical Study of Absolute Intensities of Ozone Spectral Lines in the Range 1850-2300 cm^{-1}, *JQSRT*, accepted.

Bartoshevich, S.G., V.D. Burlakov, V.V. Zuev, A.N. Maltsev, and G.A. Scripko, 1992: Source of Tunable Radiation on $Ti^{3+}:Al_2O_3$ Crystals Pumped by a Copper-vapor Laser, *Appl. Opt.*, 31, 7275-7580.

Bykov, A.D. et al., 1992: The Laser Spectroscopy of Highly Excited Vibrational States of HD^{16}O, *J. Mol. Spectrosc.*, 153, 197-207.

Bykov, A.D. et al., 1992: Database of the Shift and Broadening Coefficients for the H$_2$O Absorption Lines in the IR and Visible Regions, *Atm. and Ocean. Opt.*, 5, 604-608.

Bykov, A.D. et al., 1994: The Hot Band $v_1 + 2v_2 + v_3 - v_2$ of D$_2$^{16}O, *J..Mol. Spectrosc.*, 166, 169-175.

Chursin, A.A. et al, 1994: GEISA-PC Manual, Internal Note n. 192, Laboratoire de Meteorologie Dynamique, France.

Harris, J. E., and R. V. Greco, 1979: *Abstracts of Papers of 9th Int. Laser Radar Conf.*, Munich, Germany, 178.

Hilico, J. C.J.-P. Champion, S. Toumi, Vl.G. Tyuterev, and S.A. Tashkum, 1994: New Analysis of the Pentade System of Methane and Prediction of the Pentade Pentade Spectrum, *J. Mol. Spectrosc.*, accepted.

Lazarev, V. V., and Yu. N. Ponomarev, 1992: Measurements of the Hygrogen-induced and Self-pressure-induced Shift of H$_2$O Absorption Lines Near 0.7 µm, *Opt. Lett.*, 17, 1283-1285.

Maltsev, A.N., V.S. Korolev, and V.N. Kukharev, 1994: New Class of Tunable Al$_2$O$_3$:Ti^{3+}-Lasers with Laser and Electron Beams Pumping as a Lidars Transmitters. *Proc. 17th Int. Laser Radar Conf.*, Sendai, Japan, 279-282.

Nesmelova, L. I., S.D. Tvorogov, and V.V. Fomin, 1977: *Spectroscopy of Line Wings*, Novosibirsk, Nauka, 141 pp.

Ponomarev, Yu. N., 1991: Photo-acoustic Investigation of the Interaction of Laser Radiation with Molecules and Intermolecular Interactions in Gases, *Inf. Phys.*, 32, 377-384.

Schotland, R. M., 1964: The Detection of the Vertical Profile of Atmospheric Gases by means of a Ground-based Optical Radar. *Proc. 3rd Symp. on Remote Sensing of the Environment*, Michigan: Ann Arbor. U.S.A., 215-224.

Sinitsa, L. N., 1992: High Sensitive Spectroscopy of Highly Excited Molecular States, *JQRST*, 48, 721-729.

Tyuterev, Vl. G., J.-P. Champion, G. Pierre, and V.I. Perevalov, 1986: Parameters of Reduced Hamiltonian and Invariant Parameters of Interacting E and F_2 Fundamentals of Tetrahedral molecules: v_2 and v4 Bands of $^{12}CH_4$ and $^{28}SiH_4$, *J. Mol. Spectrosc.*, 120, 49-78.

Tyuterev, Vl. G., 1992: The Generating Function Approach to the Formulation of the Effective Rotational Hamiltonian. Simple Closed Form Model Describing Strong Centrifugal Distortion in Water Type Molecules, *J. Mol. Spectrosc.*, 151, 97-129.

Tyuterev, Vl. G. et al, 1994: Calculation of High Rotational Energies of Nonrigid Triatomic Molecules Using the Generation Function Method, *J. Mol. Spectrosc.*, accepted.

Tyuterev, Vl. G. et al, 1994: T.D.S. Spectroscopic Databank for Spherical Tops; DOS version, *JQSRT,* accepted.

Tyuterev, Vl. G., and V. I. Starikov, 1982: New Functional Form of the Dependence of Rotational and Centrifugal Distortion Parameters of Water Molecules on Bending Vibration v_2 *J. Mol. Spectrosc.*, 95, 288-296.

Zuev, V. E., 1982: *Laser Beams in the Atmosphere*, Consultants Bureau, New York and London, 504 pp.

Zuev, V. E. et al., 1977: Investigation of Structure and Dynamics of Aerosol Inhomogeneities in the Ground Layer of the Atmosphere, *Appl. Opt.*, 16, 2231-2235.

Zuev, V. E. et al., 1979: Determination of water vapor profiles in the atmosphere using a tunable ruby laser. *Abstracts of Papers of 9th Int. Laser Radar Conf.*, Munich, Germany, 240-241.

Zuev, V. V., S.L. Bondarenko, V.D. Burlakov, and M.Yu. Kataev, 1994: Lidar for Sounding of Tropospheric Ozone Using a Copper-vapor Laser and Eximer Laser. *Proc. 17th Int. Laser Radar Conf.*, Sendai, Japan, 229-230.

Zuev, V. E., V. A. Banakh, and V. V. Pokasov, 1988: *Optics of Turbulent Atmosphere*, Gidrometeoizdat, Leningrad, 256 pp.

Zuev, V. E., and M. V. Kabanov, 1987: *Optics of the Atmospheric Aerosol*, Gidrometeoizdat, Leningrad, 254 pp.

Zuev, V. E., and V. S. Komarov, 1986: *Statistical Models of Temperature and Gaseous Components of the Atmosphere*, Gidrometeoizdat, Leningrad, 264 pp.

Zuev, V. E., and G. M. Krekov, 1986: *Optical Models of the Atmosphere*, Gidrometeoizdat, Leningrad, 256 pp.

Zuev, V. E., Yu. S Makushkin, and Yu. N. Ponomarev, 1987: *Spectroscopy of the Atmosphere*, Gidrometeoizdat, Leningrad, 247 pp.

Zuev, V.E., and I.E. Naats, 1978: The Method of Multifrequency Laser Sounding of Atmospheric Aerosol Microstructure. In *Remote Sensing on the Atmosphere: Inversion Methods and Applications*, A. L. Fymat and V. E. Zuev (eds.), Elsevier Scientific Publishing Company, Amsterdam-Oxford-London, 257-264.

Zuev, V.E., and I.E. Naats, 1983: *Inverse Problems of Lidar Sensing of the Atmosphere*, Springer Verlag, Berlin-Heidelberg-New York, 260 pp.

Zuev, V. E., and I. E. Naats, 1990: *Inverse Problems of Atmospheric Optics*, Gidrometeoizdat, Leningrad, 286 pp.

Zuev, V. E., A. A. Zemlyanov, and Yu. D. Kopytin, 1987: *Nonlinear Optics of the Atmosphere*, Gidrometeoizdat, Leningrad, 256 pp.

Zuev, V. E., and V.V. Zuev, 1992: *Remote Optical Sensing of the Atmosphere*, Gidrometeoizdat, St. Petersburg, 232 pp.

Zuev, V. E., V. V. Zuev, and G.G. Matvienko, 1994: Russian Space Lidars and Stationary Lidar Complexes for Support of a Satellite Observations. *Proc. 17th Int. Laser Radar Conf.*, Sendai, Japan, 345-348.

CHAPTER 10

Global Positioning System: A Successful Example of Dual-Use Technology[1]

Helmut Hellwig
USAF Office of Scientific Research
Washington, DC

E. David Hinkley[2]
Science and Technology Corporation
Palos Verdes, California

Foreword

The U.S. Global Positioning System (GPS), made possible by technologies developed under basic research grants from the U. S. military, has led to a commercial industry that promises to be a major factor in the U.S. aerospace economy for many years to come. This chapter describes the key technological aspects of GPS and how and why they were supported through the research and development phases. Also covered is the crucial role of industry in recognizing the inherent value of GPS, and how the private sector "leapfrogged" the military in providing small, portable, and low-cost instrumentation available to the "average" person. GPS is, indeed, an excellent and timely example of Defense Conversion and Dual Use.

Introduction

Since the early days of world exploration, beginning with Columbus and the voyages of Magellan and Cook, navigation and time have been inseparable. Advances in timekeeping have been exploited nearly

---

[1]This chapter is based in part on a presentation by H.H. at the International Symposium on Defense Conversion in Orlando, Florida on 17 February 1994.
[2]Also Chairman, Aerospace Policy Committee, Institute of Electrical and Electronics Engineers (IEEE).

instantaneously for better position determination and mapping. Systems for globally networked time, satellite-based global navigation (including GPS and GLONASS[3]), and high data-rate global communication via satellites, cable, and optical fiber are currently being deployed following this historical pattern.

Current applications of GPS generally fall into two classes: *position sensing* and *information extraction*. *Position sensing* includes locations of transport vehicles (e.g., airplanes—including air traffic control, ships, trucks, buses, and automobiles), exploration (oil and gas, archeology, hiking, etc.), and public safety (search and rescue). Examples of applications for which *information extraction* is the goal include remote-sensing image rectification, environmental studies (land use planning, water quality management, atmospheric and air quality measurements, remediation, etc.), wildlife management (e.g., conservation, zoological research), farming (slope analysis for drainage, seeding, fertilizing, pesticide applications), earth movement, flood plain mapping, and time-synchronization of data for packet transmission.

Commercial Attractiveness Of GPS

In this section we focus on the factors that have made GPS such a commercially attractive undertaking: affordability, reliability, and performance.

Affordability and Reliability

In recent years, affordability and reliability have become more important than performance, and, in most cases, either one of them is actually the dominant driving force. It is interesting to note that performance (global, meter-accuracy) was the military driving force for GPS. However, once established, GPS provides a common service to a substantial number of users with geographic distributions that range from local to global. Once operational, the prime objective of any network such as GPS is to remain operational and to never disappoint a (dependent) user. Thus, the primary driver in network operation is reliability. Reliability concerns about GPS may have been originally motivated by national security, but today reliability is driven by safety, business, and other factors.

For many users the primary driver is affordability. The user will seek alternatives if the required performance cannot be afforded. One must keep in

---

[3]Global Orbiting Navigation Satellite System of Russia.

mind that affordability is a relative term; for example, the user will not acquire a clock, oscillator, receiver, or related subsystems if their acquisition or operational costs approach the cost of the host system or platform. Many years ago a proposal for an aircraft collision avoidance system floundered because the cost of a cesium clock exceeded that of some small airplanes! Once deployed and operational, the GPS system spawned (as was pointed out above) an ever-increasing multitude of uses. As a result, the GPS receiver market in 1994 was around $600 million globally, and by the year 2000 the market is expected to be between $5 billion and $20 billion, which will make it comparable to, or greater than, the very successful U.S. space communications market. GPS receivers, which in 1989 cost $3,000 each, have now been replaced by those of higher capability which now cost less than $400. Spatial accuracies range from 15 meters to better than 1 meter (in the differential mode), with position updates every second. There has been an interesting parallelism with the commercial acceptance of personal computers: Once the prices of GPS receivers and PCs dropped below the order of $1,000, the "ordinary" citizen could justify purchasing one. Clearly, as with PCs, GPS will play an important role in this *Information Age* we now live in.

Performance

Military performance needs have driven the fundamental capabilities of time/frequency, position determination, and communication/command/control/intelligence (C^3I) systems, such as GPS, and have played a major role in device and network research and development. The maturing of deployed systems in all three application areas together with their coordinated use has very recently revolutionized warfare, as demonstrated in the Gulf War of 1991. Because the military need for massive destruction by conventional or nuclear weapons was rooted in lack of precision as well as lack of knowledge about the battlefield, the new capabilities offered by time-based navigation and communication allow warfare to concentrate on military targets and avoid collateral damage. GPS proved its worth in Desert Storm as commercial firms started selling small, affordable receivers to the U. S. forces for their use in military operations (an interesting example of "spin-on"). Today's GPS receivers have wide commercial use in civilian and military aircraft, in large ships as well as small watercraft and, increasingly, in trucks, automobiles, search and rescue, and for individual (personal) uses.

GPS Technology Requirements

The key technologies on which GPS is based are:

- *Timekeeping:* Accurate and precise clocks
- *Computational capability:* Fast, small, affordable computers
- *Space access:* Appropriate launch vehicles and control systems

We shall only focus on the history of timekeeping in that it is unique to GPS, whereas computational capability and access to space are common to numerous other space-based systems.

Precision Clocks

The period from 1950 to 1970 saw great progress in stable atomic clock development at Massachusetts Institute of Technology (MIT) and Harvard University, later in government laboratories and, with DoD funding, in U. S. industry. In 1964 the first commercial atomic clock became available.

Atomic clocks and quartz crystal oscillators are essential for the functioning of today's technological world, and they have been in practical use for many decades for accurate and high-precision delivery of time and frequency signals. Despite recent scientific breakthroughs that have led to experimental devices based on stored neutral atoms or trapped ions, as well as on lasers, the instruments that still dominate the field employ just four different technological approaches: quartz crystals, rubidium gas cells, cesium beams, and hydrogen masers. Details of their operational principles may be found in the literature (Vanier and Audoin, 1988, and Hellwig, 1985). Such clocks and oscillators are complex instruments combining physical resonance phenomena with electronic means of RF and microwave signal generation, resonance interrogation, signal detection, and feedback and control circuitry. More so than with most other instruments, the truly random instrumental variations have been analyzed, understood, and reduced to a level where frequency precision is limited by environmental factors which are largely ignored in less precise instrumentation. Depending on the particular environmental conditions, clocks and oscillators will perform at often substantially degraded levels as compared to the ideal conditions of a laboratory environment. Thus anyone concerned about the performance of systems relying on clocks and oscillators in more demanding environments such as shipboard, aircraft or, in general, any uncontrolled environment, should carefully consult not only the manufacturers' specifications but also the applicable literature (Walls and Gagnepain, 1992, Riley, 1992, Audoin *et al.*, 1992, Mattison, 1992, and Hellwig, 1990).

Position Determination

The second subject of our discussions is the use of time and frequency in the determination of position and motion of objects; often, this area of application is referred to as navigation. Celestial navigation makes use of the comparison between actually observed star (or sun) positions and their time-ordered prediction with reference to an agreed-upon reference location on the globe (e.g., Greenwich). Radio navigation determines position by measuring distances from synchronized reference transmitters (of known location) through a measurement of the arrival time of the emitted electromagnetic signals. Motion can be determined by either repetitive position determinations or by measuring Doppler shifts in the frequency of the received, as compared to the emitted electromagnetic signals.

Locating an object such as a land-based vehicle, an airplane, a ship, or a spacecraft, requires a knowledge of three coordinates—longitude, latitude, and altitude. If all three are unknown, the distances to three reference radio transmitters will provide the needed information. The ranges between an object and the reference transmitters can be obtained by measuring the time of arrival of signals. Thus time enters as a required fourth coordinate in radio navigation. Because radio signals travel at the speed of light, approximately 300 m/μs, a timing accuracy of 10 ns yields a corresponding position accuracy of 3 m.

Using state-of-the-art cesium clocks, time can be predicted to within 10 ns/day after synchronization (equalizing time) and syntonization (equalizing rate or frequency). Such highly accurate time means that a vessel can establish its position with a cesium clock to within 3 m if only one day has passed since synchronization with the master clock. After a month of sailing, the ship's navigator would be able to find the vessel's location only to within 100 m; but to limit the maximum error, periodic re-synchronization to within 10 ns (via radio or laser links) will ensure retention of the 3 m positioning capability. Not all objects need to be located with such precision, but a surprising number do, as shown in Table 1. Some pleasure-boat operators, for example, may be satisfied with knowing their position to within about 1000 m, or an approximate timing accuracy of 3 μs. Military users, on the other hand, must know the whereabouts of aircraft much more precisely, to within 1 to 10 m, essentially requiring a clock accuracy of 3 to 30 ns.

Table 1. Timing Requirements for Navigation

Type of Platform	Desired positioning accuracy (m)	Required timing accuracy (ns)
Private boats and military vessels	100	300
Search and rescue	100	300
Commercial aircraft (in flight)	10-100	30-300
Deep space probes	10-100	30-300
Location of radio emitters	10	30
Natural resource exploration	10	30
Commercial aircraft (landing)	1-10	3-30
Military aircraft	1-10	3-30
Spacecraft (near Earth)	1-10	3-30
Geophysics	<1	<3

For the near ultimate in navigation, each NAVSTAR satellite comprising the space-based GPS uses several redundant cesium and rubidium clocks. The on-board atomic clocks make each GPS satellite relatively autonomous, ensuring timing accuracy to the nanosecond level, or positioning accuracy on the order of feet, with only infrequent re-synchronization. Twenty-four NAVSTAR satellites now orbit Earth. Reception of signals from four satellites simultaneously allows a user to obtain all four dimensions: the three spatial coordinates, and time. The user does not even need a precision clock! Most users, though, "carry" a clock either as part of a GPS receiver or in addition to the receiver. Knowledge of time speeds up acquisition of the GPS signal and also permits continued operation during periods of unavailability of the GPS signal (e.g., in strong electromagnetic interference, moving through a tunnel, etc.).

In order to achieve ultimate positioning accuracy, other parameters affecting the frequency and timing of the signals as received at the user location must be calculated or measured: spacecraft motion, ephemeris, ionospheric and tropospheric delays, antenna and receiver delays. It should be noted that the time and frequency signals are substantially affected by effects predicted by the theory of general relativity: the partly compensating effects of gravitational potential and second-order Doppler necessitate an on-ground offset of the satellite clocks of 4.45×10^{-10} (low in frequency) in order for them to appear "on frequency" when orbiting as measured from the surface of the Earth.

Conclusion

In this chapter we have described some of the key technologies, developed under research funding from the U.S. military, which have enabled the GPS system to be built. Reasons for the strong commercial attractiveness of GPS equipment and detailed descriptions of some uses of GPS were also given. Nowadays everyone has first-hand exposure to the pervasive nature of time and frequency. A rough estimate indicates that the number of atomic clocks serving communication and navigation worldwide is in the tens of thousands. The number of precision quartz crystal oscillators may be estimated to be on the order of one million. These numbers are small compared to the total of all time/frequency devices— if wristwatches are included, the number may well exceed one billion. The ultimate pervasiveness of GPS may rival or even exceed this!

The implications of GPS both from the standpoint of foreign policy as well as industrial commercialization are enormous. First, the cost of research which led to GPS was only a drop in the bucket when compared " .... with the enormous investment required to develop a useful new technology: satellites, microelectronics, time transfer techniques and modern data processing methods" (Kleppner, 1994). Indeed, the costs of developing and operating the constellation of 24 satellites which constitute GPS have been in the billions of dollars, whereas research costs were in the tens of millions of dollars. Second, if we are correct in assuming that the original reason for the atomic bomb was a lack of precision for military action, then GPS has effectively eliminated the need for nuclear weapons. Third, GPS owes its explosive commercial potential to the fact that military needs established a high-performance, reliable satellite network at very substantial cost; however, once operational, access to GPS has become very affordable. In fact, since the cost of GPS receivers has dropped below that of other positioning technologies, while offering the same or higher reliability and performance, it is rapidly becoming the technology of choice. By the year 2000, GPS equipment will represent a $5-20 billion industry, and we expect that GPS will represent a major aerospace market well into the 21st century. Indeed, GPS appears destined to becoming the primary technology for global navigation.

References

Audoin, C., N. Dimarcq, V. Giordano, and J. Viennet, 1992: Physical Origin of the Frequency Shift in Cesium Beam Frequency Standards-Related Environmental Sensitivity, *IEEE Trans. on Ultrasonics, Ferroelectrics, and Frequency Control*, 39, 412-421.

Hellwig, H., 1985: Microwave Frequency and Time Standards, Chapter 10 in *Precision Frequency Control*, E. A. Gerber and A. Ballato, eds., Academic Press, New York.

Hellwig, H., 1990: Environmental Sensitivities of Precision Frequency Sources, *IEEE Trans. on Instrumentation and Measurements*, 39, 301-306.

Kleppner, Daniel, 1994: Where I Stand, a brief review of the development of the GPS system, *Physics Today*, January, 9-11.

Mattison, E. M., 1992: Physics of Systematic Frequency Variations in Hydrogen Masers, *IEEE Trans. on Ultrasonics, Ferroelectrics, and Frequency Control*, 39, 250-255.

Riley, Jr., W. J., 1992: The Physics of the Environmental Sensitivity of Rubidium Gas Cell Atomic Frequency Standards, *IEEE Trans. on Ultrasonics, Ferroelectrics, and Frequency Control*, 39, 232-240.

Walls, F. L., and J. J. Gagnepain, 1992: Environmental Sensitivities of Quartz Oscillators, *IEEE Trans. on Ultrasonics, Ferroelectrics, and Frequency Control*, 39, 241-249.

Vanier, J., and C. Audoin, 1988: *The Quantum Physics of Atomic Frequency Standards*, Adam Hilger, Philadelphia, Pennsylvania.

CHAPTER 11

Fire Suppression

Charles J. Kibert
Wright Laboratory, U.S. Air Force and
University of Florida

Introduction

The phaseout of certain Halon fire suppressants has led to the development of numerous innovative approaches to fire suppression as well as to a degree of degradation in performance for the current industry offerings of gaseous Halon replacements. Industry offerings for occupied facilities have been generally limited in the United States to chemicals that are supported by the National Fire Protection Association (NFPA): HFC-227ea, HFC-23, C_4F_{10}, R-595 (blend of HCFCs), and IG-541 (blend of inert gases and CO_2). These have undergone extensive industry and military testing for a wide variety of applications, and although adequate for many applications, each has performance characteristics that will force the using community to carefully assess the criteria for each application. A recent development has been the emergence of the fluoroiodocarbon family of chemicals as potential across-the-board drop-in replacements for Halons 1211 and 1301. Extensive testing on CF_3I has indicated that it is virtually identical to Halon 1301 in fire suppression performance and toxicity. C_3F_7I is being tested as a replacement for Halon 1211 and has most of the same performance characteristics. Non-gaseous solutions are also being identified, such as aerosols, to include solid particulate aerosols, water mists, and halocarbon mists. This paper describes U.S. Air Force efforts to find replacements for Halons 1211 and 1301 with test information to date.

The U.S. Air Force Fire Protection and Crash Rescue Section, a group within Wright Laboratory, has responsibility for Halon 1211/1301 replacement in occupied critical facilities, aircraft cargo spaces, aircraft and facility portable fire extinguishers, and flightline fire extinguishers. These programs were initiated in 1988 and have had several phases that parallel developments in industry and environmental regulation directives of the U.S. Environmental Protection Agency (EPA) such as the Significant New Alternatives Policy (SNAP) that regulates chemicals allowed to serve as replacements for all Ozone Depleting Substances. A Halon 1211 program that had started in 1988 and had selected a replacement suffered serious setbacks when the replacement, perfluorohexane, was limited by the EPA in its Interim SNAP Notice to critical military applications with restrictions on training. These restrictions proved severe enough that the Air Force was forced to reinitiate the research program and search for a replacement in classes of chemicals that were in limited production for laboratory uses.

Advanced Flooding Agents

The program to replace Halon 1301 in occupied facilities and aircraft cargo spaces is called the Advanced Flooding Agent Program. The program has a dual strategy. First, replacements offered by industry and approved in the NFPA 2001 draft Standard have been part of a testing program that has evaluated the agents for Air Force applications using Air Force criteria. Second, CF_3I, a newly emerging possible drop-in replacement for Halon 1301 is being tested in a cooperative industry/military venture. The criteria for the replacement agents are important and vary among the military services for various applications. Table 1 contains a list of these criteria for aircraft, facilities, armored vehicle, and ship applications.

Table 1. Criteria for Halon 1301 Replacements for Military Applications

Criteria	Occupied Facilities	Aircraft Cargo	Acft Dry Bays, Nacelles	Vehicle Engine	Vehicle Crew	Shipboard Occupied
Toxicity	3	1	1	1	3	3
Space/Weight	1	2	3	3	3	2
Cost	3	2	1	1	1	2
Explosion Suppression	1	1	3	1	3	1

1=Minimal Problem	2=Moderate Problem	3=Significant Issue

First Generation or NFPA 2001 Approved Agents

The NFPA 2001 approved agents tested in medium scale scenarios were HFC-227ea, HFC-23, $C_4F_{10,}$ and HCFC Blend A (NAF S-III). A fifth NFPA approved agent, Inergen, a blend of carbon dioxide and inert gases, will be tested in a large-scale facility along with the other agents. The results of the cup burner and medium-scale testing are shown in Table 2 along with NFPA recommended design concentrations.

A similar pattern of behavior occurs for inertion testing with Halon 1301 having 2–3 times the inertion capability on a weight basis (Table 3).

Table 2. Test Results on NFPA 2001 Approved Agents

Agent	Cup Burner, v/v%	Medium Scale, v/v%	NFPA Design, v/v%	Weight Equivalence*
Halon 1301	2.9	4.0	5.0	1.0
HFC-227ea	5.9	8.6	7.0	2.5
HFC-23	12.4	16.0	16.0	1.9
FC-3-1-10	5.9	6.5	7.0	2.8
HCFC Blend A	10.2	12.5	8.6	1.9

* Relative to Halon 1301

Table 3. Explosion Inertion Performance of NFPA 2001 Chemicals

Agent	Laboratory, v/v%	Large Scale, v/v%	Weight Equivalence*
Halon 1301	6.1	6.6	1.0
HFC-227ea	11.5	11.5	2.0
HFC-23	20.2	20.5	1.9
FC-3-1-10	9.8	10.7	2.7
HCFC Blend A	--------------------------------not tested--------------------------------		

*Relative to Halon 1301

An issue of continuing concern in the replacement of Halon 1301 has been the decomposition products that occur because of the agent chemistry and slower fire suppression by the replacement compounds. Table 4 shows the relatively high levels of acid gases and other problematic toxics compared to Halon 1301.

CF₃I Agent Research and Development

The lack of a clear choice for replacing Halon 1301 and the penalties associated with each alternative resulted in the re-examination of non-production scale chemicals as potential solutions. One of these, CF_3I, had been thought to be unsuitable in terms of toxicity and storage stability. However, not a great deal of research had in fact been conducted on this chemical, and its powerful fire suppression characteristics made it a prime candidate for further study. A comparison of some of the characteristics of Halon 1301 and CF_3I are shown in Table 5. Note that in fire suppression, explosion inertion, and volumetric efficiency, CF_3I is equal to Halon 1301.

Table 4. Decomposition Products of NFPA 2001 Agents Compared to Halon 1301

Agent	HF, ppm	CO, ppm	CO_2, ppm	COF_2, ppm
Halon 1301	0-60	0-450	0.2-2.0	0
HFC-227ea	0-700	0-1800	0.2-2.0	0-12
HFC-23	40-1400	100-700	0.3-2.0	0-14
FC-3-1-10	0-600	0-900	0.2-1.7	0-19
HCFC Blend A	5-1400	0-3000	0.2-1.7	1-5

Table 5. Comparison of Halon 1301 and CF₃I

Parameter	Halon 1301	CF_3I
Boiling Point, °C	-57.8	-22.5
Liquid Density, g/milliliter	1.58@20°C	2.36@-42°C
Molecular Weight, g/mole	148.91	195.91
Extinguishing Concentration, v/v%	2.9	3.0
Inertion Concentration, v/v%	6.2	6.5

Solid Particulate Aerosol Fire Suppressants

A new class of fires suppressants, known generically as solid particle aerosol fire suppressants, having superior volumetric efficiency, low initial and life cycle costs, low toxicity, no known global atmospheric environmental impacts (ODP/GWP), and with the potential for a wide variety of applications, is being developed via a joint program between the private sector and the U.S. Air Force. The research program consists of developing solid compound formulations that, when pyrotechnically initiated, generate powerful fire suppressant aerosols that behave as lighter-than-air gases. Preliminary indications are that these aerosols are up to six times more powerful as fire suppressants than Halon 1301 on a mass basis. Using a solid, gel, or powder as the starting point for generation of an aerosol eliminates the need for piping and pressure cylinders, creating a potential for application in a wide variety of fire suppression roles: facilities, aircraft, portable rapid deployment shelters, fuel storage tanks, battery/UPS rooms, unmanned telecommunications facilities, and armored vehicle engine compartments. The speed of aerosol formation is dependent on system design and configuration. Mechanisms of aerosol fire suppression are discussed and the most recent test results are presented.

The search for replacements and alternatives for the Halon family of chemical fire suppressants has coincided with the development of novel materials and techniques that provide new options for fire protection. One class of materials that has good potential for filling several roles formerly performed by Halons is solid particle aerosols. Originating as solid materials, micron-size solid aerosol particles are generated via combustion of a combination of oxidizer, reducer, and binder. The U.S. Air Force is pursuing the development of solid particle aerosol fire suppressants both for their potential as an alternate to Halon 1301 fire protection systems and as the fire method of choice for certain applications. *Encapsulated Micron Aerosol Agents (EMAA)* is the title given by the U.S. Air Force to this research program.

Aerosol Science

Aerosol science or particle mechanics draws from several scientific disciplines to formulate the science that underlies its principle areas of research. Understanding the thermodynamic interaction of aerosols with fire propagation mechanisms is a new subset of aerosol science that has the potential for creating a wide variety of fire suppression options.

Aerosol refers to a system of liquid or solid particles suspended in a gaseous medium. Aerosols are generally stable or quasi-stable systems with the bulk of particles being ≤ 1 μm in diameter. Aerosols affect visibility, causing some degree of obscuration, especially in the size range of 0.1 to 1 μm. The collective term *particulate* is commonly used to refer to both solid and liquid (particle and droplet) components of an aerosol when differentiation of phases is unimportant. Several common aerosols are fumes, smoke, mists, fog, and haze (Spurny, 1986).

Fumes resulting from chemical reactions may become aerosols via agglomeration of molecules due to high Brownian diffusion rates. Particle sizes vary greatly as a function of temperature and gas volume. Once formed, separation and rediffusion become very difficult. Metal fumes have particle sizes on the order of 0.5 μm.

Smoke is an aerosol resulting from combustion of fuels. Like fumes, smoke has particle sizes on the order of 0.5 μm.

A solid aerosol particle can have a wide variety of shapes but is often considered to be virtually spherical for analysis purposes. The radius, r, or the diameter, d_p, can therefore have several definitions. Because most studies utilize the projected image of the particles, the dimension of the particle is related to the analysis technique. The *Feret diameter* is the maximum edge-to-edge distance of the particle, while the *Martin particle diameter* is the length of a line that separates the particle into two portions of equal area. The *aerodynamic diameter*, d_{ae}, is the diameter of the spherical particle of unit density that would exhibit the same aerodynamic properties as the aerosol particle. The *Stokes' diameter*, d_{St}, is the diameter of a sphere that would have the same density as the aerosol particle.

Based on the state of the suspended substance, liquid or solid, dispersion and condensation aerosols are differentiated. Dispersion aerosols are formed by the atomization of solids and liquids, while condensation aerosols are formed via the condensation of superheated vapors or chemical reactions in the gaseous phase. In general, dispersion aerosols are coarser than condensation aerosols.

Aerosol Dynamics

The dynamics of aerosols are important considerations for two reasons. First, the ability of the particles to remain suspended is obviously connected to the particle size and the residence time of the fire suppressant. Second, aerosols, if they are to replace gases in certain applications, must be able to flow around obstacles.

The suspension time of an aerosol is governed by Stokes' Law which predicts the terminal velocity of the particle through air and, consequently, the residence time of the aerosol. As particle size increases, the inertial and viscous forces of the fluid come into play. For larger particle sizes, the Stokes' Law predictions must be recalibrated for viscous drag forces.

The ability of the aerosol to flow around obstacles is necessary for the fire suppressant to be able to penetrate around and behind obstacles and into small spaces. The larger the particle size, the less able the particle will be to change direction, causing it to impinge on the obstacle. This property is called *impaction* and is governed by Stokes' number or the *impaction parameter*, the dimensionless ratio of the particle stopping distance to the characteristic dimension of the obstacle or flow geometry (Billings and Gussman, 1976).

Dispersion of an aerosol fire suppressant is an important consideration in evaluating effectiveness. The dispersion characteristics of the aerosol are a function of the aerosol particle size. In general, aerosol particles vary widely in size, from 1 nm to about 1 mm as the upper limit. Coarse particles with $r \geq$ 1 µm have a dispersion rate that is a function of diameter. Particles in the range:

$$0.1 \ \mu m \leq r \leq 1.0 \ \mu m$$

have transition properties. Very fine particle aerosols with $r \leq 0.1$ µm are dispersed proportional to r^2 and the particle velocity, v.

The loss of aerosol particles in suspension can be attributed to several phenomena: sedimentation, diffusion, and coagulation. Again the size and velocity of the aerosol particles are the driving force. Larger particles, $r \geq$ 1 µm, will tend to fall and be lost via sedimentation. Smaller, submicron particles will tend to diffuse out to the walls of containment via Brownian motion. Coagulation, the formation of larger particles from smaller particle via collisions, is caused by thermal, electrical, molecular, hydrodynamic and several other forces.

Solid Particulate Fire Suppression Aerosols

EMAA is a dispersion aerosol that is delivered to the protected space via the combustion of a solid tablet. Prior to the development of EMAA, dispersion aerosols have been created via crushing, grinding, blasting, or drilling of solid matter. The particle size reduction is directly related to the energy expended on crushing or grinding and other factors such as the brittle or plastic nature of the material, the porosity of the solid, and the presence of crystal flaws and sites of weakness. Physicochemical reactions using condensation processes have also been used to generate solid particle aerosols. Salts fused on heating wires have been used to generate aerosols via incandescence in inert gas atmospheres, the temperature being a function of the energy required to produce nuclei.

EMAA particles are on the order of 1 μm in diameter. At 1 atm and 20°C these particles will have a terminal velocity of about 10^{-4} cm/s according to Stokes' Law. Diffusion losses are also predicted to be very small. The result is that EMAA will remain suspended in the protected space for times on the order of tens of minutes to several hours.

EMAA is initially a solid material that can originate in a variety of forms: solid, powder, or gel. The active component, an oxidizer, and a reducer are combined with a filler. These components are ground into a fine powder and mixed with an epoxy resin binder. Upon ignition of the material, the combustion products are ejected as a dispersion aerosol, with the solid particles floating in the air with the gaseous components. The products of combustion of EMAA are 40 percent solid particles and 60 percent gaseous products. The gaseous products consist of N_2, CO_2, CO, H_2O, O_2 and traces of hydrocarbons. The solid particles are various solid salts, depending on the formulation of the EMAA solid.

Extinguishment Mechanisms

Successful fire suppression requires that one or more of the four factors that tend to propagate a fire be interrupted. These factors and their associated suppression mechanisms are shown in Table 6 together with the action of the aerosol as a fire suppressant. EMAA aerosols, like dry chemicals, are hypothesized to function via several mechanisms to suppress fire. Chemical inhibition of the chain reaction is hypothesized to occur via catalytic combination of the active species. There is also significant evidence that heat absorption and cooling via decomposition and vaporization of the solid particles is an important mechanism for flame extinguishment. The final mechanism may be oxygen dilution in the flame region as the chemical reaction of the particles and active species produces inert gases such as CO_2, causing localized low oxygen conditions.

Table 6. Factors Governing Fire Propagation and Solid Particulate
Aerosol Actions

Factor	Suppression Mechanism	Aerosol Actions
Fuel	Removal	- - - -
Oxygen	Exclusion	Inert gas formation
Heat	Absorption	Cooling
Chain reaction	Inhibition	Absorb active species

Chemical Inhibition Interactions

Chemical inhibition is a function of several variables. Depending on the temperature at the point of interaction, the aerosol particles act by heterogeneous or homogeneous inhibition (Birchall, 1970). The aerosol particles, due to their small size, create a large total surface area for capturing the active species of the fire chain reaction. Heterogeneous reactions occur when the particle is still in a solid state and a recombination of the fire chain propagators occurs. As the particles enter higher temperature zones, homogeneous or gaseous phase reactions occur.

Heterogeneous processes typically undergo the following general reaction sequence:

(1) $A^\circ + S \text{-----}> AS$

(2) $AS + A^\circ \text{-----}> A_2 + S$

where A° is an active species in the fire chain reaction such as OH, H, or CH_3, S is the surface of the solid aerosol particle, and A_2 represents a molecular species such as H_2O, CO_2 or C_nH_{2n+2} The newly created AS reacts with another active species in the fire chain reaction creating a stable molecule, A_2. At the same time a free aerosol particle, S, is regenerated and made available for further interactions.

Homogeneous processes have the following general pattern of interaction (Rosser et al., 1963):

(3) $K + OH + M \text{-----}> KOH + M$

(4) $KOH + H \text{-----> } H_2O + K$

(5) $KOH + OH \text{-----> } H_2O + KO$

where M is energy input from the fire, and H and OH are active species. The extinguishing process is similar to that of Halon.

Chemical precursors that interact heterogeneously with the active species are based on cations of the alkali metals: K, Na, Cs, Rb, Sr, NH_4 and anions such as CO_3, HCO_3, SO_4, and PO_4.

The alkali-metal salts have been shown to be especially effective fire suppressants. The potassium salts are generally superior to the sodium salts and the anion associated with each is an important factor in fire suppression effectiveness (Birchall, 1970). For example, alkali oxalates are particularly effective compared to bicarbonates.

In the form of dry chemicals, alkali-metal salts have to first decompose in the flame to provide a large specific area for interaction. To be effective as fire extinguishants, large dry chemical particles on the order of 70 µm in diameter decompose into submicron particles, reacting with the flames to produce inhibiting species such as alkali hydroxides. To allow such decomposition to occur, residence time in the flame is important. For large particles the appropriate residence time may be difficult to achieve because the shear mass of the particle will cause it to fall rapidly through the flame. In the case of 1 µm aerosol particles the residence time required to produce the reactive species is far shorter, and the diffusion property of the small solid particle will tend to maintain its availability in the flame. The combination of these effects is indicative of the increased effectiveness of aerosols versus dry chemical fire extinguishants of similar composition.

Thermal Cooling Mechanisms

Relatively recent evidence suggests that much of the effectiveness of dry chemicals can be attributed to thermal and heat extraction mechanisms such as heat capacity, fusion, vaporization, and decomposition (Ewing et al., 1989a) At certain particle sizes, depending on the dry chemical powder composition, a sizable increase in extinguishing effectiveness is achieved that can be explained by flame heat removal (Ewing et al., 1989b and Ewing et al., 1992). This occurs at limit temperatures that are a function of the flame and extinguishant properties. The particle size at which the step increase in effectiveness occurs is the limit size S_L, defined as the largest particle size that completely reacts with the flame. It varies with the composition of the dry chemical constituent of the formulation. Above S_L heat extraction is due to the heat capacity of the solid particle alone. Below S_L several mechanisms are effective to include heat capacity, dissociation, decomposition, and vaporization. However practical utilization of mechanically created small diameter dry chemical compounds is limited because it is difficult to store dry chemicals for extended periods of time without the onset of compaction. Humidity will also have a detrimental effect on dry chemicals and result in deterioration. The production of dry chemical solid particulate aerosols via combustion avoids these difficulties, and the solid material form has an estimated 15-year shelf-life. Packaging can be readily designed that provides protection even in fairly extreme environments.

In addition to the difference in relative effectiveness of various dry chemical formulations as noted above, it has also been suggested that for the same alkali metal the fire suppression efficiency as a function of the anion would be (Birchall, 1970):

Oxide > cyanate > carbonate > iodide > bromide > chloride > sulfate > phosphate

The generation of alkali hydroxide in the flame is cited as the reason for the relative effectiveness of the various anions.

Test Results

A series of basic tests have been carried out to assess the performance of EMAA against a variety of fires. Table 7 contains a list of preliminary laboratory scale extinguishment tests that were conducted, and Table 8 shows the results of these tests. The chamber utilized for these tests was the NMERI 170 liter LEETC device that permits testing with various fire types, with the fire and fire suppressant locations in various geometries, and with the ability to introduce obstacles for evaluating flow and penetration characteristics. Experience thus far with EMAA indicates that the more turbulent the character of the fire, the more rapid the extinguishment because convective forces tend to drive the aerosol particles into the flame region.

Table 8 provides results for a group of intermediate- to large-scale tests. The extinguishment times listed in this table include the ignition time for the solid material. Tests 4 and 5 included electrical power cable ignited together with an n-heptane fire. The suppression time is for the extinguishment

Table 7. EMAA Aerosol Laboratory Scale Test Program

Series	EMAA Location	Quantity	Fire Location	Description
1	MCSA	10 g.	Chamber Floor	Size: 4 cm dia. Fuel: n-heptane Preburn: 1 min.
2	Chamber Floor	10 g.	MCSA	Size: 4 cm dia. Fuel: n-heptane Preburn: 1 min.
3	MCSA	20 g.	Chamber Floor	Size: 4 cm dia. Fuel: n-heptane Preburn: 1 min.
4	MCSA	10 g.	Chamber Floor	Size: 10 cm dia. Fuel: n-heptane Preburn: 30 s.
5	MCSA	10 g.	Chamber Floor	Size: 10 x 8 cm fan Fuel: Brown paper Preburn: 30 s.

MCSA = mid-chamber

of the combined fuel/cable fire.   Testing indicates that EMAA has an extinguishment concentration of approximately 50 g/m^3 for n-heptane pool fires. This can be contrasted to the extinguishment concentration of Halon 1301, approximately 300 g/m^3 for the same fire.

Some of the known general characteristics of EMAA compared to gaseous agents are shown in Table 9. The major characteristics of solid particle aerosols are their extinguishing effectiveness and their low installation and life cycle costs. In contrast to the $150/$m^2$ installation cost of Halon 1301 systems, the forecasted cost of a solid particle aerosol system is $25/$m^2$. The life cycle cost differences are even greater because, unlike gaseous agent systems, solid particle aerosol systems will not require pressure cylinders that may leak and that require periodic hydrostatic testing.

Table 8. Extinguishment Times for EMAA Fire Suppressant— Medium to Large Scale Testing

No.	Form	Mass, Kg	Test Chamber	Fire Origin	Time, s
1	Tablet	0.125	3 m^3,closed	ft^{2}n-heptane	24
2	Tablet	0.150	3 m^3,closed	1ft^{2}n-heptane	21
3	Powder	0.150	3 m^3,closed	ft^{2}n-heptane	19
4	Tablet	0.250	3 m^3,closed	n-heptane+cables	60
5	Tablet	0.250	3 m^3,closed	n-heptane+cables	60
6	Tablet	0.500	3 m^3,closed	n-heptane+plastics	30
7	Tablet	0.300	55 gal drum	water/n-heptane[*]	13
8	Powder	0.250	55 gal drum	water/n-heptane[*]	4
9	Tablet	6.000	70 m^3,closed	2 x 1 ft^2 n-heptane	62

[*]EMAA initiated underwater in barrel with 75 mm n-heptane on water

Table 9. Comparison of EMAA Aerosol and Gaseous Extinguishants

Parameter	Halon 1301	Gaseous Replacement	CO$_2$	EMAA
1. ODP	High	Low/Zero	Zero	Zero
2. GWP	Mod	Low/Zero	Zero	Nil
3. Toxicity	Low	Low	High	Low
4. Conductivity	Low	Low	Low	Low
5. Corrosivity	Mod	Mod	Mod	Unk
6. Vol. Efficiency	Good	Mod	Low	Exc
7. Ext. Concentration	5%	10-15%	45%	--
8. Ext. Density, g/m^3	300	600-900	700	50
9. Cost$_a$, $/m^2	150	>250	150	25
10. Life Cycle Cost$_b$	High	High	High	Low

a - Includes piping, cylinders, installation, no detection
b - Includes initial cost, maintenance, agent replacement

Toxicity

A full toxicological study of EMAA has not yet been conducted. Preliminary analysis of gases from testing has been accomplished and the results provide some insights into the safety of EMAA. Samples of the aerosol particles and gases have been processed by various equipment and methods: GC/MS, IR spectrometry, and x-ray fluorescence.

Tests conducted by the All-Union Fire Research Institute for Fire Protection (VNIIPO) in Russia to determine the toxicity of solid particle aerosol fire suppressants utilized a 1 m^3 chamber in which a 60 mm ethanol pan fire was extinguished by varying concentrations of aerosol. After a 3-minute pre-burn, the aerosol is injected into the chamber, the fire suppressed, and the gases are fed into an animal chamber for a 15-minute exposure. The tests indicated that at a concentration of 260 g/m^3 the first adverse effects were noted, that is, a partial loss of motor control functions. This concentration corresponds to more than 5 times the extinguishment concentration (Andreev et al., 1993).

In summary, preliminary efforts at examining the overall toxicology of EMAA in neat and combustion states, including a fire test atmosphere, do not reveal any significant problems due to toxic components. The physiological effects of deep lung penetration of the aerosol particles is an issue that will be examined in future research.

Applications

The aerosol generated when an EMAA tablet is ignited has several properties that differentiate it from both gaseous agents and dry chemicals. In fact EMAA could be said to be an intermediate agent between these two extremes in fire suppression techniques. Several of the key characteristics and features of EMAA that influence the design of applications are:

a. Similar to a gaseous agent, EMAA can flow around barriers and obstacles, behaving as a gas in its basic transport properties. It can be introduced into ductwork and be delivered to an area via forced convection. Dry chemicals, in contrast, are limited by obstructions.

b. EMAA has excellent fire suppression characteristics, similar to dry chemicals, both of which are 6 times as effective as Halon 1301 per unit mass and up to 10 times as effective as the forecasted replacements for Halon 1301 such as perfluorobutane and HFC-23.

c. EMAA initiation is independent of oxygen supply and can therefore be effective under or within a liquid or at altitudes where oxygen concentrations are low.

d. Initiation of EMAA can be via electrical ignition or self-ignition due to interaction with the fire.

e. The delivery rate of EMAA is a function of its composition, form (solid, powder, gel), and the delivery system. The aerosol is generated via combustion of the EMAA material and variations in the active component, oxidizer, and reducer dramatically affect the burn rate, perhaps up to 2 orders of magnitude in difference.

f. EMAA does not require piping, pressure cylinders, or valves. A device for containing the EMAA solid material is all that is normally required. Pressure testing, weighing, pressure/leak detection, and other maintenance and testing of cylinders/pipes/nozzles/valves are not required.

The low weight to extinguishing capability of EMAA provides tremendous performance advantages for weight/space critical applications. A CO_2 cylinder weighing more than 150 kg can be replaced with about 4 kg of EMAA.

This excellent performance capability and its add-on ability will enable such applications as trucks and cars, boats and ships, engine compartment protection, fuel tanks, and numerous other applications. Where portability, expandability, simplicity, ruggedness, and cost are factors, it would appear that an EMAA system would be a consideration.

The major unknowns relative to EMAA at present are its materials compatibility performance, especially corrosion, and its application against deep-seated fires. Testing to assess EMAA performance in both of these areas is ongoing.

Conclusions on Solid Particulate Aerosol Development

The development of aerosol fire suppression systems is a newly emerging discipline that holds great promise in offering an excellent option for consideration for several fire protection roles. An ongoing Air Force research program is examining the basic physics and chemistry of fire suppression aerosols and assessing the employment of aerosol delivery systems for a variety of applications.

References

Andreev, V.A., N.P. Kopylov, V.I. Makeev, V.A.Merkulov, and V.N. Nikolaev, 1993: Replacement of Halon in Fire Extinguishing Systems, *Proceedings of the 1993 Halon Alternatives Technical Working Conference*, Albuquerque, New Mexico, 11-13 May 1993.

Billings, C.E. and R.A. Gussman, 1976: Dynamic Behavior of Aerosols, *Handbook on Aerosols*, R. Dennis, ed., NTIS, 40-65.

Birchall, J.D., 1970: On the Mechanism of Flame Inhibition by Alkali Metal Salts, *Combustion and Flame*, 14, 85-96.

Ewing, C.T., F.R. Faith, J.T. Hughes, and H.W. Carhart, 1989a: Flame Extinguishment Properties of Dry Chemicals: Extinction Concentrations for Small Pan Fires, *Fire Technology*, 25, 134-149.

Ewing, C.T., F.R. Faith, J.T. Hughes, and H.W. Carhart, 1989b: Evidence for Flame Extinguishment by Thermal Mechanisms, *Fire Technology*, 25, 195-212.

Ewing, C.T., F.R. Faith, J.B. Romans, J.T. Hughes, and H.W. Carhart, 1992: Flame Extinguishment Properties of Dry Chemicals: Extinction Weights for Small Diffusion Pan Fires and Additional Evidence for Flame Extinguishment by Thermal Mechanisms, *Journal of Fire Protection Engineering*, 4, 35-42.

Rosser, W.A., S.H. Inami, and H. Wise, 1963: The Effect of Metal Salts on Premixed Hydrocarbon-Air Flames, *Combustion and Flame*, 7, 107-119.

Spurny, K.R., 1986: Physical Characterization of Single Particles and of Particle Collectives, *Physical Characterization of Individual Airborne Particles*, K.R. Spurny, d., Ellis Horwood, Ltd., Chichester, U.K., 31-34.

CHAPTER 12

Scientific and Technological Aspects of the Problem of Utilization of Military Stores

S.G. Andreev, V.S. Solov'ev, and N.N. Sysoyev
Hydrophysics Research Center
Moscow State University
Moscow, Russia

Introduction

In the problem of utilization of military stores (MS), great importance is now assigned to the extraction of explosive material (EM) from the casings of artillery projectiles, ammunition, mines, aerial bombs, engineering supplies, and their parts. Adequate methods are presented for engineering solutions and technology constructed on their bases. Not only for each form of MS, but also for different calibers there will be choices of proper techniques, which both in technological, and also organizational features, are substantially different. The force action is characteristic for all applications and must be chosen scientifically to guarantee the safety of the processes used. In this paper we attempt to find and consider the possibility of describing the overall action and response mechanisms, with the aim of developing the scientific basis for a theory of safety in the utilization of MS.

Problems of Separating MS into their Components

Military stores represent potential sources of hazard even if their handling is professional. The danger consists of EM and, as a rule, the associated explosive initiation systems. Special safety precautions must, therefore, be taken to avoid accidental explosions during disassembly. To date, however, the requirements of safe disassembly of MS have not been adequately promoted.

Today, in connection with the MS utilization problem, it is necessary to disassemble a given technical system into its component elements in the most advantageous way, conserving as much as possible the most valuable materials. In this respect, one must take into account that the system of MS was designed and prepared in such a fashion as to eliminate the possibility of being dismantled. That is, most elements of construction of MS were pressed, cast, rolled, or set up in finishes and compounds. Furthermore, most of the MS are too old for possible utilization. Thus the basic problem of utilization is avoiding preliminary detonation and achieving ecologically safe dismantling of MS into its component elements. In view of the magnitude of the problem, when utilization amounts to millions of MS, safety has primary importance. Since military applications of all weapons require effectiveness as its first priority, this means it maintains high sensitivity and, consequently, hazardous explosive materials (EM).

In a scientifically practical plan for MS utilization, there is a chain of interconnecting problems of safety and efficiency in the engineering process of utilization. Especially hazardous are the

- extraction of EM charges from shells of MS;
- disposal of the remaining EM from the shells;
- dismantling of the fuses;
- dismantling of triggering elements (if possible);
- unscrewing the fuses from the MS (usually small caliber); and
- dissipation of the unitary explosion.

Our analysis indicates that, from the viewpoint of the level of danger and quantity of dismantled material, the main process, without previous experience, is the extraction of EM from shell casings.

As currently known, the scientific-industrial peculiarities of the basic methods of extraction of EM from shells are: melting the MS with a low-melting base, vaporization of the EM, washing out the EM by a stream of liquid (gas), gasification and subsequent extraction of the EM from the casings, cryogenic treatment of the charge with subsequent extraction, burning out of the EM (especially for small-size systems of ignition), abrasive hydrocutting of the shells with washing out of the charge using ultrasound, weak spark high-frequency shock-wave action on the charge through the casing, use of partial low-order decomposition of the high explosive in shock waves and by action of cumulative jets, centrifugation of the high explosive, boring out of the EM, magneto dynamic destruction of the shell, and annihilation by explosion.

It is not hard to see that these methods of extraction all use one form or another of intense thermal, mechanical (including shock wave), and combined action at the stage of extraction. In the process of extraction, and in subsequent stages, structural (rheological) characteristics of the EM charge are substantially changed and, consequently, the degree of hazard changes. One must add that concerning the new state of EM, as a product, it must have further uses. Thus if one discards the possibility of chemical transformation in all stages of "live" EM, the sequence of changes of structural characteristics of a charge of EM is described in the following manner: the original EM, stabilization, preparation of the charge in some fashion (casting, pressing, boring out, rolling), change of the charge for storage, thermo-mechanical action on the charge in the process of extraction from the shell casing, granulation of the EM or other preparation. Considering the whole action on the charge of EM both before separation and during the process, the technology may be divided into the following groups:

Group I: Procedures are characterized by the situation that nothing need be done, but it can be treated as an inert construction material with known properties and unchanging during the processes applied. Formation of any regimes of explosive transformation is absent. This group of actions is characteristic in performing different technological operations in preparing the charge, extracting it from the shell, auxiliary conversions (transportation), and also in recycling for making industrial EM.

Group II: Procedures are characterized by the fact that we know only a limited range of actions on the charge of EM, which may be changed within limits. This situation may exist for principal changes in the charge, down to particular chemical reactions. Similar treatments are characteristic for heating, when the charge temperature is not constant, but depends on time. However, for each type of EM it is necessary to insure that after the series of treatments, the functional possibility of the EM exists for fabrication into articles from it, for reuse.

Group III: Procedures are characterized by occasional actions when accidents happen, not only from the point of view of the parameters of the treatment, but also the character of the response of the EM to the treatment. The effect of such a treatment on the surroundings may be as large as normal sanctioned explosions. This group of treatments is characterized by a large spectrum of reactions, triggering mechanisms, and features of development. Most of all, in relation to the character of the charge container, for example, thick and strong casings, the process, starting as a slow reaction, may develop into a normal detonation.

Present domestic and foreign methods for evaluating the response of EM to external actions are unusually diverse and may be systematized in relation to the state of the article acted upon: filled batch of EM; charge of EM, prepared by pressing or casting; shielded charge; and charge of EM in thin or thick and strong shell. There is a definite difficulty in establishing a correlation between different methods of testing and their results to permit the achievement of reliable information and reduction of the number of tests. A peculiarity of most tests is the absence of complexity. Accordingly, the safety characteristics of manipulation of EM, in processing of military stores with the aim of maximum safety and resistance to intense external actions, require special indicators of the possibility of direct transfer to the problem of utilization.

Theoretical and experimental studies of processes which take place in MS utilization showed that their physical essence is universal and suitable for a wide range of problems. So a number of both technical and fundamental aspects of the MS utilization problem must be investigated today. The contents of fundamental investigation of elementary processes, which occur because of force and thermal action on an EM charge when it is extracted from the MS shell, are the following:

- Mechanism of creation and evolution of thermal fields in the charge and MS shell (including EM transition into a plastic state in the field of frictional interaction (Averson, 1980; Andreev and Solov'ev, 1984)

- Dynamics of plastic destruction of cavity and dissipative heating of material in the vicinity of the cavity (Belyaev et al., 1973; Attetkov and Solov'ev, 1987; Selivanov et al., 1990)

- Dissipative heating in plastic flow processes with the problems of adiabatic pressing of gas and heat exchange between EM and gas (Attetkov and Solov'ev, 1987)

- Problems of thermal theory of ignition, especially for conditions of force and thermal action in extraction from MS shell (Averson, 1980; Attetkov and Lazarev, 1989; Andreev et al., 1979; Andreev et al., 1993)

- Dynamics of EM deformation under the shock by hard surface and analysis of thermal fields lacking place in EM and especially in the zone of contact with surface which is the most dangerous from the possible burning point of view (Andreev et al. 1982; Zemskikh and Leipunskii, 1987; Afanas'ev and Bobolev, 1968; Selivanov et al., 1990)

- Problems of the dispersing regime of extracting of EM charge from MS shell through filler in high-speed centrifugation (Jensen et al., 1981; Andreev and Solov'ev, 1992)

- Problems of finishing of burning processes in partly full volume of MS chamber with dust fraction (Kabirov et al., 1992; Kolobov et al., 1992; Andreev and Solov'ev, 1984; Ermolaev et al., 1977)

- Problem of starting and development of burning processes in air-EM mixture with concentration more than kg/m^3 (Kabirov et al., 1992; Ermolaev et al., 1977)

- Problems of ignition of air-EM mixtures by spark-discharge which is a consequence of high-speed motion of big masses of dielectrics

- A number of problems of EM ignition analyses and their results in a form of development of processes and force action factors upon neighborhood (Andreev and Solov'ev, 1992; Andreev and Solov'ev, 1984)

- Problems of weak shock-wave action with partly local emission of energy which excludes the development processes and some others (Andreev and Solov'ev, 1992; Attetkov and Solov'ev, 1987; Andreev et al., 1979; Hubbard and Tomlinson, 1989)

High-Speed Centrifugation of EM from Explosive Devices

The basic questions in analysis of high-speed centrifugation of EM are the conditions when centrifugal forces are insufficient for EM extraction from the shell and safe conditions for dampening out the dispersed EM thrown out from the shell into the catcher. The answer to the first question is given as a first approximation by an analysis of the dependence of the mean "equilibrium" stresses on the cross section of the cylindrical body of EM of density ρ, diameter d on distance x from the "free" face opposite the opening (this end is removed from the rotational axis j by the distance R). On the assumption that the tangential stresses on the surface of the cylindrical body at the moment of "breaking equilibrium," which is the beginning of the ascent of the body or its fragments from the circular trajectory (emergence from the casing), are equal to the limiting value of τ (in particular, the shear strength of the EM), whereas the external pressure p_o we have (p may be equal to atmospheric pressure p_A),

$$\overline{\sigma}=(vR \ / \ A)^2 \ \overline{x}^{(2-x)} \ / \ 2 - 4\overline{\tau} \ \overline{x}R \ / \ d - p_0 \ / \ p_A,$$

where n is the rotational frequency; $A = \sqrt{p_A/\rho}/2\pi$, $\quad \overline{x}=x/R$; $\quad \overline{\sigma}=\sigma/p_A$; $\quad \overline{\tau}=\tau/p_A$

Analysis of data on the range of possible values of τ (characteristic shear strength of EM or its adhesion to the shell casing), the limiting value of s (characteristic strength of EM in rupture or its adhesion to the casing bottom) and size of the chamber, indicates the possibility of ejection of a cylindrical charge either intact or in pieces (broken into small fragments, which may be ejected also through the ejection openings). In both cases the EM, ejected to the catcher with speed on the order of $2\pi nR$, has a new, damaged structure. The parameters of the process are angular speed of rotation of 200 radians per second and speed of ejection of the material is 200–300 m/sec.

Especially dangerous from possible situations, arising particularly upon impact of friction of the EM into the damping material, would be excitation of local burning on the broken structure of the charge pores. Analysis of the local breakdown of the EM, initiated by the initial impulse of the shock wave with a given level of pressure p and speed of its collapse $\partial p \ / \ \partial t$, indicates that in the case of an insignificant exceeding of the threshold level of pressure p_i, a non-trivial, two-stage mechanism of evolution of an explosive transformation is probable. This leads to a strong destructive action if the value of the parameters of the two, p and $\partial p \ / \ \partial t$ are at the limits g(p, $\partial p \ / \ \partial t$)=0, and s($p$, $\partial p \ / \ \partial t$)=0. These limits, determining the respective critical level for extinguishing the EM, being ignited upon collapse of the pores, $\partial p \ / \ \partial t = -3\pi B^2 p^3 \ / \ 2k$, and the absence of growth of the seat of disintegration behind the front of the shock wave (SW) in the first approximation, are described by the relations

$$\partial p/\partial t = -(\Pi \ / \ r[k/(k+1)]\left[P_{cj}/p\right]^{vk}Bp^2\xi^2, \xi = r_i/r,$$

where B is the constant in the law of combustion, $U=Bp$; k is thermal conductivity of the EM; Π is porosity of the charge with pores of radius r; k is the indicator of adiabatic products of detonation; P_{cj} is pressure in the Zhug plane; and r_i is the radius of the pore at the moment of ignition. At the same time, at the first stage (depending on the drop in combustion velocity in the points of origin, without extinguishing the EM) behind the shock wave front in the struck charge or its fragments, "smoldering" in the course of a long time (up to tenths of a microsecond) decomposition begins with an infinitesimally small velocity. Depending on the structure and rheological properties of the EM, determining upon shock damping the damage of the structure and chemical activity of the material on the formed surfaces of the second stage is possible—intensification of the seat of decomposition in the part of struck EM (due to increasing at first of the burning surface) leading to excitation of detonation in the peripheral zones of the EM with the damaged and sensitized structure (originating by the quenching SW with pressure falling below the threshold level of p(T) for ignition on the pores), or to "volume" explosive burning of particles of EM, dispersed in the air.

The computational methods, based on the adduced relationships and experimental data of initial charge temperature influence on the characteristic combustibility of the EM on the inhomogeneity of the structure and its intercrystalline strength, predict the necessity of preliminary heating of charges of EM to a temperature of 60–90°C for a practical accomplishment of safe centrifugation from the housing of explosive materials based on phlegmatized hexogene.

Low-Speed Centrifugation of EM from the Housing of MS

For MS with subdivided explosives, when t and s are relatively small, it is possible to extract the charge of EM with relatively low speeds of rotation, v>10 radians/sec, by use of preliminary heating. In this case a realization of motion of the segments or charge as a whole as an unbroken unit is possible.

In the process of extraction, the EM is under intense frictional action due to the pressing of the charge or its fragments against the wall of the chamber of the shell because of developing Coriolis acceleration, which may be evaluated as

$$\alpha_k = 4\pi v V_R, v_R \approx 2\pi v R \sqrt{1 - (\frac{R_{cp}}{R_k})^2},$$

neglecting the damping action of tangential forces in the EM at the stage of its "sliding" along the wall (here R_{cp} and R_k are distances between the axis of rotation of the centrifugal and center of the mass of the charge or its fragment at the beginning of taking off the chamber walls and the following instant of time in motion). V_R is the radial speed of motion of the EM.

The emergence of the EM from the projectile chamber ends by shock brake action on the damping material, which for non-dispersing low-rotational speed centrifugation is expediently accomplished in the form of a construction, not moving with respect to the projectile. At the stage of damping, the action on the EM may be conditionally subdivided in general into frictional, shock, and a combination "friction-shock" (a type of oblique shock). For a shock action one must distinguish the initial shock-wave stage with peak of pressure, determined by dynamic strength of the damping catcher elements and EM and also the speed of the co-stress and subsequent "post-shock-wave" stage, differentiated from the shock wave by its significant duration and lower pressure, determined in a considerable degree, especially in a finite stage, by strength characteristics of the charge of EM and the dynamic pressure.

For non-dispersive or low rotational speed centrifugation for damping in the damping catcher of the EM charge thrown out of the chamber, one must anticipate either a quasi-plastic "crumpling" of phlegmatized EM in a compact mass or a practically complete retention of the shape of the damping charge depending on the speed of the shock, prescribed peculiarity, and its temperature. Thus, for low-speed centrifugation the potential danger is connected with the processes of sliding of the charge along the walls of the catcher and the impact at the bottom of the catcher. To evaluate the potential hazard of the processes in the damping catcher, it is possible to use a general nomogram, constructed on the basis of the theory of thermal ignition by means of the sources, on the frictional surface.

One should emphasize the potential hazard which is due to sealed cavities in the charge (cavity under the igniter) upon impact on the bottom of the catcher. How far the conditions of low-speed centrifugation are from critical hazards is illustrated in Figure 1. In the figure there is the dependence of the diameter of the spherical hole necessary for its ignition from the pressure on impact. Also the levels of pressure are noted on shock in the catcher with velocities corresponding to rotational frequency of 6 and 12.5 radians/sec.

Already for insignificant speeds of extraction and shock, low-speed centrifugation does not exclude deformation of the charge in a single piece.

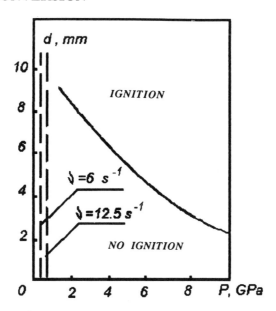

Figure 1. Ignition dependence on P and d.

Thus for shock speeds in the range of up to 100 meters/sec, temperatures do not exceed a few degrees. However, on spreading the EM over the surface, the picture is quite complicated; local regions are realized with increased parameters, presenting a genuine hazard. The information necessary for a reliable description of the degree of danger, may be obtained from a solution of the two-dimensional deformation, with subsequent evaluation of thermal effects of friction and disintegration on the walls of the damping catcher.

Boring Charges out of the Shells of MS

The boring out of charges by a special cutter is an alternative technique of extracting EM from the structure of a missile with undercutting, in comparison with high-speed centrifugation. The cutter must be flexibly turned relative to the axes of the shell to follow close to the wall of the chamber of the charge (Andreev et al., 1993).

The shape of the cutting blade of the tool in plan, the force of clamping it to the side walls of the chamber, and the frequency of turning relative to the axis of the shell for a practically complete cleaning of the wall of the chamber along the entire length of the missile are in definite relations. The degree of avoidance of self propagating explosive reactions, possibly in the vicinity of interaction of the cutter with EM and the wall of the chamber, is determined to an extent by the stress and area of pinching the EM in the vicinity of contact of the tool with the chamber wall. Numerical analysis and physical experiments on shock-wave acting on local parts of the surface of the charge of high-density EM, with high dispersion of mechanical energy flow, show that for pinched EM under hypothetical conditions of excitation of even detonating transformation in it is not capable of initiating an explosion in the high-density surrounding charge. However, it may still cause an explosive reaction in the powdery products of boring, the degree of localization and destructiveness of which is determined by the volume concentration of EM particles and aluminum in the charge chamber, and by the system of removal of the turning products.

Construction parameters of the basic elements of the setup should be chosen in conditions of hazard-free work for different unofficial situations, such as breaking tools, output from a line of different elements of drives, etc. The EM layer remaining on the wall of a missile chamber in an unintended regime of a turning by a broken instrument (by reserve elements with the additional function of duplicating the basic outline ones) is of the same thickness as the Michelson layer and therefore does not burn through from the intense heat output in the body of the shell.

A natural model of sparking from sparks of "frictional origin," potentially possible in extreme stress regimes, was devised in the first approximation, by the burning or exploding of thin steel wires. With the energy of an electrical discharge, including the stage of development and cooling of a plasma cloud (fuse), up to 600 Joules (in a time of about five milliseconds), which corresponds to 0.1 gram of EM, an optical method is able to fix only a local, not self-propagating luminous zone, abutting the place of the discharge and not having noticeable mechanical and thermal action. Spreading of the zone depends mainly on the speed and concentration of the aerodispersed flow.

Measurements of the strength of feed, cutting moments and corresponding speeds indicate that the process of EM extraction from the inside of the shell is energy-saving in comparison with other (mechanical) methods because no energy is expended on the heating of the shell and EM charge. The basic energy expenditure in use of the method of boring is connected with the high degree of purity of the air. After the dust-air mixture goes through the first cyclone with storing of boring chips of EM, the concentration of EM in the air falls to the level of a safe value, which permits carrying out a final purification of the air for ejection into the atmosphere, maintaining ecological requirements in standard filtration equipment outside the armored chamber with boring modules.

A comparison of the dependence on time for heating of the powdered product of the boring process, and original composition used for the outfitted shells before explosion, indicates the absence of boring product stability reduction by reason of newly sharpened tools with prescribed composition, and consequently, the possibility of accumulation in sufficient amount for subsequent use for different objectives, including as explosive material.

Extraction of Charges Connected with their Disintegration (Shear, Fracturing, Pressing, Extrusion)

It is evident that the force used for extracting a charge from a shell of MS and the force used pressing the charge into it will be different. The differences will be a consequence of the fact that in pressing, a volume compaction will be produced of powdered material, whereas the nature of resistance to extraction consists in overcoming the force of mutual attraction of randomly oriented grains. In this case, intercrystalline effects appear.

In contrast, when the charge is sheared or squeezed out (Figure 2) the transition is realized from intercrystalline strength into transcrystalline strength. The basic causes of such transitions are the roughness of surfaces of the MS housing with the scale such as the size of grains, fixing the relation between diameters of the dies and the inner surface of the chamber. For small clearances by virtue of the indicated sources the extrusion is made substantially more difficult; for large (larger characteristic size of roughness on the casing surface, and grains of EM) sizes of irregularities, a significant amount of EM is left on the walls of the chamber, which must be cleaned afterwards.

The die stresses, necessary for pressing out the EM charge from the chamber, cylindrical, truncated-conical, and also approximating these surfaces, may be determined by assuming a dependence of limiting tangential stresses on the mean hydrostatic pressure. In this approximation when the Poisson's ratio is equal to 0.5,

$$P = (p_0 + \frac{\tau_0}{\tau})\exp(\varepsilon\tau l/r) - \frac{\tau_0}{\tau}$$

where p_0 is pressure, acting on the end-plate to which the extruder is not clamped; τ_0 and τ are parameters of linear approximate dependence of limiting tangential stress to the mean hydrodynamic pressure; and l and r are length and radius of the cylindrical charge.

From the point of view of the strength of polycrystalline EM related by hydrostatic pressure, $\tau = \tau_0 + \tau p$ is caused by transition from the intercrystalline mechanism of rupture to a transcrystalline one. Figure 3 illustrates the results of computations and experiments.

Determination of the basic parameters of the charge extrusion regimes may be found in terms of thermal diffusion and the thermal theory of ignition. Within the framework of the first approach, the size of EM (hexogene) grain may be evaluated, the energy of elastic deformation, upon formation of transcrystalline zones of sliding, heated layers, corresponding to the conditions of flame front propagation. At the same time, the maximum probability of EM ignition at the beginning of the polydispersed charge extrusion, by a pressure is equal to the probability of striking the zone of EM monocrystal fracture with size larger than $a_{cr}(p)$ (Figure 4).

Within the scope of the second approach, we must determine the critical speed for safe extrusion V_{cr}, at which the heat flow during the time of breakdown t, is sufficient to reach the ignition temperature ($t=x/V_{cr}$, where x is the upper estimate of the path of shear for tangential stress close to l).

A computational evaluation indicates that at the heating temperature of the charge of 60–80°C, and a speed of 50 m/sec, critical conditions are not reached with 2 or 3-fold margin, whereas strengths and forces generated under extrusion lie in the range 20–200 kN and 1–10 kWt respectively.

Explosive Methods of Splitting EM and the Housing of MS

In the category of explosive methods of separating charges and structures, there are methods leading to the destruction of the shells without developing of the EM explosive destruction process, or partial local energy generation, leading to formation of such a quantity of gaseous products, that it is sufficient for opening the MS shell, but not enough to lead to an explosion or detonation of the fuel. The forms of explosive methods are:

– a procedure for opening and separating the EM from the metal by use of prolonged cumulative explosions;

– opening and cleaving the structure of the MS by use of excitation in the equipment of low-order local exploding processes by contact explosion;

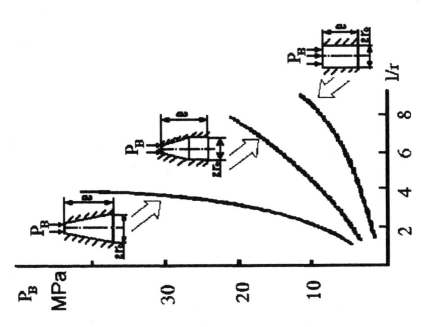

Figure 3. Pressure vs 1/r in transitions from intercrystalline to transcrystalline states for various shapes.

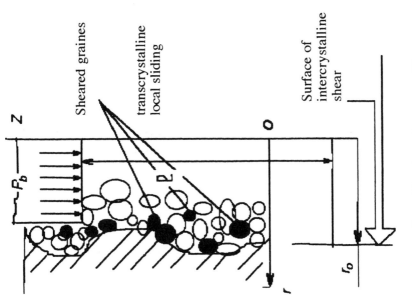

Figure 2. Transition from intercrystalline to transcrystalline states.

– opening and cleaving the structure of the MS by exciting in the equipment low-order local explosive processes by cumulative jets. These techniques are suitable for large-scale MS of complex non-recurrent geometries.

All of these methods are based on the knowledge of weak shock wave propagation in the EM charge enclosed in a stout shell. For realization of the indicated technologies, not allowing the development of a process towards explosion or detonation, it is necessary to predict accurately the critical conditions for initiation of chemical reactions in the action of weak shock-wave processes. The essence of the problem is how much we can exceed the threshold level of initiating the chemical reaction without causing development towards higher levels (convective burning, low-speed wave processes, explosions, detonation).

Critical conditions of initiation of a chemical reaction in the EM charge, of suitable structure, are such a pressure of a shock wave, below which only the physical-mechanical changes are possible in EM, without chemical processes leading to formation of gaseous products of decomposition. In conformity with [(7)] an expression for threshold pressure may be written in the form:

$$P_{i\sigma} = \frac{2Y}{3}\ln\left\{1 +(\alpha_0 -1)^{-1}\exp\left[\frac{3e_s}{2Y}\right]^{\eta}\right\}$$

$$\eta = \begin{cases} 1, R = 0 \\ \dfrac{1}{2}, R \gg 1 \end{cases}$$

where $\alpha=(1-m)^{-1}$, and m is porosity, $e_s=c_p(T_s -T_o)$—the increment of specific internal energy per unit of volume which is necessary for EM ignition (for typical EM, $e_s =(0.8-1.2)$ GPa, Y is the limit of fluidity of the EM).

$$R = \eta/a_0\sqrt{\rho Y}; \ \eta = (1 \div 10^2)$$

is fluidity of the material. Dependence of the threshold pressure for initiating the chemical reaction on the initial porosity of the EM (Y=0.2 GPa, e_s=1.0 GPa) is presented in Figure 5. The curve shown, constructed for EM of the TNT type, gives a range of conditions of chemical reactions initiation , above which a reasonably broad spectrum of explosive and similar processes is observed.

Nonideal Regimes of Development of Explosive Processes upon Shock-Wave Action on EM in a Stout Casing

In a number of cases at a specified level of initial impulse, different forms of explosive processes are possible: burning out of all the EM without bursting the shell; destruction of the shell in the process of accelerated burning; and cessation of burning (collapse of burning) at the moment of the shell bursting and burning transitions into normal detonation. The speeds of propagation of the process of 2.0-2.5 km/s with the level of pressure in the shock wave of 0.7-1.5 GPa are registered especially frequently. This process is close by its parameters to the NSD process, for which the speed of the plastic wave, initiating a reaction because of the features of dynamic compression of solid organic materials, is constant. The existence of a critical amplitude of a shock wave p_{cr} was established for which excitation of detonation takes place. In the first approximation the pressure of shock-wave initiation of detonation can be considered as the critical pressure P_{cr} of transition to detonation. Usually the evolution of a detonation-like explosion to normal detonation is not accompanied by an anomalous strength of action, and a monotonic transition is observed. The depth of the transition L changes within a wide range for different EMs. It may be presumed that the transition to detonation does not depend on primary causes, which initiated the EM burning within a stout shell (white hot surface, a splinter, large-scale defect, leading to ignition of the surrounding volume, etc.).

The number of magnitudes of P_{cr} and ℓ determined by different methods: pile driver tests Pd/pcr, the Andreev KK tube $P_{cr}{}^{At}$, and magnitudes computed from the relation

$$Pcr = \frac{(E/\mu c) - Ttr}{\alpha_p}; \quad T_{tr} = T_{tr}^{o} + \alpha_p P$$

are collected in Table 1.

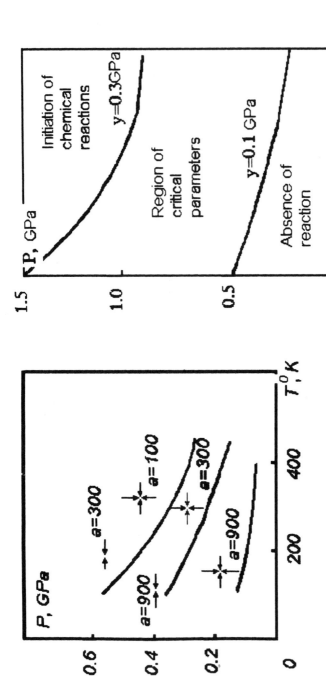

Figure 4. Critical pressures for grain destruction leading to ignition at various temperatures. Experimental: Opposing arrows for linear compression; crossed opposing arrows for three dimensional compression. Theoretical: curves for cases in Figure 3.

Figure 5. Threshold pressure for initiating chemical reaction vs initial porosity.

Table 1. Critical Parameters for Various Explosives

EM	$P_{cr}^{pd}(GPa)$	$P_{cr}(GPa)$	l_{SM}	$\alpha_p\left(\dfrac{K}{P_a}\right)$
TNT	1.39	1.19	–	2.9	3.1*10
Dina	1.17	–	2.0	3.7	2.2*10
Picric Acid	0.98	0.95	–	12-13	2.9*10
Tetryl	0.99	0.85	–	4-6	2.9*10
Hexogene	0.95	0.7	–	1.5-3.0	2.5*10
TEN	.41	0.48	0.6	1.0	2.0*1.0

From the data of Table 1, it follows that for evaluation of the possibility of EM ignition in a stout shell, one may use values of P_{cr} obtained by either of the methods presented. In this connection, MS can be set up according to the degree of the tendency to transition into detonation arising from the process of burning in it (independent on the excitation source) in the following sequence: engineers' MS, MS for close combat, usual MS of shells, _fugas_ MS of the rockets, aerial bombs, artillery projectiles, and penetration shells with hardened casings.

We present a series of critical values of external action for TNT, leading to one or another regime of explosive transition (ET) or transition of one regime into another (thickness of shell casing 10-12 mm, external diameter 70-100 mm): threshold of pressure below which at normal temperatures for a charge in a stout casing, processes of chemical decomposition do not begin amounts to 0.25 GPa; safe loading pressure below which no break in continuity (original geometric dimensions) occurs even for development and subsequent extinction of the process of chemical decomposition, 1.8 GPa: pressure of splitting (blowing up) of the shell, leading to its destruction due to the pressure of gaseous products of the EM decomposition, 2.0 GPa; critical pressure for transition from burning to detonation, 2.25 GPa; critical pressure for shock-wave initiation of detonation, 6.2 GPa. Each of the pressures presented for initiation of explosive processes in MS development leads to one or another degree of complete energy generation.

Each explosion and detonation-like process in MS development is the consequence of improper choice of a regime of the charge extraction. One must especially note that they exist in real scale MS. It must be especially emphasized that with increase in EM sensitivity, transition to oxygen-containing compositions, the shock-wave methods of the charges extracting will be problematical because they approach unsafe and explosion-dangerous actions.

Conclusions

An investigation of the problem of utilization of MS confirms that one of the main problems is extraction of the explosive charge from the shell of the MS, a process especially difficult and dangerous. A cycle of investigations, including a broad spectrum, both of fundamental development and development of models of different principles of extraction of EM from the shell, permits demonstrating not only the effectiveness of these methods, but also the limits of their safe application for sufficiently high efficiency.

References

Afanas'ev, G.T., and V.K. Bobolev, 1968: Initiation of solid explosive materials by shock, M.: Nauka, 174 pp.

Amosov, A. P., S.A. Bostandzhiyan, and V.S. Kozlov, 1972: Ignition of solid EM by heat of dry-friction, *Physics of Combustion and Explosion*, 8, No. 3, 362-68.

Andreev, S.G., O.N. Eroshkin, and V.S. Solov'ev, 1993: Development of methods of extraction of infusible explosive materials from used projectiles, *Defense Technology*, No. 9, 47-52.

Andreev, S.G., and V.S. Solov'ev, 1992: On an analysis of Centrifugation of EM charges from usable explosive devices, *Physics of Combustion and Explosions*, 28, No.5, 132-3.

Andreev, S.G., A.E. Solov'ev, and A.E. Novitskii et al., 1991: Longitudinal-transverse instability of initiating shock waves, All-Union Conference on Detonation; Collection of papers, Krasnoyarsk, 330-334.

Andreev, S.G., L.N. Usenkov, V.S. Solov'ev, and V.V. Zyuzin, 1990: Increasing the precision of a model of the source of explosive material decomposition behind the front of an initiating shock wave, Moscow

State Technical University im, N.E. Bauman, M., 26 pp., Dep. v BINITI 18.02.91, N 794-891.

Andreev, S.G., and V.S. Solov'ev, 1984: Basis of the theory of explosive transformation of energy-generating materials, M TsNIINTI, 252 pp.

Andreev, S.G., A.N. Isaev, and V.S. Solov'ev et al., 1982: Limits of the EM ignition, *Physics of Combustion and Explosion*, 18, No. 6, 3-9.

Andreev, S.G., M.M. Boiko, and I.F. Kobilkin et al., 1979: Hotbeds formation in trotil and tetryl under the weak shot action, *Physics of Combustion and Explosion*, 15, No. 6, 143-48.

Andreev, S.G., M.M. Boiko, and V.S. Solov'ev, 1976: Initiation of EM on stepwise loading, *Physics of Combustion and Explosion*, 12, No. 1, 117-120.

Andreev, S.G., and V.S. Solov'ev, 1985: Basis of the theory of sensitivity of energy-producing materials. M.:TsNIINTI, 177 pp.

Attetkov, A.V., and V.V. Lazarev, 1989: Initial heating and ignition of fuels by compression of gas in pores, *Trudy MVTU*, No. 530, 3-19.

Attetkov, A.V., and V.S. Solov'ev, 1987: On the possibility of breaking down of heterogeneous EM in front of a weak shock wave, *Physics of Combustion and Explosion*, 23, No. 4, 113-25.

Averson, A. E., 1980: Theory of ignition, Heat-mass exchange in the burning process, *Chernogolovka*, 16-36.

Belyaev, A.F., V.K. Bobolev, and A.I. Korotkov et al., 1973: Transition of burning of condensed systems to explosion, M. Nauka, 292 pages.

Ermolaev, B.S., B.A. Khasainov, and A.A. Borisov et al., 1977: On a theory of stationary convective combustion, *Physics of Combustion and Explosion*, 13, No. 2, 169-76.

Hubbard, P.J., and R. Tomlinson, 1989: Explosiveness and shock-induced deflagration of large confined explosive charges, 9th International Symposium on Detonation, Portland, U.S.A., 580-92.

Jensen, R.L., E.J. Blommer, and B. Brawn, 1981: An instrumented shotgun possibility of an impact-initiated explosive reaction, *Seventh International Symposium on Detonation*, Maryland, 155-62.

Kabirov, S.A., V.M. Blldnikov, and L.K. Chekalina, 1992: Investigation of detonation capabilities of aerosols of hexogene, Chemical physics of the processes of combustion and explosion, Detonation: materials of the 10th symposium on combustion and explosion, *Chernogolovka,* 92-3.

Keef, R.L., 1981: Delayed detonation in card gap test. *Seventh International Symposium on Detonation*, Maryland, 233-240.

Khasainov, B. A., A.A. Borisov, and B.S. Ermolaev, 1988: Development of the source of reaction in porous energy-generating materials, *Chemical Physics*, 7, No. 7, 989-98.

Kolobov, V.I., L.M. Makarov, A.S. Shteinberg, and P.F. Drozhzhin, 1992: On the burning out of compact samples on emergence of a fresh metal surface, *Physics of Combustion and Explosion*, 28, No. 5, 8-11.

Lyubchenko, I.S., and V.V. Matveev, 1981: On the thermal theory of ignition of materials by surface heating, *J. Phys. Chem.*, 55, No. 6, 1465-69.

Selivanov, V.V., V.S. Solov'ev, and N.N. Sysoev, 1990: Shock and detonation waves: methods of investigation, M. Izd. MGY, 260.

Zemskikh, V.I., and O.I. Leipunskii, 1987: Secondary ignition of condensed reacting materials, *Physics of Combustion and Explosion*, 23, No. 2, 3-10.

CHAPTER 13

Retrofit Engineering: A Methodology For Conversion

Ali Seireg
University of Florida
University of Wisconsin

Introduction

For almost a half century, the lion's share of the world's material and human resources has been allocated to the development of military technology and products. The result is an overabundance of military hardware and an enormous investment in related manufacturing facilities, material supply systems, infrastructures, management organizations, and highly sophisticated physical, chemical, biological and mathematical sciences.

The race for quantitative and qualitative advantages in armaments and the growth of the so called "Military-Industrial Complexes" severely impacted the economics of the U.S.A. and the former U.S.S.R. Now that the threat of a global nuclear war has diminished and is being replaced by growing mutual trust between Russia and the United States, it is high time that some of the enormous scientific and technological resources join forces to find solutions to the problems that truly count for the people, such as abundant production of food, better housing and transportation, cleaning the environment, caring for the sick and the elderly, managing waste disposal and responding to natural or accidental disasters.

Due to the significant reductions in demands for defense products, the U.S. Government and the governments of the Commonwealth of Independent States are placing a high priority on helping the defense industries speed their transition to commercial production. In the U.S. there are approximately 9,000 primary suppliers of defense products in more than 200 industry sectors. Defense conversion seems to be a way to avoid massive layoffs and plant closings of industries which are on the cutting edge of advanced technology. Over the next 5 years the annual loss to these industries from procurement and

R&D is expected to be in the order of $50 billion. Since most defense products do not have direct commercial analogs, the process of conversion can be difficult and financially risky. The task is not simply to change from defense to commercial production, it is to restructure the industry into highly focused market driven and sustainable companies which take advantage of the quality of the defense technological base. Such a process is critical and can be painful. If not pursued knowledgeably, objectively and consciously, it can have negative or even disastrous consequences. In the time of crises well-meaning decision makers can embark on courses of action that produce adverse effects unless the change with all its aspects and impact potential are well analyzed and clearly thought out. There are numerous examples of unsuccessful conversion such as Rockwell's attempt to produce electronic calculators and watches, Textron's production of VCR equipment and motorhomes, McDonnell-Douglas' medical systems venture, Northrop's and Martin Marietta's environmental services, and Grumman and Boeing ventures into urban transportation. On the other hand, the aerospace division of Lockheed was very successful in profitably transferring their government-supported Dialog database service to the industrial markets. Similar activities are currently underway in the former U.S.S.R. with different degrees of success.

An important and potentially dangerous situation facing the world today is the vast stockpiles of nuclear, chemical, biological and conventional arms which have to be disposed of. This is creating a "flea market" of military hardware and production facilities. Careful attention should be given to their conversion or disposal for maximizing the extraction of any value they can add to the civilian economy and minimizing the impact of disposal on world security and the environment.

The Need for Systematic Methodology

In previous times, and certainly in Biblical times, the systems, the processes and the technical skills used in military production were few and simple. The conversion to peaceful use—"swords into plowshares"—could be easily conceived and implemented. Now, with a good share of the world's natural, financial, and technical resources devoted to military purposes, the systems are extremely complex. Economic conversion and efficient and safe disposal of nonusable products are understandably proportionally complex. Human conceptual approaches, although necessary and important, cannot by themselves deal with the complexity of the process. New analytical and synthesis techniques have to be applied in order to meet the difficult challenges.

It is fortunate that military needs which created the problem have also created the tools that can be used to solve it. The miraculous developments of computer systems, software, databases, programmable machines and robotics can provide the knowledge base and tools necessary for guiding the optimum conversion to civilian use and the safe disposal of the non-usable elements.

This chapter presents the framework of a methodology for the conversion process based on decomposition and reconstructive composition to meet civilian needs. The methodology takes advantage of the advances made in recent years in computer-aided design, manufacturing, assembly, production planning and database management. Illustrative examples of perceived areas of needs will also be given.

The Conversion Problem

The motivation to devise new systems or modify existing systems to improve the quality of life is an inherent characteristic of humans. It has controlled their actions since prehistoric times. Humans are equipped with the means to visualize, plan, and execute their plans. They are uniquely endowed with introspective ability to reflect on their needs and to modify their environment in a purposeful way to satisfy the perceived needs. The basic needs have always been, and continue to be, the provision of food, improvement of the habitat and protection from hostile intruders.

The traditional practice of design is based on intuitive conception of a feasible device capable of performing the specified task. Analytical tools are then applied to check the adequacy of the design. Changes and readjustments are made, usually one at a time, whenever necessary to insure the satisfactory behavior of the device under the expected operating conditions. While this approach guarantees an acceptable solution, it does not necessarily produce the best solution.

A common characteristic of all design problems is the existence of many feasible solutions. The selection of the best possible solution depends on a clear definition of the interaction of all the pertinent variables affecting the problem, an explicit statement of a merit criterion and an efficient search method for selecting the system with the highest merit among all feasible alternatives. The design problem is a task-oriented activity and, consequently, the first stage must be the definition of the required task using abstraction. Following this stage is the conceptual phase, the preliminary design and its optimization to generate the final design. The human design activity incorporates unconscious as well as conscious activities. The unconscious incorporates unconscious as well as conscious activities. The unconscious activity can be very powerful and should be given appropriate consideration and not be disturbed by any forced consciousness. Perhaps the first attempt at systematizing the design of machines is due to the Hero of Alexandria in the first century A.D. He classified the basic elements to be combined for performing different tasks as: the lever, the wheel and axle, the pulley, the inclined plane and the screw.

In the last two decades a great deal of interest in design methodology research was inspired by the challenges of developing high technology systems for defense and exploration of space. This type of research is still receiving considerable attention in the microelectronic, aerospace and defense-related industries. The abstraction of many mechanical-technical phenomena based upon their essential unity and the formulation of synthesis steps based on a "plan of events" provided a systematic framework for creating new systems.

The task definition as a product planning phase has been given considerable attention by design researchers. Pahl and Beitz give a complete overview of this approach. In their perception, this phase must answer the following questions:

- What is the objective of the problem?

- What are the implicit desires and expectations involved in the problem?

- What are the constraints and do they actually exist?

- What are the possibilities of future development?

For the design of a system, the following questions must be answered:

- What objectives must be satisfied by the solution?

- What are the desirable properties?

- What are the nondesirable properties?

Selecting and optimizing standard machines to fulfill the requirements of any specific problem can then be accomplished by piecing together in an optimal fashion existing standard elements to generate a total system capable of performing the entire task requirements. This approach receives considerable attention from European researchers, and interested readers may refer to the book by Pahl and Beitz (1984). This method of designing is implemented in highly developed design software and can be used in the composition of new systems from disassembled and properly catalogued parts if such parts can be directly adapted to the system. However, this may not be applicable in many cases, and a generalized methodology for conversion and retrofitting is outlined in the following.

A Structure for Retrofit Engineering

The five basic elements of retrofit engineering can be stated as:

1. The knowledge base of the existing system or product.
2. The functional analysis of the need.
3. The selection of components from the knowledge base which can be used or converted to match the different functional requirements.
4. The composition and optimization of an integrated system from components in the knowledge base with minimum added value.
5. Objective assessment of the economics and social cost of a restructured system and its candidacy for implementation.

Creating Feature-Based Models

A feature-based product model would greatly facilitate automated implementation of the conversion process. A growing portion of recent research and development has focused on methods to create such a product model. Recognizing or inferring features from a previously created model of a part is commonly called "feature recognition." Incorporating features into the design or product model definition process is called "design by feature."

Feature Recognition

Feature Recognition involves scanning a model of a product and recognizing or inferring features from its characteristics. This process can be done by human interpretation or by a software program.

Design by Feature

The design by feature method generates a feature-based product model by requiring that the model be described in terms of features as it is first created. The features are then saved in some form in the database and become part of the definition which describes the product. Applications should then be able to query the product model in terms of features. The concept of using features to communicate and store a product definition is relatively new. It was only made possible in recent years with the advent of powerful computer-based modeling systems and associated hardware.

Functional Feature Database

A number of factors influence the representation methods chosen for the functional feature database. These factors include the following:

(1) A desire for a canonical feature definition such that new feature definitions could be created by specially trained designers.

(2) An ability to retain design intent at both a topological and geometric level.

(3) A provision for enforcing design guidelines in the context of feature interaction. Incorporation of these capabilities must be possible at the feature and engineering part family definition level.

User Interface

The objective of the user interface is to present the product model to the user in a manner consistent with the overall objective. It is especially important that the interface communicate in terms meaningful to the functional aspects of the product that is being designed.

This objective was in part born from experience with conventional CAD system user interfaces. These interfaces force the user into abstract thinking often mismatched with actual design processes. When editing of a conventional product model is required, the designer is often forced to examine in detail the model construction method. The designer then modifies some sequence or parameter of the construction not directly associated with the aspect (or feature) of the design to be edited.

The concept of a constantly coherent product model requires the development of engineering part families and functionally minimal designations. The idea is similar to structured editors for some programming languages. The functionally minimal designation defines the starting point for a particular engineering part family. Coherency checking is accomplished through rules governing feature interaction at a feature level and at a part family level.

Creating and Interacting With the Product Model

The interaction of the user/designer with the Design by Functional Feature System is crucial to the viability of the entire concept. Making the interface even more critical is the difference between the design by feature approach and current methods. The main underlying concept is to only allow user interaction with the actual product model on a functional feature basis. This concept could be called a type of structured editor where the model is edited in terms of functional features in order to constantly enforce a particular structure on the product model representation. This enforced structure is somewhat controlled by the feature definitions themselves and also through the part family designation chosen by the designer.

Part Family and Feature Hierarchy

A part family is a set of criteria that establish an engineering-related functional grouping for product models. These criteria are enforced through feature hierarchy and functionally minimal designation.

A feature hierarchy has two purposes: (1) to define which features are valid for use within the particular part family, and (2) define a hierarchy for those features to establish rules for feature interaction in order to enforce design guidelines for the particular part family.

A functionally minimal designation is the minimum configuration of the valid features for a part family that satisfies the functional requirements of the part family. A particular instance or instances of each required feature type must be defined from the feature types contained in the hierarchy subgraph. This is done by defining an instances name or names for each feature type. These names will then be referred to in the remainder of the functionally minimal designation.

Benefits of the Design by Functional Feature Approach

In an integrated retrofitting or conversion environment, the product model created during the design process provides the data to guide and drive engineering and manufacturing applications from design inception through analysis, planning, manufacture and final inspection. Given the widespread effect of the product model format and contents, it is essential that any design method that creates the product model be evaluated in the context of the entire integrated system. The following evaluates the benefits of the design by functional feature approach in the conversion process as well as in other areas where the data in the product model can be used.

Retention of Design Intent. Defining a product model by specifying functional features, parameters and relationships allows retention of design intent. The function feature model represents the highest level design information available. This could also be called the highest level of abstraction. Tolerencing information might be attached to the features both internal to the features and between features. Explicitly modeled dependencies such as those possible with geometric constraints and geometric relational operators could aid in automatic modifications, assembly, inspection, and tooling.

By designing in terms of features one can always be assured that the product model is understandable (or coherent) in terms of features. This is an important capability in order to allow feature-based analysis of a product model at any stage of its development, especially in the early stages.

Design engineers generally envision the part they are to design in terms of functional features. The initial model is probably based on common aspects of previously designed parts in the same part family. Specific functional requirements of the new design will then form the basis for modifications. Design changes are directly communicated to the modeler.

Given the individual feature definitions, engineering part family definition, and functionally minimal model initialization input, a design by functional feature system could then automatically generate a rough cut design. Starting with this rough model, the designer can quickly add and/or modify features to create design adaptations.

Mapping of functional features to other equipment is a very important benefit to users of the design data in manufacturing modifications, assembly and cost estimation.

Mechanical System Decomposition Representation

A mechanical system can be viewed as an interlinked hierarchically-based network of subassemblies and components. Disassembly can be viewed as breaking component links, while assembly is the creation of links and the appropriate connectivity between components. To enhance the conversion or the environmentally safe recyclability of products, Ishii et al. (1993) developed a method of grouping components called "clumping." A clump is a collection of components and/or subassemblies that share a physical relationship and some common functional characteristics based on the user intent. They used four types of nodes for the design description: component, subassembly, fastener and fastening process. In general the data for the four nodes consist of item cost, removal time, installation time, tools and training required to perform the action, the name of the item or process, a user defined part number, part code and the next higher assembly. Clumping then seeks to form aggregations of components for reuse which require minimum disassembly and reprocessing costs. Knowledge representation of the subsystems and components can therefore be accomplished. The information storage and retrieval can be expedited by a Knowledge Based Expert System. Two procedures can be used for the system representation as follows:

1. Topological Approach: The system structure is represented abstractly using graph theory where the graph represents the entire system. A hierarchical graph of the system topology places the overall system at the top level. The major subsystems form the next level. These subsystems are further decomposed into lower levels until the basic component levels are reached.

2. Functional Approach: The system is viewed as being composed of a set of components that perform certain functions. Functional diagrams are then used to develop abstract representation of the system with all its subsystems and components.

The flow diagram shown in Fig.1 illustrates the decomposition process and the generation of the knowledge base for the products or systems which are candidates for retrofitting or conversion.

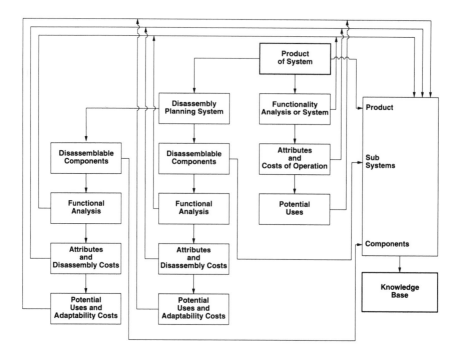

Figure 1.   The decomposition process.

Disassembly/Assembly Planning

Several machine assembly/disassembly planning systems have been developed to create an optimal disassembly and assembly sequence of machine systems for any goal such as replacing parts, modifying the original structure or reassembly of components to form new systems.

The systems generally incorporate expert knowledge and are adaptable for implementation with automated processing and robotics.

Function Description for the Knowledge Base

An important first step for retrofitting, conversion or reuse of a product or system is the creation of a functional description of the system or the product for use in a knowledge base. Functional entities consist of a formalized description which is organized in a hierarchy representing the function decomposition. There are main and auxiliary functions for the product's use. All product functions which describe physical values can be organized in a functional flow characterizing the physical functionality of the product. This can be derived by the definition of the predecessor/successor relations between the subfunctions and by hierarchically relating the subfunctions of the functional structure to the system, subsystems and components of the product.

Products or components are modeled by classes rather than by treating each product on a discrete basis. A given object class can be fully described by a minimal list of features representing key geometrics, material, functions, cost of production, interfaces and connectivity. "Set Theory" is the theoretical framework of the process of naming, describing, organizing, relating and constructing a given domain of parametrization. "Information Engines" form the principal components of the design package for retrofitting or conversion.

Functional Analysis of Need

As in any design process, a functional analysis of the need is the activity that controls the final outcome. The designer has to carefully address the following:

- Determining what is needed and what is to be achieved. This represents in broad terms the design objectives

- Breaking down the overall task into a set of subtasks with their attributes

- Establishing the connectivity between the subtasks

- Defining the constraints on the overall function and the subfunctions

Figure 2 outlines the functional analysis process which leads to a tabulation of the required functions and the attributes of potential systems or components capable of achieving these functions.

Product Development from Disassembled Parts

New product development in general relies on methods of conceptualization, and integrated design and manufacturing. In order to achieve success, the process requires strong innovative input, access to a broad spectrum of information, techniques for management of the information and a reliable cost management system.

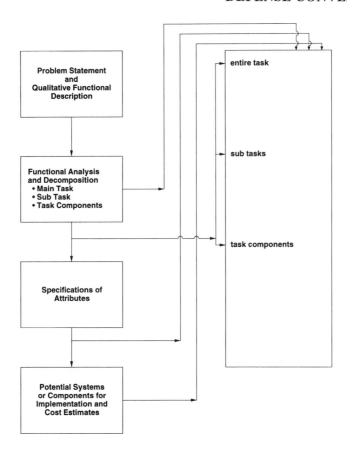

Figure 2. Analysis of need.

This section describes a formal structure for the process of retrofitting an existing system by replacements of parts or generating a new system by reassembling disassembled parts. The methodology is based on the feature-object concept and assumes the availability of a knowledge base with the functional and feature tabulation of subsystems and components of the considered military systems.

Conceptual Design

In conceptual design one attempts to find as many solutions as possible for satisfying the need. The intuitive process of selecting subsystems which are capable of performing the different subfunction can be greatly enhanced by searching the knowledge base. Combinations of possible solutions can then be generated for the subfunctions, and the human involvement in the process can make it tractable. A major concern in conceptual design is the relationship and connectivity between the different components that make up the entire system and discarding all solutions that are difficult to combine into an integrated design. Hierarchically Structured Database Management Systems can provide valuable assistance in component selection from the knowledge base for suitable retrofitting or conversion. It is well recognized that the conceptual phase of generating alternative solutions is an iterative process involving considerable input and qualitative judgement from the designer.

The recent advance made in network representation based on Graph Theory and Inference Engines with access rules for automatic induction can be utilized towards this goal. The selection of the most feasible concept among the alternative solution can be accomplished by a "Quality Audit" based on the sum of weighted objectives. These include the cost of value added relative to the final value, the time needed for conversion and the economic and societal benefits of the retrofitted or reassembled product. Careful evaluation of parallel concepts prevents committing to a single poorly conceived idea too quickly.

Conversion Modification and Reassembly

A critical element of retrofitting and conversion is the cost of disassembly and reassembly. The design of systems for automated assembly/disassembly may be needed for cost reduction especially for large volume products. Knowledge-Based Expert Systems can be applied to optimize the sequence of operation and to minimize the assembly/disassembly time. Design or manufacturing modifications and the addition or substitution of parts to simplify the process would be an inherent element of the conversion process.

The flow diagram in Fig. 3 illustrates the morphology of the conversion or retrofitting process. The essence is to iteratively optimize the match between a need for the civilian market with converted military products or facilities. The matching between need and available systems is the element of the process which is most responsible for its ultimate success. Although the conversion activity relies heavily on creativity and intuitive identification of potential applications, it can benefit greatly from quantitative and systematic procedures that stimulate the generation of alternative uses for surplus products and facilities. Many techniques are now available that can effectively handle the

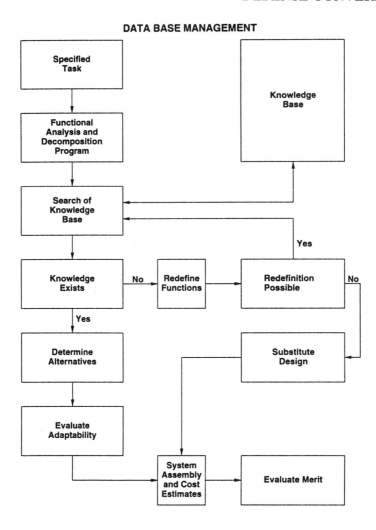

Figure 3. The retrofitting or conversion process.

large combinational problems that arise in the synthesis of engineering systems. They integrate the best capabilities of the designers and knowledge-based computers. The generation of a system topology can be effectively accomplished by employing and integrating different retrofitted or dis-assembled segments into a coherent system. The generated system can be iteratively optimized for best performance and minimum cost of conversion.

Database Management

An effective database management scheme for use in retrofitting and conversion should be able to automatically convert data from the format in which it is stored to the format which the user expects to receive it. Since military products involve many corporations who have their own databases, it is therefore necessary to develop database management systems capable of integrating data from a variety of sources. This would provide greater flexibility and allows the users to access the specific data they want without having to instruct the system on how to obtain it. Ideally, a single request from the user can retrieve single or multiple records using one or more search keys. The user, for example, can request information about parts for a certain function and receive a description, cost, and inventory level and then order the list by increasing cost. Database management systems, such as those currently used in the military and aerospace industries, can be valuable in maximizing the benefits of the conversion process.

Conversion Economics and Cost Management

In order to maximize the economics of conversion it is necessary to employ models for quantitative assessment of the costs involved for candidate applications and the benefit to society from reusing the military products. Cost accounting practices developed for the computer age enable designers to make strategic decisions on retrofitting and any necessary investment in new capital equipment as a part of the conversion process. Input-output technical economic models can be effectively used to evaluate the economic impact of conversion with the following considerations:

- Short-term and long-term allocation of resources

- Appropriate timing for investment in a particular venture

- Return on investment for the conversion efforts in a selected area

- Market and profit potential of planned new products

- Ripple effects on the economy from the introduction of the converted products

- Comparative effects of alternative materials, designs and manufacturing processes

- Needs for labor, energy, material resources, infrastructure and
environmental controls

- Optimum return from alternative product mixes

- Productivity of human resources and capital investment

- Competitiveness, both nationally and internationally, in quantitative
measures

Technology as a Resource

Most of the current economic decisions, corporate investments and
government practices do not adequately account for technology and innovative
engineering as a resource. They are still based on concepts that originated in the
past when the level of technical input was relatively low. The complexity of
modern military systems can create a wide gap between those who can make
engineering advances for their conversion and those who manage the
enterprises that can affect the change. The decision required for putting the
process in motion will require considerable input from knowledgeable and
innovative scientists and engineers who have the vision to see beyond "what is"
to "what can be."

Human Resources and Expert Knowledge

The arms race has produced great numbers of highly trained scientists
and engineers who are finding now that their talents and skills are no longer in
high demand. This has created a crisis situation which is felt around the globe
and especially in Eastern Europe and the former U.S.S.R. The latter accounts
for approximately one third of the world scientific and engineering output and
holds over 20 percent of all the patents registered worldwide. They have more
machines than the U.S.A., Japan and Germany combined. In spite of these
numerical advantages, there is now realization of the inefficient use of these
resources and that 60 percent of the engineering industries are in need for
renovation in order to make their products meet world standards. Academies
of Sciences have difficulty turning enough basic research into profitable

products. The problem is not the lack of good research but finding a way to utilize it in the civilian economy. This presents a great potential which can be tapped for the conversion activity as it was once tapped for the military effort. Any management system for conversion should pay considerable attention to the optimum utilization of the available human resources and the wealth of knowledge they represent.

Political Consideration and Overcoming the Barriers

There are many obstacles which will inevitably be encountered in the face of any conversion efforts. Besides the very challenging technical organizational and financial problems, there are formidable political and social barriers which have to be overcome on a global scale. Among these are the problems of ownership, secrecy, regulations, cooperation between the agencies involved, the establishing of priorities, the different governmental and industrial bureaucracies and above all the generation of consences, commitment and open-minded attitude for investigating the possibilities and willingness to take risks.

Some Candidate Areas for Retrofitting and Conversion

There are many thoughtful ideas for areas of human needs which can benefit from retrofitting and conversion of excess military systems. Some of these are already identified by the technology applications advisory groups for agencies such as NASA and SDI. All the National Laboratories of the Department of Energy (with an annual research budget of approximately six billion dollars) have active committees for transferring the advanced technology inspired by the defense needs to the civilian economy. The following are examples of some of the frequently discussed global areas of application:

1. Modernization of the physical plants and technology for the consumer goods industries
2. Small business development including conversion and retrofitting industries
3. Water resource technology such as desalination of ocean waters and irrigation networks
4. Energy generation and transmission networks

5. Agriculture and food production, development of a variety of farming implements, storage systems and means of delivery to the markets
6. Transportation in air, sea and land
7. Housing industries
8. Communication systems
9. Health care industries for the elderly and the handicapped. Medical diagnostics, devices and delivery systems including remote delivery
10. Urban renewal and industrialization
11. Cleaning the environment and creating sustainable forestry
12. Ecologically sensitive harvesting of ocean resources
13. Recreation facilities and industries
14. Peaceful use of space
15. Mining and excavation
16. Monitoring of climatic changes
17. Fast response to natural disasters and emergencies
18. Enhancing security and fighting crimes

There are many elements of these areas which can be effectively addressed by innovative conversion of existing military systems and technology.

Conclusion

The threat to world peace and security of nations is no longer military aggression. Military buildup to ward off conceived and real military threats was the focal point of the strategic planning of the superpowers. It held the top ranking in priorities for 50 years and overshadowed the social, economic and environmental programs. No country suffered from the consequences as did the former U.S.S.R. Meanwhile the Third World population has been exploding, and the only concern the superpowers had for them was where they stand in the balance of the ideological confrontation. The result is a world situation now where the efforts to achieve a superpower status of the former U.S.S.R. simultaneously created a "Third World" economic status. In the U.S.A., the neglect of domestic programs caused the inner cities and the infrastructure to be stressed to the breaking point. Unregulated and ill-conceived industrialization of developing countries wasted valuable resources and created uncalculatable damage to the environment. The time is right now that the unnecessary investment in human and material resources, which has been directed to the military effort, should be redirected to improving the national and international human conditions instead of simply disbanding it to unemployment and waste by benign neglect. A new global mission should be to provide incentives for the military industries to retool for the change. There should also be incentives for recycling the human and technological resources that were firmly absorbed in the military industries and establishments into useful enterprises for addressing the pressing human needs on a global scale. This can be accomplished by rearranging and adapting building blocks that already exist to provide a wide spectrum of employment opportunities for economic developments. By well conceived retrofitting and conversion, the excess capacity of the world military establishments can be refocused to play a major role in realizing the important goal of a better world society and living environment.

Modern military technologies are too complex and too diverse for individuals to fully comprehend, utilize and manage their conversion. Only groups and organizations can manage the knowledge, skills and material resources necessary for useful reuse. Although ideas usually originate with creative individuals, the development of ideas into useful products requires the pooling of many skills. This presents challenges to the development of managerial approaches to define the viable conversion opportunities, appraise their relevance and convert plans into actions. There is a great need for clear vision to transform the current problem into an opportunity for a brighter future. A central requirement for the success of the conversion process is the generation and continuous maintenance of comprehensive knowledge bases, database management systems and action plans for implementation. Ideas alone are not sufficient to make it happen.

References

Ishii et al., 1993: "Life-Cycle for Recyclability," Proc. JSME-ASME Joint Workshop on Design, Tokyo, Japan.

Pahl, G. and W. Beitz, 1984: Engineering Design, Springer-Verlag, New York.

Bibliography

Accounting in the Automation Age, Computers in Mechanical Engineering, (CIME), July/August 1987, Springer-Verlag, New York.

Andreason, M.M., "The Systematic Design in Practice," Proc. of ISDS, 1984, Tokyo, Japan, pp., 165-170.

Baron, S., "Overcoming Barriers to Technology Transfer," Research and Technology Management, 33, No. 1, 1990.

Bennett, J., Creary, L., Englemore, R. and Melsoh, R., "SACON: A Knowledge-Based Consultant for Structural Analysis," Technical Report, STAN-CS-78-699, Stanford University, Sept. 1978.

Biggioggero, G.F. and Rovida, E., "Proposal for Methodic Design in the Mechanical Field," Proc. of ISDS, 1984, Tokyo, Japan, pp. 211-215.

Chung, J.C., R.L. Cook, D. Patel, and M.K. Simmons, "Feature-Based Geometry Construction for Geometric Construction," 1988 ASME Computers in Engineering Conf., San Francisco, California, August.

Corser, T. and Seireg, A., "Optimizing a Design for Production, Inspection and Operation," Computers in Mechanical Engineering, 4, No. 2, Sept. 1985.

Cross, N., "Engineering Design Methods," John Wiley & Sons, NewYork, 1989.

Cunningham, J. and J. Dixon, "Designing with Features: the Origin of Features," 1988 ASME Computers in Engineering Conf., San Francisco, California, August.

Data Bases for Design, Computers in Mechanical Engineering CIME, ASME, Special Issue, March 1987.

Defense Industry and the Environmental Agenda, Symposium 91, National Security Industrial Association, Washington, DC, 1991.

Dhillon, B.S. and Reiche, H., "Reliability and Maintainability Management," Van Nostrand Reinhold Co., New York, 1985.

Dittmayer, S. and Sata, T., "Systematic Product Development," proc. of ISDS, 1984, Tokyo, Japan, pp. 237-242.

Descotte, Y. and J. Latombe, "GARI: Expert System for Processing Planning," in Solid Modeling by Computers from Theory to Application, eds. M.S. Pickett, and J.W. Boyse, New York: Plenum Press, 1984, pp. 329-345.

Dixon, J.R., "Designing with Features: Building Manufacturing Knowledge into More Intelligent CAD Systems," Proc. ASME Manufacturing International '88 Conf., Atlanta, Georgia, April 17-20, 1988.

Fulton, R.E., "A Framework for Innovation," Computers in Mechanical Engineering, pp. 26-40, March, 1987.

Harker, S.D.P and K.D. Eason, "Representing the User in the Design Process," Design Studies 5, No. 2, 1984, pp. 79-85.

Hasegawa, M. and H. Mizoochi, "ICAD System for Automated Assembly Line Design Using the Technique of Autonomous Change of Structural Model," Proc. JSME-ASME Joint Workshop on Design, Tokyo, Japan, June 1993.

Henderson, M.R. and D.C. Anderson, "Computer Recognition and Extraction of Form Features: A CAD/CAM Link," Computers in Industry, pp. 329-339, May 1984.

Hubka, V., "Attempts and Possibilities for Rationalization of Engineering Design," Proc. of ISDS, 1984, Tokyo, Japan, 159-164.

Hongo, K., N. Nakajima, T. Ishida, and J. Kohno, "Self-Organizing Database for Conceptual Design," Proc. of ICED, Rome, Italy, 1981, pp. 425-434.

Hongo, K., "On the Significance of the Theory of Design," Proc. of ISDS, 1984, Tokyo, Japan, pp. 204-210.

Imamura, S. et al., "Assembly Planning by Cooperative Agents," Proc. JSME-ASME Joint Workshop on Design, Tokyo, Japan, June 1993.

Kubota, A. and T. Taura, "A Conceptual Design Process Model Based on Functional Similarity," Proc. JSME-ASME Joint Workshop on Design, Tokyo, Japan, June 1993.

Leontief, W. and A. Seireg, Engineering Economics, A Special Issue of Mechanical Engineering, ASME, January 1987.

Luthy, C., "Proposed: A Feature-Oriented CAD Database," Manufacturing Systems, pp. 26-27, March 1987.

McDermott, J., "R1: An Expert in the Computer Systems Domains," Proc. of the 1st Annual National Conf. on A.I., Stanford University, 1980, pp. 269-271.

Maher, M.L. and S.J. Fenves, "HI-RISE: Design of High Rise Building," Private Communication, 1984.

Manoocherhri, S. and A. Seireg, "Computer-Aided Generation of Machine Topology for Specified Tasks," CIME, 6, No. 3, 1987.

Maes, P., "The Dynamics of Action Selection," Proc. IJCAI-89, 1989.

Morse, W.J., H.P. Roth, and K.M. Poston, "Measuring, Planning and Controlling Quality Costs," National Association of Accountants, Montvale, New Jersey, 1987.

Nicolai, W., "Design System for the Development of a Standard Product into a Special Product," Proc. JSME-ASME Joint Workshop on Design, Tokyo, Japan, June 1993.

Pighini, V., G.D. Francesco, D.Z. Yuan, A.V. Schettino, and A. Rivalta, "The Determination of Optimal Dimensions for a City Car Using Methodical Design with Prior Technology Analysis," Design Studies 2, No. 2, 1983, 233-243.

Pollalis, S and W.S. Habib, "Selection and Predimensioning of Structural Systems," Presented at 4th Intl. Symp. on Offshore Mechanics and Arctic Eng., Feb. 1985.

"Product Definition Data Interface," Materials Laboratory, U.S. Air Force Wright Aeronautical Laboratories, Wright-Patterson AFB, Ohio, 1984-1987, see especially System Requirement Document SRD560130000, July 1984.

"Product Definition Exchange Specification (PDES) Working Group Documents," as available August 1988, National Bureau of Standards, United States, and Individual PDES Group Leaders as designated by the National Bureau of Standards.

Quality, A Special Issue of Mechanical Engineering, ASME, January 1988.

Redford, A.H., "Design for Assembly," Design Studies 4, No. 3, 1983, pp. 170-176.

Roth, K.H., "Foundation of Methodical Procedures in Design," Design Studies 2, No.2, April 1981, pp. 107-115.

Rzevski, C., D. Woolman, and D.B. Trafford, "Validation of a Design Methodology," Design Studies 1, No. 6, 1981, pp. 325-328.

Seireg, A., "Research Needs in the Mechanical Sciences," Paper Presented at ASME-Winter Annual Meeting, Washington, DC, Nov. 1981.

Seireg, A., "A Survey of Optimization of Mechanical Design," J. of Eng. for Industry 94, No. 2, 1972, pp. 495-499.

Seireg, A., "Recent Developments in Design Tools and Methods," Proc. of the International Conference on World Progress in Mechanical Engineering CMES, Beijing, China, June 1991.

Sekiguchi, H. et al., "Study on Automatic Determination of Assembly Sequence," Annals of CIRP, 32/1, 1983.

Sekimoto, S. and M. Ukai, "Hierarchically Structured Database for Mechanical Design," Proc. JSME-ASME Joint Workshop on Design, Tokyo, Japan, June 1993.

Serrano, D. and D. Gossard, "Constraint Management in Conceptual Design," in Knowledge Based Expert Systems in Engineering Planning and Design, eds. D. Sriram, and R.A. Adey (Computational Mechanics Publications, 1987), pp. 211-224.

Shah, J.J. and M.T. Rogers, "Feature Based Modeling Shell: Design and Implementation," 1988 ASME Computers in Engineering Conf., San Francisco, California, August 1988.

Shah, J.J. and A. Bhatnagar, and D. Hsiao, "Feature Mapping and Application Shell,"1988 ASME Computers in Engineering Conf., San Francisco, California, August 1988.

Staley, S.M. and D.C. Anderson, "Functional Specification for CAD Databases,"Computer-Aided Design, 18, No. 3, 132-137, April 1986.

CHAPTER 14

Nuclear Technological Perspectives

Alex E.S. Green
Nuclear Engineering Sciences Department
University of Florida
Gainesville, Florida

Nuclear Energetics and Fission

Nuclear fires, first harnessed a half century ago, are based upon nuclear reactions in which the basic constituents of nuclei are rearranged from less stable to more stable configurations. They are like chemical fires, first harnessed some 5000 centuries ago, which are based upon reactions in which atoms, the fundamental chemical constituents of nature, are rearranged from less stable to more stable molecular forms. Nuclear burning in many respects is simpler to understand since there are only two basic nuclear constituents (neutrons and protons, together called nucleons). The mass number A is the total number of nucleons in a nucleus and the element number Z is the number of protons. There are now 110 elements whose atoms can form innumerable molecular sources of chemical energy.

The mass of any nucleus is always less than the unassembled mass of its protons and neutrons, the missing mass constituting the binding energy of the nucleus. The release of nuclear energy is accomplished by nuclear reactions in which the nucleons are rearranged from loosely bound structures to more tightly bound structures (i.e., missing more mass). This principle applies whether splitting nuclei in fission or combining nuclei in fusion. The suitability of a substance as a nuclear fuel can thus be visualized by considering the tightness of the binding of potential imputs as represented by the nuclear binding energy per nucleon (b). Figure 1 shows the trend of b vs A for beta stable nuclear species in mMU (thousandth of a mass unit), where a mass unit (MU) is approximately the mass of each nucleon. Note that the b's of the very lightest nuclei fall off precipitously with A and go into a deeper energy hole as A approaches mass numbers about 60. As one goes to higher mass numbers b rises slightly (i.e., gets less missing mass per nucleon). Fusion processes,

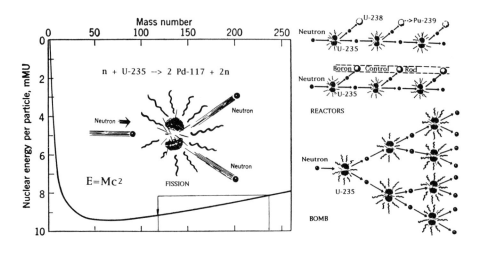

Figure 1.   Left: Trend of nuclear binding energies per nucleon vs. mass number
             and illustration of the neutron-fission process. Right: n-f applications:
             (top) Reactors for plutonium production and energy generation with
             unit multiplication; (bottom) Bomb with multiplication by 2 (adapted
             from Green, 1955 and Benedict et al., 1981).

including those in our sun and in proposed fusion reactors, move nuclear matter
to the greater nuclear stability of the 60 mass region. Fission processes use the
small mass loss that occurs when a heavy nucleus is split into two parts. The
downward arrow for the example n + U-235-->2Pd +2n process in Figure 1
represents such a mass loss.

In Figure 1, n represents a neutron that because it is electrically neutral
is not repelled by the electric charge of nuclei, U is uranium (Z=92), and Pd is
Palladium (Z=46). In effect, excited by neutron capture, the compound
nucleus, U-236, splits into two equal parts and also produces two neutrons that
can initiate further fissions (a chain reaction). Since the b of U-236 ~ 8 mMU,
whereas b of Pd-117 ~ 9.1 mMu, about 1.1 thousandth of each nucleon mass
(~MU) is converted to energy via Einstein's mass-energy law. Thus the fission
of one kilogram of U-235 releases

$$Q = (1.1) \text{ x } (.001) \text{ x } (1 kg) \text{ x } (3 \text{ x } 10^8 \text{ m/s})^2 \sim 10^{14} \text{ joules}$$

The fact that this is about four million times the chemical energy of a kilogram of coal illustrates the tremendous potential of nuclear energy. Fusion has even greater potential and has been successfully used in "hydrogen" bombs. However it has been difficult to overcome the electric charge repulsion of nuclei in fusion reactors.

The heavy radioactive elements including thorium (Th, Z=90), protactinium (Pa, Z=91), and uranium, (Z=92) that are naturally present are all members of three chains whose mass numbers satisfy $A = 4n+i$ where n is an integer=51 or larger and i =0, 2 or 3 (Green, 1955). The existence of these natural chains is attributed to the exceptionally long half-lives of three members: Th-232, 14 billion years; U-235, 0.7 billion years; and U-238, 4.5 billion years. U-235 is present to the extent of 0.7 percent in natural uranium, which is 99.3 percent U-238.

The large thermal neutron capture cross section of U-235 and its still appreciable natural abundance has made it possible since World War II to "breed" the transuranic elements neptunium (Np, Z=93); plutonium (Pu, Z=94); americium (Am, Z=95); curium (Cm, Z=96) and additional elements now up to Z=110. By this modern alchemy it has been possible to reproduce many members of the three natural radioactive families as well as a fourth (i=1) family whose longest lived member is neptunium-237 (Np-237, Z=93), with 2.2 million years half-life. All of these nuclides undoubtedly existed in our geological past but had long ago decayed away to insignificant quantities. Were the Earth another U-235 half -life or so older it would probably have been too difficult to launch the nuclear age of bombs and reactors in the 20th century. With only 0.7 percent U-235 in natural uranium it is possible to "breed" large quantities of Pu-239 from U-238. Similarly, potentially large quantities of U-233 can be bred from Th-232.

Nuclear Reactors

Almost immediately after nuclear fission, induced by neutrons, was identified by Hahn and Strassman in 1939, it was recognized that fission reactions fulfilled the two requirements for a sustained nuclear-energy process. Not only is the reaction markedly exoergic, but it also automatically reproduces the initiators (neutrons) of the reaction. Whether a sustained process could actually be attained under practical conditions was recognized to be dependent upon the values of cross sections for neutron capture followed by fission and the cross section for neutron capture followed by loss of energy by gamma radiation. The fact that these parameters were found suitable for U-235 has made it possible to release nuclear energy in a slow controlled manner (reactor) or explosively (bomb).

The nuclear age was launched on December 2, 1942 with the successful operation of a graphite moderated natural uranium reactor at the athletic field of the University of Chicago. The pile was first operated at the 0.5-watt level and later achieved 200 watts. A higher-power pile designed primarily to serve as a pilot plant for plutonium production was built in 1943 at Oak Ridge, Tennessee. Original plans were made for a uranium-graphite pile that would produce significant quantities of plutonium; for this purpose a power level of 1000 kilowatts was specified. Final plutonium production was transferred to a reactor constructed at Hanford, Washington.

A nuclear reactor releases nuclear power by providing the conditions for reproduction or regeneration of the fission reaction and the multiplication of neutrons which are initiators and products of the reaction. Since some neutrons inevitably escape through the surface of the reactor, a sustained process will take place only when the reactor is large enough. To secure a reactor of reasonable size, the fissionable fuel must meet several stringent requirements. Because of the large thermal fission cross section of U-235, it has proved possible to operate a controlled reactor using natural uranium. For such a reactor, moderators must be used to slow down or thermalize the fast neutrons ejected during fission and thereby improve their chances for capture and fission with respect to capture and production of gamma radiation or loss out of the surface. Moderators like heavy water and graphite are especially useful since they have very low probabilities for neutron capture; nevertheless with uranium slightly enriched in U-235 light water can be used as a moderator as in modern pressurized and boiling water reactors.

At thermal energies the radiative-capture cross section of U-238 is large and its fission cross section is small, so it is not directly suitable as a fuel for thermal reactors. However a natural uranium reactor "breeds" plutonium (Pu-239) when the neutrons from the fission of U-235 are captured by U-238. The compound nucleus U-239 loses energy instantly by gamma emission and then produces the easily fissionable Pu-239 via the successive negative beta decays

$$\text{U-239} \dashrightarrow \text{Np-239} + \beta \, , \, \text{Np-239} \dashrightarrow \text{Pu-239} + \beta$$

Th-232, an abundant nuclide, can also be bred into a fissionable nuclide (U-233) in a U-235-fueled reactor by the sequence of reactions:

n + Th-232 -> Th-233, Th-233 -> Pa-233 + β, Pa-233 -> U-233 + β

Natural U-235 and artificial Pu-239 and U-233 have the common property of having an even number of protons and an odd number of neutrons. The compound nuclei formed from such an even proton odd neutron (EO) nuclide after capturing a neutron becomes an even proton, even neutron (EE) nuclide, which in its ground state has extra stability due to double outer shell pairing (Green, 1955, Green and Lee, 1955, Green, 1958). In consequence, even when the neutron captured is slow the compound nucleus is formed in a highly excited state and can overcome the inherent barrier to the fission process with its large release of energy (about 200 Mev.). Actinides with EE (like U-238) or OE (like NP-237) proton and neutron numbers can release comparable fission energies; however, fast neutrons are required to overcome the inherent fission barrier, as in U-238.

Most reactors operate with slow or thermal neutrons that are very effective in the fission of U-235, Pu-239 and U-233 and in some case also effective for breeding (e.g.,Th-232-->U-233). Thermal neutrons are produced by slowing fast neutrons in moderators such as graphite, heavy water or light water. The reactor cores are usually cooled with water or a gas (e.g., helium). Some reactors have no moderator, operate with fast neutrons, and are normally cooled by a liquid metal (e.g., sodium) (NRC, 1992). These reactors can serve as breeders and under appropriate arrangements can make use of all actinides as fissionable fuel.

Commercial water reactors are of three classes: (1) pressurized water reactors (PWR) are light-water reactors (LWR) that maintain the water adjacent to the fuel elements at high pressure to prevent boiling; (2) boiling water reactors (BWR) are LWRs in which the water adjacent to the fuel elements boils; and (3) heavy water reactors (HWR) are reactors in which heavy water (deuterium oxide or D_2O) serves as both coolant and moderator instead of ordinary (light) water, and only the coolant is pressurized. In current HWRs the reactor fuel is natural or slightly enriched (~1 percent) uranium, and in LWRs the fuel is uranium enriched to contain 3 or 4 percent U-235 isotope (NRC, 1992). These reactors produce electricity by generating steam to drive steam turbines (Rankine Cycle), usually achieving a conversion efficiency of about 33 percent. Their power ratings are given in megawatts thermal (MWt) or megawatts electrical (MWe). Table 1, adapted from a survey in the September 1994 issue of Nuclear News lists the worldwide operational nuclear power units by total installed capacity (in gigawatts electrical) and number of units. Table 2 lists the installed capacity; that is, the number of units operational and under construction by the thirteen nuclear electricity producers. The totals for 20 other countries, each having installed capacities below 3.5 GWe, are also given.

Table 1. Operational Nuclear Power Units Worldwide by Reactor Type *

	GWe	# Units
Pressurized light-water reactors (PWR)	214.2	243
Boiling light-water reactors (BWR)	74.9	91
Gas-cooled reactors, all types	12.2	36
Heavy-water reactors, all types	18.6	33
Graphite-moderated light-water reactors (LGR)	14.8	15
Liquid-metal fast breeder reactors (LMFBR)	0.9	3
Total	335.6	421

*(adapted from Nuclear News, September 1994)

Table 2. Nuclear Power Plants in Operation and Under Construction (UC)

Country	GWe	#Units	UC	Country	GWe	#Units	UC
U.S.A.	99.5	109	2	United Kingdom	11.5	34	1
France	57.6	56	4	Sweden	10.0	12	-
Japan	39.9	47	6	Korea	7.2	9	6
Germany	22.7	21	-	Spain	7.1	9	-
Russia	19.8	25	4	Belgium	5.5	7	-
Canada	15.4	22	-	Taiwan	4.9	6	-
Ukraine	12.1	14	6	20 others	22.4	51	-

*(adapted from Nuclear News, September, 1994)

Nuclear Bombs

The neutrons released following fission divide naturally into "prompt" neutrons and "delayed" neutrons. The yield of prompt neutrons from fast neutron fission of isotopically purified U-235 and Pu-239 is large enough so that a highly critical mass can be made by the rapid assembly of sub-critical masses. In the Trinity and Nagasaki bombs Pu-239 was used in an implosion arrangement driven by chemical explosives to achieve prompt neutron criticality in fractions of a microsecond. In the Hiroshima bomb two subcritcical masses of U-235 were driven together by chemical propellants in a gun barrel-like system to achieve prompt neutron criticality. During the short period before these bombs burst, an appreciable part of the material undergoes fission with the release of energies equivalent to that of many thousands of tons of TNT with 1 kg fissioning yielding 17 kT (Lovins, 1994). Temperatures and pressures close to those at the interior of the sun are created and the devastation possible is widely known.

Physical methods that depend upon isotopic mass differences have been used for the separation or purification of U-235 to achieve highly enriched uranium (HEU) suitable for bombs. These have been advanced greatly in the last half century from the original electromagnetic separators and gaseous diffusion plants used during WWII. Centrifugal separation and laser separation have been added to the battery of available isotopic techniques in recent years (May, 1994). While less costly, these still constitute complex technologies.

Chemical methods can be used to separate isotopically pure Pu-239 from the residual uranium and the fission products in reactor fuel that has been exposed in a reactor for relatively short times (low burn-up). Such highly enriched Pu-239 can be used to make very efficient implosion bombs. If the reactor fuel is left in a reactor for its useful lifetime as a nuclear energy source (high burn-up), Pu-240, Pu-241 and other superheavy nuclides are formed. These isotopes have substantial spontaneous fission rates and other undesirable properties so that high burn-up was once considered an approach to "denaturing" plutonium chemically separated from spent reactor fuel. Unfortunately with sophisticated design and greater difficulty, mixed isotopic plutonium can also be made into bombs, albeit not as efficient as weapons made of isotopically pure Pu-239. This relationship between reactor technology and weapons fuel generation complicates efforts to separate nuclear energy and nuclear weapon technologies (Lovins,1994; May, 1994).

"Little Boy," a bomb fueled by Uranium-235 was dropped on Hiroshima on August 6, 1945, and "Fat Man," a bomb fueled by Plutonium-

239, was dropped on Nagasaki on August 9, 1945. Together with the Trinity plutonium bomb exploded in the first test on July 16th these nuclear explosives opened a new and troublesome era for mankind. There are at least four contrasting views as to the role of these atomic bombs in World War II. This topic is of particular interest to the author who participated in a reconnaissance flight that found the then "missing" Japanese fleet, immobilized for lack of oil, near Hiroshima in March 1945 prior to our Okinawa landings (Green, 1993, 1994). No matter what view is accepted, "Hiroshima" played a major role in bringing the Cold War between the United States and the former Soviet Union (F.S.U.) to a very costly level.

Under the MAD (mutually assured destruction) military doctrine in the early 1960s the population of the U.S.A. and the former Soviet Union (F.S.U.) became hostage to the large nuclear arsenals of both countries. Then as a flexible response doctrine evolved that could be described as Nuclear Utilization Target Selection (NUTS) (Keeny and Panofsky, 1981), the combined arsenals grew further to achieve a destructive capability possibly many times more than that needed to destroy human civilization.

With the breakup of the U.S.S.R. in December 1991 the fate of their 45,000 nuclear bombs and the U.S.A.'s 30,000 nuclear weapons became an overriding concern. In view of the very serious economic bind the F.S.U. is in, and the 4.7 trillion dollar national debt of the U.S.A., a specific project directed at converting our vast supplies of destructive nuclear weapons irreversibly into useful and safe energy sources would appear to be helpful.

In October 1991, at a conference on "Climate Change and Energy Policy" at Los Alamos National Laboratory (Rosen and Glasser, 1992) the use of nuclear energy as an eventual "Greenhouse Mitigation" (Green, 1989) measure was discussed. This solution, however, is impeded by the poor public image of nuclear energy due to "Hiroshima," the Three Mile Island accident and the Chernobyl meltdown, the nuclear waste storage problem and nuclear weapon proliferation. These, plus the high capital costs of reactors are serious obstacles to the use of nuclear energy in the U.S.A. and the F.S.U. A method to convert irreversibly nuclear "weapons to inherently safe reactors" (WISR) might provide an accommodation to these public perception problems (Green,1992, 1994).

WISR Concepts

It must be recognized that the Cold War was launched in the last phases of the Hot War with Germany and Japan in a confrontation between a

Stalin-dominated F.S.U. and a Truman-led U.S.A.. Since this past no longer inhibits current relationships, perhaps the two major "victors" of WWII can now collaborate to regain some industrial and economic strength relative to the "losers." An imaginative Defense Conversion program would preferentially help the U.S.A. and the F.S.U., now overly encumbered with debt from five decades of capital investments in military equipment and production facilities. On the other hand, after WWII Japan and Germany invested in facilities to make consumer products that generate capital, now the key to advanced technology and economic prosperity and the construction of advanced reactors.

Climate change has emerged as a global issue and the international drive to reduce carbon dioxide emissions has been a source of embarrassment to the U.S.A. Since Three Mile Island we have become more reliant on our excellent reserves of coal for electricity generation, and among the fossil fuels (coal, oil, natural gas) coal gives the most carbon dioxide per energy output. Nuclear electrical generation and the use of electric vehicles are natural ways of lowering carbon dioxide emissions. Unfortunately, the capital costs of individually designed nuclear power plants in this country are very high. In addition there is a very strong anti-nuclear movement. Yet engineers, scientists and systems analysts who dispassionately examine how we might practically reduce global carbon dioxide emissions inevitably face the dilemma that nations with large populations, such as China and India, and other developing countries that have large coal reserves, can only achieve higher living standards by increasing their use of coal (Jones and Fulkerson, 1989; Green, 1980, 1989).

If a global cap on carbon dioxide emissions is needed, such a policy will almost inevitably require advanced nations to back-off their use of coal in favor of emissionless or low carbon dioxide emission energy resources. While renewables (solar, hydro, wind power, biomass) can pick up some of the load, most quantitative estimates find a large need for a nuclear contribution. Other measures will also be needed such as reforestation, energy efficiency, control of chlorofluorocarbon, methane and nitrous oxide emissions, possibly carbon dioxide scrubbing, and certainly global population stabilization. Ironically, for lack of capital and because of the bad public image of nuclear energy, the nuclear component of the Greenhouse solution is practically dead in the U.S.A. and F.S.U., the two largest carbon dioxide emitters (Hammond et al., 1991).

The nuclear waste disposal problem is frequently cited as the basis for rejecting nuclear energy. There are, however, potential nuclear transmutation and chemical separation solutions to this problem (Schnitzler and Schneider, 1976; Marriott, 1976; Arthur, 1992). However, it is probable that the "Hiroshima" proliferation and the Chernobyl disaster are the main reasons many countries and organizations are rejecting nuclear energy. The WISR (weapons to inherently safe nuclear reactors) concept (Green, 1992) was proposed with the hope of providing a pull for deproliferation and a push for the use of nuclear energy as a Greenhouse mitigation measure.

Such efforts to rebottle the bad (weapons) nuclear genie while helping the good (reactor) nuclear genie reach its full potential for service to humankind are certainly not new . The Baruch Plan of 1946 and Eisenhower's "Atoms for Peace" program of 1953 had similar objectives. However with the end of the Cold War, the tremendous excess of nuclear weapons and weapons-grade nuclear fuel, the widespread proliferation of nuclear weapons technology, and the emergence of climate change as a global issue presented a new opportunity to drive home these peace objectives. Some of the steps necessary to initiate a WISR-type program have already been taken in connection with the Strategic Arms Reduction Treaties on lowering the nuclear weapons threat by destroying delivery vehicles. However with the breakup of the U.S.S.R. several independent countries have displayed ambiguous feelings about proposed arrangements. A "weapons to inherently safe reactors" program combined with "denaturing" weapons-grade fuel could allay such concerns. Table 3 presents a list of potential special advantages of a WISR-type solution for the U.S.A. and the F.S.U..

The United States has embarked upon an extensive program to retire plutonium production reactors. At the Hanford Site eight nuclear reactors have been retired from service and are ready for decommissioning (Miller et al., 1994). These projects are technically complex, since each reactor block weighs about 10,000 tons and must be transported 5–14 miles to the disposal site. In Russia the problem is further complicated by the fact that their plutonium production reactors have provided district heat and electricity to some cities; thus, replacement power systems are needed. Solutions to this problem are now being addressed on a joint U.S.-R.F. basis (DOE, 1994).

Advanced Reactors

As a result of intensive studies in response to Three Mile Island and Chernobyl, there are under development a number of advanced reactor technologies including passive and inherently safe nuclear reactor systems (Jones and Fulkerson, 1989; American Nuclear Society, 1991; Forsberg and Reich, 1991; Gas Cooled Reactor Assoc., 1991; EPRI, 1991; National Research

Table 3. WISR* Advantages to USA and FSU

---

1. recaptures some of Cold War investments
2. reduces CO_2 and other anthropogenic emissions
3. reduces oil imports and balance of payments problems
4. revitalizes nuclear industries
   - (a) employs nuclear engineers and scientists
   - (b) lower nuclear weapons threat
   - (c) provides mission for weapons laboratories
   - (d) replaces Chenobyl type reactors by ISR
   - (e) ends sell-out to foreign countries
   - (f) fosters seawater desalinization
   - (g) fosters electric vehicles
   - (h) facilitates hydrogen fuel production
5. USA and FSU can become energy exporters
6. USA and FSU can assume environmental leadership
7. reduces defense externalities cost
8. fits a general "Swords to Plowshares" program
9. favors U.S.A. and F.S.U. with their large stockpiles
10. sets a deproliferation pattern for other countries
11. provides a simple path for denaturing U-235
12. provides long range paths for plutonium denaturing

---

*Weapons to inherently safe reactors

Council (NRC), 1992; Nuclear News, 1992). These advanced reactors include advanced light-water reactors (ALWR). (APWR and ABWR mean "advanced"; AP means "advanced passive"; SBWR means "simplified"; CANDU means "Canadian deuterium uranium"; SIR means "safe integral reactor"; and PIUS means "process inherent ultimate safety") (NRC, 1992). The liquid metal-cooled fast neutron reactor has variations known as LMR (liquid metal reactor), PRISM (power reactor, innovative small module), the Integral Fast Reactor (IFR) and the European Fast Reactor (EFR). Table 4 is a listing and recent assessment of advanced reactor technologies.

General Electric's 1300-MWe Advanced Boiling Water Reactor (ABWR) is the first advanced nuclear plant to receive a final design approval (FDA) from the U.S. Nuclear Regulatory Commission (NRC). Design certification of standardized nuclear power plant designs means that utilities will save significant time and money when constructing a nuclear power plant. With the certification of standardized plant designs, nuclear vendors design the entire nuclear plant and are responsible for pre-licensing their power plant designs before utilities commit to expensive projects. Costs are reduced

Table 4. Advanced Power Reactors

	Power Lic	Type	Lead designer	Neutrons	Fuel	NRC Rank
System 80+	1300 92	press water	ABB-CE	thermal	UO_2 or PuO_2	H
ABWR	1300 91	boil water	GE	ther	UO_2	H
SBWR	640 95	boil water	GE	ther	UO_2	H
APWR-1300	130 95	press water	Westinghouse	ther	UO_2	H
AP 600	600 94	press water	Westinghouse	ther	UO_2	H
MHTGR	538(4) 02	gas-cooled	General Atomic	ther	UCO/ThO_2	L
CANDU-3	450 93	press heavy water	AECL Candu	ther	$Nat.UO_2$	M
PIUS	640 02	press water	ABM Atom	ther	UO2	L
EFR	1450	liq. met. breeder	EFR Assoc.	fast	MOX	L
ALMR	1440 03	liq. met breeder	GE/Argonne	fast	MOX,Zr	M
EPR	1450	press water	NPF	ther	UO2, MOX	
GT-MHR	600	gas cooled	GE/Ga/ORNL	ther		

H - high   M - medium   L - low

because standardized nuclear power plants are built in as little as half the time because lengthy construction and licensing delays are eliminated. Two ABWRs are under construction in Japan and on schedule for operation in 1996 and 1997. Several additional ABWR units will soon be built for other Japanese utilities (Nuclear News, September 1994).

General Electric also has underway studies of a 640-MWe Simplified Boiling Water Reactor (SBWR) that is expected to show improvements in plant availability, operating capacity factor, safety and reliability while reducing power generation costs, construction duration, occupational radiation exposure and radwaste.

ABB's (Asea Brown Bovary) System 80+ standard design has become the first pressurized water reactor to obtain final design approval under the new U.S. NRC regulations for licensing standard plant designs (ABBCE Nuclear Systems, Fall 1994). The System 80+ standard plant design is rated at 1350 MWe and meets all applicable U.S. NRC regulations. It also complies with the Electric Power Research Institute's ALWR Utility Requirements Document. This is an evolutionary design based on the three System 80+ units in operation in Arizona and four units under construction in The Republic of Korea.

Westinghouse Electric Corp. is developing the AP600, a simplified, standard 600-MWe nuclear power plant design that it says combines proven pressurized water reactor technology with innovative passive safety systems. Westinghouse is leading the AP600 design effort. Major contractors on the team are Bechtel Power Corp. (nuclear island buildings and systems), Burns and Roe (annex, access, diesel generator and solid radwaste buildings and systems), Avondale Industries, Inc. (modularization), MK-Ferguson Co., (construction planning and management), Chicago Bridge and Iron, Inc. (containment vessel design), and Southern Electric International (turbine island buildings and systems design), (Nuclear News, September 1992).

A European Pressurized Water Reactor (EPR) was launched as a joint development project in 1991 by nine German electricity utilities and Electricite de France (EdF) together with nuclear power plant vendors active in Germany and France (Siemens and Framatome) and with their joint subsidiary, Nuclear Power International (NPI). A declared objective of the cooperation is the exploitation of the experience accumulated in Germany and France in order to achieve further improvements in plant operation and technical plant safety. Choosing the evolutionary design path takes into account the time available, the limitations of development and construction costs, and the fact that the acceptance of technical safety by the regulatory and supervisory authorities can be achieved more easily by a development of existing technology in small steps than by trying some completely new development. Measures to control core meltdown accidents and to limit the consequences of such accidents to the environment are integrated into pressurized water reactors of the classical design. A plant capacity of 1400 to 1500 MWe was chosen for the joint German-French plant development since assessments of the specific electricity generating costs in nuclear power plants have revealed a decrease in capital costs with increasing plant size, while the costs contributed for plant personnel and for annual revisions are almost independent of plant size. NPI concludes that a plant of the evolutionary type in the 1400 to 1500 MWe power category will cause lower specific electricity generating costs than a technically simplified plant of half the size (Brocker, 1994).

Canada continues to direct its attention to Pressurized Heavy Water Reactors (PHWR) that use deuterated water as a moderator and natural uranium as fuel. The CANDU reactors in service have a record of safe, reliable and economic performance (Snell and Feinroth, 1993). Atomic Energy of Canada Limited (AECL) is completing the design of an advanced evolutionary CANDU, known as CANDU-3, with a nominal rating of 450 MWe. This plant has improvements in reliability, safety, operability and constructability and can be constructed in a little over three years (Nuclear News, September 1992).

Japan has embarked upon extensive nuclear energy programs based upon evolutionary LWR designs (Forsberg and Reich, 1991). These reactors include the Hitachi Small Boiling-Water Reactor (HSBWR-600) with the rated capacity of 600 MWe; the Mitsubishi Simplified PWR (MS-600) rated at 600 MWe; the Japanese System-Integrated Pressurized-Water Reactor (SPWR) rated at 350 MWe and the Toshiba SBWR-900 rated at 310 MWe.

Advanced reactor technologies that do not use water as a coolant or moderator include the gas-cooled graphite-moderated reactor known as the MHTGR (modular high-temperature gas-cooled reactor) and the liquid metal reactor (LMR). In the MHTGR the elementary fuel particle is a refractory coated spherical kernal about 0.5 mm in diameter with multiple layers of refractory material such as pyrolytic carbon and silicon carbide. The elementary fuel particle is intended to retain fission products at the highest temperatures (Gas Cooled Reactor Assoc., 1991). The fissile fuel is a two-phase mixture of 20 percent enriched uranium dioxide and uranium carbide. Fertile material such as natural uranium or thorium can be incorporated into the pellet. The MHTGR uses a heat exchanger to convey heat from the high temperature helium coolant to a steam generator. The steam drives a standard turbine (Rankine cycle) to generate electricity. Secondary containment in MHTGR is an underground steel vessel that can conduct heat to the soil so as to avoid core meltdown by decay heat if the reactor is spontaneously shut down.

The recently proposed Gas Turbine-Modular Helium Reactor (GT-MHR) couples the passively safe MHTGR to a high efficiency power conversion system, the aeroderivative gas turbine (Brayton cycle). Power rating investigations and design studies (McDonald et al., 1994; Silady et al., 1994; LaBar and Simon, 1994) have led to the selection of a nominal power rating of 550 MWt (260 MWe) and a stretch capability of 600 MWt. The major component in the direct cycle system is a helium closed-cycle gas turbine rated at 286 MWe. The rotating group consists of an intercooled helium turbo-compressor coupled to a synchronous generator. The vertical rotating assembly is installed in a steel vessel, together with the other major components (i.e., recuperator, precooler, intercooler, and connecting ducts and support structures). The rotor is supported on an active magnetic bearing system. The turbine operates directly on the reactor helium coolant and with a temperature of 850°C (1562°F). Projected efficiencies of approximately 50 percent might be achieved with advanced turbine technologies. The selected configuration forms the basis for more detailed investigations and meets the requirements for a second generation inherently safe nuclear power plant that, according to its proponents, could be in service in the first decade of the 21st century.

Japan has demonstrated a strong interest in MTHGRs. According to the revision of "Long-Term Program for Development and Utilization of Nuclear Energy" issued by the Japanese Atomic Energy Commission, the High Temperature Engineering Test Reactor (HTTR), which is the first High Temperature Gas-Cooled Reactor (HTGR) in Japan, is being constructed by the Japan Atomic Energy Research Institute (JAERI). Its purpose is to establish and upgrade the technology basis for an HTGR, serving at the same time as a potential tool for new and innovative basic research and international cooperation. The JAERI is proceeding with the construction of the HTTR, focusing on criticality in FY 1998 (Shiozawa et al., 1994).

The LMR, PRISM, IFR, and EFR use liquid metal cooling and metallic fuel. The IFR works together with a new pyroprocessing stream that provides another approach to burning uranium, plutonium and actinides in general, (Till and Chang, 1992; Quinn and Thompson, 1993; Quinn, et al., 1994). According to its advocates, pyroprocessing separates fission products from residual actinides of the nuclear waste from light-water reactors. This offers a synergy between LWR and IFR fuel cycles that might lead to a large mitigation of the nuclear waste storage problem. Whereas U.S. fast reactors have focused on small units, the EFR attempts to achieve economies of scale at 1500MWe (3600 MWt).

In addition to designing and developing inherently safe advanced reactors the prime movers in building reactors are actively involved in designing, building, and installing elements of advanced instrumentation and control (I&C) systems, (Deutsch and Reid, 1993; Yudate and Suzuki, 1993; Nishiyama et al., 1993; O'Neil, 1993)). The architectures are intended to meet the requirements specified in the Electrical Power Research Institute (EPRI) Advanced Light-Water Requirements (ALWR) document, Chapter 10, Man-Machine Interface Systems. Key elements of these design approaches include continual focus on coordinating the I&C design with the overall plant design, the use of a consistent, integrated approach for enhancing plant operation and reducing operator burden, and continual recognition of the need for maintenance, extensive testing, and inspections on the installed equipment throughout the plant life. The advanced I&C architecture provides for flexibility in meeting specific plant requirements without requiring extensive hardware changes. Portions of this advanced I&C architecture are being incorporated as upgrades to existing facilities thereby enhancing the safety margins of current reactors. Additional elements of this advanced I&C architecture are also being incorporated into plants that are currently under construction and are scheduled for operation with the next few years.

Inherently safe reactor systems or upgraded current commercial reactor systems can be adapted for burning weapons-grade highly enriched uranium (HEU) (95 percent U-235) diluted with natural uranium (99.3 percent U-238 and 0.7 percent U-235) to reactor-grade low enriched uranium (LEU) (about 3 percent U-235). An agreement between the U.S.A. and Russia has been reached and adopted in which Russia will convert 500 tons of HEU to diluted U-235 and sell it to the U.S.A. for further conversion to LEU. This weapons-to-existing-reactor use has achieved wide acceptance.

At this time the leading candidates for denaturing weapons-grade plutonium by burning it as a fuel are standard light-water reactors (Washington Public Power Service, 1987), or in the future, an ALWR (Buckner and Parks, 1992; Buckner et al., 1993). The Integral Fast Reactor (IFR) using liquid metal cooling and metallic fuel together with a new pyroprocessing stream provides another means to burning uranium, plutonium and actinides in general (Quinn, et al.,1993). Indeed, the possibility of using pyroprocessing to separate fission products from residual actinides in the nuclear waste from light-water reactors offers a possible mitigation of the nuclear waste storage problem.

With the low cost of oil, natural gas and coal and the relative capital costs of gas-fired combined cycle systems (about $500/kW), coal plants (about $1500/kW) and nuclear plants (of the order of $2500/kW) the direct economic incentive for the construction of new inherently safe reactors at this time is not favorable. In the near term most additions to electrical generation systems in this country and most other countries are being made using natural gas with aeroderivative gas turbines in combined cycle or cogeneration systems. In the former case conversion efficiencies from fuel to electrical energy now exceed 50 percent. In cogeneration systems leading to electrical and steam output, even greater use of fuel energy might be achieved. Thus as long as the bulk of the weapons-grade fuel (U-235), after simple denaturing by dilution with natural uranium or depleted uranium, can be used in existing or upgraded reactors there is little immediate economic drive towards a Weapon to Inherently Safe Reactor (WISR) type program. The longer range picture, however, must reflect our long-range national interests in maintaining an advanced position on the nuclear energy option and must consider long-range environmental and defense externalities.

Economically the use of weapons-grade plutonium in a WISR-type program is even more unfavorable at this time since a plutonium processing facility will be needed that will add considerably to the effective cost of the reactor fuel (Panofsky, 1993). Thus the use, disposal or storage of weapons-grade plutonium must largely be examined in relation to other strategic national considerations. Such considerations will be the subject of the chapters that follow.

References

ABB CE Nuclear Systems, 1994: System 80^{+TM} receives design approval from the NRC, *Power Perspective*, Windsor, Connecticut.

American Nuclear Society, 1991: *Proceedings of the Topical Meeting on The Next Generation of Nuclear Power Plants: A Status Report*, La Grange Park, Illinois. Nov. 10-14, 1991.

Arthur, E., 1992: Radioactive Isotope Destruction and Accelerator-Driven Nuclear Reactors, *Proc. of the Conference on Global Change* at Los Alamos, Oct. 1991, American Institute of Physics, New York.

Benedict, M., T. Pigford, and H. Levi, 1981: *Nuclear Chemical Engineering, 2nd Ed.,* McGraw-Hill Series in Nuclear Engineering, New York.

Brocker, B., 1994: Status Of The Development Of The European Pressurized Water Reactor, ASME Joint International Power Generation Conference, Phoenix, Arizona, 94-JPGC-NE-22.

Buckner, M. R., and P.B. Parks, 1992: Strategies for Denaturing the Weapons-Grade Plutonium Stockpile, prepared for the U.S. Department of Energy, Aiken, South Carolina, October.

Buckner, M. R., J.A. Radder, J.G. Angelos and H. Inhaber, 1993: Excess Plutonium Disposition Using ALWR Technology (U), prepared for the U.S. Dept. of Energy, Aiken, South Carolina, February.

DOE, 1994: Replacement Power Fact Finding Mission For Plutonium Producing Reactors, U.S. Delegation to Tomsk and Krasnoyarsk-26, Office of Nuclear Energy, Washington, DC.

Deutsch, K.L., and J.B. Reid, 1993: Advanced Instrumentation and Control Systems for the Next Generation of Nuclear Reactors, ASME International Joint Power Generation Conference, Kansas City, Missouri, NE-Vol.12.

EPRI/CRIEPI, 1991: GE Nuclear Energy Passive Plant Natural Circulation BWR Core Studies, Joint EPRI/CRIEPI Advanced LWR Studies, EPRI NP-7186-M Project 2660-57.

Forsberg, C.W., and W.J. Reich, 1991: *Worldwide Advanced Nuclear Power Reactors with Passive and Inherent Safety: What, Why, How, and Who,* ORNL/TM-11907, Oak Ridge National Laboratory/Martin Marietta for DOE.

Gas-Cooled Reactor Associates, 1991: *Utility/User Requirements For and Assessment of the Modular High Temperature Gas-Cooled Reactor,* GCRA 91-002 , San Diego, California.

Green, A.E.S., and K. Lee, 1955: *Proceedings of International Conference for the Peaceful Uses of Atomic Energy,* United Nations, New York, 107-112.

Green, A.E.S., 1955: *Nuclear Physics,* International Series of Physics, McGraw-Hill, New York.

Green, A.E.S., 1958: Nuclear Sizes and the Weizsacher Mass Formula, *Rev. Mod. Phys.,* 30, 580-584.

Green, A.E.S., Ed.,1980: *Coal Burning Issues*, Chapter 1: Introduction and Summary by Interdisciplinary Center for Aeronomy and Other Atmospheric Sciences, University Presses of Florida, Gainesville, Florida, 1-32.

Green, A.E.S., 1989: *Greenhouse Mitigation*, FACT Vol 7 Amer.Soc. of Mechanical Engineers, New York., New York, 1-77.

Green A.E.S., 1992: Peacetime Application of Weapons-Grade Fuel, short synopses by Jason Makansi in *Common Sense,* February and *Power,* March.

Green, A.E.S., 1993: Finding the Japanese Fleet in March 1945, *INTERFACE,* an international Journal of The Institute of Management Science and Operations Research Society of America September/October.

Green, A.E.S., 1994: An Operations Analyst with the 21st Bomber Command *Alex Green Festschrift*, A. Deepak Publishing, Hampton, Virginia, 1-15.

Hahn, O. And F. Strassman, 1939: Uber den Nachweis und das Verhalfen der bei der Bestrahlung des Uransmittels Neutronen Entstehenden Erdalkalzmetalle, *Die Naturwissenschaften* 27.

Hammond, A.L., E. Rodenberg, and W.R. Moomaw, 1991: Calculating National Accountability for Climate Change, *Environment*, 33, No.1, 11-15.

Harms, A.A. and D.R. Kingdon, 1993: Passively Fail-Safe Fission Reactor Based on Pellet Suspension Technology, presented at ASME International Joint Power Generation Conference, Kansas City, Missouri, NE-Vol.12.

Jones, J.E. Jr., and W. Fulkerson, 1989: *Global Warming—the Role for Nuclear Power,* Chap. 5, Green, A.E.S., *Greenhouse Mitigation.*

Keeny, S.M. Jr., and W.K.H. Panofsky, 1981: MAD versus NUTS Foreign Affairs 60, pp. 287-304.

LaBar, M.P., and W.A. Simon, 1994: Comparative Economics of the GT-MHR and Power Generation Alternatives, General Atomics Project 4962, presented at the ASME Joint Power Generation Conference, Phoenix, Arizona, Oct. 3-5.

Lovins, A. B., 1994: Plutonium Disposition, *Physics and Society*, 23, No. 4, 2.

Marriott, R., 1976: Transmutation and Chemical Processing of Nuclear Waste patents: U.S.A., 4,721,596; France, 0.030.404; Germany, P3071586.7-08 and other countries.

May, M. M., 1994: Nuclear Weapons Supply and Demand, *American Scientist,* 82, No. 6, 526-537.

McDonald, C.F., R.J. Orlando, G.M. Cotzas, 1994: Helium Turbomachine Design for GT-MHR Power Plant, presented at the ASME Joint International Power Generation Conference, Phoenix, Arizona, 94-JPGC-NE-12.

Miller, R.L., E.W. Powers, J.M. Usher, Y. Oktay, 1994: Engineering For The Surplus Production Reactor Decommissioning Project At The Hanford Site, Richland, Washington.

National Research Council, 1992: "Nuclear Power," National Academy Press, Washington D.C.

Nishiyama, H., M. Makino, and H. Sakamoto, 1993: Integrated Digital Control System for Nuclear Power Plants, ASME Intern. Joint Power Generation Conf., Kansas City, Missouri, NE-Vol.12.

Nuclear Engineering International, 1994, 39, 482.

Nuclear News, 1992: The New Reactors, September.

Nuclear News, 1994: The Latest World List of Nuclear Power Plants, September.

O'Neil, T.J., 1993: Operator Interface Design for GE's Advanced Light-Water Reactors, presented at ASME International Joint Power Generation Conference, Kansas City, Missouri, NE-Vol.12.

Panofsky, W.K.H., 1993: National Academy of Sciences, Science at the Frontier, *A Symposium in Honor of Frank Press*, The Academy and Arms Control, preprint April 25, 1993.

Quinn, J.E. and M.L. Thompson, 1993: The ALMR Actinide Recycle System's Mission and Status, ASME Intern. Joint Power Generation Conference, Kansas City, Missouri, NE-Vol.12.

Quinn, J.E., P.M. Magee, M.L. Thompson and T. Wu, 1994: ALMR Fuel Cycle Flexibility, GE Nuclear Energy, San Jose, California, *Proceedings of the American Power Conference.*

Rosen, L., and R. Glasser, 1992: *Proceedings of the Conference on Global Climate Change Its Mitigation Through Improved Production and Utilization of Energy,* held at Los Alamos National Laboratory, October 21-24; 1991: published by American Institute of Physics, New York.

Schnitzler, B.G., and R.T. Schneider, 1976: Application of Gas Core Reactor for Transmutation of Nuclear Waste, *Third Symposium on Uranium Plasmas*, Princeton University, June 10-12.

Shiozawa, S., S. Maruyama, and K. Sawa, 1994: Present Status and Future Program of HTGR in Japan, presented at the ASME Joint International Power Generation Conference, Phoenix, Arizona, 94-JPGC-NE-15.

Silady, F.A., A.M. Baxter, T.D. Dunn, G.M. Baccaglini, and A.A. Schwartz, 1994: Module Power Rating For GT-MHR Helium Gas Turbine Power Plant ASME Joint Intern. Power Generation Conf., Phoenix, Arizona, 94-JPGC-NE-17.

Snell, V., and H. Feinroth, 1993: Advanced CANDU Reactors: Status and Future Plans, ASME International Joint Power Generation Conference, Kansas City, Missouri, NE-Vol.12.

Till, C. E., and Y.I. Chang, 1992: Integrating the Fuel Cycle at IFR Nuclear Engineering International, November.

Washington Public Power Service, 1987: Technical Feasibility Task Force WNP-1 Conversion Preinvestment Analysis Report Summary, U.S. Department of Energy, Office of Nuclear Materials, February.

Yudate, T., and T. Suzuki, 1993: Application of a Digitalized Safety Protection System for the Advanced Boiling Water Reactor, presented at ASME International Joint Power Generation Conference, Kansas City, Missouri, NE-Vol.12.

CHAPTER 15

Plutonium Options

John W. Landis
Chairman
Public Safety Standards Group

Problems With Plutonium

Plutonium is an extremely poisonous element—not as dangerous as concentrated caffeine or nicotine or pure heroin or arsenic—but hazardous enough to require that it be handled very carefully and not taken into the body in more than trace quantities. If inhaled, its alpha emissions may cause lung damage. If ingested, its chemical properties allow it to become permanently embedded in bone structures, where its alpha activity destroys the marrow.

Frightening as these health hazards are, they are not the main cause of our concern about the hundreds of metric tons of this element that now reside in nuclear warheads, in weapons plants, in weapons scrap piles, in nuclear generating stations, in military and civilian nuclear waste, and in reprocessing plants. We are afraid that these sources of plutonium will not be tightly controlled and that substantial quantities will be acquired by renegade nations or terrorist groups and used to make bombs or non-explosive devices for criminal purposes.

This is not a new fear. Heeding the admonitions of foresighted scientists like Glenn Seaborg and Eugene Wigner, the global public has been aware of the dangers inherent in the proliferation of weapons-grade nuclear material for almost five decades, and through its representatives in government has demanded the development of adequate plutonium safeguards.

Reasonably effective safeguards have indeed been set up through bilateral and multilateral agreements and through the establishment of the International Atomic Energy Agency (IAEA). The statutes of the IAEA, for example, authorize the Agency to store plutonium that is "in excess of the peaceful needs" of its members. How this particular provision would be implemented is not clear, but the fact that it is on the books, so to speak, indicates a serious intention to severely restrict the availability of plutonium.

Obviously, there is a similar international intention to severely restrict the availability of weapons-grade uranium. This restriction can be accomplished fairly easily, however, by simple dilution with U-238 or natural uranium to concentrations that are usable as fuel for current nuclear generating stations. There is an overwhelming international consensus that this is the appropriate way to reduce the extensive stockpiles of weapons-grade uranium. In view of the fact that Russia and the United States have already started down this path, this chapter focuses on the real problem—*the use or disposal of weapons-grade plutonium.*

Weapons-Grade Plutonium

Weapons-grade plutonium has to encompass any plutonium that can be fabricated into an explosive device, no matter what the efficiency of the device is. Therefore, for our purposes, the term "weapons-grade" includes the plutonium produced in commercial nuclear generating stations. Since the process of producing plutonium is irreversible, the options for use or disposal are quite limited. Generically, they are:

1. Recycling in commercial nuclear generating stations.
2. Destruction in specially designed power-producing reactors.
3. Storage in relatively pure form for future use or disposal.
4. Storage in adulterated form in permanent repositories.
5. Storage in adulterated form in monitored retrievable facilities.

Recycling of plutonium in commercial nuclear generating stations is an inordinately difficult operation. In theory it can be accomplished with varying degrees of effectiveness in all types of power reactors, ranging from the ubiquitous light water reactors to the planned liquid-metal reactors. In practice, the technical, economic, institutional and political problems for each type are daunting. Without discussing these problems in detail, let us consider a few examples.

First of all, any present-day commercial station manager worth his (or her) salt would not undertake such a financially questionable venture without requiring very large premium payments for the effort. These payments may be substantial enough to make the option uneconomic. The exorbitant prices that probably will be charged for reprocessing spent fuel from commercial stations, conversion of recovered plutonium to suitable oxide form, mixing of plutonium oxide with uranium oxide, and fabrication of mixed-oxide fuel assemblies would certainly compel the owners of the plutonium to look for alternative methods of using it.

Second, assessing and solving the safety and environmental problems associated with use of mixed-oxide fuel in current commercial nuclear generating stations is a complex task requiring considerable time and a sophisticated effort. Although the task has been performed satisfactorily in Europe, the delays and disruptions it would cause and the money it would cost in the United States are additional deterrents to the use of the recycle option.

Finally, the recycle option may not be politically acceptable because it ties nuclear installations approved by the public for the sole purpose of producing electricity into another purpose that is not well understood and has a confusing relationship with nuclear weapons.

Destruction of plutonium in specially designed power-producing reactors appears to be a more attractive technical option than recycling it in commercial nuclear generating stations. One reason is that these reactors would be designed from scratch for this purpose, eliminating some potentially troublesome backfits and maximizing the net reduction of plutonium. A 1000-MWe burner reactor, for instance, would reduce the total plutonium inventory by about one metric ton each year, or about ten times as much as would a standard commercial LWR of the same size.

The big disadvantages of this option are (1) the enormous cost of the new facilities, (2) the political and technical constraints on siting, (3) the new and complicated licensing regulations required for the non-fertile fuel forms that will be employed, and (4) the maze of financial arrangements that must be negotiated whether the facilities are located in the United States or in Russia. Also, like the first option, this option would require reprocessing of spent fuel from commercial plants and other steps which would make plutonium in its free form more susceptible to diversion.

Storage of plutonium in relatively pure, or free, form for use or disposal, say one hundred years from now, is of course only a stop-gap measure. It is a measure that offers the great advantage of time, however, for the nuclear nations to collectively think through and develop the options for ultimate treatment and decide which should be applied to each of the extant basic sets of circumstances.

Nuclear Nations

The "extant basic sets of circumstances" of nuclear nations can be briefly categorized as follows:

1. Nations with extensive programs in both nuclear power and nuclear weapons. (a) With reprocessing of spent fuel. (b) Without reprocessing of spent fuel.

2. Nations with extensive programs only in nuclear power. (a) With reprocessing of spent fuel. (b) Without processing of spent fuel.

3. Nations with minor programs in both nuclear power and nuclear weapons.

4. Nations with minor programs only in nuclear power.

5. Nations with minor programs only in nuclear weapons.

6. Nations with no programs in nuclear power or nuclear weapons, but which have possession of weapons-grade plutonium made by the nuclear nations.

This categorization clearly indicates that the solution to the problem of ultimate disposal or the use of plutonium will be different for different parts of the world, which unfortunately greatly complicates the challenge that humanity faces. The fundamental differences regarding plutonium disposal or use already exist. The United States has eschewed the reprocessing of spent nuclear fuel. Nuclear nations in Western Europe and Asia have not. Russia employs some of its nuclear generating stations to produce both electricity and plutonium. Most other nations separate these functions. These differences may decrease with the passage of time. No one can guarantee that they will, however.

In a sense, the nations that reprocess spent nuclear fuel have already implemented the storage option and, according to responsible IAEA officials, the techniques being used are quite satisfactory. France has alleviated its storage problem by selling a large quantity of plutonium to Japan. During a recent visit to Japan, the author was assured by Japan Atomic Power Company executives that elaborate precautions are being taken to prevent the diversion of any of this material to military applications, but the basic problem still exists. Only the locale has changed!

Nevertheless, seeing a multiplicity of plutonium-storage arrangements springing up around the world makes many non-proliferation experts somewhat uneasy. They would much rather have all excess plutonium stored in one or more IAEA facilities. This, they feel, would minimize the proliferation risk. Working out the necessary agreements between the IAEA and the nations that own either the plutonium or the selected storage sites will take at least a decade, however.

IAEA storage and control does not solve the plutonium-safeguards problem entirely. The storage facilities will have to be located on sovereign territory somewhere and, wherever that somewhere is, national priorities may at some point overwhelm the force of the international agreements and cause the nation or nations involved to take possession of the plutonium.

Storage of plutonium in adulterated form in permanent repositories is a superficially attractive option to two groups: (1) those who want to make future use of plutonium as unlikely as possible and (2) many advocates of nuclear-power growth who want to "wipe the slate clean" and revitalize the worldwide nuclear-power industry by developing and deploying reactors that produce little or no plutonium or that recycle the plutonium until what is left is no longer useful as an explosive. These and other groups who are promoting this option seem to have forgotten the regulations currently in force in several countries that stipulate a long period of retrievability (50 years in the United States) for the waste put into so-called permanent repositories. These regulations have a sound environmental basis. We need to find out what happens in the repositories, particularly if they have the extra heat and radioactivity burdens imposed by the presence of actinides, before we permit geologic forces to seal them.

Despite the above, this option does have certain advantages. One is that it obviates the need for spent-fuel reprocessing. Another is that plutonium recaptured from weapons or the weapons complex can be placed in the waste streams from either commercial nuclear generating stations or military reactors and disposed accordingly. This option has little appeal in countries like Japan and France where, largely because of worries about energy security, most people do not want to see the vast plutonium energy reserves thrown away.

There is a finite possibility that a monitored retrievable storage (MRS) system for high-level radioactive waste will be built in the United States before a permanent repository is constructed. Initial disposal of weapons-grade plutonium in such a facility would have some of the same drawbacks as initial disposal in a permanent repository, but not all of them. There would be hope for many years that the plutonium so stored could be recovered with minimal trouble if the world—or at least a portion of the world—needed it for energy supply or some other important peaceful purpose. Conversely, a determined proliferator could probably pilfer it with somewhat less difficulty than he would have in getting it out of a permanent repository.

This approach has great merit in that it would yield much more definitive information about storage of high-level radioactive materials than would immediate confinement in a permanent repository and would perhaps prevent mankind from making serious mistakes about the effectiveness of below-ground storage. We would learn, among other things, what effects a large decrease in fission-product activity and/or heat load would have on the stored material and its containers. We would also learn how best to recover the material, if such recovery is desirable.

On the negative side, many countries, in addition to the dozen or so that now have the capability, will be able to process the waste and recover the plutonium for military purposes by the time the MRS testing is complete and this may encourage renewed proliferation activity at that time. We have no clear view of what will happen. All we know is that the primary barrier against proliferation will then be, as it is now, rigorous political and regulatory control.

CHAPTER 16

PLUTONIUM: MILITARY AND CIVILIAN

W. K. H. Panofsky

Stanford Linear Accelerator Center
Stanford University
Stanford, California

Plutonium

The management of plutonium, the only man-made element produced in large quantities, poses unprecedented challenges to man's wisdom. Plutonium plays a dual role: It is one of the two fissionable materials each of which can serve as an essential ingredient for the manufacture of nuclear weapons and it is an integral part of the nuclear fuel cycle which feeds civilian nuclear power.

These two functions are separate in many respects but are also linked both physically and politically. They are linked physically because all isotopes of plutonium can be used to make nuclear explosives. While what is called weapons grade plutonium containing more than 94 percent of the isotope Pu 239 is the material of choice of the nuclear bomb maker, reactor grade plutonium, which is the isotopic mixture of plutonium produced from U238 after extensive burnup in nuclear reactors, can also be used to manufacture nuclear weapons of elementary design with an assured yield of at least one to two kilotons. They are linked politically because the separation (reprocessing) of plutonium in the civilian fuel cycle increases the risk that that material can be diverted to military use, yet it is such reprocessing which can extend the energy value of the finite uranium resources of the world by perhaps two orders of magnitude.

In this discussion I would like to address first the problem engendered by the release of unprecedented amounts of <u>military</u> plutonium resulting from the reduction of the nuclear weapons stockpiles of the U.S. and Russia. I will then discuss briefly the future of <u>civilian</u> plutonium and the controversies which swirl around that future among different countries in the world.

Excess Military Plutonium

With the end of the Cold War, nuclear arms reductions on an unprecedented scale are underway. If current plans are successfully implemented, tens of thousands of nuclear weapons will be dismantled over the next decade. This represents an historical moment of great hope, but also of danger.

The weapons to be dismantled contain 100 tons or more of plutonium and several hundreds of tons of highly-enriched uranium. Since these materials are the essential ingredients of nuclear weapons, limiting access to them remains the primary remaining technical barrier to the spread of nuclear weapons in the world today. Managing and protecting these materials and securing and accounting for them—when even a grapefruit-sized ball weighing only several kilograms would be enough to make the fissionable core of a nuclear bomb—will be a monumental task. Indeed, this is one of the most pressing security challenges facing our country, Russia and the world today. Plutonium poses special difficulties; as unlike highly-enriched uranium, it cannot be "blended down" to a proliferation-resistant form, and it cannot today compete economically in the current market for nuclear fuels.

In the former Soviet Union, this security challenge is further complicated by the enormous political, economic, and social upheavals now underway. Ukraine has now decided not to go the nuclear road, a possibility that would have dealt a devastating blow to arms reduction and nonproliferation. And the risk that weapons-grade materials could be stolen in the former Soviet Union remains all too real. Unless urgent action is taken, any day now we could wake up and read in the morning newspaper that enough material for a dozen bombs really had been stolen. There have been many false alarms and minor diversions already.

Faced with this situation, the U.S. National Security Council asked the National Academy of Sciences' Committee on International Security and Arms Control to make recommendations on appropriate policy steps for the management and disposition of excess weapons plutonium. The report was released in January of 1994. It covers three stages of the process of reductions—dismantlement of nuclear weapons, storage of the resulting fissile materials, and long-term disposition of those materials—as well as a broad transparency regime designed to apply to all nuclear weapons and fissile materials and, therefore, to all three of these stages. An additional report providing more detail on the reactor-related options for long-term disposition of plutonium, prepared by a separate panel commissioned by the Committee, will be released in the middle of 1995. All of the main conclusions of that future report, however, are included in the parent document.

These excess weapons materials, particularly those in the former Soviet Union, pose a "clear and present danger" to international security. Reducing that security risk must be the driving force in deciding our policy; exploiting energy value of this plutonium (which is tiny on the scale of global energy needs), or influencing the future of nuclear power, are secondary issues. The recommended steps are designed to meet three key security objectives:

- To minimize the risk that either weapons or fissile materials could be obtained by unauthorized parties;

- To minimize the risk that weapons or fissile materials could be reintroduced into the arsenals from which they came, halting or reversing the arms reduction process;

- To strengthen the national and international arms control mechanisms and incentives designed to assure continued arms reductions and prevent the spread of nuclear weapons.

Management of this plutonium must also meet high standards of protection for environment, safety, and health.

The recommendations of the Academy Committee fall into four major areas:

First, a series of sweeping new agreements under which the United States and Russia would exchange information on their entire stocks of nuclear weapons and fissile materials. This declaratory regime would be coupled with cooperative monitoring to confirm the information exchanged. A verified cut-off of production of fissile materials for weapons and monitoring of weapons dismantlement would be key parts of this regime. Technically weapons dismantlement can be monitored without compromising sensitive information and without imposing substantial delays and costs. Such improved openness and accounting would strengthen efforts to reduce nuclear arms and stem their spread, reduce the risks that nuclear materials might "go missing," and allow more democratic participation in decision making. Little of this regime is yet in place, though the Department of Energy's recent declassifications of the amounts of plutonium produced for the U.S. nuclear arsenal is a most welcome first step, and negotiations on the other components of a new open regime of plutonium management are being actively pursued by the United States and Russia.

Second, the United States and Russia should pursue a reciprocal regime of secure, internationally monitored storage of fissile material, with the aim of ensuring that the inventory in storage can only be withdrawn for non-weapons purposes. Both nations should explicitly commit a very large fraction of their nuclear materials from dismantled weapons to non-weapons use or disposal under international safeguards. No such international transparency arrangements are yet in place, though President Clinton announced on 27 September 1993 that U.S. excess weapons materials would be placed under safeguards, and President Yeltsin's government has announced its willingness to do the same, and further discussions are proceeding.

Third, with respect to long-term disposition, the Committee did not offer a final answer but a road map for arriving at one: the criteria on which decisions should be based are proposed. All but two of the proposed options have been rejected, and the questions to be answered before one of the remaining contenders could be confidently chosen as the preferred approach are defined. The United States and Russia should pursue long-term disposition options that:

- minimize the time during which the plutonium is stored in forms readily usable for nuclear weapons;

- preserve accounting and security during the disposition process, seeking to meet a "stored weapons standard"—that is, maintaining the same high standards of security and accounting applied to stored nuclear weapons;

- result in a form that meets a "spent fuel standard"—that is, making the weapons plutonium as difficult to recover for weapons use as the larger and growing quantity of plutonium in commercial spent fuel increases worldwide;

- meet high standards of protection for environment, safety, and health.

The two most promising alternatives for this purpose are:

- the *spent fuel option*, in which the plutonium would be used as fuel in existing or modified nuclear reactors (such as U.S. and Russian light water reactors, or Canadian CANDU heavy water reactors), which would consume a fraction of the plutonium in a "once-through" mode and embed the rest in highly radioactive spent fuel similar to that now produced by these reactors; and

- the *vitrification option*, in which the plutonium would be mixed with intensely radioactive high-level wastes, which are scheduled to be mixed with molten glass to form glass logs for ultimate disposal in an underground repository.

A third option, burial in deep boreholes, has until now been less thoroughly studied than the first two, but could turn out to be comparably attractive.

Advanced nuclear reactors should not be specifically developed and built for the mission of transforming weapons plutonium into spent fuel, because that aim can be achieved more rapidly, less expensively, and more assuredly by using existing or evolutionary reactor types. Decisions on design and construction of advanced reactors and fuel cycles should be based on the needs for civilian nuclear power, not the requirements for weapons plutonium disposition.

Fourth, the immediate need to deal with excess weapons materials is an opportunity to set a standard of improved security and accounting that would be applied to *all* fissile materials worldwide. The excess weapons plutonium is only a small part of the global plutonium stock, which includes many hundreds of tons of plutonium in spent fuel, almost 90 tons of separated civilian plutonium, plutonium in scrap and residues, and other materials. The United States should pursue new agreements to ensure that *all* civil fissile materials worldwide are under safeguards with stringent standards of security and accounting. Most urgently, we must take steps to cooperate with Russia to reduce the real danger that weapons-usable materials might be stolen; the spread of nuclear weapons is perhaps the greatest threat to U.S. and international security today, and this risk of theft is one of the greatest current sources of that threat.

None of the approaches that have been identified can eliminate the dangers posed by these materials. All they can do is to reduce the risks. Even the best of the disposition methods cannot make a significant dent in the stockpiles of excess plutonium for more than a decade. Thus the world is condemned to "baby-sit" this dangerous stockpile for many years to come. It is essential that the U.S. Government elevate the priority given to these issues.

A more systematic interagency approach is needed within the government with leadership from the top and new initiatives to cooperate with Russia in addressing these challenges. Precisely because management of this plutonium will be a long and complex endeavor, it is important to begin now.

The Future of Civilian Plutonium

The "value" of plutonium

The major source of controversy concerning the role of plutonium in the civilian nuclear fuel cycle is derived from the fact that there are three different values associated with plutonium. These are its energy value, its economic value, and its military value.

As a source of energy plutonium yields about the same quantity of fission energy as does Uranium 235 on a weight-by-weight basis. This is roughly one gigawatt year of electricity per ton of material. This however does not mean that the economic value of these two materials is the same. The basic fuel for the vast majority of today's nuclear reactors is Low Enriched Uranium (LEU) which contains between three and four percent Uranium 235 with the balance being Uranium 238. This material is today abundant and cheap, has only weak radioactivity and is not a nuclear proliferation risk since the fraction of Uranium 235 is too low for use as bomb material.

In contrast, if plutonium is substituted for Uranium 235 as is done in the so-called Mixed Oxide (MOX) fuel, the resulting material is more expensive to fabricate, is a significantly larger radiation hazard, and is a proliferation risk since weapons-suitable plutonium can be extracted using only chemical processing. Translated into economic terms this difference means that even if metallic plutonium withdrawn from nuclear weapons is made available to the civilian nuclear industry as a "free" good, even then the cost of MOX fuel would be substantially higher than that of LEU-based conventional reactor fuel. Under current U.S. economic conditions the difference is roughly $1,500 per kilogram of heavy metal amounting to a higher cost of electricity in the ten percent range. Thus on a comparative basis the "economic" value of plutonium is negative compared to LEU, at least in the U.S.

In contrast, the military value of plutonium is extremely high to a potential nuclear weapons proliferator or subnational group. For such a group to produce plutonium indigenously would require large reprocessing facilities. These are both expensive and would have to be acquired clandestinely if the country is subject to international non-diversion inspections by the International

Atomic Agency. Thus to a country bent on acquiring nuclear weapons or to a subnational group wishing to acquire nuclear weapons for terrorist use, buying existing plutonium would be a preferred alternative. Thus the military value of plutonium is in the millions of dollars per kilogram.

This disparity among the three alternate values of plutonium is a reason for divergent plutonium utilization policies among nations and for the need of strict safeguards against diversion of ostensibly civilian material to military customers.

"Once-through" vs. reprocessing

Currently, the United States is continuing the policy originally adopted during the Carter administration of using nuclear fuel in a "once through" fuel cycle where the plutonium contained in spent fuel rods is not reprocessed but is instead stored in tanks or caskets near the power plant until a deep geological disposal is ready to receive it. The high radioactivity of spent fuel makes the risk of theft very low for many decades. This policy is based both on the concern with the proliferation risk of reprocessed plutonium and on the lack of economic incentive for reusing that material either in the form of MOX or in future breeder reactors in which more plutonium would be produced from Uranium 238 than would be produced in fresh reactor fuel.

In contrast, some other nations have not followed that path. Japan is having its spent fuel reprocessed in Europe with the resulting plutonium returned to Japan for use as MOX and some of it to be used eventually in a breeder. Several European countries are following a similar path, and Russia is reprocessing spent fuel both for future use in the civilian economy but also, at least until recently, for use in weapons.

Decisions to deviate from U.S. policy were made by other countries many years ago on the basis of general assumptions which are currently no longer valid. In the past, forecasts for electrical energy demand have been much too large, and forecasts for the availability for the economically mineable uranium have been too small. As a result, future economic incentives for reprocessing and thereby extending the energy value of uranium have been overstated in the past.

Separately from this consideration, the Japanese are concerned about energy security: they have feared a cutoff from overseas uranium suppliers and they therefore wish to be able to extract the maximum energy value from a given amount of uranium. These perceptions have been translated into investments in reprocessing strategies and into contractual commitments between the countries concerned and reprocessing authorities—the lack of clear economic justification notwithstanding.

The question to be faced is whether a worldwide consensus on worldwide plutonium should be sought, both in the interest of minimizing nuclear weapons proliferation risks and in order to pursue the wisest course in terms of energy policy. There is no great urgency to achieve such a worldwide consensus since current uranium supplies are so abundant that an increase in the cost of uranium based on future scarcity of that material will not be faced until many decades hence. The exact time at which the civilian use of plutonium will become economically justifiable, or even mandatory, cannot be forecast precisely, since it depends on forecasts of population growth, on the level of industrial development of the lesser developed world, and on the success of energy conservation measures worldwide.

One should recognize that even today *de facto* half of the nuclear energy produced in the world is derived from plutonium, even if the only once-through fuel cycle is used as is the case in the overwhelming fraction of the world's nuclear power plants. The reason is that during the burnup of the conventional LEU fuel in a reactor plutonium is generated from Uranium 238; as the burnup of Uranium 235 proceeds, an increasing larger fraction of energy generation in the reactor core stems from the fission of plutonium. Thus, with reasonably efficient burnup, roughly one half of the energy in today's nuclear reactors comes from plutonium with the balance generated by Uranium 235. If most or all the remaining Uranium 238 was convertible into plutonium, then the total energy resource from uranium could be extended by perhaps a factor of fifty. But this requires separating (reprocessing) the plutonium and recycling it in a reactor. The question is when, where, and whether such resource extension should be utilized.

Energy resource extension vs. non-proliferation

In view of all the foregoing, wise decisions concerning the future of the use of plutonium in the civilian fuel cycle depends on a balance between the proliferation risks on the one hand and the need for extending the energy resource contained in a given amount of uranium. The wisest balance may well appear to be different in the different countries of the world. In the United States, with both ample coal and uranium resources, plutonium may not be needed for a long time, perhaps well over a century, and it may never be needed, depending on the future of fusion or other forms of energy not tapped today. The United States has an overriding interest in stemming the proliferation of nuclear weapons with its equalizing implications for the smaller states. In contrast, many countries in the lesser developed world, in their need for industrialization, require a great expansion of their electric supply; nuclear energy may well become an essential element of that expansion. This is, for instance, clearly true in the case of China and other countries where indigenous coal resources per capita are low and of poor quality. Moreover, the burning of fossil fuels worldwide may well become constrained by global warming considerations, and this increases the pressure for expansion of nuclear energy.

While the United States as a nation has lesser need for plutonium as part of the nuclear fuel cycle relative to other countries, it has to face the issue of whether to participate in the development of technology of recycling uranium for breeders even if in the foreseeable future this is a matter of direct interest primarily to other countries. Specifically the United States has a direct interest in the development of more proliferation-resistant fuel cycles for plutonium. Again this is a difficult question. If you push technology which is only needed in the distant future too soon, then there is a risk of placing an obsolete technology on the shelf. If one delays too much, then the viability of the American nuclear industry is interrupted or at least impaired in competition with foreign suppliers. All this paints a complex pattern which does not point toward a unique solution.

Before an optimum policy can be developed the following questions must be answered:

(1) What are the current forecasts for the availability of uranium for different parts of the world, and what are the demand forecasts for nuclear electricity, taking into account the environmental risks inherent in continued burning of fossil fuels and the availability of fossil fuels in various parts of the world? Will the extraction of Uranium from seawater ever make sense on energy grounds, or is it only too costly today on economic grounds?

(2) What are the proliferation risks inherent in civilian use of plutonium, and how can they be reduced by such means as integrating reprocessing and the use of plutonium fuel at a single location? What technical means can be developed, such that plutonium in civilian nuclear fuel cycles is more proliferation resistant than in the traditional chemical separation processes?

(3) What is the lead time with which the question on the future role of civilian plutonium must be addressed, in particular in respect to the needs of the less developed world? When will the scarcity costs of uranium have grown to such an extent as to make the civilian plutonium use economically attractive, and how large a lead time is required for developing a reliable breeder technology?

(4) To what extent should one seek international agreement and standardization of a worldwide approach to the future role of civilian plutonium, or to what extent is it acceptable that countries like the United States with her large fossil fuel resources and other parts of the world with varying resources pursue diverse policies?

I suggest that studying these questions in a manner not distorted by ideological "pro-nuclear" and "anti-nuclear" sentiments and as isolated as possible from the institutional interests of reactor suppliers and reprocessors is a matter of urgency. After better understanding of the answers to these questions, it is time for trying to arrive at an international consensus on the future role of civilian plutonium.

CHAPTER 17

Nuclear Options: Russian Perspectives

MINATOM*

Conversion Programs of MINATOM

The success of the reforms of Russia's economy depends very much on the effectiveness of defense conversion. Russian defense enterprises at the start of economic restructuring produced up to 60 percent of the total volume of civil products and consumer goods. A significant portion belonged to MINATOM industry. During the last three years this portion has grown. This fact reflects the great scientific, technological and production abilities of MINATOM's institutes and enterprises.

Russia derives approximately 12 percent of its electricity from twenty-four operating nuclear power plants all supplied by MINATOM. Twelve of these, producing 9.06 GWe, are pressurized light-water reactors (PWR or VVER); eleven, producing 10.18 GWe, are light-water cooled graphite moderated reactors (LGR or RBMK); and one, producing 5.66 GWe, is a liquid metal fast breeder reactor (LMFBR or BN). One PWR, one LGR and two LMFBR are under construction to add an additional 3.37 GWe capacity.

The Conversion Program of MINATOM, being a part of the Federal Defense Conversion Program, includes the following state targeted comprehensive scientific and technological directions:

1. Microelectronics, computer and automation facilities;
2. Development and manufacture of the modern medical engineering;
3. Rehabilitation of the territories contaminated with radioactive and toxic substances as a result of the operation of nuclear material production enterprises;
4. Advanced materials;

---

*Compiled by A.E.S. Green.

5. Development of fiber-optical communicational system;
6. Mechanical engineering for milk processing enterprises, the agroindustrial complex;
7. Development of a new generation of enhanced-safety reactors;
8. Development and commercial production of electric power equipment and facilities with SF6 insulation;
9. Radionuclide materials, preparations, manufactured articles and related perspective technologies.

An extended description of each program includes the following parts:

– main targets
– stage development
– enterprises involved
– finance requirement
– final industrial products
– state-of-the-art review
– critical problems

Weapons-grade Plutonium Utilization in Nuclear Power Plants

The process of nuclear arms reduction now underway will inevitably result in a release of a considerable amount of fissile material. This result has directed international attention to the potential use of highly enriched uranium (HEU), weapons-grade plutonium (WGP) and reactor grade plutonium (RGP) originating from spent fuel reprocessing. There is general agreement on the use of weapons-grade uranium. It is a traditional product of the nuclear industry and can be effectively used for nuclear power plant fuel fabrication. Furthermore, there is considerable experience on the problems arising regarding its storage.

About 500 tons of highly enriched uranium (HEU) from Russian warheads will be sold to the U.S.A. during the next 20 years. Russia will dilute this with 1.5 percent low enriched uranium (LEU) to produce about 15,780 tons of LEU at 4.4 percent which will be provided in the form of UF_6 to the U.S. Enrichment Corporation (USEC).

About 100 tons of weapons-grade plutonium are also expected to be recovered during the process of nuclear arms reduction. Projects for using plutonium for nuclear power production began in Russia with the implementation of the program of development of fast breeder reactors (FBR).

However, it is acknowledged that the situation with plutonium is quite different. The world's nuclear power industry is characterized by a decreased development rate caused primarily by:

(a) lower public confidence in its safety;
(b) overproduction of, and low prices for, uranium fuel;
(c) unsolved problems in the economy and ecology of the closed fuel cycle; and
(d) the absence of a sound solution for the problem of nuclear waste disposal.

Plutonium especially presents an acute problem due to the public desire to make the disarmament process irreversible. There are two opposing points of view on plutonium—one that it is a radwaste, another, that it is a national asset. In MINATOM's view this difference in viewpoint is based more on the difference in the technological development status of nuclear power industries in particular countries than on any subjective division into nuclear experts and environmentalists.

If a country's technology for the use of plutonium is sufficiently developed to:

(a) follow the non-proliferation policy;
(b) provide a safe and ecologically acceptable fuel cycle; and
(c) be economically competitive;

then plutonium is considered to be a national asset. Otherwise, it is a permanent global threat.

In Russia, MINATOM believes that plutonium management—production, separation, storage and utilization—is a result of solving numerous, very complex problems. It is one of the most important branches of technical culture in the worlds largest countries. As far as nuclear disarmament and nonproliferation move us toward a nuclear-free world, strict international control of the production and use of nuclear materials is necessary. This might possibly be carried out under the auspices of the IAEA. But with nuclear power efforts channeled more and more into peaceful applications, the attitude towards costs will be determined by safety and ecology.

The situation in Russia with the secondary nuclear fuel, plutonium, is different from that in Western countries in one important aspect. For the West, uranium is one of many things they can buy. For Russia, it is one of the things

Russia can sell on the international market. In the case of enriched uranium, to say nothing of finished nuclear fuel, what is mainly sold is not a raw material but a high technological product with a high added value. That is why Russia can assume that the potential price for plutonium would be comparable with the price of the highly enriched uranium (HEU) that it replaces.

From the very beginning, efforts in MINATOM connected with the use of plutonium in nuclear power have been quite extensive. These include studies of the uranium-plutonium fuel cycle and related technologies, physical investigations, and analyses of fast and other thermal reactors' potential. The industry is young and Russia is at the beginning of the road to a real mastering of nuclear fission.

Utilization of Plutonium in Fast Reactors

Up to now, two cores of weapons-grade plutonium oxide have been tested in the experimental reactor BR-10 at the Institute of Physics and Power Engineering (in Obninsk, near Moscow). Using different technologies from different isotope oxide mixtures, large batches of mixed oxide (MOX) fuel pins have been made and tested at the research reactor BOR-60 (Research Institute of Atomic Reactors in Dmitrovgrad). At this reactor, work has been conducted for many years on MOX and commercial reactor grade plutonium.

At the industrial pilot-plant BN-350, MOX-fuel assemblies (350 kg of weapons-grade plutonium) were tested, reprocessed and examined. Up to now, over 2000 MOX-fuel pins have been made for BN-type reactors. Not a single leak has occurred at power density 490 Wt/cm, cladding temperatures 690 C, burning up to 10 percent.

Designed for the Yuzhno-Uralskaya (or "Mayak") nuclear power plant, the BN-800 reactor is to use 2.3 t of plutonium for the initial loading and 1.6 t annually. Along with the development of fast reactors, extensive research has been done on technologies using secondary MOX-fuel in fast reactors:

(a) About 50 per cent of the construction has been completed at the fuel Complex 300;
(b) The RT-l (Mayak) plant reprocesses VVER-440 and BN reactor irradiated fuel;
(c) On the same site, the "Paket" pilot plant produces MOX-assemblies for BN reactors; and
(d) A pilot facility that produces plutonium fuel assemblies by vibrotechnology is also working at RIAR.

As a next step of the national fast reactor program, it has been planned to construct three or four MOX-fueled BN-800 nuclear power plants as well as complete the Complex 300 for the remote-controlled production of MOX-fuel assemblies. The construction of two BN-800 nuclear power plants has begun at the Beloyarskaya and Yuzhno-Uralskaya sites. While Complex 300 is one-half built, the current economic situation has halted those activities. If MINATOM can continue construction of the BN-800 and Complex 300, fast reactors will be ready for large-scale plutonium utilization early next century.

A country's decision on the use of weapons-grade plutonium is a part of its national plutonium strategy, which will be different for different countries. Each country considers a number of factors in determining its strategy:

(a) The chosen national concept for long-term nuclear energy development;
(b) The scientific and technological background and readiness of plutonium utilization technologies; and
(c) Specific features of the evolution of the national nuclear complex.

While plutonium use presents problems, plutonium utilization can also help solve a few problems. It can:

(a) Promote non-proliferation;
(b) Increase the energy potential of the nuclear industry;
(c) Reduce the dangers of actinide-containing radwaste; and,
(d) Simplify the initial development stage of uranium-plutonium fuel cycles for fast and thermal reactors.

The first issue—non-proliferation—is not an easy one. Reducing or even curtailing the accumulation of international plutonium stocks, especially weapons-grade plutonium, is certainly a positive development. But reactor-grade plutonium can also be used to make a primitive nuclear explosive. Thus it is essential to take into account accumulated plutonium in the nuclear power industry when considering the utilization of excess weapons-grade plutonium. Most of this plutonium, that from commercial use of nuclear power, is in the form of spent fuel. However, extracting this plutonium from spent fuel is a complex, technical problem and a serious obstacle to the unauthorized use of plutonium for non-peaceful purposes.

Russia has accumulated approximately 30 tons of reactor grade plutonium produced from spent uranium-based fuel. Reactor-grade plutonium is produced at the RT-1 plant ("Mayak") during the chemical reprocessing of spent fuel assemblies from VVER-40, BN-600 and BN-350 reactors. The major purpose of the reprocessing is to extract under-burned uranium for use in RBMK-type reactors' fuel fabrication. Performing such reprocessing also enables us to gain experience in fuel chemical processing and long-term waste storage. Extracted plutonium is stored for its further use in fast reactors. At present, the RT-1 plant works at partial capacity, producing 0.6 tons of plutonium per year. At full capacity, the RT-1 plant could produce 2.5 tons of reactor-grade plutonium per year.

MINATOM estimates show that the problem of reactor-grade plutonium accumulated and produced at the RT-1 plant, as well as the likely 100 tons surplus of weapons-grade plutonium, can be solved at the nuclear center being created at the "Mayak" site, which includes Complex 300 and three or four BN-800 nuclear power plants.

To minimize the time of "disarming" the extracted plutonium by transforming it into spent fuel, it is advisable to use fast reactors with open fuel cycles. The expected "disarming" times for reactor-grade and weapons-grade plutonium depend on the RT-1 factory's capacity and the number of BN-800 reactors. At current capacity, RT-1 can "disarm" 100 tons of reactor-grade and weapons-grade plutonium through the year 2036, 2023 and 2018 if two units, three units and four BN-800 units, respectively, are operational. At maximum capacity at RT-1, weapons-grade plutonium will be completely transformed in 2041 and 2027, if three and four units, respectively, are operational.

In general, it is possible to "disarm" plutonium at the Mayak facilities using light-water reactors as suggested by the United States and already being done in France. For Russia, however, this solution is unacceptable for several reasons. First, Russia has only just begun its experimental research using MOX fuels for VVERs (PWRs). Russia is considerably behind our foreign partners in this field. There is no thermal reactor operating in Russia designed to use MOX fuels. Safety levels at the VVERs, even operating with uranium, do not meet long-term safety requirements for new generation reactors. Hence, licensing a changeover from uranium fuel assemblies to MOX fuel assemblies at operational VVERs is highly doubtful.

Second, to "disarm" weapons-grade plutonium would require twice as many MOX-only core VVERs as the number of BN-type reactors. This is because annual consumption levels of plutonium for fabricated fuels for VVER and BN reactors are different. In France, for example, they load one-third of the core with MOX assemblies. Thus for this pattern six times more VVERs will be needed (compared with BNs). This cannot be recommended for the Mayak site.

Third, the question of radiotoxicity of spent fuel is important. It is well-known that long-lived isotopes in spent fuel such as Am, Np and Cm complicate both MOX-fuel recycle technology and finding solutions to the long-term waste disposal. To a great extent, these problems are attributed to the accumulation of plutonium-241 in spent fuel. The specific radio toxicity of plutonium-241 is 40 times higher than that of the basic isotope plutonium-239. Furthermore, the plutonium-241 isotope is transformed during storage into the more toxic Am-241 with a half-life of 433 years. This isotope is the main contributor to the radio toxicity of transuranium elements in the spent fuel after the decay of short-lived fission products. About 250kg/GWt(e)* years of reactor-grade plutonium are built up during the operation of light-water reactors with uranium. About 30 kg of this mass is plutonium-241. "Disarming" or burning-up weapons-grade plutonium in thermal reactors increases three-fold the annual build-up of plutonium-241, compared with burning uranium based fuel in VVERs. If this spent fuel is stored for the long-term, a considerable amount of the plutonium-241 will be transformed into Am-241, highly complicating further utilization of plutonium and waste disposal.

Fourth, in addition to the undesirable accumulation of plutonium-241, the burning of weapons-grade plutonium at VVERs may produce several times more minor actinides as compared with the VVERs using uranium-based fuel. The burning of the basic isotope plutonium-239 during weapons-grade plutonium utilization at "Mayak" facilities would result in an accumulation of nuclides with a total radio toxicity three times higher than when uranium based fuel is used in VVERS.

The situation is quite different however, if we use BN-type reactors to utilize weapons-grade plutonium. The radiotoxicity of the "disarmed" plutonium does not, for all practical purposes, exceed that of the initially loaded plutonium. Efficiency index comparisons for weapons-grade plutonium utilization in VVERs and BNs show that BN gives the best radioecological effect; it is the most effective burner of plutonium-241. All other conditions being equal, it is more logical initially to utilize reactor-grade plutonium and only after weapons-grade plutonium. The radiotoxicity index factor is highly important for the "Mayak" plant conditions with its difficult ecological situation.

The question of plutonium utilization in thermal reactors in many countries is connected with the relatively high cost of fast reactors. In Russia, the electricity generated by the first BN-600 is 40 percent more expensive than that of VVER-1000. But the experience of BN-600 was taken into account in the BN-800 project and the metal fuel consumption factor is only 80 percent of the BN-600 project. This improved economic characteristic of the BN-800 fuel cycle has been reached through the transition from uranium (which is ineffective for fast reactors) to MOX fuel and the further improvement of the burnup factor.

The economic characteristics of the fast and thermal reactors have also been compared, based on the increased safety standards required in Russia after Chernobyl. The inherent characteristics of fast reactors, as well as new technical solutions, facilitated the upgrading of the BN-800 project to that of a world-level nuclear power plant of a new generation, with improved safety characteristics. It is the only project which has passed all, including ecological, necessary certifications. Local authorities have already approved the project and have reached an agreement with MINATOM.

But work is not completed on new projects with new, safer uranium reactors (VVER-500, VPBER-600). Preliminary estimates show that average capital investment in these projects is higher than in VVER-1000, but corresponds approximately to the investment necessary for the construction of three BN-800 units at Yuzhno-Vealskaya. Another factor that must be considered is that Russia has no industrial-scale MOX fuel fabrication for VVER. Such a technological line is to be built at the RT-2 facility to be commissioned after 2010.

As mentioned before regarding BN-type reactors, the Complex-300 is 50 percent completed. With sufficient investment, it can be commissioned by the end of the century, before the commissioning of BN-800's first unit. After putting into operation four BN-800 units, Complex 300 will reach its maximum capacity in MOX fuel fabrication. So, using plutonium in fast, BN-type reactors is, for Russia, a natural and inevitable step.

A computational examination of how the BN-800 reactor would reduce the radiotoxicity of plutonium and minor actinides accumulated in the reprocessing of spent fuel from VVER-440 reactors accumulated by the year 2000 has been given in the March 18, 1994 issue of Post Soviet Nuclear Complex Monitor and Exchange Publications.

The addition of 3.5 percent minor actinides to BN-800 fuel guarantees the annual burnup of about 100 kg of these isotopes. This quantity of minor actinides is produced by three VVER-1000 reactors per year. Such limited volumes of minor actinides added to the fuel effect little change on the operation of fast reactors.

Even more effective burnup rates may be reached in the specialized BN-800 core when U-238 is replaced by an inert component (for example, zirconium carbide or thorium). This fuel composition leads to an optimal balance that approximately corresponds to the 1:3 ratio of minor actinides content to the main fissile isotope in the fresh fuel. Under these conditions, one BN-800 of 2000 MWt(th) reactor can burn up annually 350 kg of minor actinides, thus servicing ten VVER-1000s. Thus, actinides can be used in fast reactor fuels in different ways that can help compensate for the inevitably growing costs of actinide chemical reprocessing.

In MINATOM's computation analyses three situations are considered. The BN-800 reactor

(a) is not put into operation and the actinides are stored until the year 2060;

(b) is put into operation in the year 2000 and burns traditional MOX-fuel without minor actinides (MA); and,

(c) is put into operation in the year 2000 and uses MA containing MOX-fuel. Irretrievable actinide losses are assumed constant and equal to 2 percent, but the results are also presented for a case when this key parameter is improved to 0.2 per cent for plutonium and Am.

The resulting data on the radionuclides inventory and their total radiotoxicity in 2060 for the three scenarios show that if the fast reactor recycles plutonium and minor actinides, it reduces by at least an order of two the volume and toxicity of the actinides going to waste. Thus, the long-term ecological effect of the transmutations in a BN-800 reactor is enough to justify R&D in this direction. It opens new opportunities to control radiotoxicity of the irradiated nuclear fuel in the closed fuel cycle using fast reactors. The Institute of Physics and Power Engineering attaches the highest priority to the development of work on transmutation within the framework of the plutonium project.

Pu-Th-U Fuel Cycles

Traditionally, fast breeder technology (both in Russia and other countries) was based on economical and safety factors, as well as on intensive breeding of plutonium for a future transition to closed uranium-plutonium fuel cycles. While burning considerable amounts of actinides, traditional fast breeders build-up their own plutonium, which is extremely toxic. However, the newly developed specialized cores with inert material instead of U-238 make it possible to burn some, including weapons-grade, plutonium. But they are unable to get rid of the ecologically dangerous plutonium and minor actinide isotopes.

Research reveals the possibility of solving the above-mentioned problems using the so-called "mixed fuel cycle" on uranium, thorium, uranium-233 and plutonium in fast and thermal reactors. In this case, fast reactor cores are loaded with plutonium. Thorium is used as a fertile material in which uranium-233 is accumulated and this U-233 is eventually used for loading light-water reactors.

The principal results of realizing these mixed fuel cycles is that the 3-fuel cycle (Pu-Th-U cycle) reduces existing plutonium stockpiles to minimal levels within the next century. The transition to uranium-233 and thorium for VVER-type reactors performs two important tasks:

(a) Upgrades safety due to the inherent characteristics of reactors on uranium-233 and thorium; and,

(b) Reduces high transuranium and transplutonium elements in the fuels down to the lowest levels possible.

The development of specialized fast reactors on Th with a relatively "hard" neutron spectrum will make it possible to burn plutonium intensively with any content of high actinides and build-up a needed amount of uranium-233. The module-type reactors with metallic fuels, such as the PRISM in the United States, is a suitable reactor. Using Th, moreover, will improve the safety of fast reactors. The positive results from this include:

(a) Improved technical, economic and safety characteristics of nuclear power plants with thermal and fast reactors; and

(b) Establishing a basis for a future nuclear power industry free from accumulated plutonium which poses a permanent problem for nuclear waste disposal.

Further comprehensive radiological assessments of the Th cycle should be carried out that include both the role of the short-lived uranium-232 and the formation of highly toxic Th 229 and 230 through the decay of U233 and 234. The described system of fuel cycles is flexible enough to

(a) develop light-water reactors and a new generation of higher safety standards;

(b) balance plutonium; and

(c) assign fast reactors the new missions of burning up other actinides and building up uranium-233.

This system neither contradicts nor rejects the historical experience of the nuclear power industry. On the contrary, it shows new perspectives for light-water and fast reactors. Moreover, only the current developmental state of plutonium technology can be the starting point for realizing this concept.

Prospects for Using Civilian Marine Nuclear Power Facilities for Power and Heat Production

MINATOM's enterprises have developed the following marine nuclear power facilities:

(a) 36 MW(e) KLT-40 ice-breaker nuclear power facilities;

(b) ABV facility of 6 MW(e) capacity + 12 GCal/h;

(c) KN-3 facility and 50-70 MW(e) nuclear power units;

(d) 50 MW(e) LM reactor;

(e) 150 MW(e) BRUS facility with LM reactor.

The development of 36 MW(e) floating nuclear power plants based on KLT-40 type plants is the most feasible, as well as most economically and ecologically acceptable. The first plant of this type can be developed within five or six years, with subsequent deployment of one or two plants per year.

A series of medium-capacity nuclear power plants should be developed as an immediate response to the shortage of heat and electricity in the remote areas of the North, Siberia and Far East, as well as in other former Soviet republics.

At present cogenerating mini plants are being developed on the basis of unattended ship and satellite facilities which directly convert thermal power into electricity under natural circulation of coolant in all circuits.

Summary and Conclusions

In summary, MINATOM's concept for using plutonium is based on the evolutionary development of technologies mastered in Russia:

(a) Solution to the problem of reliable and safe pre-reactor storage of recovered weapons-grade plutonium (WGP);
(b) Initial use of plutonium in FBRs (including studies on the use of WGP in BN-600);
(c) Orientation for the use of WGP and reactor-grade plutonium (RGP) within the scope of nuclear power centers (MAYAK; RT-1 Plant; "300 Complex"; BN-800 reactor);
(d) Development of a safe fast breeder reactor as an efficient "utilizer" of plutonium and producer of uranium-233;
(e) Analysis of the potential for development of a light-water reactor (LWR) for the use of WGP;
(f) Development of an enhanced safety LWR that operates on uranium-233 fuel; and
(g) Development of a technology for a safe closed fuel cycle based on plutonium and uranium-233.

Accordingly, MINATOM's concept of weapons plutonium utilization is based on Russia's evolutionary development of reactor technologies. Any short-term plutonium management program must be based on the safe and reliable storage of weapons-grade plutonium until it can be used in reactors. Reactor-grade plutonium should be utilized first, and in the BN-800. Weapons-grade plutonium should be utilized later, and its reprocessing technology should be initially tested on the BN-600. The future orientation on nuclear power centers (first "Mayak" facilities: RT-I, Complex 300, BN-800) should include a reliable solution to the non-proliferation problem.

The foregoing chapter is largely based upon a paper presented by V.M. Murogov, general director of the Institute of Physics and Power Engineering in Obninsk, Russia, at the International Policy Forum. Management and Disposition of Nuclear Weapon Materials, held March 8-11, 1994 in Leesburg, Virginia, sponsored by the Duffy Group and the Post-Soviet Nuclear Monitor. Mr. Murogov presented the paper on behalf of V.N. Mikhailov, Minister of the Russian Federation Nuclear Energy (MINATOM), Mr. E.V. Bogdan, MINATOM staff; and V.M. Murogov, V.S. Kagamanian, N.S. Rabotnov, V.Ya. Rudneva, and M.F. Troyanov, from the Institute of Physics and Power Engineering in Obninsk. The chapter summarizes material provided by Yuri Lipatov and V. Vasiliev.

Thorium is used as a fertile material in which uranium-233 is accumulated and this U-233 is eventually used for loading light-water reactors.

CHAPTER 18

AFTERWORD

Alex E.S. Green
University of Florida

Introduction

The purpose of this chapter is to summarize important recent developments in defense conversion with emphasis on nuclear weapon control, the central problem of the Cold War. Nuclear defense conversion is greatly complicated by the intimate relationship between civilian and military applications of nuclear energy and the great scale-up in military destructiveness of nuclear weapons unleashed some 50 years ago. The previous chapters by Green, Landis, Panofsky and MINATOM deal with this very difficult dual technology issue. An international consensus has emerged as to civilian applications of weapons-grade uranium by denaturing and use in conventional reactors. However, in the words of Panofsky, "the management of plutonium poses unprecedented challenges to man's wisdom." The recent "Nuclear Posture Review" by the U.S. Department of Defense directly addresses the issue of nuclear weapons.

Nuclear Posture Review (NPR)

This section is largely a condensation of NPR material released on September 22, 1994 by the DoD Office of Public Affairs and remarks delivered on September 20, 1994 by Secretary of Defense William J. Perry (DoD, 1994; Perry, 1994).

Nuclear weapons are the most vivid and significant symbol of the Cold War that was characterized by: (1) an application of enormous resources on strategic nuclear programs reaching a peak of about $50 billion a year, (2) an arms race between the United States and the Soviet Union dangerous to both countries and to the world, (3) a web of treaties intended to control the arms race and reduce the danger, and (4) a unique military strategy, mutually assured destruction (MAD). The U.S.A.'s nuclear policy during the Cold War did not presume to solve the nuclear problem, but only to keep it from exploding.

With the end of the Cold War the threat of nuclear war has dramatically reduced. In response to this radically changed security situation the United States, over the past six years, has made dramatic reductions in its nuclear forces. These are summarized in the NPR chart entitled **A Historical Perspective.** In the light of the positive changes indicated in this chart and some uncertainties as to how far and how fast to go, the NPR was conducted by the Office of the Secretary of Defense, the Joint Staff, and the services and the commanders of U.S. unified commands. This was the first such review of U.S. nuclear policy in 15 years and the first study ever to include policy, doctrine, force structure, command and control, operations, supporting infrastructure, safety and security, and arms control in a single study.

The overall conclusions of the NPR are given in the chart entitled **Conclusions.** The DoD NPR release noted that Russia has made tremendous strides toward reform. Political stability has increased markedly in Moscow since the siege of the Russian White House in October 1993. Even more impressively, Russian economic reform is moving full speed ahead, with privatization as its centerpiece. In the security domain, Russia is cooperating on many fronts, from denuclearization to joint exercises, diplomatic efforts in Bosnia and the Mideast, and membership in the Partnership for Peace. The Russian people have been trying, in a few short years, to change from an authoritarian government to a democratic government and from a state-controlled economy to a market economy. While Russia has succeeded in dismantling the controls of the previous system, the new institutions are still being created. Ukraine is experiencing similar successes and uncertainties. In short, Russia and the other states of the former Soviet Union are struggling and will continue to struggle with the historic changes under way.

The NPR concluded, however, in contrast to the U.S.A., Russia has deactivated just over half of the ballistic missiles required under START agreements. Its non-strategic nuclear warhead stockpile greatly exceeds that of the U.S.A., and each of the Russian armed services continues to retain a nuclear role. This lag is partly due to internal turmoil and old thinking about the role of nuclear weapons in military security. But more importantly it is costly and complex to denuclearize. The major concern of the DoD is that Russia still has about 25,000 nuclear weapons—many more than enough to threaten the national survival of the U.S.A.

A Historical Perspective

❑ **Significant reductions in US nuclear forces are underway**
    ❑ **Weapons (since 1988)**
        ❑ Total active stockpile reduced by 59%
        ❑ Strategic warheads reduced by 47%
        ❑ Non-strategic nuclear force warheads reduced by 90%
        ❑ No nuclear weapons remain in the custody of US ground forces

    ❑ **Operations**
        ❑ Strategic bombers taken off day-to-day alert
        ❑ ICBMs and SLBMs detargeted
        ❑ More SSBNs patrolling on "modified alert" rather than "alert"
        ❑ Naval NSNF no longer routinely deployed at sea
        ❑ Reduced airborne command and control operations tempo

    ❑ **Programmatic (1989-Present)**

Program Terminations	Program Truncations	Systems Retired; No Replacement
• Small ICBM	• Peacekeeper	• Artillery Fired Atomic Projectile
• Peacekeeper Rail Garrison	• B-2	• FB-111
• Lance Follow-on	• B-1 Nuclear Role	• Minuteman II
• New Artillery Fired Atomic Projectile	• Advanced Cruise Missile	• Lance
• Tactical Air to Surface Missile	• W-88	• Short Range Attack Missile-A
• Short Range Attack Missile II		• Nuclear Depth Bomb
		• C-3 SSBN

Conclusions

❑ **Post-Cold War environment requires nuclear deterrent**
    ❑ Rebalanced Triad
    ❑ START II levels remain in US interest until START I implementation complete, Russia nears START II levels, and we're confident of Russia's future

❑ **Major reductions and cost savings underway**
    ❑ US forces will be smaller, safer, more secure and maintained at lower alert rates
    ❑ Reduce infrastructure, but maintain people and technical base

❑ **US Nuclear Posture must help shape future**
    ❑ Create world in which role of nuclear weapons reduced
    ❑ Stem proliferation
    ❑ Preserve options if reform fails in Russia
    ❑ Maintain good stewardship

❑ **Difficult but vital challenge for US Posture is to both lead and hedge**

In view of the above, the U.S.A. will: (1) maintain selected portions of the defense industrial base that are unique to strategic and other nuclear systems, (2) maintain a strong working partnership between the Department of Defense and the Department of Energy to ensure the soundest stewardship for our deterrent stockpile, without nuclear testing, and (3) ensure it has the ability to reconstitute nuclear forces if needed as it draws down these forces. The **Main Results of the NPR** are given in the two following charts.

On the positive side the Nuclear Posture Review indicated that the United States could make further reductions in its non-strategic nuclear force (NSNF) and, assuming START I and II are implemented fully by 2003, consider further reductions in its strategic nuclear force (SNF). It suggested that if Russia rethinks its security needs and budget realities, it too will revise its plans downward, especially in the area of NSNF. For improved security Russia should consolidate these non-strategic weapons in the smallest possible number of storage sites; store them under stricter safeguards and inventory control; and dismantle its older and excess weapons sooner. The chart labeled **Initiatives Considered for Improving Russian Safety, Security and Use Control** reflects suggestions from the NPR on reducing uncertainties.

The NPR recognized that if U.S.A.-F.S.U. programs of denuclearization stay on course the remaining global threat to security will be the proliferation of weapons of mass destruction (WMD) including biological weapons (BW) and chemical weapons (CW). The chart **Counterproliferation Initiatives** summarizes the NPR proposals on such problems.

All these initiatives recognize that even though the superpower nuclear standoff is over, the nuclear age is not. We cannot shut the lid on the nuclear Pandora's box, but we can—and must—limit and control the dangers it has released. During the Cold War era the acronym MAD perfectly captured the insanity of the superpower nuclear standoff. The U.S.A. and F.S.U. now have the opportunity to create a new relationship based not on MAD, but rather on Mutual Assured Safety (MAS).

This new arms control outlined in the NPR has four new approaches that emphasize: (1) nuclear safety, in addition to stability, (2) cooperation to reach shared objectives, rather than pressure to make concessions, (3) carrying out existing agreements, actually eliminating the weapons we've agreed to eliminate, and (4) the real issue of nuclear safety, stability, and proliferation of bombs and bomb materials, in addition to missiles, silos, bombers and submarines. The conclusions of this NPR review are intended to give the

Main Results of the NPR

- Strategic Forces
  - No more than 20 B-2 bombers required for nuclear role
  - Reduce B-52 bomber force (94 to 66)
  - Reduce Trident submarine fleet size from 18 to 14; but modernize SLBM force for very long service life by equipping all submarines with D-5 missiles
  - Maintain single warhead Minuteman III ICBMs (500/450)
  - Maintain flexibility to reduce further or reconstitute
- Non-Strategic Nuclear Forces
  - Maintain European NSNF commitment at current level (less than 10% of Cold War level)
  - Eliminate nuclear weapons capability from US Navy surface ships
    - Eliminate nuclear DCA capability from aircraft carriers
    - Eliminate nuclear cruise missile capability from surface combatants
  - Retain nuclear cruise missile capability on submarines
  - Retain land-based dual-capable nuclear aircraft capability

Main Results of the NPR (cont)

- Safety, Security, and Use Control
  - Equip all US nuclear weapons systems, including submarines, with coded control devices or PAL by 1997
  - Upgrade coded control locking devices on Minuteman III ICBMs and B-52 bombers
  - Conduct regular NCA procedural exercises
- Infrastructure
  - Stockpile stewardship "customer plan" for DoE
  - Sustain ballistic missile industrial base by Minuteman III sustainment and D-5 production
  - Sustain reentry vehicle and guidance system industrial base
- Command, Control, Communications, & Intelligence and Operations
  - Continue adjustments to post-Cold War alert/operational requirements
  - Support selected C3I programs for assured NCA survivability and continuity
- Threat Reduction and Proliferation
  - Support Cooperative Threat Reduction program to promote steps to prevent unauthorized/accidental use or diversion of weapons or materials from/within the FSU
  - Support counterproliferation initiative to provide conventional responses to use of WMD in regional conflict

Initiatives Considered for Improving Russian Safety, Security, and Use Control

Forces
- ☐ Further NSNF reductions
- ☐ Accelerating removal of warheads down to START II levels
- ☐ Further SNF reductions beyond START II
- ☐ Removing warheads from all ICBMs

Operational Practices
- ☐ Cooperative warning and verification of alert status
- ☐ Delaying ICBM/SLBM launch ability

Weapon Stockpile
- ☐ Stockpile data exchange
- ☐ Transparency/acceleration of warhead dismantlement
- ☐ Stockpile inventory cap
- ☐ Storing weapons/material under international custody

Counterproliferation Initiatives

- ☐ Develop effective theater defenses against ballistic missile and air-breathing threats
- ☐ Enhance conventional capabilities to counter the proliferation threat and support funding for principal Deutch Committee report recommendations
    - ☐ Improved real-time detection and characterization of BW/CW agents
    - ☐ Underground structures detection and characterization
    - ☐ Hard underground target defeat, including advanced non-nuclear weapons producing low collateral damage
- ☐ Provide DoD capabilities in support of UN and other international non-proliferation efforts
- ☐ Fully implement nuclear arms control agreements and support NPT, BWC, and CWC
- ☐ Continue assistance to FSU to enhance safety and security of nuclear weapons

United States a prudent balance between the arms control accord, the current and anticipated deterrent requirements, the conviction that the U.S.A. needs to protect the inherent advantages of its triad structure, and the concern that the actual number of warheads possessed by the F.S.U. is coming down much more slowly than the warheads in the active military stockpiles of the U.S.A.

Dr. William Perry said "the most important NPR results concern decisions made to *further* reduce the strategic nuclear force structure the United States plans to retain after the START II Treaty is implemented. As adjustments in the future plans for the U.S. nuclear posture are made, uppermost is the fact that the states of the former Soviet Union are yet in the early stages of implementing the agreed reductions called for by the START I and START II agreements" (Perry, 1994). The U.S.A. is trying to hasten that process through, among other things, Cooperative Threat Reduction programs with Russia, Ukraine, Kazakhstan, and Belarus.

The Nunn-Lugar Cooperative Threat Reduction Program

The Nunn-Lugar Cooperative Threat Reduction program, first legislated late in 1991, provided $400 million in United States Government (USG) funds to help dismantle the former Soviet nuclear arsenal, convert the Soviet weapons industry to civilian production, and generally help reduce the former Soviet force structure. The program had a slow start associated with mutual suspicions as to intent and the need for confidence building. Much of the funds to date have been expended on the problems of weapon dismantlement, transport and storage. The recent transfer of one-half ton of highly enriched uranium from Ust-Kamenogorsk in Kazakstan to Oak Ridge, Tennessee is a successful and dramatic example of this program (Gordon, 1994).

The part of the Nunn-Lugar program concerned with the conversion of the F.S.U. weapon facilities to civilian applications is beginning to move ahead at a respectable pace. Table 1 lists contracts and joint venture arrangements awarded from April 1994 through April 1995 (DNA, 1995).

The Nunn-Lugar program is specifically directed towards cooperative threat reduction, and most of its funds are utilized in weapon dismantlement and storage. However there are a number of other United States Funding Organizations fostering defense conversions in the F.S.U. These are listed in the following section (DNA,1995).

Table 1. Defense Conversion Contract Summary

1. Russia, NPO Mashinostroyenia (formerly cruise missiles, ICBM's, maneuverable satellites). The U.S. partners (USP) are Double Cola Company, PA. The project is to establish a complete cola bottle manufacturing facility and bottling plant. The total value (TV) is $6.1 M (with USP contributing 16 %).

2. Russia Leninats (radar, avionics systems), USP, International American Products, SC, Joint venture to produce dental chairs and supplies. TV $3.9 M, (50%).

3. Russia Istok, (Electronic and communications gear for space and military applications, radar, lasers), USP, Hearing Aids Intern., NH to produce low cost, high performance hearing aids. TV $7.4 M, (24%).

4. Russia GosNIIAS (Design and testing of military avionics), USP Rockwell International, TX, to produce Russian traffic control hardware and software based on GPS and GLONASS. TV $4.7 M, (13.5%).

5. Belarus Integral (Nuclear hardened chips for Soviet military), USP KRAS Corp, PA, For retooling, Mgt, marketing & manufacturing low end ICs. TV $6.7 M, (14%).

6. Belarus BelOMO (Satellite systems, night vision devices, range finders) USP Byelocorp, NY, to manufacture and sell laser pointers. TV $104 M, (8%).

7. Ukraine Frigate (shipbuilding), USP Bill Harbert International Construction, AL, for prefabricated housing construction in Pervomyask. TV $10.4 M, (5%).

8. Ukraine NPO Hartron, Kharkiv, Ukraine, (Developed, produced & installed control systems for missiles and space systems), USP Westinghouse Electric, PA, instrumentation and control devices for nuclear power plants. TV $19 M, (74%).

9. Ukraine, Kiev: Central Design Institute and Montazhnik "K" (formerly designed and constructed silos and other strategic facilities). The USP are ABB SUSA, Inc., NJ. and American International Services Inc., VA. Design and construct 135 apartment units with associated on-site facilities. TV $16.1 M, (0%).

10. Ukraine, Kharkov: Kommunar (electronics manufacturer for Aerospace and other military/commercial fields). USP, Federal Systems Group (FSG) of VA and OMNI Telecommunications, IL. Manufacture distribute and sell cellular phones in Asia, Ukraine and other non-USA markets. TV $7.5 M, (55%).

11. Belarus, Minsk: MCA (military main frames). USP-FSG, radio controlled modems and battery chargers. TV $6.3 M, (62%).

12. Kazakhstan, Kazinform Telecom (Missile testing and tracking), AT&T Wireless Syst., NJ, international telecommunications link. TV $16 M, (69%).

13. Kazakhstan, Biomedpreparat (Biological warfare research & production), USP, Allen & Assoc., Int'l., DC, Manufacture & distribute vitamins, pharmaceuticals, & antibiotics. TV $5.8 M, (54%).

14. Kazakhstan, Gidromash, (Missile systems, aircraft hydraulics, motors, & machines), USP, Byelocorp Scientific Corp., NY, Manufacture, service & distribute valves and ASME certified pressure vessels. TV $6.2 M, (52%).

15. Kazakhstan, Nat'l Nuclear Center, (Nuclear weapons testing; reactor testing), USP, KRAS Corp, PA, Printed circuit board production, TV $7.6 M, (48%).

Other United States Funding Organizations

Agency for International Development (AID)
Nine enterprise funds have been created for the Newly Independent States (NIS) of Russia, Ukraine, Kazakhstan and Belarus to assist in the successful privatizing of defense industries and conversion of military technologies and capabilities into civilian activities. These USG funded but privately operated funds are empowered to provide loans and take equity shares in joint ventures between U.S. companies and privately owned NIS companies.

Trade Development Agency
Provides grants to U.S. companies for Phase I assessment studies of potential projects in the NIS.

United States Industry Coalition
Provides partial funding for R&D type projects involving U.S. companies, U.S. DOE Laboratories, and former Soviet military science laboratories.

Overseas Private Investment Corporation
Provides loans and equity shares for investments with U.S./NIS joint ventures. Also provides political insurance for currency convertibility, seizure and other national actions by the host nation.

Department of Commerce
Provides an information service on NIS companies and a clearinghouse for potential partnerships between U.S. companies interested in working in the NIS.

Defense Enterprise Fund
This recently established fund will make both equity investments and loans and may make grants to qualified joint venture projects. It will seek to develop financial transactions and instruments which are appropriate to the existing circumstances of the NIS economy and financial sector. The Fund will concentrate on providing financial assistance or making investments in those qualified joint venture initiatives which include personnel and/or facilities currently or formerly involved in research, development, production, or operation and support of the defense sector of the former Soviet Union, with focus on weapons of mass destruction, components of such weapons, and

delivery or support systems for such weapons. In the context of Fund activities, these include nuclear, biological, and chemical weapons, guided missiles and aircraft that can deliver these weapons, and weapons platforms such as aircraft carriers, surface ships and submarines that carry nuclear-equipped guided missiles and aircraft.

Also eligible for Defense Enterprise Funds are firms associated with the production of command, control and communications equipment for military forces associated with the above weapons as well as with the production of strategic defense systems (such as ABMs and systems to counter strategic bombers). Fund investments may also be made in facilities and personnel associated currently or formerly with other segments of the NIS defense sector that are converting to civilian activities. The Fund will seek to encourage NIS private sector participation in the ownership and management of the entities in which the Fund invests. Towards this end, the Fund will make investments only in initiatives involving privatized NIS enterprises or involving enterprises or spin-off enterprises that commit in writing to privatization. An enterprise will be considered to be privatized when greater than 50 percent of the ownership is in the private sector.

Major Funding Sources For Economic Conversion

The U.S. Government programs described in the previous section primarily foster Defense Conversion in the F.S.U. Recently much larger sources of funding for joint ventures have developed for Economic Conversion (White House, 1994). These programs are relevant to this work because formerly the same centralized authority controlled both the civilian and defense sectors of the F.S.U. economy. For example, an Export-Import (Ex-Im) Bank loan guarantee to Russia supports the $293.4 million export of oil drilling equipment by Ramoil Management Co. to Nizhnevartovskneftegas (NNG), one of Russia's largest oil production associations located in Western Siberia. The financing will rehabilitate 2,000 inactive wells and drill 240 more wells, dramatically reducing NNG's declining production.

An Ex-Im Bank loan guarantee supports $124 million in exports by IBM, AT&T and American Airlines to International Technology Corp. Sirena (ITCS) of Moscow to provide Aeroflot with new systems for passenger reservations and ticketing, departure control, and information management.

During the 1994 Washington summit between Russian President Boris Yeltsin and President Clinton, the Overseas Private Investment Corporation (OPIC) signed contracts, commitment letters, and protocols for more than one-half billion dollars in U.S. Government support to American-Russian joint ventures (White House,1994). Pratt & Whitney, a division of United Technologies Corp. obtained $250 million in combined OPIC insurance and loan guaranty. It is joining with Motoren and Turbinen Union GmbH of Germany, the Russian aerospace manufacturer Perm Motors, and Aviadvigatel, the Russian design bureau, to redesign and market an existing aero-engine.

SFMT, Inc., a telecommunications company, received a $60 million loan guaranty and will use the OPIC funds for sub-projects: to set up satellite antennas to improve phone service; to expand the number of lines for international calling; and to provide data transmission services for banks and business.

Swift Energy was awarded $165 million in insurance and finance. With Senaga, a Russian joint stock company in Novi Urengoi, Swift plans to develop and produce oil and gas in western Siberia.

Mid-Com Communications obtained $30 million in insurance and $24 million in finance through an insurance contract and finance protocol respectively. Mid-Com plans to acquire part of Dal Telecom International, a phone company in the Far East. Services will be expanded to provide wire and wireless phones to thousands of people who have never had one.

All Alaskan Seafoods, Inc., obtained a $13 million loan guaranty for a fish processing boat in a venture with Dalmoreproduct, Russia's largest fishing company, based in Vladivostok.

NC International obtained a $8 million contract in political risk insurance. NC International plans to sell Caterpillar mining equipment in the gold producing region around Magadan in the Russian Far East.

Another channel of economic conversion is provided by a memorandum of understanding between the U.S. Trade and Development Agency (TDA) and Russia's Ministry of Foreign Economic Relations. TDA has provided $25 million for feasibility studies on more than 65 projects. These include U.S.-R.F. coproduction of trucks at Zil, and KamAZ, the joint production of the IL96M aircraft and the construction of an oil refinery in Krasnodar. TDA funding has been confirmed on the coproduction of a small helicopter with a Russian airframe and U.S. engines, the upgrade of the smelter technology at the Volgograd Aluminum Works, the upgrade of the air traffic control system in the Russian Far East, a joint venture between the Volga Pipe Factory and Pacific Roller Die Work to produce pipeline quality pipes for the oil and gas industry, the construction of new power plants to replace the power and steam lost by the shutdown of the Tomsk Plutonium Reactor and other joint ventures.

In summary, during the week of the September 1994 Yeltsin-Clinton summit the United States and Russia signed commercial agreements worth more than $1 billion. The two governments also agreed that, given the right conditions, bilateral trade between the two countries could more than double its current level of $4.7 billion a year by the turn of the century. The commercial agreements included: $689 million in Export-Import Bank loan guarantees for oil, gas, communications, computer and airline projects; $475 million in Overseas Private Investment Corporation support for U.S.-Russian joint ventures; and $3 million in non-reimbursable feasibility grants by the Trade Development Agency for special projects in Russia. U.S. exports to Russia grew by 40 percent in 1993, and exports of manufactured goods grew by 114 percent. Russian exports to the United States doubled in the same period.

The numerous commercial agreements signed during the Washington Summit underscores the strong interest by American firms wanting to do business in Russia. The dozen formal agreements and contracts signed by the U.S. Department of Commerce, the Overseas Private Investment Corporation, the Export-Import Bank, and the U.S. Trade Development Agency represent hundreds of millions of dollars in trade and investment and herald a new business partnership.

The Washington visit of Ukraine's new president, Leonid Kuchma, on November 22, 1994 also occasioned the announcement of a large number of awards for joint ventures closely tied to defense conversion and to economic conversion. These include $200 million in additional economic aid, another $100 million in assistance for student exchanges, privatization and small business and a $100 million emergency grant to Ukraine—with no strings—for importing food and fuel. These awards will make Ukraine the fourth largest aid recipient after Israel, Egypt and Russia (Greenhouse, 1994).

During his 1994 visit the U.S. administration provided Mr. Kuchma with security assurances in return for having persuaded his Parliament to vote to eliminate Ukraine's 1,800 nuclear warheads. These assurances included a promise never to use nuclear weapons against Ukraine, to talk with its Government if Ukraine is ever threatened militarily and, if necessary, to present Ukraine's case to the United Nations Security Council (Perlez, 1994).

Defense Conversion and the 104th Congress

The ascendancy of the Republican Party in the 104th Congress has raised questions as to the continuity of U.S.A. support for F.S.U. defense conversion. In support of continuing bilateral defense conversion efforts, U.S. Secretary of Defense William Perry has pressed the argument that helping former Soviet republics dispose of their weapons and refit military plants for peaceful uses is a sound investment in mutual security. He has noted that the United States spent "just under 1 billion dollars" over the past three years for the Nunn-Lugar program. As a result, he said, more than 2,600 warheads had been removed from missiles or planes, more than 900 had been shipped from Ukraine, Belarus or Kazakhstan to Russia for dismantling, 750 missiles had been dismantled and 575 launchers and bombers destroyed (BBC, 1995).

Charts 1, 4 and 6 used in Secretary of Defense William Perry's statement before the House Budget Committee (DOD, 1995) are displayed on the following pages. His FY 1996 budget request is for $246 billion representing an estimated 3.4 percent of our gross domestic product (GDP). This compares with 6.3 percent in the 1985 period, 9.1 percent in the Vietnam era and 11.9 percent in the Korean War era. Just before the celebrations in Moscow of the 50th anniversary of victory in Europe Russia's Foreign Minister, Andrei V. Kozyrev said that the progress made on arms control during the last few years between the United States and Russia had been impressive. He said this is a tribute to Start 1, the first strategic arms reduction treaty. He was concerned that U.S. development of enhanced short range antimissile systems would alarm Russians, including members of Parliament who must now ratify Start II, the second strategic, or long range, arms reduction treaty. That treaty is also nearing a vote in the United States Senate, where it is expected to have an easier time. If Start II is ratified by both countries perhaps they could move on to serious discussion of Start III, a third strategic arms reduction treaty (Crossette, 1995a).

Hard-liners in Russia are also mounting pressure to reexamine Russia's moves toward converting defense factories to civilian use. Many of them view upgrading defense factories and selling armaments to other nations as their most effective form of defense conversion. The recent relative lack of success of these efforts may, however, foster conversion to civilian production. The Rosvoomzheniye (Russian Arms) State Company for the export and import of weapons and military hardware, reported that Russian arms exports in 1994 amounted to only $1.7 billion. The sales for 1993, were $2.50 billion and for 1992, $2.33 billion. These results contrast with arms exports exceeding $20 billion in the 1980s.

Defense Challenges

- Managing Use of Military Force in Post Cold War Era

- Preventing Reemergence of Nuclear Threat

- Managing Drawdown in Post Cold War Era

Preventing Reemergence of Nuclear Threat

- Nuclear Posture Review
  - Hedge strategy
    - Retains nuclear deterrence
    - Ballistic Missile Defense
      - TMD
      - NMD
- Cooperative Threat Reduction
- Counterproliferation
  - North Korea Framework Agreement

COOPERATIVE THREAT REDUCTION
(Dollars in Millions)

	FY 1995	FY 1996	FY 1997
Budget Request	400.0	371.0	364.4

Primary objectives of cooperative threat reduction:

- Assist the former Soviet Union in destroying nuclear, chemical, and other weapons of mass destruction.

- Transport, store, disable, and safeguard weapons in connection with their destruction.

- Establish verifiable safeguards against the proliferation of such weapons.

- Facilitate demilitarization of defense industries and conversion of military capabilities and technologies.

Managers of enterprises in the military industrial complex are also in despair over their need to sell bartered goods in the form of Chinese and Indian civilian "junk." According to the State Committee for the Defense Branches of Industry, the armaments complex urgently needs to find customers among the Arab oil sheiks, who will pay real money. More than 250 Russian officials, arms manufacturers, merchants and military men went to an exhibition in Abu Dhabi in the United Arab Emirates. The Russian delegation tried to prove that "our hardware is no worse and maybe even be better than foreign equipment." The overall psychological and material damage done by the winter campaign in Chechna appears to be a problem (Post-Soviet Press, 1995).

Some recent developments provide momentum to the defense conversion of the F.S.U. Thus an International Monetary Fund (IMF) loan of $6.6 billion has been made to support Russia's economic reforms. A key element of the program is to cut the federal deficit in half, which will entail spending cuts and revenue measures, including taxes on the energy sector. In announcing the loan IMF's Director cited important and irreversible progress by Russia in privatization, freeing prices, unifying the exchange rate and liberalizing the exchange system, and lifting restrictions on imports. The IMF has previously made three loans to Russia totaling some $4 billion since Russia joined the multilateral organization in June 1992 (BNA-ITR, 1995).

Export-Import Bank loan guarantees, worth about $1 billion, cover the U.S.-built portion of 20 Il-96M/Ts that Ilyushin plans to sell to Aeroflot International Airlines. Boeing and MacDonald concerned about the subsidy for an airframe manufacturer hope to block the loan guarantees. However, Pratt & Whitney and Rockwell Collins support them since each Il-96M/T wide-body aircraft is to be powered by four U.S.-built Pratt Whitney PW2337 engines and feature Collins cockpit avionics. Pratt estimated cancellation of the sale would cost about 2,500 U.S. jobs (Aviation Week, 1995).

A bilateral U.S.A.-R.F. investment treaty would grant U.S. investors national treatment and protect them from arbitrary expropriation. A bilateral tax treaty went into effect in 1994, aimed at giving American firms greater stability in their treatment under Russian tax law and avoid their being taxed twice on the same profits. But since the treaty's effective date Russia has announced a new tax on wages that is inconsistent with the intent of the treaty. There is an ongoing "dialogue" with the Russian government on this matter (BNA-ITR 1995). An oil and gas framework agreement under which the U.S. Export-Import Bank has committed $1.4 billion in loans to Russia to supply capital equipment to Russia's oil fields will require regulatory changes by the Russian government before the money can be disbursed. Perhaps the forthcoming Moscow summit will resolve these issues.

Regional Approaches to Defense Conversion

One of the most striking features of the economic geography of the F.S.U. was the high concentration of defense activities in particular locations, regions and oblasts (equivalent to states in the U.S.A.). Some areas depended almost entirely on the defense sector for their income, employment and for most of their social infrastructure, including schools, hospitals, housing, and leisure facilities. As a result, the sharp reductions in the defense budget have torn at the economic and social fabric of thousands of communities. It is difficult for many Russians to 'pack up and leave,' owing to family ties, housing shortages, an absence of information about labor markets in different regions, and a lack of training for new jobs. Thus a large number of people are still tied to their oblasts, if not to their cities (Kapstein and Mills, 1995).

Some major assistance programs are beginning to recognize the need to address more micro-economic problems in aiding the transition process. For example Moscow and St. Petersburg, which had among the highest concentrations of defense enterprises are doing (relatively) well economically during this period of transformation. However, cities and oblasts that are far from transport and supply networks, by contrast, are having more difficulties. Their problems are compounded by a variety of social assets, from day-care centers to vacation resorts, that these defense communities enterprises often manage. Enterprise-oriented approaches recognize the regional and local dimension of industrial restructuring. Thus the assistance program of the European Union (Technical Assistance for the Commonwealth of Independent States, or TACIS), and the U.S.-based International Executive Service Corps (IESC) are focusing on the specific problems of defense-dependent communities in providing technical assistance.

TACIS, in carrying out its program has engaged Russian experts to produce economic surveys of several of these regions. They are considering industrial restructuring–employment generation–local administration, finance and the restructuring of social assets such as housing, schools, hospitals and leisure facilities and the quality of infrastructure and the environment. Of course, Russia is too big for a single solution and it is unlikely that foreign assistance will play a decisive role. Yet, small developments can have a large economic multiplier effects, and by assisting the transition in a few regions, this regional approach might point the way to successful defense conversion (Kapstein and Mills, 1995).

Assistance by Japan to states of the F.S.U. also have a regional character. All formal restrictions have been lifted between Russia and Japan's export and import bank with respect to a $400 million credit to be extended by Japan. The creation of fuel producing joint ventures are to be important parts of the Japan-Russia defense conversion efforts. Russia also welcomes the establishment by Japan of a special $50 million fund, to finance the development of small and medium-sized business in Russia's far east and eastern Siberia (TASS, 1995a).

The Export-Import Bank of Japan granted credit to the National Bank for Foreign Economic Activity of the Republic of Uzbekistan to a total sum of around 8.9 billion yen (approximately $85 million) (TASS, 1995b). The credit will be used to purchase equipment from Japan and other countries to implement the Kondumalak oil and gas project which is to be executed by the Uzbek oil and Gas agency Uzbekneftegaz. The project is an area of cooperation between Japan and the United States and is financed jointly with the export-import bank of the United States.

U.S.A.-Russia Space Collaborations

From its earliest days, the Space Race was a surrogate form of Cold Warfare with the goal of achieving recognition as the planet's technological leader. When U.S.S.R. was the first to launch a satellite (Sputnik) and man in orbit the U.S.A. retaliated by sending a man to the moon. After this tremendous technical triumph the U.S.A.'s space program lacked focus and soon settled into a broad technological rivalry with the Soviet Union. With the cold war won, battling the Russians was no longer relevant and NASA seemed adrift, if not lost in space.

Space, however, is now one of the most promising large scale arenas of Russian-American collaborations. NASA is now merging many of its leading activities with those of the Russian space program (Broad, 1994a). The East-West partnership involves much more than building an orbital outpost for astronauts, which is to be assembled piecemeal in space between 1997 and 2002. The two sides are also cooperating in manned space flights, aeronautics research and Earth monitoring.

Daniel S. Goldin, NASA's Administrator, appointed by President George Bush in March 1992, said prudent interaction will strengthen the science programs of both countries and symbolize a new era of East-West cooperation. By engaging Moscow in constructive space work the hope, in part, is to end practices like exporting advanced rocket gear to developing countries. Goldin pledged an era in which NASA's endeavors would be "smaller, cheaper, faster, better," ending a trend to bigness and complexity that marked many aspects of NASA's rivalry with Moscow. The cost-cutting goals foster a broad partnership with the Russians in cooperative space projects. The intent, in part, is to help stabilize the Russian economy, and do more, cost less and be in orbit faster than by working exclusively with its Western partners, Europe, Japan and Canada.

In one developing program, NASA is to fly gear for mapping atmospheric ozone and aerosols aboard a Russian satellite. Another would have American teams fly as many as five new Earth-monitoring experiments aboard Russia's Mir space station. In earth-resources monitoring, NASA and the Russians are working to monitor the volcanoes of the Makchatka Peninsula in eastern Russia, 29 of which are active, at times explosively so. A Russian co-pilot carried a $1.2 million infra-red multispectral scanner and an advanced camera over some of the volcanoes in a study meant to help predict eruptions. The area, rich in top-secret facilities, has been off limits to Westerners.

NASA is also working closely with Moscow on the possibility of joint explorations of the planet Mars. Russia would provide a rocket for the launching and some of the exploratory gear, including vehicles that would descend through the thin atmosphere to crawl on the planet's surface. The United States would provide the overall carrier vehicle, that would probably orbit the red planet to make remote observations after releasing the descent module.

NASA is negotiating to test American scramjet engines on Russian rockets, and plans to use the Russian Tu-144 supersonic transport jet from the Tupolov Design Bureau as a flying test bed for high-speed aeronautic research. Perhaps the most visionary aspect of the emerging alliance centers on joint missions to send robotic probes to such places as Pluto, the outermost and most mysterious of the planets, the only one never visited by a spacecraft. NASA planners found that tight budgets allowed them either to design a probe or buy a rocket for its launching, but not to do both.

The Russian Space Agency (RSA), only three years old, has recently accepted the tremendous management responsibility of harnessing the extensive space capabilities of the former Soviet Union to this cooperative effort. Originally formed with only four major space institutes and facilities, RSA today has funding control over 42 significant enterprises ranging from research to industrial capability. RSA has also successfully negotiated with Kazakhstan the operations and maintenance of the Baikonur Cosmodrome from which the Russian human space program is launched (Stencil, 1995).

Activities for a cooperative space program between NASA and RSA, to include the enhancement of Mir, joint space flights and the design, development, utilization and operations of the international Space Station were initiated in a series of agreements spanning the Bush and Clinton administrations. In June 1994, RSA and NASA signed a $400 million contract for supplies and services relating to Mir-1 and the International Space Station Alpha (ISSA).

The Russian capabilities enable humankind to permanently man a Space Station at a much earlier date and greatly reduce the complexity and scheduling of extra-vehicle activity as the Space Station is built. Extra-vehicular activities (EVAs) do not need to be tied to a single, ten or fourteen day Shuttle mission but can be choreographed over a prolonged exposure. The Russian contribution will lean heavily on Russia's proven Proton rocket, the work horse of the Russian space launch fleet. Initial launch of a 20 ton energy block will be made in November 1997 and other blocks and modules will be added at intervals until completion of ISSA in 2002 (Kiselev et al, 1995).

Some view these NASA-Russia efforts as laden with political and technical risks. Problems have already come up in initial cooperative endeavors. However NASA officials look upon these problems as a part of the process of learning to work together (Broad, 1994b). NASA is taking precautions to make sure these space mergers work as well as possible, and notes that not everything it plans to do in the future is tied to the Russians. New entirely indigenous programs are underway such as a series of small satellites for solar-system exploration and Earth monitoring. The merger is a judicious gamble needed to help Russia maintain its equilibrium and to help balance centrifugal forces in that country. As noted in the Foreword of this book such joint engagements and relationships working toward common goals can help build bridges of understanding and foster global peace.

Without exception, national space programs face tough budgetary challenges in every part of the world. Alone, no one nation can really afford to build and operate a space station without sacrificing other areas of space exploration. The new concept for the space station maximizes on the various expertise within the partnership while recognizing the requirement each nation has to deliver their share on time and at cost. The space station now takes into consideration the benefits of using multiple space transportation vehicles, increasing reliability and simultaneously broadening opportunities for all partners.

The International Space Station Alpha (ISSA) is to be in a low Earth orbiting facility for conducting research in the life science, microgravity, earth observations, astrophysics, space processing, and engineering disciplines. The ISSA will be assembled on-orbit at an altitude of 220 nautical miles with contributions from the United States, Canada, Japan, the European Space Agency, and Russia. The ISSA provides a shirt-sleeve environment for conducting research in the U.S. Laboratory (US Lab), the Centrifuge Module, the Japanese Experiment Module (JEM), the European Columbus Orbiting Facility (COF), and three Russian Research Modules. The Mini Pressurized Logistics Module (MPLM) provided by Italy serves as a conditioned pressurized transport carrier to replenish and return passive and perishable payload cargo (Hartman, 1995).

Space activities tend to bring forth great technical challenges, many leading to inventions that have commercial applications. One intriguing proposal is to destroy asteroids on a collision course with the Earth with nuclear weapons (Johnson, 1995). Many other applications of aerospace technology to everyday life have been identified. The greatest duel use inventions in NASA's programs have been summarized recently (Curto, 1995). With successful international cooperation perhaps humankind can find solutions to its major long-range problems. Space cooperation would be particularly helpful in elucidating and resolving environmental issues of global concern such as the climate change and stratospheric ozone depletion problems. When the instruments of all participants in these joint international scientific missions give similar results it should be easier to reach an international consensus on these global environmental issues.

Emerging Military Technologies

As noted in Chapter 3 military research and development in many important technologies have been overtaken by the commercial sector in this and many other countries. Indeed it has been suggested that "major savings could be achieved by abolishing virtually all the Defense Department and military service laboratories" (Odum, 1993). In the absence of a superpower adversary, U.S. military research and development increasingly derives from advances in the commercial sector. According to the National Research Council (NRC, 1992) it is quite possible that the way that war is fought will change much more between 1990 and 2020 than it did between 1915 and 1945. A recent extensive survey (Aftergood, 1995) describes in detail how the revolution in information technology is being exploited for war. Aftergood notes that ever greater quantities of data can be transmitted faster and more widely than ever before. Enthusiasts say that the military applications of information technology, embodied in microminiature weapons systems, will drastically alter the shape of future military forces.

The Secretary of Defense in late 1993, established a Revolutionary in Military Affairs project "in order to better understand and exploit the potential for revolutionary changes in warfare." The current, or pending, revolution in military affairs is predicated largely on the exploitation of new information technologies. These promise an unprecedented degree of detailed and near-instantaneous data on battlefield conditions along with the ability to coordinate and execute battle plans with extraordinary precision and lethality.

New technologies are also creating a capability to conduct war fighting simulations with unprecedented realism. The important new capability promises to improve military training, to enhance battle preparedness, and to streamline the weapon acquisition process. Whatever its limitations, computer technology appears to be an increasingly important and cost-effective tool for the military of the future (Aftergood, 1995).

The global reach of television, particularly since the advent of Cable News Network, has fundamentally altered the flow of information throughout world political systems. "TV news carries information directly and immediately to both the public and top leaders, bypassing the entire apparatus of intelligence, diplomacy, and national security."

Biotechnology is also undergoing an inverse defense conversion and is emerging as a prominent near-term military biotechnology with a potential role in biological warfare. For as little as $40 one can 'depopulate' a square mile using anthrax spores, which are easily producible, viable in air for hours, and over 95 percent fatal. The biotechnology revolution is unfolding more quickly than its consequences can be understood and assimilated. Consequently, an important near-term priority is to improve defensive capabilities against military or terrorist use of biological weapons (Aftergood, 1995).

One important technology trend that is already manifest is an increasing reliance on unmanned vehicles (UAVs) for certain military missions. In the future, the role of UAVs in military operations will only expand and diversify. With the microminiaturization of sensors and computers, and new developments in materials and weapons technologies, we will even see swarms of UAVs that are each "the size of a songbird," says the National Research Council (NRC, 1992).

There are potential negative aspects to the information revolution. The overwhelming dependence on advanced information technologies in the U.S. economy, and in the military and space programs all but guarantees that information systems will become an increasingly important target in times of conflict. The creation of multiple new mechanisms of accessing information tends to flatten existing hierarchies and, perhaps, to 'empower' small social units and individuals. "The information revolution disrupts and erodes the hierarchies around which institutions are normally designed. Current international trends toward democracy may reverse, as computational technologies shift economic and military power from the masses to technical elites" (Aftergood, 1995).

Some also believe the growing availability of cheap, compact and powerful information systems is not likely to change the conduct of warfare in ways that cannot be fully anticipated. For example, Army General Paul E. Funk has observed that "With the increased speed, range, lethality and real-time communications capabilities of the modern battlefield comes a directly proportional increase in the chaos on that battlefield."

In countering these "plowshares to swords" type defense conversions new opportunities are developing for averting war and promoting peace. Just as technology is used to magnify, extend and focus human abilities in other domains, it can also be applied to reduce the likelihood that violent conflict will erupt and to ameliorate the consequences of warfare. The Department of Energy has established a new Cooperative Monitoring Center (CMC) at Sandia National Laboratories that can be used to verify compliance with regional arms control and environmental agreements.

So-called non-lethal weapons, slowly emerging from the secret "black budget," are among emerging military technologies. In the aftermath of the Gulf War, the Pentagon created an initiative to coordinate these diverse research programs and to plan the acquisition of non-lethal weapons and their incorporation into military training and doctrine. Note, however, that the NRC concludes that future weapons systems, "like any revolutionary technical development, will disrupt existing military structures and industrial competencies." They will be expensive and often will not work. When they do work, they will remain vulnerable to enemy countermeasures. They cannot be trusted blindly or simply substituted for humans; they require understanding on their own terms. They are often surrounded by cycles of exaggerated expectation and disillusionment (Aftergood, 1995).

The Feasibility of Defense Conversion

In pursuing various approaches to Defense Conversion (DC) our hope was to uncover patterns that would be helpful in guiding further efforts at DC. It is gratifying to the editor, a World War II operations analyst, that the Nuclear Posture Review, the Nunn Lugar program, and other U.S. Government programs reflect approaches to defense conversion that can reasonably be viewed as derived from extensions of World War II Operations Analysis. The recent progress noted in the preceding sections is impressive, logical, and reflects more common sense than manifested during the tenure of "best and the brightest ."

In our organizational efforts over a three-year period to uncover promising DC programs we found that many firms experiencing severe defense cuts were actively involved in applying their defense technologies to civilian markets. Some could not take time to write a chapter because they were *too busy at defense conversion* (TBADC). Others were concerned with proprietary or competitive aspects of their programs and felt that it was *premature to disclose their work* (PTDTW). Still other firms were *active but were seeking military clearance* (ABSMC). The three groups (TBADC), (PTDTW) and (ABSMC) include a number of very promising military to civilian or dual use type defense conversions, some of which are underway with private sources of capital. Recapitulating, some of the promising DC examples that have been described in this work we list:

(1) Global Position System (GPS). Chapter 12 gives an excellent and timely example of Defense Conversion to Dual Use. Here the civilian sector in pursuit of large markets has substantially lowered the costs of positioning systems for both military and civilian applications.

(2) Aeroderivative Gas Turbines. Chapter 3 describes how the enhanced performance requirements of military aircraft turbines have been applied to the civilian aircraft sector and to low capital cost combined cycle electrical energy generation systems, another example of dual use.

(3) Environmental Measurements with Optical Systems: Chapters 8 and 9 discuss environmental applications of ultraviolet spectroscopic and laser optical systems whose development were mainly stimulated by military requirements. Optics is a very rapidly growing technology with many dual applications. The use of infrared spectroscopy for environmental measurements, another very promising growth area, did not make it into this edition simply because the invited author was TBADC.

(4) Electronic Hardware. Due to the competitive pressures of the market place, advancement in consumer electronics while borrowing earlier from defense programs has in many cases moved beyond military electronics. Thus this area is a natural case for the dual use mode of Defense Conversion in which the defense sector will benefit from plowshares to swords conversion.

(5) Computer Software. Here, too, the market place has stimulated a large civilian industry that is now blossoming. Evidence for this is the fact that the individual who has accumulated the most capital in the U.S.A. (the richest man) comes from the software sector. As noted in Chapter 6, top flight institutes in the F.S.U. previously confined to the military sector are now competing in the highly sophisticated civilian software sector.

The foregoing are but a few successful or promising, examples of defense conversion. Examples from TBADC, PTDTW, and ABSMC groups as well as conversion or dual use applications arising out of the space program would add considerably to these cases. Then it would be very apparent that the assessment "defense conversion is a concept unblemished by examples of success" (Chapter 7) was premature and is no longer valid. On the contrary, considerable progress has already been made and is now being made towards converting significant sectors of the U.S.A. and F.S.U. defense enterprises to civilian or dual purposes. Success in Russia, Ukraine and other F.S.U. states would foster the development of a middle class which, having a stake in their new economies, would certainly favor the politics of the middle ground.

Final Perspectives

The 20th century's most successful examples of defense conversions are those of Japan and Germany following World War II. With the almost total destruction of their military production facilities by Allied military action, and restrictions from rebuilding, Japan and Germany built industries to make consumer products. In time this led to large capital accumulations, the essence of economic power. While this World War II model is hardly a defense conversion methodology to be recommended, a comparison of the current economic strengths of the "losers" with those of the "winners" conveys some important lessons. The F.S.U., a big "winner" is now dismembered and Russia, Ukraine and other F.S.U. states are experiencing great economic difficulties. The U.S.A., the other big "winner", is some \$5 trillion in debt. In their cold war and surrogate wars (space, big science) they grossly over expended capital.   These trends were exacerbated by the Vietnam and Afghanistan wars thanks to "leadership" by the "best and the brightest" (McNamara,1995).

This simple explanation of the current economic status of Japan, Germany, the U.S.A. and the F.S.U. will probably be challenged. Be that as it may, the question is how can the F.S.U. and the U.S.A. recover from the cumulative impact of the cold war? More importantly how can we reduce the tremendous nuclear threat built up during the cold war to manageable levels?

There are no simple answers to these questions.   Threat reduction slowed by mutual suspicions is now complicated by the proliferation of nuclear weapon making capability that is physically associated with the use of nuclear energy. In the short term it is absolutely necessary that Russia and U.S.A. continue on the Start I, Start II tracks and hopefully advance to some Start III levels that further lowers nuclear weapons levels. Since this can only be accomplished bilaterally by U.S.A. and the F.S.U. it necessitates a close relationship that would be more productive as cooperative rather than adversarial. Issues in which our near-term interests appear in conflict should be examined from longer term perspectives to seek courses of action leading to mutual benefits. Cooperation in space appears already to be heading in this direction. Perhaps cooperation on more devisive issues such as the use of plutonium, sales of nuclear reactors and on development of short-range missile defenses could also be developed towards mutual advantages.

As noted above, Japan and Germany with their successful defense conversions are now major economic powers and hence their attitudes must also be considered. It is ironic that the U.S.A. following the WW II nuclear weapons project was the first to develop nuclear reactors for power but this industry is now in decline. Japan, however, is now the only nation with the capital to construct advance nuclear reactors to satisfy its future energy needs.

A comprehensive survey of attitudes was made recently by the Wall Street Journal in the U.S.A. and top   German and Japanese financial newspapers (Hunt, 1995) with about 1,500 citizens from each country. The combined survey indicated that Germans overwhelmingly think Japan is the world's strongest economy, while Americans rate Japan and the U.S. as the most powerful.   The Japanese think that the U.S. now has the strongest economy, but that in a decade or so China will. Despite economic tensions Germany, Japan and the U.S.A. view each other as diplomatic allies who will not repeat the conflicts of a half-century ago. Each nation has a clear sense of its own strengths. For Germans, it's economic success; for Japanese, it's technological achievements; and for Americans, it's leadership in world affairs.

In focusing this book on downsizing the MAD nuclear levels of the U.S.A. and Russia we must be mindful of nuclear developments in Asia (Shenon, 1995) and in other countries. There are already 115 commercial and research reactors in operation in East Asia, most in Japan, South Korea, Taiwan and China. In the next decade, dozens of new reactors are expected to be built across the continent at a cost of more than $100 billion. China, which only opened its first commercial complex last year with technical and financial help by France has plans for 30 more reactors. While reactors may power Asia's thriving economies into the next century, they also pose problems of safety and cost and issues now under scrutiny at the United Nations.

Diplomats are now negotiating extensions of the Nuclear Non-Proliferation Treaty (NPT), a 25-year-old treaty designed to limit the spread of nuclear arms, that is about to expire. Since the need for UN inspection of power plants to verify that atomic material is not diverted to weapons use is increasing we must hope that these NPT negotiations are successful. Halfway into a month-long conference the possibility of an indefinite extension of the treaty or a 25-year renewal plan looks favorable. Some observers reason that the latter would provide greater leverage for prodding nuclear weapons nations into more rapid disarmaments (Crossette, 1995b).

Finally it should be noted that the opening lines of the Executive Summary by Isaiah were written some three millennia ago and there have been very few periods in history since then that the world has been without war. As we approach the 50th anniversaries of the first two demonstrations of the power of nuclear weapons one cannot but be amazed that the world has thus far escaped a global nuclear holocaust despite the number of wars since then and the large number of nuclear weapons scattered around the globe. Clearly the ultimate achievement of Isaiah's goal will require the cooperation of all nations. However before global denuclearization can really begin the U.S.A. and the F.S.U. must undo much of the MADness of the half century U.S.A.-F.S.U. Cold War. Cooperative nuclear threat reduction to SANE levels should set the stage for general global threat reduction. Furthermore by simultaneously pursuing Defense Conversion the former antagonists might recover some of Cold War costs that had such deleterious social, economic and financial impacts. This should help lower the indebtedness of the U.S.A. and F.S.U. and help restore the nations involved to their rightful places of influence in world affairs. International cooperation towards further disarmament could then follow more naturally. Hopefully this book will provide some useful guidance towards these objectives.

Acknowledgments

The author thanks Dolores Jenkins and Barry Hartigan of the University of Florida Library, Octavio Durao of the Brazilian Institute for Space Research, Paul Boren of Defense Nuclear Agency and Sally Horn of DoD Policy Analysis Section for their help in assembling information used in this Afterword.

References

Aftergood, S., 1995: Journal of the Federation of American Scientists (FAS), 48, No. 1, January/February.

Aviation Week and Space Technology, 1995: McGraw-Hill, Inc., April 3.

BBC, 1995: British Broadcasting Corporation, April 3.

BNA-ITR, 1995: The Bureau of National Affairs, Inc., International Trade Reporter, 12, No. 14; 638, April 5.

Broad, W. J., 1994a: NASA's New Ploy, Meld with Moscow, New York Times, July 19.

Broad, W. J., 1994b: NASA-Russian Space Problems, New York Times, Nov. 29.

Crossette, B., 1995a: New York Times, April 25.

Crossette, B., 1995b: New York Times, April 30.

Curto, P.A., 1995: NASA's Greatest Inventions and Contributions of Dual-Use Technologies in the 1990s, 7-1. Canaveral Council of Technical Studies, *Proceedings of the 32nd Space Congress, Cocoa Beach, FL,* April 25-28.

DNA, 1995: Listings of contract awards and funding channels distributed by the Defense Nuclear Agency, Spring.

DoD, 1994: Nuclear Posture Review Recommends Reduction in Nuclear Force, News Releases No. 541and 546, Sept. 22.

DoD, 1995: Statement of Secretary of Defense William J. Perry before the House Budget Committee in connection with the FY 1996-97 Department of Defense Budget, April 27.

Gordon, M.R., 1994: U.S. Negotiates Deal to remove Bomb Fuel in Ex-Soviet Republic, New York Times, Nov. 22.

Greenhouse, S., 1994: Ukraine Gets a $200 Million 'Thanks', New York Times, Nov. 23.

Hartman, D.W., 1995: International Space Station Alpha Payload Accommodations, 4-40 - 4-50, ibid. Curto.

Hunt, A.R., 1995: The Wall Street Journal, April 24.

Johnson, L. N., 1995: Preparing for Planetary Defense, 32 Space Congress, 2-17 - 2-27, ibid Canaveral.

Kapstein, E.B. and C.M. Mills, 1995: Organization for Economic Co-operation and OECD Observer, February, 1995.

Kiselev, A.I., A.k. Nedaivoda and V. K. Karask,1995: Energy Block of ISSA, 4-28, ibid Curto .

McNamara, R. S. with B. Van De Mark, 1995: The Tragedy and Lessons of Vietnam, Random House, New York, 414 pp.

NRC, 1992: National Research Council, STAR 21; Strategic Technologies for the Army of the Twenty-First Century, National Academy Press, 311 pp.

Odom, W.E., 1993: America's Military Revolution: Strategy and Structure After the Cold War, American University Press, 186 pp.

Perlez, J., 1994: Ukraine Gets Reformer at Helm, New York Times, Nov. 29.

Perry, 1994: Address of Secretary of Defense William J. Perry to the Henry L. Stimson Center, DoD News Release No. 535-94, Sept. 20.

Post-Soviet Press, 1995: Current Digest, April 5.

Shenon, P., 1995: New York Times, Sunday, April 23.

Stencil, J.C., 1995: International Partnership in the Space Station Program 4-23 ibid. Curto.

TASS, 1995a: April 13, 1995.

TASS, 1995b: April 3, 1995.

White House, 1994: Press Release, September 27.